MANUFACTURING MATERIAL EFFECTS: RETHINKING DESIGN AND MAKING IN ARCHITECTURE

EDITED BY **BRANKO KOLAREVIC** & **KEVIN R. KLINGER**

 Routledge
Taylor & Francis Group

NEW YORK AND LONDON

First published 2008 by Routledge
Reprinted in 2010
270 Madison Avenue, New York, NY10016

Simultaneously published in the UK by Routledge
2 Park Square, Milton Park, Abingdon, Oxon, OX14 4RN

Routledge is an imprint of the Taylor & Francis Group, an informa business

© 2008 Branko Kolarevic & Kevin R. Klinger, selection and editorial matter; individual
chapters, the contributors

Designed and typeset in Bell Gothic by Branko Kolarevic

Printed and bound in China by Everbest Printing Co. Ltd.

British Library Cataloguing in Publication Data
A catalogue record for this book is available from the British Library

Library of Congress Cataloging- in-Publication Data
A catalog record for this book has been requested

ISBN10 0-415-77574-4 (hbk)
ISBN10 0-415-77575-2 (pbk)

ISBN13 978-0-415-77574-8 (hbk)
ISBN13 978-0-415-77575-5 (pbk)

CONTENTS

ACKNOWLEDGMENTS

We thank with the deepest gratitude the contributors to this book – their creative ideas and their highly innovative work were the main inspiration for this volume and the eponymous symposium that preceded it. In April 2007, we gathered in Indianapolis for two days to examine the synergetic relationships between design and making in architecture and the increasing attention devoted to intricate, often complex *effects* in material and surface articulation. The intention of the symposium content and the ensuing discussions have been refined and captured in this book.

The "Manufacturing Material Effects" (MMFX) symposium (www.bsu.edu/imade/mmfx) was organized by the Institute for Digital Fabrication at Ball State University (BSU) and held at the Indianapolis Museum of Art (IMA) on April 6 and 7, 2007. We are most grateful to the symposium sponsors: Autodesk, Inc., McGraw-Hill Construction Information Group, auto•des•sys, Inc., Bentley Systems, Inc., IMA and Center for Media Design and College of Architecture and Planning at Ball State University; without their support, the symposium and this book would not have been possible. Major funding for the initial formative research was provided through the Center for Media Design; our deepest gratitude to the Lilly Endowment for their funding of research and educational initiatives at BSU.

We are profoundly appreciative of Ball State University, a unique institution at the crossroads of the Midwest. We are particularly grateful to Jo Ann Gora, the University President, David Ferguson, Director of the Center for Media Design, Joseph Billelo, former Dean of the College of Architecture and Planning, Jon Coddington, former Chair of the Department of Architecture, and the Irving Distinguished Professorship for the inspiration, encouragement and support of our work. We also want to thank the Indianapolis Museum of Art, Maxwell Anderson, the Museum Director, and Linda Duke, Director of Education, for embracing this project from its inception, for providing a platform for its success, and for encouraging and hosting a follow-up exhibition in the spring of 2008 with the help of David Russick, David Chalfie, Rosanne Winings, Sue Ellen Paxson, Andy Stewart, and the rest of the IMA staff.

At the University of Calgary, we would like to express our gratitude to Loraine Fowlow, Interim Dean of the Faculty of Environmental Design, and the Haworth Research Chair Professorship in Integrated Design, for their support in the later stages of this project. The production of the book was supported in part through a grant from the Graham Foundation for Advanced Studies in the Fine Arts.

Finally, and most importantly, we want to thank our students and our colleagues for the stimulating conversations about the subject of this book. In particular, we want to acknowledge Joshua Vermillion at Ball State University for his ideas, enthusiasm, hard work, and infallible support in our efforts. We also want to thank the students who were involved with the ideas, content, and organization of the symposium and subsequent activities and Jennifer Weaver Cotton for minding many details.

We are grateful to Caroline Mallinder at Taylor and Francis for her enthusiastic support of this project and Katherine Morton for patiently navigating the editing of the manuscript and production of the book. Special thanks to Frank Barkow of Barkow Leibinger Architects for kindly providing us with an image for the book cover.

At a personal level, we are indebted (in so many ways) to our spouses; our special thanks to Stephanie LaBeau Sisco Klinger and Vera Parlac, respectively, for their patient support during the endless refinement and crafting of this project, and to our boys, J. Wesley and Ethan Frederick Klinger, and Marko Parlac Kolarevic, for allowing us to focus attention on this work during the formative years of their lives. This book is dedicated to them.

Kevin R. Klinger and Branko Kolarevic
Indianapolis and Calgary, Spring 2008

PROTOTYPING ARCHITECTURE'S FUTURE, AGAIN

**BRETT STEELE
ARCHITECTURAL ASSOCIATION**

The future is already here. It's just unevenly distributed.
(William Gibson)

Modern architecture came into being as something first glimpsed, later recognized, and finally capitalized upon thanks to a bunch of clunky, often awkward and frequently just-plain-lucky prototypes.

The legacy of twentieth-century architectural innovation is that of countless stumbling discoveries by people calling themselves architects who were – especially at the outset of their careers – often paying the bills by doing something else entirely. Consider a quick laundry list of examples: Mies van der Rohe's glass-and-metal working model of the 1917 *Friedrichstrasse Tower*, where he claimed: "I had to make the model using the building's actual materials just to learn what the reflective qualities would be like", or his later series of 1:1 villa mock-ups or wall-sized simulations, assembled over and over again at countless expositions and exhibitions before actually building a full "live" piece of architecture. We have Le Corbusier's child-like wire and string "toy" model of the *Brussels Pavilion* (visualizing the form of ruled-surface structure), or around the same time Charles and Ray Eames's plywood splints pressed out of the "Kazaam" machine in a back bedroom of their Los Angeles apartment. Consider Antonio Gaudí's material computers assembled as inverted form-finding chain models consisting of hundreds of carefully arranged weights and cords, or Frei Otto's no-less complex analogue model, a stereoscopic photography set-up that he designed to record and analyze the essential loading experiments applied to cable models of his Munich stadium. Scanning the history of modern architecture's underlying prototypers we come across quirky inventor-figures like the French craftsman-engineer Jean Prouve with a sheet-metal bending press (purchased at the outset of his setting up his own office; a kind of rapid-prototyping machine of the 1930s). Or we have, at the ideological end of modernism's revolutionary impulse, Vladimir Tatlin's massive timber tests of his never-realized *Monument to the Soviets*. The birth of corporate architecture is no less prototype-bound: remember the large-scale mock-ups and testing that went into the invention of an odd one-off steel and aluminum cleaning cradle that had to be designed on the fly in order for *SOM* to realize the *Lever House*, the world's first all-glass tower in the early 1950s. More recently, consider the career trajectory of Frank Gehry and how it was sent in new directions only after he grabbed on to cheap corrugated cardboard as the ideal working material for a line of furniture whose experimental forms profoundly changed his subsequent architectural work (including especially that of his own Venice house, assembled as a hands-on, full-scale, constantly re-arranging prototype in the architect's thinking in the 1970s).

This book provides an important and comprehensive survey of how this kind of enduring "material" sensibility for the making of experimental prototypes within – and as – architecture has taken on a new and compelling form of its own in recent years, thanks to the arrival of new digital, connective, and output technologies fundamentally transforming the idea of manufacturing itself in relationship to architecture. The following projects show how willing a new generation of experimentalists with architecture are, at least in being willing to learn from free-wheeling, open-ended, but doggedly focused forms of design research.

Branko Kolarevic and Kevin Klinger have done a marvelous job of convincingly demonstrating not only something of the breadth, but also the considerable depth, of this vital area of renewed architectural interest; something that was on display in 2007 at an international conference that served as the basis for this volume. Plenty of the examples included in this book testify to a sweeping realignment within architecture today, decidedly at odds with either the journalist/information gathering models of contemporary architectural research focused on distinct geographies and urban settings, or any of the historical (post-modern, deconstructive) forms of architectural knowledge that have dominated recent decades of architectural culture and thinking. As hinted at above, there are numerous architectural prototypes hovering around the topic of manufacturing, if we look past the conventional personalities and attributions of modern architecture. When we do, we can look up to see in an entirely new light today projects like Eiffel's tower, Mies's *Barcelona Pavilion*, Buckminster Fuller's geodesic domes, as well as a million other examples, all pointing to prototype after prototype having been the result of their architects' interest in concepts of manufacturing, making, and experimentation.

My point here is a straightforward one. The kinds of architectural prototyping on display in this collection are only the latest – albeit increasingly influential and optimistic – iteration of work on the effects of material experimentation. The settings for such investigations today are of course radically different from that of their predecessors in their digital, informational, and networked design realities. But this, I would argue, is more of a change in degree than kind (I say this for the especially youngest part of a new generation today that tends to see the world as a radically different one owing to the advent of personal computing – something that is very much not the case, as the various examples of material computing listed above make obvious).

One quality stands out especially in the projects compiled in this book, when reading through some of the accompanying explanations by their architects: incredibly narrow and carefully constrained areas of research interest. You will find some of these designers talking about one particular kind of laser cutting (or kind of cutter), one specific software platform (and way of modifying it), one of dozens of possible scripting or programming languages used to conceive and code the project work. This is work understood by its practitioners in terms of release dates, model numbers, and material alloys; or cutting speeds, tool paths, and matrix arrays. But it is work that is not automatically, I would claim, indicative of equally narrow fields of architectural vision or ambition. Quite the opposite, I would suggest. What you see here is common among all kinds of advanced industrial and manufacturing enterprises: new initiatives and projects carefully calibrated to work within the niches of already ongoing technologies, below the

radar of known technique, or in the realm of entirely new kinds of project definition. Such is the nature of knowledge production today in a world of global learning economies; a strange (architectural) space for sure, where it is not what you know so much as how you know the possible ways you can get to where you want to go. (The challenges this situation poses to the traditional form and expectation of schools and offices are, of course, the real sub-text here.)

There is much I could write here that would fulfill the normal textual obligations of writing a foreword to a collection of works as distinguished as this, by the many different contributors. An introduction (like this one) is always intended to "set up" the coherence of what it is you are about to read – to manufacture and then justify the monolithic composition of the compilation itself. It is easy to perform that task here owing to the editors' success in bringing together such a coherent selection of work being done from within the informational ecology where more and more aspects of all architecture work are being undertaken, across diverse networks of all kinds.

You will see in what follows a bias towards the surface, specifically surface operations, effects, manipulation, and deformation. In projects like these, the concept of the surface operates like that of mass, volume, or figure did for previous architectural generations. Architectural entities or properties once brought into order and organization via geometry and composition have been displaced by much more iterative design operations controlled now through various kinds of machinic iteration, repetition, and variable arrays across surfaces. These are the kinds of "things" (or conceptual entities) that sit as the essential operands of the hidden artificial languages built upon by the machine codes, operating systems, and finally software applications in use throughout this work. Within the design worlds of these projects, how surfaces are divided, assembled, machined, or modeled are central questions. That is not a coincidence, nor some kind of imaginary, epistemological imperative. We must remember that nearly every aspect of projects like these is being driven by software that is entirely surface-oriented in its underlying mathematics, the very same surface mathematics that are, of course, now also being utilized in the machines, making possible new output technologies, such as 3D printing, milling, or laser-cutting.

Another obvious and shared trait of the contributors to this volume is something I alluded to above: their inherently collaborative, multi-disciplinary ways of working. These are works undertaken, by and large, by young practices still in the formative stages of their careers. What is worth our attention here is the way in which the collaborative impulses of certain younger and emerging practices today are literally turning on its head a conventional and familiar modern business expectation of architectural practice, whereby the expanded scope and project size of one's later career tended to associate itself with larger and larger design teams and work arrangements. What is different today in the work presented in this book, and for reasons that are obvious owing to the technological complexity of the undertaking, is the much more real need for multi-disciplinary expertise within design teams, and from the very beginnings of young architects' working lives. This I believe to be the single greatest change in architecture today from its recent past – one generational, and perhaps even historical, change in the shaping of what is taken to be architectural knowledge (let alone expertise). The familiar twentieth-century professional categories of supporting engineering, costing, and other disciplines around which most of the architectural practice is

today organized (if not fossilized) are clearly giving way. This is a book where you can see the hands of not only computer programmers, machinists, artists, and composite material engineers, but also laser cutters, rubber workers, new media animators, mathematicians, and countless others, all of whom seem as capable, if not more so, of working out the problems of three-dimensional form, machinic assembly, network design, and composite material performance that are all immeasurably more advanced than that of conventional construction and manufacturing trades.

All kinds of effects are being manufactured by the projects that follow, which is obviously why its editors followed the tried and true form of titling this book in a way that lets you judge it by its cover. You will learn plenty about the specific results of the strange teams and collaborations across machinic domains on a case-by-case basis in the chapters that follow. The point to stress in an introduction like this is simply that we should resist efforts to flatten the forms of differentiation that underlie each of the individual contributors' interests and results.

Instead, and looking for a way out of this introduction, let's just stand back and look at what this collective effort really shows us: something in contemporary form today that architecture has long proven itself most capable of doing best – manufacturing its own future, one project at a time. That is the effect that matters most, among all the other beautiful ones depicted in this book.

1
MANUFACTURING /
MATERIAL /
EFFECTS

BRANKO KOLAREVIC & KEVIN R. KLINGER

Materials and surfaces have a language of their own. Stone speaks of its distant geological origins, its durability and inherent symbolism of permanence; brick makes one think of earth and fire, gravity and the ageless traditions of construction; bronze evokes the extreme heat of its manufacture, the ancient processes of casting and the passage of time as measured in its patina. Wood speaks of its two existences and time scales; its first life as a growing tree and the second as a human artefact made by the caring hand of a carpenter or cabinetmaker.

(Juhani Pallasmaa)[1]

Over the past decade we have seen in architecture the (re)emergence of complexly shaped forms and intricately articulated surfaces, enclosures, and structures, whose design and production were fundamentally enabled by the capacity of digital technologies to accurately represent and precisely fabricate artifacts of almost any complexity. Some buildings produced by this digital technological shift feature smooth, "liquid" forms, while some are simple "boxes" with complexly patterned envelopes; many blend both approaches. These new buildings are attractive to many who relish their innovative potential; to others they are merely provisional distractions from the historically distilled essences of the discipline. Beyond the valuation verdict ("good" or "bad"), the proliferation of these types of expressive projects is undeniable; often lacking historically affirmed subtleties, they provoke established formal and material conceptions of architecture. For example, the first projects that exploit the newfound capacity to digitally design and manufacture highly crafted surface effects are being realized, featuring series of panels with unique decorative reliefs, cut-out patterns, striated surface configurations, etc., hinting at the emergence of new "ornamentalism" in contemporary architecture. Experimental building skins with dynamic, adaptive behavior are also beginning to materialize, challenging prevalent assumptions about tectonics and the permanence of material conditions in buildings. Fundamental to this technological and material experimentation is that *atypical* buildings realized over the past decade or so – whether complexly shaped, complexly patterned, or behaving dynamically – are *affecting* in novel ways our perceptions of surface, form, and space through carefully crafted *effects*, explorations of inventive material organizations pursued across a wide range of scales.

In addition to new forms of architectural expression, and new means of conceptual and material production, increasing advances in material science have radically affected architectural thinking. New materials are offering unparalleled thinness, dynamically changing properties, and functionally gradient compositions. Coupled with the means of digital technology, advances in material science have led to renewed interest among architects in tectonic expression, material properties, and the ability to produce the desired surface and spatial effects, both with emerging materials and with innovative applications of "conventional" materials. A particularly interesting trajectory is the pursuit of material and tectonic unity of skin, structure, and effect (as a contemporary expression of Vitruvius' *firmitas*, *utilitas* and *venustas*) that provides variability in volume, shape, composition, texture, and appearance in a single material product. To that end, composite, layered materials, commonly used in automotive, aerospace, shipbuilding and other industries, are directly interrogated for possible architectural applications, as they offer the unprecedented capability to directly formulate material properties and effects by digitally controlling the production of the material itself. The composition of such materials can be engineered precisely to meet specific performance criteria, so that properties can vary across the section to achieve, for example, a different structural capacity in relationship to local stress conditions, or variable fiber density to achieve different opacity and appearance. By manipulating material variables in composites for local performance criteria, entirely new material, tectonic, and ornamental possibilities open up for architecture. Furthermore, wiring, plumbing, and mechanical systems can be embedded into layers of the composite material. The design and tectonic ambition are remarkable: the manufactured material *is* the building component, or as Toshiko Mori recognized, the "production of materials and fabrication of building components will soon be simultaneous."[2]

MANUFACTURING

Recent advances in digital technologies of design, analysis, and production have set in motion a remarkable affect not only on the practice and the discipline of architecture, but on the entire disciplinary and professional structure of the building industry.[3] Technology, as has always been the case, lies at the core of the examination of new working protocols in architecture and building. Today, the effective digital exchange of information is vital to the realization of the new *integrative* capacity of architecture.[4]

Manufacturing of material effects is a powerful contemporary actualization of the potentialities opened up by highly collaborative, highly integrated design, engineering, fabrication, and construction knowledge. It is intriguing to note that this emerging, technologically enabled transformation of the building industry in the "digital" age has led to a much greater integration of "mechanical" age processes and techniques into conceptual building design. The twentieth-century separation of the disciplines and the standardization of components have given way to the collaboration of diverse interests and a rigorous exploration of distinctive, atypical, non-standard design solutions, often realized in close association with the manufacturing sector. As observed by Toshiko Mori, "The age of mechanical production, of linear processes and the strict division of labor, is rapidly collapsing around us."[5]

Accepting informed *manufacturing* potentialities is a principal strategy in realizing innovative contemporary architectural design intentions. Thus, a close, collaborative relationship with industry is critical early on, during the conceptual stages of design development. Such an approach confronts traditional modes of practicing architecture with an exchange of information unrestricted by antiquated legal mechanisms, i.e. the legal "firewalls" designed to keep architects (and the risk of litigation) away from the shop floor and the construction site. While much of industry has not "retooled" to take advantage of the digitally driven design and production, each new experiment and each new collaborative pursuit will help broker the change as projects move towards redefining techniques and methods of design conception and material realization.

In light of these technologically enabled changes, innovative practices with cross-disciplinary expertise are forming to enable the design and construction of new formal complexities and tectonic intricacies. *Front Inc.* from New York is perhaps the most exemplary collaborative practice to emerge over the past decade; acting as a type of free agency, they fluidly move across the professional and disciplinary territories of architecture, engineering, fabrication and construction, and effectively deploy new digital technologies of parametric design, analysis, and fabrication. Similarly, entrepreneurial enterprises, such as *designtoproduction* from Zurich, Switzerland, have identified an industry niche in the translation of model scale prototypical designs into full-scale buildings. Design firms, such as *SHoP Architects* and *LTL Architects* in New York and *Gang Studio Architects* from Chicago, have integrated in-house design and production in many of their projects. Meanwhile, informed fabrication specialists such as *3form, Inc.* in Salt Lake City, *A. Zahner Company* in Kansas City, and *Octatube* in Delft, the Netherlands, represent an industry-oriented broadening to engage the emerging innovative design processes directly and more effectively through close collaboration with designers.

MATERIAL

In a dramatic departure from the formally and materially reductive norms of much twentieth-century architecture, it is now possible to materially realize complex geometric organizational ideas that were previously unattainable. Furthermore, in a paradoxical way, the new techniques and methods of digitally enabled making are reaffirming the long forgotten notions of craft, resulting from a desire to extract intrinsic qualities of material and deploy them for particular effect. As such, interrogating materiality is fundamental to new attitudes towards achieving design intent. (After all, architecture is fundamentally a *material* practice.)

Utterly conventional materials are put to unexpected uses: Shigeru Ban has used paper tubes as structural material on projects of different scales (figure 1.1). New technical capacities are uncovered in traditional materials by out-of-the-box thinking: glass is used in compression, as shown by the work of *Front Inc.*, and stone in tension, as in Jeanne Gang's *Marble Curtain* installation at the National Building Museum in Washington, DC. These material experiments result from a much more informed knowledge base of material performance and the systemic behavior of its assembly.

1.1.
The structural enclosure of the *Japan Pavilion* at *Expo 2000*, Hannover, Germany, designed by Shigeru Ban, is made from paper tubes.

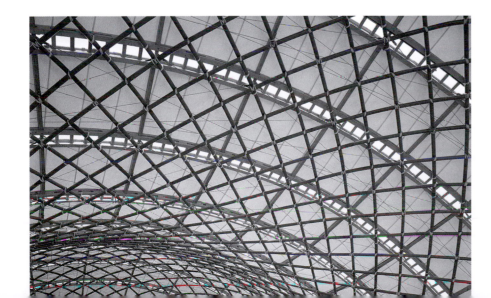

Concrete, metal, and wood are losing their *opacity*. In the past few years, we have seen the emergence of *translucent* concrete,[6] developed by *LiTraCon* from Hungary (figure 1.2), and *translucent* metal and wood panels, developed by *3form Inc.* of Salt Lake City, Utah. Such unconventional articulation of conventional materials brings into focus long-established notions of material *truth* and *signification* in architecture. The new *effects* teased out of "old" materials are deployed to *affect* in new ways the "old" perceptions of space, precisely because of the expectations of how the familiar materials should behave.

Aluminum is applied in new ways, as doubly-curved structural skins. The curvaceous building envelope of the *Media Centre* at the *Lord's Cricket Grounds* in London (1999), designed by *Future Systems*, is a semi-*monocoque* aluminum shell, inspired by "stressed skins" long used in automotive, aerospace, and shipbuilding production. In airplanes, for example, the cage-like structure called the *airframe*, made from aluminum alloys, is covered by aluminum panels to form a semi-monocoque envelope in which the structure and skin are separate tectonic elements acting in unison to absorb stresses. By defying the binary logics of the Modernist tectonic thinking, structure and skin are re-unified into one element in semi-monocoque and monocoque shells, thus creating self-supporting forms that require no armature.

Other commonly available materials, such as fiberglass, polymers and foams, rarely used in the building industry, are being closely scrutinized today for potential because they offer several advantages over typical materials. They are lightweight, high strength, and can easily be shaped into various forms, making them ideal for structural skins. These "old," overlooked materials, however, require curvilinear geometries to enable the monocoque skins to perform structurally. Thus, an interesting reciprocal relationship is established between the new geometries and new materialities: complex geometries open up a quest for new materials and vice versa.

The physical characteristics of fiberglass make it particularly suitable for achieving complex forms. It is cast in liquid state, so it can conform to any mold shape and produce a surface of exceptional smoothness – a liquid, fluid materiality that produces liquid, fluid spatiality. The "liquid" materials arousing particular interest among architects today are composites whose composition can be precisely designed and manufactured to meet specific performance criteria. Composites are actually solid materials created, as their name suggests, by combining two or more different constituent material components, often with very different properties.[7] Together the constituents make more than the sum of their individual parts. The result is a new material that offers a marked qualitative improvement in performance, with properties that are superior to those of the original components. Among composites, the *polymer* composite materials (or simply "plastics") are being considered anew by some architects, primarily because of their high formability,[8] relatively low cost, minimum maintenance, and a relatively high strength-to-weight ratio.

By optimizing material variables in composites for local performance criteria, entirely new material and tectonic possibilities open up in architecture: transparency can be modulated in a single surface, and structural performance can be modulated by varying the quantity and pattern of reinforcement fibers,[9] etc. For example, *structural polyurethane foam*, produced by *reaction injection molding* (RIM), enables a wide range of density and rigidity to be designed and engineered into a wall panel. Two liquids are injected into the mold, reacting upon entry, and forming the polyurethane with the desired properties.[10] A solid surface with a foam core is easily achieved using this process.

Mutability of materials is also recognized as a design opportunity. The capacity of materials to transform and change over time, i.e. deteriorate through ageing, weathering, and use, was something to be avoided in much twentieth-century architecture, and was rarely embraced as a design opportunity. Decay is seen as the enemy in buildings, and a great deal of technical effort is aimed at combating and arresting it. However, weathering is a potent surface strategy[11] and has been pursued by a number of well-known architects, such as Peter Zumthor, whose work

1.4a–c. (below)
Chromogenic Dwelling,
proposed by Thom
Faulders, features a
constantly changing
pattern of visible
solids and voids.

1.3a–b. (left)
Liquid Crystal Glass House,
proposed by Michael Silver,
features an adaptive glass
enclosure that can shift
from transparency to
opacity and vice versa.

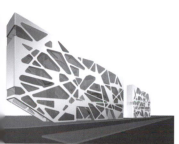

expresses a profound understanding of materials. The contemporary successor to this legacy can be found in the digitally designed and fabricated patterns of perforation and embossing in the skin of the *de Young Museum* in San Francisco, designed by *Herzog & de Meuron* in collaboration with the *A. Zahner Company.* Over time the copper skin will take on an anticipated patina, whose green coloration will eventually blend the dotted field of abstract tree canopies of the building skin with the verdant greenery of the park in which the building is situated, and thus realize a design intent in partnership with nature that will be years in the making.

Other possibilities are opened up by materials that change their properties dynamically in direct response to external and internal stimuli, such as light, heat, and mechanical stresses. Sulan Kolatan and William MacDonald have explored materials such as "plastics that undergo molecular restructuring with stress," "smart glass that responds to light and weather conditions," "anti-bacterial woven-glass-fiber wall covering," and "pultruded fiberglass-reinforced polymer structural components."[12] Michael Silver's *Liquid Crystal Glass House*[13] (figures 1.3a–b), proposed for a site in Malibu, California, features a responsive, constantly adapting electronic building skin made from panels which consist of a layer of liquid crystals sandwiched between two sheets of glass, enabling an

electronic shift from transparency to opacity and vice versa.[14] The interconnected liquid crystal glass panels are computationally controlled and can create different patterns of transparency and opacity, producing an envelope that is infinitely variable and visually unpredictable. Thom Faulders pursued a similar strategy in his *Chromogenic Dwelling* design proposal (figures 1.4a–c) for the Octavia Boulevard Housing Competition in San Francisco (2005). *Electrochromic* glass was used to create a changing pattern of visible solids and voids, where the building's occupants could electronically switch the exterior glass into an opaque, transparent, or translucent surface in response to climate, light effects, and privacy requirements.[15]

UN Studio, the Dutch design practice led by Ben van Berkel and Caroline Bos, has developed a polychromic laminated glass, with a reflective thin film between two sheets of glass that changes color depending on the light angle. It was used for the first time in the *La Defense* office complex in Almere, the Netherlands (2004); depending on the angle of incidence of sunlight, the façades facing the courtyard of this office complex change across the entire color spectrum during the day, from yellow to blue and red and from purple to green (figures 1.5a–b). The architects van Berkel and Bos were interested in "painting space,"[16] by testing "the malleability of colors almost as if [they] were de Chirico or Jeff Koons," achieving "both phenomenological and literal transparency."[17]

1.5a–b.
La Defense office
complex in Almere,
the Netherlands
(2004), designed
by *UN Studio.*

1.6a–f.
The dynamic
skin of the *Aegis
Hyposurface,*
designed by Mark
Goulthorpe/
dECOi.

1.7.
SmartWrap
ultra-thin building
envelope developed
by *KieranTimberlake,*
a Philadelphia-based
design firm.

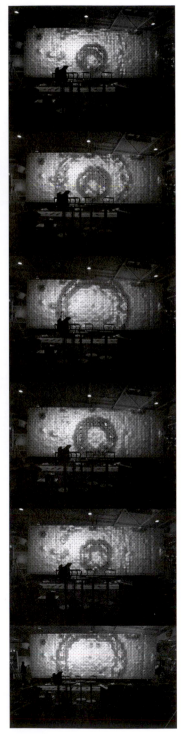

1.6a–f.
The dynamic skin of the *Aegis Hyposurface,* designed by Mark Goulthorpe/ *dECOi.*

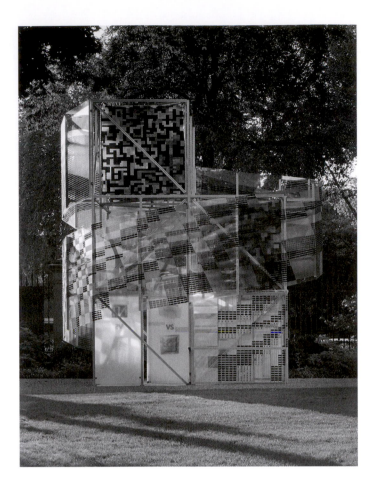

1.7. *SmartWrap* ultra-thin building envelope developed by *KieranTimberlake,* a Philadelphia-based design firm.

New skins can change not only their transparency and color, but also their shape in response to various environmental influences, as demonstrated by the *Aegis Hyposurface* project (figures 1.6a–f) by Mark Goulthorpe/*dECOi.* It features a faceted metallic surface, which is deformable, resulting from a flexible rubber membrane covered with tens of thousands of triangular metal shingles. The surface can change shape in response to electronic stimuli resulting from movement and modification of sound and light levels in its environment, or through parametrically generated patterns. It is driven by an underlying mechanical apparatus that consists of several thousand pistons, controlled digitally, providing a real-time response.[18]

Goulthorpe's *Aegis Hyposurface* dynamic skin, a highly complex, electro-mechanical hybrid structure, whose sensors, pneumatic actuators, and computational and control systems provide it with what could be called "smart" behavior, points to a material future in which a building envelope could become a fairly thin, single "intelligent" composite material[19] with a "neural" system fully integrated into its layers. Such a possibility has been already demonstrated in the *SmartWrap* project[20] (figure 1.7) by *KieranTimberlake,* a Philadelphia-based design firm. This "building envelope of the future," as it is referred to by its designers, is an ultra-thin composite material that integrates separate functional components of a conventional wall into one single element. The polymer-based material consists of a substrate (the same material used in plastic soda bottles) and printed, laminated layers that are roll-coated into a single film. This multi-functional building envelope prototype, besides providing shelter and interior climate control, also differentiates its aesthetics by changing color and appearance, as well as providing light and power to the building. Light and heating technology are simply printed on the surface.

Finally, designers and researchers increasingly are looking for inspiration in nature to discover new materials and new material behaviors, so that buildings (or rather, building enclosures) can respond dynamically to changing environmental conditions. In addition to mimicking the intricate complex *appearance* and *organization* of patterned skins and structures in nature, their *behavior* is also being investigated for possible new ideas about the performance of building skins and structures. In such "form follows performance" strategies, the impulse is to harness the generative potential of nature, where evolutionary pressure forces organisms to become highly optimized and efficient (nature produces maximum *effect* with minimum means). A nature-imitating search for new material effects, based on biological precedents – often referred to as *biomimicry* or *biomimetics*[21] – holds much promise as an overarching generative driving force for digitally driven contemporary architecture.[22]

EFFECTS

There is a close relationship of materiality in architecture to the extended realm of *effects* and *affects.* Articulation of surface and formal effects can have a tremendous affect on the experiential veracity of architecture. Peter Eisenman makes the distinction between effect and affect rather clear.[23] He states, "*Effect* is something produced by an agent or cause. In architecture it is the relationship between some

1.8.
Detail of the
*Goldman and
Salatsch Building*
("Looshaus") at
Michaelerplatz in
Vienna (1911),
designed by Adolf
Loos.

1.9.
The *Barcelona
Pavilion* (1929),
designed by Mies
van der Rohe,
features a broad
material palette,
including richly
patterned onyx and
Tinian marble.

Materials and their particular properties make architecture multi-sensory – we not only see the material surfaces, but also touch and hear them, all of which contribute to our comprehension and experience of spaces. In other words, material effects are not only visual effects; they are *experiential effects*. According to Juhani Pallasmaa, "Authentic architectural experiences derive from real or ideated bodily confrontations rather than visually observed entities ... The visual image of a door is not an architectural image, for instance, whereas entering and exiting through a door are architectural experiences."[25]

To inform our discourse today, it is useful to examine the notion of material effects from previous eras. As observed by Juhani Pallasmaa, Modernist architecture preferred materials and surfaces that could provide the "effect of flatness, immaterial abstractness, and timelessness."[26] In other words, the Modernists were after the *immaterial effects*:

> The Modernist surface is treated as an abstracted boundary of volume, and has a conceptual rather than a sensory essence. These surfaces tend to remain mute, as shape and volume are given priority; form is vocal, whereas matter remains mute. The aspiration for geometric purity and reductive aesthetics further weakens the presence of matter.[27]

object and its function or meaning; it is an idea that has dominated Western architecture for the last 200 years." In contrast, "*Affect* is the conscious subjective aspect of an emotion considered apart from bodily changes. Affect in architecture is simply the sensate response to a physical environment."[24] As architecture privileges human engagement, interaction, visual and sensual reading, well-crafted material effects can engender powerful affects.

Material effects are *performative*: we can verify how materials work by sensing what they do. Performative dimensions of materiality in architecture are primarily physical and perceptual: how the material looks matters as much as how the material performs structurally, thermally, acoustically, etc. Building materials can be manufactured mechanically through slicing and cutting, for example, shaped by force through bending, extruding, expanding, casting, etc. They are used in structural systems, in building envelopes, as surface finishes, etc., i.e. for different *effects*. More importantly, however, they are used to *affect* the perceptions and experience of the forms, surfaces, and spaces; they can embody meanings, evoke feelings ...

But, it wasn't so in the early days of Modernism. The rich, "organic" decorative qualities of materials (often richly patterned marble) were often used to counterbalance the sensory reductivism of the Modernism's formal minimalism. Adolf Loos, who at the beginning of the twentieth century decried the use of ornament in architecture,[28] in his buildings extensively deployed the natural decorative qualities of materials. In the *Goldman and Salatsch Building* ("Looshaus") at Michaelerplatz in Vienna (1911, figure 1.8), the exterior of the lower stories is surprisingly ornate, primarily through the use of richly veined green marble. Mies van der Rohe's *Barcelona Pavilion* (1929) was an ode to the sensory richness of materials, with walls made from four different kinds of stone, including richly patterned, rust-colored onyx, green Tinian marble, and white travertine (figure 1.9), cruciform chrome-plated columns, tinted glass (green, white, and clear), black carpet, scarlet velvet, plus shallow, reflective pools of water. In these examples of early Modern architecture, the material expression operates on human scale and as such elicits a more acute sensory response from the observer.

1.10.
The "*Bubble*,"
BMW pavilion at the
IAA'99 Auto Show in
Frankfurt, Germany,
designed by Bernhard
Franken.

1.11. (far right)
The "*Dynaform*,"
BMW Pavilion at the
IAA'01 Auto Show in
Frankfurt, Germany,
designed by Bernhard
Franken.

If we examine the deployment of material-driven ornamental strategies in the context of formal minimalism in early modern architecture, we realize that, while not intended as decorative, there was an inherent expression of material in its natural form, or even as affected by the machine process that manufactured it.[29] In fact, there is a subtext of manufacturing that underlies the material realization during the mechanical age, in its perfectly sliced and polished marble, repetitive standardized components, etc. According to Umberto Eco, in Renaissance and Baroque times, machines were used periodically to achieve effects, but it was the ornamental result of the effect that was celebrated, and not the procedural mechanic (machinic) operations, as we see in early Modernism. "Machines were definitively associated with the production of aesthetic effects and were used to produce 'theater,' or stunningly beautiful and amazing architectures."[30]

Phenomenological potency of material is increasingly given primacy over fluid, supple potential of the digitally derived complex form and further is in opposition to the Baroque attitude. This recognition of the affective appeal of the material affirms the significance Gaston Bachelard assigned to "material imagination." In *Water and Dreams*,[31] his phenomenological investigation of poetic imagery, Bachelard makes a distinction between two forms of imagination: a formal imagination ("images of free forms") and material imagination ("images of matter"). According to Bachelard, both are present in nature and mind; in nature, the "formal imagination" creates the beauty it contains; the "material imagination," on the other hand, produces that which, in being, is both primitive and eternal. For Bachelard, "images of matter" project deeper and more profound experiences than "images of free form." In acknowledging Bachelard's phenomenological distinctions between the images of matter and the images of form, Juhani Pallasmaa notes that "matter evokes unconscious images and emotions, but modernity at large has been primarily concerned with form."[32]

In his essay in 1992, Peter Eisenman went a step further, and lamented: "Architecture not only does not deal with affect but it no longer deals with effect."[33] That is no longer true: in contemporary architecture, materials and their inherent properties are often fundamental points of departure for discovering and exploring new spatial possibilities (*effects*) and for designing different perceptions and experiences of architecture (*affects*). For example, as discussed later in this chapter, in many projects by *Herzog & de Meuron*, the material is often foregrounded as an effect; the effect cannot be decoupled from the material.

In returning architecture to both the realm of effects and affects, we should avoid instrumentalizing the links between design intentions and their material manifestations. The typical tactic is to resort to material "determinism" by presuming that "correctly" selected materials will provide the desired effects both aesthetically and performatively. That passive mode of material deployment must be challenged. As Toshiko Mori noted in *Immaterial/Ultramaterial*, "By understanding materials' basic properties, pushing their limits for greater performance, and at the same time being aware of their aesthetic values and psychological effects, an essential design role can be regained and expanded."[34]

FROM SMOOTH TO PATTERNED

Digitally based technologies and techniques have introduced new spatial and formal capacities in architecture.[35] This digital technological shift led to several lines of investigation in contemporary architecture: one aimed at seamless materiality, in which fluid smoothness was a primary design consideration, a second trajectory explored the outcome of digitally crafted, two- and three-dimensional non-uniform patterns and textures, and a third sought out the unity of skin, structure, and pattern.

Soon after the curvaceous forms started to appear on computer screens in early 1990s, the ambition in the material realm was to express the seamlessness and the smoothness of form. Bernhard Franken, for example, described several of his projects[36] for BMW (figures 1.10 and 1.11) as an explicit attempt to hide the connections between components and achieve the smooth appearance characteristic of the cars manufactured by his client. *Future*

1.12. (left)
The *Media Centre* at
the *Lord's Cricket
Grounds* in London
(1999), designed by
Future Systems.

1.13. (right)
The "shredded" skin
of the *Embryological
House* proposed by
Greg Lynn.

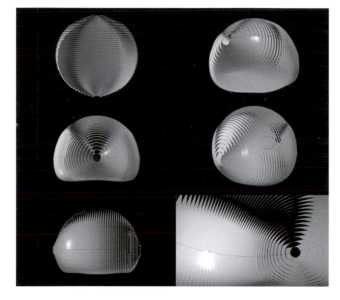

1.14.
Signal Box in Basel,
Switzerland (1999),
designed by *Herzog &
de Meuron*.

Systems expressed a similar strategy for smoothness of appearance in several of their projects, such as the *Media Centre* at the *Lord's Cricket Grounds* in London (1999, figure 1.12). To a large extent, the smoothness and seamlessness provided only one reading that mattered in those projects: overall form and shape were primary – nothing was allowed to distract from the articulation of the expressive and atypical geometry of the exterior skin.

The infatuation with complex geometry in mid-1990s soon was replaced by the exploration of highly crafted, non-uniform *surface effects* based on complex *patterning*, *texturing*, or *relief*. This aesthetic shift led to a re-emergence of the discourse related to ornament and decoration, out of favor with architecture for a large part of the twentieth century. The reasons for this move towards the ornamental or decorative stemmed partly from pragmatic requirements that building skins have to satisfy, partly from purely aesthetic considerations, and partly because of the old-fashioned need for scale and tactility in buildings.

Greg Lynn, for example, developed various strategies of creating apertures in the curvy skins of his buildings through "shredding;" the smooth morphology was adapted to the pragmatic requirements of bringing light and air into the buildings. The resulted striated, shredded surfaces attain a changing, but smooth rhythm, a pattern of alternating voids and solids that can dematerialize parts of the skin or render it almost entirely opaque depending on the viewing direction (figure 1.13); the "shredding" also adds a much needed sense of scale. In addition, the "shredding" can provide a subtle, dynamic optical effect resulting from the changing angle of the viewer's eyes to the surface, which was aptly demonstrated by the "shredded" skin of twisted copper strips in the *Signal Box* in Basel, Switzerland (1999, figure 1.14), designed by *Herzog & de Meuron*.

Among contemporary design practices, *Herzog & de Meuron* stand out in their unapologetic exploration of pattern, texture, and relief and the resulting material and surface effects they can produce. The "ornamented minimalism" – a seemingly minimalist geometry of the building, often wrapped with a highly decorative skin – has become their signature. In the Library of the *Eberswalde Technical School* in Eberswalde, Germany (1999), a

1.15. (far right)
Library of the
*Eberswalde Technical
School* in Eberswalde,
Germany (1999),
designed by *Herzog &
de Meuron*.

1.16. (right)
New addition to the
Walker Art Museum
in Minneapolis,
Minnesota (2005),
designed by *Herzog &
de Meuron*.

conventional, "box" building with horizontal, alternating strips of concrete and glass, images were silk-screened onto glass and concrete panels, literally blurring the material distinctions between the two (figure 1.15). The new addition to the *Walker Art Museum* in Minneapolis, Minnesota (2005, figure 1.16), for example, features a skin made from stamped, aluminum mesh panels, "a blur between solid, translucent, and transparent" in the words of Jacques Herzog. The "ornamental" is not limited to the building skin only; the interior surfaces of the museum addition are decorated by swirling, lacy patterns cut in wood (figure 1.17) or embossed in metal panels (figure 1.18).

1.17. (right)
Walker Art Museum:
Swirling, lacy patterns
were cut in wood in the
interior surfaces.

1.18. (far right)
Walker Art Museum:
Swirling, lacy patterns
were embossed
into panels in the
auditorium.

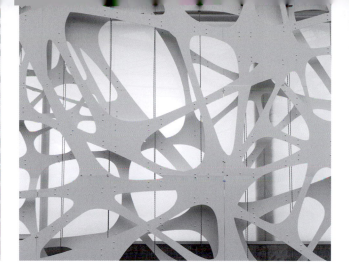

1.19. (above)
The embossed and perforated rain screen panels in *de Young Museum* in San Francisco (2005), designed by *Herzog & de Meuron*.

1.20a–b. (above right)
The *Airspace* façade in Tokyo, Japan (2007), designed by *Thom Faulders Architecture* with *Proces2*.

The scale of decoration in the buildings by *Herzog & de Meuron* can vary greatly, from several feet to several hundred feet. The large surfaces of the rain screen at the *De Young Museum* in San Francisco are made from over 7,000 copper panels, each of which features unique halftone cut-out and embossing patterns abstracted from images of the surrounding tree canopies (figure 1.19). The rain screen cladding is obviously decorative, but it also has a purely functional purpose – to hide an integrated ventilation system and to diffuse exterior light falling into the galleries. Such a *functional* approach to ornamentation is typical of many of the projects by *Herzog & de Meuron*. A project with a similar functional intent can be found in the Thom Faulders-designed layered, porous skin of the *Airspace* façade in Tokyo, Japan (2007, figures 1.20a–b): "sunlight is refracted

along its metallic surfaces; rainwater is channeled away from exterior walkways via capillary action; and interior views are shielded behind its variegated and foliage-like cover."[37]

Patterned surfaces of the *Federation Square* building in Melbourne (figure 1.21), designed by *LAB Architecture Studio*, are based on what is known in mathematics as *pinwheel aperiodic tiling*, enabling the designers to apply different scales of the same pattern across the building as needed. There are other notable examples in which patterning is based on mathematics. For example, *Voronoi tessellation*[38] is a particularly popular algorithm today (figure 1.22). Daniel Libeskind, as well, proposed a patterned skin based on fractals for the extension he designed (with Cecil Balmond of *Arup*) for the *Victoria & Albert Museum* addition in London (figure 1.23).

1.21. (right)
The *pinwheel aperiodic tiling* in the patterned skin of the *Federation Square* buildings in Melbourne, Australia (2002), designed by *LAB Architecture Studio*.

1.22. (far right)
The patterning of the *C-wall* project by Andrew Kudless is based on *Voronoi tessellation*.

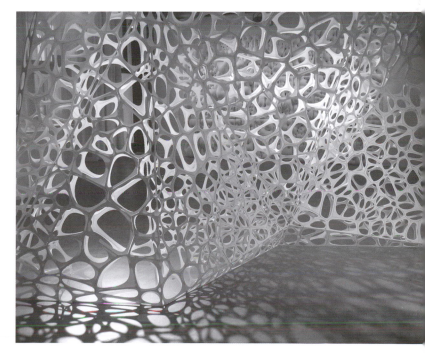

1.23. (right)
The fractal skin of
the proposed *Victoria
& Albert Museum*
addition in London,
designed by Daniel
Libeskind.

1.24a–b.
The three-
dimensional
Voronoi
patterning
by Andrew
Kudless.

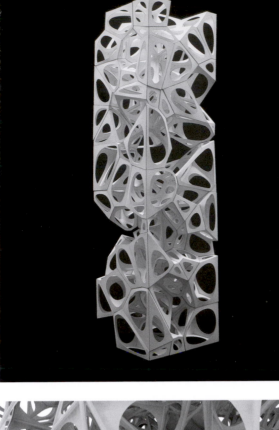

Many of these patterning schemes can be extended from a two-dimensional to a three-dimensional realm (figures 1.24a–b) and emerge from basic mathematical operations in order to achieve complex results. A simple patterning scheme was used by Cecil Balmond and Toyo Ito in their design for the *Serpentine Pavilion* in London (2002, figure 1.25) to produce a complex-looking outcome. The apparently random patterning that wraps the entire pavilion is produced by incremental scaling and rotation of a series of inscribed squares, whose edges were extended and trimmed by the pavilion's unfolded box shape (figure 1.26) to create a beautiful, seemingly irregular-looking pattern of alternating voids and solids. The "bird nest" random-looking structural pattern for the *National Stadium* in Beijing, China (2008, figure 1.27), designed by *Herzog & de Meuron* with *Arup*, is also based on a relatively simple set of rules to create the "extra-large" material effect. The nearby *National Aquatics Center* (2008, figure 1.28), designed by *PTW Architects* from Australia (with *Arup*), provides another example of a large-scale material effect. The *Water Cube*, as the project is nicknamed, is a simple box that features a complex three-dimensional bubble patterning. Its geometric origin is the so-called *Weaire-Phelan* structure[39] (figure 1.29), an efficient method of subdividing space using two kinds of cells of equal volume: an irregular *pentagonal dodecahedron* and a *tetrakaidecahedron* with 2 hexagons and 12 pentagons. This regular three-dimensional pattern was sliced with a

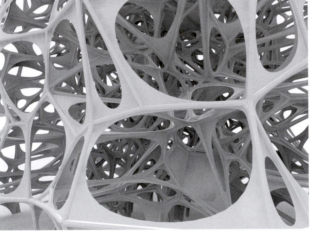

1.25. (right)
The *Serpentine
Pavilion* in London
(2002), designed by
Cecil Balmond and
Toyo Ito.

1.26. (far right)
Serpentine Pavilion:
the irregular-looking
pattern is based on
incremental scaling
and rotation of a
series of inscribed
squares.

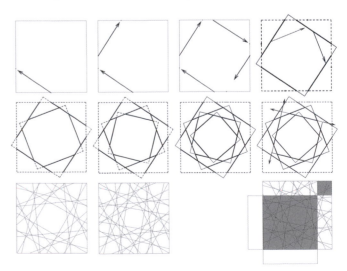

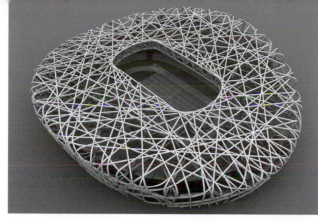

1.27.
The "bird nest" structural pattern of the *National Stadium* in Beijing, China (2008), designed by *Herzog & de Meuron* with *Arup Sports*.

1.28. (right)
The *National Aquatics Center* in Beijing, China (2008), designed by *PTW Architects* with *Arup*.

1.30. (right)
The *CCTV* building in Beijing, China (2008), designed by *OMA* in collaboration with *Arup*.

1.31. (far right)
Ministry of Culture and Communication in Paris, France (2005), designed by Francis Soler.

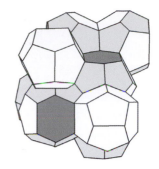

1.29. (right)
National Aquatics Center: the three-dimensional pattern is based on *Weaire-Phelan* structure made from *dodecahedrons* and *tetrakaidecahedrons*.

non-aligned, i.e. slightly rotated rectilinear box to produce the seemingly irregular patterning effect on the exterior. Voids between structural members on the exterior and interior of the building are filled with inflated, pillow-like layers of plastic film called *ethylene tetrafluoroethylene* (*ETFE*).[40] The material effects of this translucent, white, bubble-like skin is ethereal, literally inducing a sensation of being immersed into a giant foam-like structure. Finally, the *Central Chinese Television Center (CCTV)* located further away in the newly emerging Beijing business district (to be also completed in 2008), also features an extra-large complex patterning scheme (figure 1.30), resulting in this case from the structural analysis of the stresses in the envelope of the building's simply shaped spatial loop.

In many recently completed projects, patterning, however, is primarily decorative, i.e. there is little of the "functionalist ornamentation" as seen in the work of *Herzog & de Meuron*, described earlier. A good example of this purely decorative application of patterning is the recently completed *Ministry of Culture and Communication* in Paris, France (2005), designed by Francis Soler, wrapped in what C.C. Sullivan referred to as a "tech-nouveau" latticework screen of stainless steel with six recurring, symmetrical motifs[41] (figure 1.31). The function of this decorative "wrapper" is to create a visual unity of two distinctly different buildings: the old, neo-classical building and its contemporary glass addition; technically, it is largely superficial.

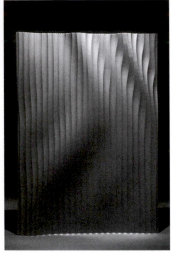

1.34. (below)
CNC-carved panels
are commercially
produced in variable
series (*Esthetic Panels*,
manufactured by
Marotte, France).

1.32a–b.
Objectiles,
parametrically
designed and
produced by
Bernard Cache.

1.33.
The use of CNC
"corrugation"
in Greg Lynn's
work.

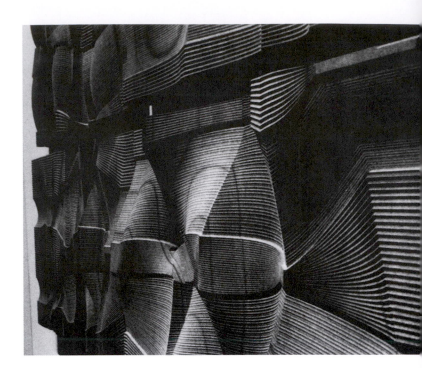

Working on a much smaller scale, Bernard Cache explored the decorative realm of pattern, texture, and relief, which also seems to be the current preoccupation of Greg Lynn, who, for example, in recent projects uses "surface geometry to emit texture information so that, like an animal skin, the pattern and relief is intricate with the form."[42] For Cache, "objects are no longer designed but calculated,"[43] allowing the design of complex, variable shapes and laying "the foundation for a nonstandard mode of production."[44] His *objectiles* (figures 1.32a–b), mainly furniture and paneling, are procedurally calculated in modeling software and are industrially produced with numerically controlled machines. The modification of parameters of design, often random, allows the manufacture of unique objects in a same series, thus making mass-customization, i.e. the industrial production of unique objects, possible.[45]

In many of his *objectile* designs, Cache exploits the decorative effect of the tooling path patterns that can be produced in the material by CNC milling machines. These material effects are directly related to how the surfaces are crafted in CNC milling.[46] In CAD/CAM post-processing software, a NURBS surface is interpreted and converted into precise tool paths that produce a corrugated pattern in the material.[47] By designing the tool paths carefully, richly patterned surfaces can be produced by carefully choreographing the milling sequence. Slight deviations in tool paths can produce surprisingly interesting effects in the material. The same two-dimensional (XY) tooling pattern, if varied in Z direction for each manufactured instance, can produce a series of repetitive, yet differentiated objects. This and similar carefully crafted tool path strategies have been used by Cache very effectively in a number of his *objectiles*;[48] they appear as the information-driven, machinic tectonics inheriting (and redirecting) the modernist notions of ornament as resulting from manufacturing processes. Similar patterning techniques were used by Greg Lynn for interior wall panels (figure 1.33), as an "ornament [that] accentuates the formal qualities of the surface."[49] There are now several commercially available product lines that feature

paneling systems with repetitive and differing patterning produced in automatic fashion through CNC milling[50] (figure 1.34).

Finally, evocative visual effects can be produced by mimicking the appearance of one material in another; this is a time-tested technique practiced by stone masons over centuries. *Belzberg Architects* produced fabric-like simulated effect in wood panels for the *Patina Restaurant* (in Frank Gehry-designed *Walt Disney Concert Hall*) in Los Angeles (figure 1.35) by laminating standard wood planks and then CNC milling the desired curtain-like "topography" in the resulting laminate. Such visual and tactile material strategies need not be (entirely) digitally driven. In the *p-wall* project, Andrew Kudless used elastic fabric to cast a series of plaster panels, arranged in a large field (figure 1.36). This project, inspired by the experiments in flexible concrete formwork by Spanish architect Miguel Fisac in the 1960s, is based on a cloud of points generated from the grayscale values of pixels in a digital image. The points are used to constrain the elastic fabric in the formwork, as it expands under the weight of poured plaster. As observed by Kudless, "The resultant plaster tile has a certain resonance with the body as it sags, expands, and stretches in its own relationship with gravity and structure." The resulting supple surface invites visitors to touch it, to sense its smooth undulations. *The affect is in the material effect, whether small, medium, large, or extra-large.*

1.35.
The *Patina
Restaurant* in Los
Angeles, designed
by *Belzberg
Architects*.

MATERIAL AND SURFACE EFFECTS: ORNAMENT REDUX?

> Ornament shapes, straightens and stabilizes the bare arid field on which it is inscribed. Not only does it exist in and of itself, but it also shapes its own environment – to which it imparts form. (Henri Focillon)[51]

The projects presented so far raise the perennial questions of surface and form versus structure, of *appearance* versus *substance* (or *superficiality* versus *essence*, as seen by some) in contemporary architecture. While the digital technologies of parametric design and fabrication opened new possibilities for non-uniform, non-monotonous, variable patterning and texturing of surface, the question of appropriateness, i.e. of cultural significance of such ornamental treatment of surfaces in a contemporary context also emerged.

Following the famous manifesto Adolf Loos published in 1908, polemically entitled "Ornament and Crime," in which he described ornament as a need of the primitive man, arguing that the lack of decoration is a manifestation of a progressive, advanced culture,[52] the emergence of the Modern Movement entrenched

1.36.
The *p-wall*
project by
Andrew
Kudless.

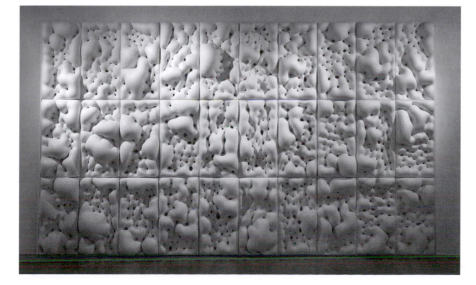

a perception that to be authentically "modern," one has to categorically remove all ornament, which consequently led to the barren surfaces of much twentieth-century architecture. It was the absence of historically traditional surface ornamentation that arguably made the minimalist aesthetics of Modernism less *affectionate*, contributing in part to its demise. The façades didn't shed the rhythm and the pattern – but their monotonous grids didn't give much to the eye. Moreover, in Loos' articulation of the minimal ornamental expression of modern architecture, he decried the potential for lineages in this manner of thinking: "Modern ornament has neither forbears nor descendants, no past and no future."[53]

We take the "Semperian" position that "architecture comes to be defined in its essence as an ornamental activity."[54] After all, throughout history (bar the second half of the twentieth century) ornamentation was used in buildings, both on the exterior and in the interior, to enhance and amplify presence and appearance, give scale and texture through intricate treatment of surfaces, and demonstrate the mastery of artisans and craftsmen. Ornamentation had largely a symbolic function – it embodied values and ideals that defined a particular culture, simultaneously acting as a symbolic construct and enabling the construction of symbolic meaning. Such an approach to ornamentation is in line with the view that the buildings are shaped by and are expressive of the social, economic, political and cultural context, i.e. buildings are *representational*, while simultaneously being active agents in defining that very same context.

Given the increasing presence of ornamentation in contemporary design (and not just in architecture but also in a range of design disciplines), an obvious question to ask is if there is any deeper significance, some kind of profound relevance of ornamentation today. A possible answer to that question could start with a definition of what constitutes an ornament in a contemporary context. As there are many possible definitions, perhaps it would be more appropriate to begin by making some basic distinctions about different kinds of ornament in architecture.

In general, ornamentation can be *decorative* or *applied*, *functional* or *integral*, and *mimetic* or *imitative*. Ornament, when purely decorative, relies on its application to an already existing surface or an object; hence, such ornamentation could be classified as *applied*. Structural ornament is considered an integral part of the building's structure, i.e. the structural components act simultaneously as ornaments, as was the case, for example, in gothic architecture. Such ornamentation can be described as *functional* or *integral*. *Mimetic* or *imitative* ornamentation is characterized by unambiguous meanings or symbolic significance – it is purely representational.

Today, however, when "decorative" is used to describe an artifact, the meaning is negative in most cases, suggesting that the work itself is superficial, devoid of any deeper meaning. The perception of superficiality often stems from the surface application of ornamentation – it is often seen as nothing more than an (unnecessary) embellishment to an "other," as was the case for most of the twentieth century.

When decoration is deployed in a contemporary context, it is often used to hide something unpleasant to the eye – a *functional* application that is often judged as acceptable (*Herzog & de Meuron* used an ornamented rain screen to hide an integrated ventilation system on the façade of the *de Young Museum*). Decoration, however, is increasingly seen as *performative* as well, as it can produce effects that can directly affect an emotional response; it can be

excessive or minimal, "loud" or "quiet," "serious" or "cheerful." It can accentuate a specific quality of the object or the surface to which it is applied.

Another way of understanding the significance of ornament is to compare it to pattern which could be described as an abstract construct characterized by repetition. As such, patterns exist in nature in all sorts of imaginable shapes, forms, and sizes. It is only when a particular pattern is recognized and represented in some physical manifestation, such as decoration, for example, that it becomes a cultural artifact – an ornament.

The human need to perceive, organize, and structure the world around us into patterns and rhythms is seen as intrinsic; decoration and ornament are recognized as indicators of neurological synergy of the eye and the brain. E.H. Gombrich offers evolutionary arguments that ornament is a result of a biological need to generate underlying structure in the surrounding environments: "I believe that in the struggle for existence organisms developed a sense of order not because their environment was generally orderly but rather because perception requires a framework against which to plot deviations from regularity."[55] According to Gombrich, the human mind has an intrinsic need for "careful balance" between complexity and order. The mind has no trouble deconstructing a simple, regular grid (i.e. recognizing the monotonous); it quickly "disconnects" in reading complex configurations if it cannot recognize an underlying structure. Gombrich argues that a "careful balance" between these two conditions, i.e. between monotony and complexity, is what the mind looks for in its constant processing of the surrounding environments.

In other words, one could argue that patterning – or ornamentation – is a necessity, and perhaps as such, it should be given back the significance it once had in architectural discourse. The challenge is to avoid creating a singular, outstanding image, pattern, or form (*the* effect), but a subtle, sensory, contextually responsive and responsible experience (*an* affect).

AFFECTING ARCHITECTURE

It seems that the computational potential for generating complex forms and complexly patterned surfaces and structures is virtually inexhaustible. The precise digital representation of these complexities and the capacity of digital fabrication technologies to reproduce in material *any* shape or form regardless of its complexity seem to have expanded infinitely the boundaries of what is possible geometry- and material-wise. This liberation from the orthogonal grid and the constraints of standardization raises not only the obvious question of what (and where) the new *limits* are, but, more fundamentally, to what ends – to what *effects* and *affects* – should this new formal and material liberty be directed. If seemingly any complexity is describable and producible in a plane or in space, what is the new formal and material "discipline"?

Beyond the pragmatic instrumentality implications of manufacturing material effects lies a provocation of new (and old) ways of thinking about architecture. The idea of a harmonious "whole" being greater than and dependent upon the sum of its "parts" is examined today directly through interconnected relationships, layers of information, and a search for "elegance" in architecture. An example of the integrated application of the multiplicity of information about a project can be seen in the proliferation of ecological and biological design considerations surfacing in contemporary architecture in relation to greater availability of information about natural and human circumstance.

Engineering, scientific, and aesthetic ideas are part of the great subtext of greater information and digitally driven methods. Concepts such as minimizing waste are engineering tactics that are increasingly applied to architecture as design intention, and stemming from a deeper and early connection to information about a given project. Other engineering concepts, such as optimization, are finding favor, not just in budgetary considerations and fabrication procedures, but also in formal and organizational strategies. Greater attention is given to calculating performance criteria and scientific analyses of simulated building behavior as essential feedback criteria in the design process. Refuting the longstanding aesthetic traditions arising from standardization of industrial techniques, we are also finding a much more productive position for the return of notions of ornament, eschewed from architectural fashion for much of the twentieth century.

Each new project brings us closer to a more complete picture of the implications of these new methods, although, the solutions will most likely be a range of possibilities. At present, more manageable scales dominate the cases of these new methods, as economies of scale in deploying these techniques have yet to be replicated in the complexity of major building projects. In most projects, the building skin and its surface effects remain the most potent territory for this discourse. The trajectory of these applications, however, lies not in the final form, but in the retooling of how we consider architecture. Manufacturing material effects is now finding increasing application, with growing scales and complexity resulting from closer relations between designers and fabricators, as the learning curve of adopting these techniques ripples through the discipline.

More fundamentally, the developing materials and the digital technologies of production, touched upon in this chapter, may substantially redefine the relationship between architecture and its material reality. Current research efforts, such as the *SmartWrap* project described earlier, point to a material future of architecture in which conventional building cladding will be compressed into a "plastic sheet" that is ultralight, fairly inexpensive, and that can be erected in a fraction of time compared to present practice. This is a dramatic technological development with the potential to transform all aspects of building design and production, with broad social, economic, and cultural implications.

The *SmartWrap* project offers a glimpse of future building envelopes based on *functionally gradient polymer composite* materials, in which structure, glazing, mechanical, and electrical systems are synthesized into a single material entity. By producing materials in a digitally controlled layer-by-layer fashion, as in *additive fabrication*, it is possible to embed various functional components, thus making them an integral part of a single, complex composite material. This, in turn, implies designing with heterogeneous and non-isotropic materials, i.e. with materials in which variation is present not only in surface articulation, but also in material composition.

We already have the technological capacity to design and manufacture materials that do not have uniform composition, properties, and appearance. With digital parametric design and production, variation becomes possible not only in spatial layouts and component dimensions, but also in material composition and surface articulation, offering unprecedented freedom from standardization that defined design and production for much of the twentieth century. Such variability presents a radical departure from the present normative practice. Whether the new "freedoms," afforded by almost infinite variability in design and production, result in better architecture remains to be seen.

NOTES

1 Juhani Pallasmaa, "Hapticity and Time – Notes on Fragile Architecture," *The Architectural Review*, vol. 207, no.1239, May 2000, pp. 78–84.

2 Toshiko Mori (ed.), *Immaterial/Ultramaterial: Architecture, Design, and Materials*, New York: George Braziller, Inc., 2002, p. xv.

3 For an in-depth discussion of the structural shifts within the building industry, see Branko Kolarevic (ed.), *Architecture in the Digital Age Design and Manufacturing*, London: Spon Press, 2003, and Branko Kolarevic and Ali Malkawi (eds), *Performative Architecture: Beyond Instrumentality*, London: Spon Press, 2005.

4 For more on the exchange of information, see the chapter by Kevin R. Klinger in this book.

5 Mori, op. cit., p. xv.

6 Translucent (light-transmitting) concrete is produced by mixing glass fibers with crushed stone, cement and water, introducing a slight variation to a process used for centuries. The process was devised by Hungarian architect Aron Losonczi in 2001, who founded the company that offers translucent concrete products under the name of *LiTraCon*.

7 A composite material is produced by combining two principal components – the reinforcement and the matrix, to which other filler materials and additives could be added. The matrix is, typically, a metallic, ceramic or polymer material, into which multiple layers of reinforcement fibers, made from glass, carbon, polyethylene or some other material, are embedded. Lightweight fillers are often used to add volume to the composites with minimal weight gain, while various chemical additives are typically used to attain a desired color or to improve fire or thermal performance.

8 The actual components made from composite materials are usually formed over CNC-milled moulds, as in boat-building to produce boat hulls or large interior components, or in closed moulds by injecting the matrix material under pressure or by partial vacuum, as is done in the automotive industry for the production of smaller-scale components. In the building industry, composite panels are produced either through continuous lamination or by using the resin transfer molding.

9 Bettum, Johan. "Skin Deep: Polymer Composite Materials in Architecture," in Ali Rahim (ed.), *AD Profile 155: Contemporary Techniques in Architecture*, London: Wiley Academy Editions, 2002, pp. 72–76.

10 A polyol and an isocyanate mixture are used in a product called *Baydur*, manufactured by *Bayer*, Germany.

11 For a discussion of weathering as a continuation of the building process rather than as a force antagonistic to it, see Mohsen Mostafavi and David Leatherbarrow, *On Weathering: The Life of Buildings in Time*, Cambridge, MA: MIT Press, 1993.

12 Sulan Kolatan and William MacDonald, Kol/Mac Studio, http://www.kolmacllc.com.

13 See http://www.vrglass.net.

14 This new category of glass is more commonly known as "smart glass" or "switchable glass." It is also technically known as *electrochromic* glass. Smart glass can change its light transmission properties when voltage is applied, i.e. it can switch from transparency to opacity, and vice versa. A thin film laminate of rod-like particles suspended in a fluid is placed between two glass layers. In the absence of electrical current, the suspended particles are randomly arranged and absorb light, and the glass panel looks opaque. When an electric current is applied, the suspended particles become aligned and let the light pass, thus making the glass transparent.

15 Described online at http://www.beigedesign.com/proj_chromogenic.html.

16 As quoted in Lucy Bullivant, "Non-standard Networking," *Atlas*, no. 23, November 2005, p. 99.

17 Ibid.

18 For more information about this project, see Mark Goulthorpe/dECOi, "Scott Points: Exploring Principles of Digital Creativity" in Branko Kolarevic (ed.), *Architecture in the Digital Age: Design and Manufacturing*, London: Spon Press, 2003, pp. 163–180.

19 "Intelligent," "smart," "adaptive" and other terms are used today to describe a higher form of composite materials that have sensors, actuators, and computational and control firmware built into their layers. According to another definition, intelligent materials are those materials that possess adaptive capabilities to external stimuli through built-in "intelligence." This "intelligence" of the material can be "programmed" through its composition, its microstructure, or by conditioning to adapt in a certain manner to different levels of stimuli. The "intelligence" of the material can be limited to sensing or actuation only. For example, a sensory material is capable of determining particular material states or characteristics and sending an appropriate signal; an adaptive material is capable of altering its properties, such as volume, opacity, color, resistance, etc. in response to external stimuli. An active material, however, contains both sensors and actuators, with a feedback loop between the two, and is capable of complex behavior – not only can it sense a new condition, but it can also respond to it. For an in-depth discussion of "smart" materials, see Michelle Addington, *Smart Materials and Technologies in Architecture*, Oxford: Architectural Press, 2005.

20 Described online at http://www.kierantimberlake.com/research/smartwrap_research_1.html.

21 The term *biomimetics* refers to man-made processes, substances, devices, or systems that imitate nature. It was coined by Otto Herbert Schmitt (1913–1998), an American engineer and biophysicist, best known for establishing the field of biomedical engineering. *Velcro*, the hook-loop fastener, is perhaps the best-known example of material *biomimetics*: it was created in 1948 by George de Mestral, Swiss engineer, who was interested in how the hooks of the burrs clung to the fur of his dog.

22 Imitating forms and structures found in nature also has a long history in architecture: Joseph Paxton's *Crystal Palace* was allegedly inspired by the lily pad's structure.

23 Peter Eisenman, "The Affects of Singularity," in Andreas Papadakis (ed.), *Theory and Experimentation*, *Architectural Design*, London: Academy Editions, 1992, pp. 42–45.

24 Peter Eisenman (ibid) goes on to discuss the technological shift vis-à-vis the notions of effect and affect: "The mechanical paradigm dealt with the shift in value from the individual hand, as in the hand of a painter as an original maker, to the value of the hand as intermediary, as in the developer of raw film; from the creation of an individual to the mediation of the multiple. The photograph can be manipulated by an individual to have more contrast, more texture, more tone. Thus there remains within the mechanical repetition of a photograph a unique, individual quality; it remains a particular object even within the idea of the multiple. And within the process, the individual subject is still able to effect as well as affect."

25 Pallasmaa, op. cit. p. 79.

26 Ibid.

27 Ibid.

28 Adolf Loos, "Ornament and Crime" (originally published in 1908) in Michael Mitchell (trans.), *Ornament and Crime: Selected Essays*, Riverside, CA: Ariadne Press, 1997.

29 "But what is most remarkable, in view of later developments, is to find within the line of descent from the English Free architecture and the Deutscher Werkbund, no sense of impropriety in the ornamentation of machinery, engineering structures and machine products. The development of such a sense is a tribute to the revolution in taste effected by Loos himself and the Abstract aesthetics of the war years." In Reyner Banham, "Adolph Loos and the Problem of Ornament," in *Theory and Design in the First Machine Age*, London: Architectural Press, 1960, p. 91.

30 Umberto Eco (ed.), *History of Beauty*, New York: Rizzoli International Publications, 2004, p. 388.

31 Gaston Bachelard, "Introduction," in *Water and Dreams: An Essay On the Imagination of Matter* (1942), Dallas Institute, Texas, 1983.

32 Pallasmaa, op. cit.

33 Eisenman, op. cit. p. 43.

34 Mori, op. cit., p. xiv.

35 For more information, see Branko Kolarevic (ed.), *Architecture in the Digital Age*.

36 Bernhard Franken, "Real as Data," in Branko Kolarevic (ed.), *Architecture in the Digital Age*, pp. 121–138.

37 As described online at http://www.beigedesign.com/proj_airspace.html.

38 Voronoi diagrams are named after Russian mathematician Georgy Voronoi, who studied the general n-dimensional case of the conceptually simple decomposition scheme in 1908. In *Voronoi tessellation*, the decomposition of space is determined by distances to a specified discrete set of objects (points) in space.

39 The *Weaire-Phelan structure* is a complex three-dimensional structure devised in 1993 by Denis Weaire and Robert Phelan, two physicists based at Trinity College in Dublin, Ireland.

40 This extremely lightweight material was also used in the enclosures of the *Allianz Arena* in Munich, Germany (2005), designed by *Herzog & de Meuron*, and the *Eden Project* in Cornwall, England (2001), designed by *Grimshaw and Partners*.

41 C.C. Sullivan, "Screen Gem," *Architecture*, September 2005, p. 67.

42 Online at www.glform.com.

43 Bernard Cache, *Earth Moves: The Furnishing of Territories*, Cambridge, MA: MIT Press, 1995.

44 Ibid.

45 The digitally driven production processes introduce a different logic of *seriality* in architecture, one that is based on local variation and differentiation in series. In buildings, individual components could be customized using digital technologies of fabrication to allow optimal variance in response to differing local conditions in buildings, such as uniquely shaped and sized structural components that address different structural loads in the most optimal way, variable window shapes and sizes that correspond to differences in orientation and available views, etc.

46 In addition to careful crafting of the CNC tool paths (whether for milling or cutting) for each object produced in series, particular attention must be given to the overall *field effect* that is created by assembling the seemingly similar objects into a larger composition. This field effect can be described as a secondary pattern that emerges through the composition of primary, object-related tool path patterns. In many projects, however, it is the field effect that is the primary surface effect that is sought.

47 In a typical CNC production, however, the desired outcome is a smooth, featureless surface which is produced by using milling bits with a fairly small radius and tool paths that are closely spaced.

48 Another technique that Cache used was to work with flat-sheet laminated materials into which a certain topographic design is inscribed through milling, producing a contouring effect that reveals the laminate in subtle ways. In some projects, he used a parametrically controlled and varied spline curve to inscribe it into series of solid panels or to carve out complex shapes that can produce intricate screens with repetitive, yet differing patterns.

49 N. Leach, D. Turnbull and C. Williams (eds), *Digital Tectonics*, London: Wiley-Academy, 2004, p. 65.

50 Cache's *Objectile* website, now defunct, permitted customers to design their own patterns by varying the parameter values that control the geometry of patterning. The parameter values are then automatically transmitted to the fabricator and translated into CNC machine code for manufacturing.

51 Henri Focillon, *The Life of Forms in Art*, (trans. George Kubler), New York: Zone Books, 1992, p. 66.

52 Loos, op. cit.

53 Ibid.

54 Godfried Semper (originally published in 1860–1863; Introduction by Harry Francis Mallgrave), *Style in the Technical and Tectonic Arts; or, Practical Aesthetics*, Los Angeles: Getty Research Institute, 2004.

55 E.H. Gombrich, *The Sense of Order: A Study in the Psychology of Decorative Art*, Ithaca, NY: Cornell University Press, 1979.

2

RELATIONS: INFORMATION EXCHANGE IN DESIGNING AND MAKING ARCHITECTURE

KEVIN R. KLINGER / BALL STATE UNIVERSITY

2.1.
The *Parthenon* in
Athens, Greece
(5th century BC).

Architecture depends upon its time. It is the crystallization of its inner structure, the slow unfolding of its form. That is the reason why technology and architecture are so closely related. Our real hope is that they will grow together, that some day the one will be the expression of the other. Only then will we have an architecture worthy of its name: architecture as a true symbol of our time.

(Mies van der Rohe)[1]

Digital technology has engendered a profound affect on modes of architectural production. While technological change has always been a catalyst for new ideas in architecture, today, digital information technology is the essential agent of innovation in a total process of architecture. The central requirement is clear, reliable, and consistent exchange of information among all parties involved in creating and realizing a given project. Software enables architects to manage complexly articulated designs, while digital models facilitate the exchange of information with collaborative teams, interweaving a diverse range of expertise and feedback into the design process. As a result, analysis, simulation, fabrication, and assembly information are revealed at earlier stages in the process of formulating architecture.

A critical examination of data in a *total process of design through production* sets in motion a well-informed series of architectural intentions. Several factors, which may seem obvious, must be stated as essentials: first, the projects need to be built. Second, *design is central* to the equation, and must be privileged in the development of solutions, augmented by feedback about production realities. Third, *early collaboration* is necessary with a diverse range of expertise. Finally, and most importantly, numerous inputs of information about the project must be *effectively managed* during all stages of realization of a project; while the master model is the central storage mechanism of project information as it evolves toward built form, it is the information that adds value through an iterative process and critical reflection, resulting in useful data stored in the model. Rigorous application of these informed methods leads to abundant solutions that address an array of design and performance concerns. Through a reflective process-oriented crafting of shared information, the effective means of communication and information exchange is vital to the achievement of new methods for design and production for an architecture aligned with the spirit of our age.

ANCIENT HARMONY

The ancient Greeks turned to interrogating nature to reveal its secrets. In a sense, they endeavored to discover the codes of nature and use them with mathematics and geometry as organizing devices, which, if applied judiciously, led to "harmony" in architecture[2] (figure 2.1). (The golden section *is* true; it *does* occur in nature.) Today, we do not talk about "harmony" (let alone "beauty"). Yet, like the ancient Greeks, we are operating at the level of the *code* – whether found in nature or not – by manipulating information that remains largely invisible in the final form.

The ancient Greeks translated codified geometry into fundamental principles that could be applied as universal solutions for design strategies. The analog application of geometry has given way today to the algorithmic definition of complex geometry. This algorithmic, *procedural* geometry, while still governed by a mathematical rigor of an internal logic, has its own inherent nature, resulting in formal strategies that seem to lack the certainty of a universal principle;[3] each solution can be unique depending upon selected input variables (figure 2.2). Yet, it is difficult to critique an algorithmic, generative procedure for its formal implications; we can only evaluate its particular formulaic potentialities. So instead, our focus has shifted mostly to an effective interrogation and revealing of information specific to the formulations of architectural intent; "harmony" remains out with the discussion.

2.2.
Manifold Project:
Andrew Kudless:
Architectural
Association, MA
dissertation,[4]
London (2004).

The ancient Greek temple, elevated high on the hill was dedicated to the gods, but in effect, they were elevating their own understanding of order derived from interpreting the natural realm.[5] If we examine our high places today, such as tops of buildings, mountains, and even the exosphere, we find the signification of ubiquitous information flow: cell towers, dishes, satellites in geosynchronous orbit, all radiating dense waves of invisible bits of information. How do we organize and articulate architecture in this ocean of information? The answer is obvious — by steering in relation to information, and navigating the bits. As such, with a diversity of expertise and fluidity of information exchange, new structural conditions for building can flourish, and we can turn our attention to the fundamental relations of architecture (i.e. the natural world), and its greater affects (i.e. the human realm).

ENCOMPASSING INFORMATION

Contemporary methods in architecture promote computational processes, which demand dynamic flows of information. Layers of embedded intelligence are interlaced with formal generative techniques. Parameters take into account behaviors in relation to sun, gravity, environment, or hundreds of other considerations. While algorithms assist in the examination of complex strategies, human reasoning still governs the selection of appropriate input parameters for consideration. Choices are born out of a human capacity, even though we could still envision an architecture that is the result of a direct output of specified inputs and formulaic calculations by computational devices, as envisioned by Nicholas Negroponte in *The Architecture Machine*[6] in the early and radical days of computational speculation of the late 1960s and early 1970s. To set up his argument, Negroponte offers a useful articulation of the human capacity for incorporating information into design:

> What probably distinguishes a talented, competent designer is his ability both to provide and to provide for missing information. Any environmental design task is characterized by an astounding amount

of unavailable or indeterminate information. Part of the design process is, in effect, the procurement of this information. Some is gathered by doing research in the preliminary design stages. Some is obtained through experience, overlaying and applying a seasoned wisdom. Other chunks of information are gained through prediction, induction, and guesswork. Finally some information is handled randomly, playfully, whimsically, personally.[7]

At about the same time, however, Buckminster Fuller raised serious questions about the human ability to cope with issues of complexity.[8] Today, the very notion of involving human choice in relation to complexity underscores the necessity for a greater evolution of architectural principles relevant to a *total process of design-through-production* that privileges the exchange of information. This is the hinge. Many new digital design languages import terms and reflect qualities specific to the jargon of the digital tools we use, yet a "clear and critical definition of new principles has yet to materialize."[9] This doesn't mean that the old principles are irrelevant; rather, a broader definition of architectural principles should emerge in relation to the digital age, and in relation to a much more significantly informed understanding of an interconnected world.

DIGITAL EXCHANGE

An effective exchange of information is fundamental in achieving architecture materially, and is increasingly reliant upon close collaboration between architects, manufacturers, fabricators, material suppliers, engineers, and many others in the early, conceptual stages in design. This new structural condition has led to innovative architectural opportunities, well articulated in the resonant call for changing the profession led by Phillip Bernstein[10] and others. Roles of collaborators vary on a per project basis, and in reality, many potential players must retool their operations to more effectively participate in the digital exchange.[11] Ironically, the evidence that the information age has advanced inter- and intra-relations of diverse participants is the ultimate realization of notions proposed during the height of the mechanical age by Walter Gropius[12] and others, who lamented the separation of the trades.

2.3.
This communitarian town plan was based on a model community at *New Harmony*, Indiana, by Robert Owen (1825).[13] Key elements include functions that elevate the social and human realm: a central conservatory and "Pleasure Grounds" flanked by four major buildings for social gathering, assembly, concerts, libraries, reading rooms, museums, laboratories, artists' rooms, lecture rooms, committee rooms, and places of worship.

More often than not, presentations by those who identify the potentials of new structural conditions for the building industry include some form of diagram that represents a *new* way of organizing the building enterprise. Typically the point of view of the person presenting is what ends up in the center of these diagrams, whether a software developer, regulating institution, developer, contractor, or architect. These diagrams are like so many utopian settlement diagrams, which privilege the central idea of each utopia by placing a building related to that idea in the center of the town plan: communitarian utopia = socializing edifices (figure 2.3); industrial utopia = factory and administration buildings (figure 2.4). To solidify a diagram for operation within a transformed building enterprise may be merely an exercise in affecting control. Yet, the fundamental condition of every diagram is its reliance upon information exchange. Flows are integral, while configurations vary (most likely because each project is unique due to the operative strategies necessary for its completion). As such, diagrams representing changing conditions for the building industry will likely continue to fluctuate, as in some instances, innovative architects will control more of the building process, or clever developers will deploy data exchange mechanisms to exert more influence on the process, while contractors craving more deliverable control and fewer change orders may also formulate new models. The result of this diversity will be a range of different types of projects that can all claim the primacy of information as their driving force. This diversity is desirable.

In light of the necessity for fluid information transfer, contractual arrangements in the building enterprise must evolve more swiftly to facilitate information exchange at *all* stages of the process. Still, we must observe caution in a race to facilitate information flows to avoid instrumentalizing change through rigid systemic control of the enterprise. The capacity for fluid aggregation of diverse input hinges upon the flexibility of arrangements. The opportunity for diverse arrangements is in part what is so exciting about this new structural condition. Exacting, yet flexible arrangements (similar to associative design) will serve to engender innovative new architectural solutions.

Since data files are the chosen medium of exchange (for communication, testing, modeling, prototyping, and manufacturing), all bits must be in order prior to coordinating the atoms. Well-organized information during the design process leads to decidedly *informed form*. As such, the craftworkers have reappeared,[14] only their focus has shifted from direct engagement with the material to creating information for materialization, digital fabrication, and assembly, in relation to material knowledge; encoding information is a form of craft that directs the craft of form.

INPUT PARAMETERS

Selection of input parameters during the design process can be made lightly or in great detail, as a multiplicity of combinatorial possibilities exists. Also, feedback loops can multiply infinitely, thus enabling continuous refinement of a project based on deeper levels of information revealed in subsequent iterations. It is up to the collaborative design group – and ultimately human decision – to determine which parameters are admitted into the process. Critical reflection about appropriate strategies, however, must be articulated at the outset. For example, a range of formal strategies can result from choosing appropriate *scripting* techniques, or operations for producing form (i.e. *sectioning, nesting, unfolding*, etc.).[15] Performative information may be incorporated, revealed by interrogating the digital model via testing, simulation, and analysis (using techniques such as *spatial visibility, daylighting, finite element analysis, acoustic behavior*, to name just a few).[16] Materialization and production parameters can inform the design in many ways, by understanding the operative constraints of the machines, customized detail solutions that replicate through the entire system, tolerance criteria, limits of tooling such as drill bit influence on final fit, as well as complexities involved in shifting from model-scale to full-scale.[17] Assembly factors such as labeling, bar coding, and transportation size limitations are also important; they too reveal information that can affect the final design. Given the diversity of operative techniques, potential parameters that inform the design solution can expand *ad infinitum*.[18] Thus, it is critical to look beyond the operative conditions and ask what the ethical responsibilities for architecture are in relation to natural systems, human behavior, social conditions, etc.

2.4.
The *Ideal City* and *Royal Salt Works* at Chaux, France by Claude Nicolas Ledoux (1775): industrial city for living and working with central buildings for the director's villa and the industrial evaporation of brine.

INFORMING THE COLLABORATIVE

In light of the fact that design strategies vary dependent upon the team and the project (i.e. levels of complexity, site, scale, materials), some critical topics can be considered in general during the total process of design-through-production:

Consultation: All disciplines have something to input into design thinking, depending on the conditions of the problem. Expertise in fabrication, engineering, scientific analysis, mathematics, systems behavior, environmental performance, construction assemblies, and financial planning are some privileged, obviously beneficial, inputs into design thinking. However, other kinds of knowledge are increasingly relevant to the equation, such as biological sciences, environmental conditions, information management, etc.

Fabrication: Working with the operative particularities of laser cutters, water jets, joinery machines, etc. can be daunting. Knowledge workers with digital fabrication expertise are more than just automatons of the industrial machine, but rather technical experts skilled at interrogating the machine potentials in light of information inputs derived directly from the master model. As such, well-informed fabrication experts armed with an understanding of design knowledge (at the very least) are essential.

Software and coding: Scripting is a particularly effective strategy for creating necessary design information. It is based on crafting bits of information to achieve certain goals, for a customized solution when software fails to provide a particular operation. Even still, the operative capacity of software has expanded, and further increasing transparency between software facilitates import/export of needed data. Yet, the range of software one needs to adequately inform design and production is still burdensome. Expertise in managing information for modeling can be of fundamental value in translating data and embedding information into useable form to better guide the design and production of building. Perhaps some day, information management experts may even guarantee that all exchanged information is reliable!

Research: Direct research related to problems considered in the design process is essential. As most companies do not have the time or resources to invest heavily in research and development, potential linkages that transgress traditional boundaries between academia and industry are important. Engaging university research centers, as well as collective research and development within particular industries, can address this need. Such an applied form of research can better inform the design process, while potentially leading to innovation. As such, educational programs need to break free from traditional notions of architectural practice by encouraging deeper-connected applied research. Students encouraged to innovate will likely lead in pioneering the necessary changes within the ossified professions that comprise the building industry today.

MASTER MODEL

The *master model* (even though it may involve multiple types of models) provides a three-dimensional representation of a project and all of its individual components. Value is added by evolving iterations of the model, as each agent in design and production weighs in with knowledge, expertise, and decision-making. The master model contains important design and production information related to geometry, material properties, simulation, performance, fabrication, and assembly. The model can be used in several interrelated ways. First, the master model encourages systems of associations and constraints that describe relations between formal strategies and components, assemblies, and context. In this way, inevitable design changes are propagated through the entire model, eliminating repetitive elemental modeling tasks and ensuring greater freedom for variety.[19] Second, the master model allows the simulation, analysis, and testing of a project, using digital tools to evaluate performance considerations related to gravity, wind, acoustics, and other simulated influences. Third, prototypes, scale models, and mock-ups can be created without expensive tooling, providing means to inform the master model based on prototyping material production, through "physical-to-digital" feedback loops. Fourth, the master model contains all the geometric information needed to directly fabricate final building components. Fifth, the master model facilitates the assembly

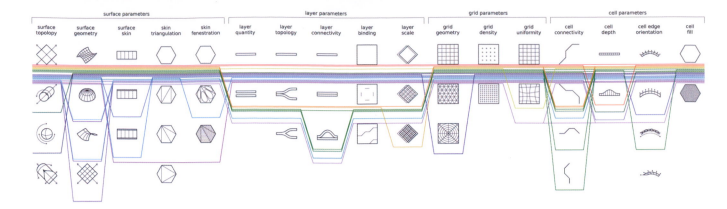

surface parameters					layer parameters					grid parameters			cell parameters			
surface topology	surface geometry	surface skin	skin triangulation	skin fenestration	layer quantity	layer topology	layer connectivity	layer binding	layer scale	grid geometry	grid density	grid uniformity	cell connectivity	cell depth	cell edge orientation	cell fill

2.5.
Manifold Project by Andrew Kudless (*Architectural Association*): parametric matrix exploring geometric and topological properties of the honeycomb system.

2.6.
Digital information flow relationship tree at the *A. Zahner Company* for the detailing and fabrication of the copper skin panels of the *de Young Museum* in San Francisco.

of complex products and projects by serving as a database of parts and locations by translating data into bar-code scanning, laser positioning, material tracking, and part inventories. Even shipping and delivery can be phased, choreographed, and coordinated through project completion with data obtainable from the master model. The master model is the catalyst for enabling collaborative information exchange, which sets the stage for new structural conditions in the building industry.

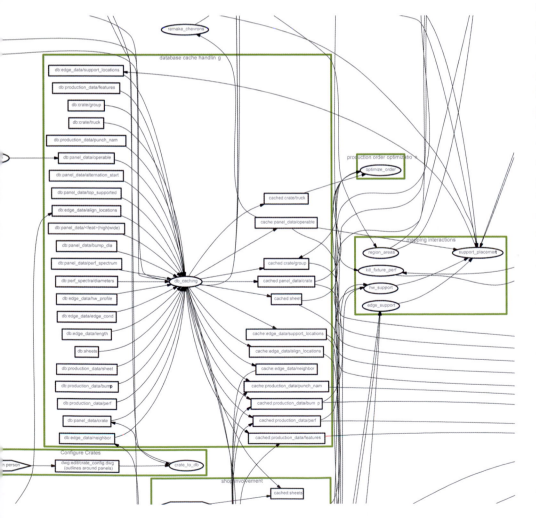

REPRESENTING RELATIONS

Beyond the master modeling strategies, changing techniques for communicating process information are evolving to facilitate the exchange of information.[20] Plans and sections have given way to nesting diagrams, unfolding operations, surface optimization, material tolerance simulation, and more.[21] New representational techniques emerge from the need to direct machines to cut, bend, and fold precisely the physical shapes and the capacity to guide form. However, some representations also allow envisioning design iterations used to evolve design. *Matrices* and *relationship trees* permit prompt visualization and prioritization of solutions in relation to one another, while providing a capacity to trace a genetic history of design decisions, operations, or even related projects. They are also useful in arranging morphological variants resulting from scripting. As digital tools provide the opportunity for serial differentiation, countless design variants (good and bad) are generated during the design process. Matrices and relationship trees allow the designer to manage and examine this repetitive complexity and direct the next set of decisions for further exploration. For example, the matrices that Andrew Kudless[22] used in the design and making of the *Manifold Project*, produced with the *Architectural Association*'s *Emergent Technologies* (*EmTech*) *Group* (figure 2.5), kept track of the lineage of strategies and parameters used to produce a set of prototypes until the optimal combination was identified using feedback loops and a final path to resolution selected.

A. Zahner Company constructed an operative flow relationship tree (figure 2.6) to manage the complexity of digital information for the fabrication of the *Herzog & de Meuron*-designed copper skin cladding for the *de Young Museum* in San Francisco. Digital model files were charted according to the operations performed (such as shearing, punching, perforating, and dimpling) and the timetable of the fabrication and assembly process.

2.7.
Calibration Channel,
Mounds State Park,
Anderson, IN (2006).

2.8.
Calibration Channel:
digital model.

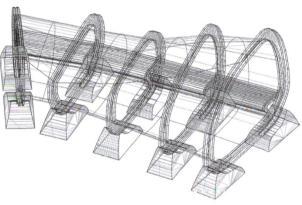

2.9.
Calibration Channel:
prototype model.

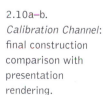

2.10a–b.
Calibration Channel:
final construction
comparison with
presentation
rendering.

IMMERSIVE EDUCATION: DIGITAL DESIGN AND INDUSTRY PARTNERSHIPS

We need a new academic model; one that is not satisfied with architecture as it is typically practiced today. Diverse course offerings are still separated from one another, with little opportunity for integrated techniques and innovative multidisciplinary collaborations. Within accredited professional degree programs, much attention is paid to satisfying the set of skills students may need for real-world practice, while not deviating from sole author project-driven design investigations. While serving the profession is still necessary, a spirit of innovative partnership between the academia and profession can discover new potentialities. It is critical today to impart to students the imperative for directed research, experimentation, teamwork, and collaboration with industry partners in *design-focused* investigations. There are broad implications about how we train architects for a future that relies upon digital exchange. As such, the educational system needs to be more flexible. Digitally driven *immersive education* involves students in the application of digital research in real-world projects with industry partners. Through experimentation, academia-and-industry collaborations examine methodologies and a total process of design-through-fabrication at various scales – from furniture to building components.

As the American Midwest has a long tradition of making things through manufacturing and material processing, the *Ball State University* (*BSU*) in Muncie, Indiana, has created a fertile territory by engaging regional industry partners through immersive education in an attempt to test and apply new methodologies for designing and making architecture. In the spring of 2006, students enrolled in a special seminar with the *Virginia Ball Center for Creative Inquiry* at *BSU* in which they developed a number of full-scale installations at strategic locations along Indiana's White River in partnership with key Midwest industry partners.

One particular installation, *The Calibration Channel*, located at Mounds State Park, in Anderson, Indiana, was designed and manufactured in partnership with the *Indiana Limestone* industry and the *Indiana Hardwood* industry (two strong regional material interests within the state). The design was developed in response to the aural presence of the river as it flowed across a ripple zone in the riverbed (figure 2.7). Students generated a design solution with the intention of capturing, channeling, and condensing the sound of rippling water as it traveled up a promontory bluff, thus calibrating the sensory experience. Initial design ideas were modeled, laser cut, and developed with feedback of fabrication realities of hardwood and limestone (figures 2.8, 2.9, and 2.10a–b). Students crafted assembly configurations for the red oak and ash donated by one of the major regional hardwood mills, the

2.11.
Calibration Channel:
rib component nesting/
material matrix.

2.12.
Calibration Channel:
catalog/shop tickets for
a portion of the skin
panels; each panel was
checked off the catalog
as fabrication was
completed.

2.13. (below)
Calibration Channel:
precise translation of
the model data into
the final form.

2.14. (right)
Calibration Channel:
final limestone
footers.

2.15. (far right)
Calibration Channel:
Virginia Ball Seminar
students[23] testing the
affect.

Frank Miller Lumber Company, in Union City, IN. Structural decisions were made in accordance with both the limits of the bed size of the in-house 3-axis mill, as well as the variable nominal dimensions of the donated lumber; we received an assortment of board lengths and widths, which were first inventoried into a matrix of available size configurations (figures 2.11 and 2.12). Additionally, a working protocol for the exchange of information was central to the fabrication of the Indiana limestone footers for the structure. Data translated from *Rhino* into *SurfCAM* was exchanged directly between the students and the *Indiana Limestone Fabricators* in Spencer Indiana, who ultimately used the final model information to directly mill the stone using their *Sawing Systems, Inc* 5-axis stone-milling machine. The fabricator had never received information from architects in that format before, which was translated with precision into the final fabrication of the form (figures 2.13 and 2.14). The fabricator now encourages architects to send their information in that particular fashion and format.

The lesson of the *Calibration Channel* was revealed when, following the seamless translation of design intention into fabricated components, and accurate final assembly procedures, students climbed inside the installation, and it worked precisely as designed, affecting the occupant with a much more amplified sound of the water in the distance (figure 2.15). As such, *Calibration Channel* was both a success as a device for connecting the user to the resonance of the natural surroundings, while demonstrating the potential for managing and sharing information in a total process of design-through-production.

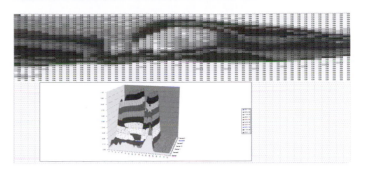

2.18.
SmartScrap: database of available limestone scraps arranged in an overlay configuration of final form.

2.16.
SmartScrap: rendering as wall panel system.

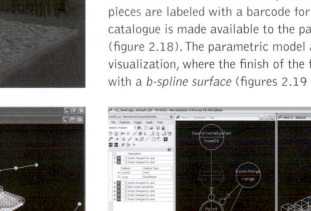

2.17.
SmartScrap: landscape installation.

MATERIAL PROCESSING, MINIMIZING WASTE RESEARCH: SMARTSCRAP

The *SmartScrap* project[24] engages the Indiana limestone industry with direct research and experimentation through the *Institute for Digital Fabrication* at *Ball State University*, by using a digital database of component pieces based on available sizes, shapes, and quantities of leftover/waste stone scrap material. Through a (developing) digital catalog of waste products from the Indiana limestone industry, computational means are deployed to supply the catalog information to parametric design models (figures 2.16 and 2.17) – thus connecting with the broader aim to effectively reuse typically wasted limestone material.

SmartMosaic is a pilot study within the *SmartScrap* project that came into existence by deploying associative modeling and scripting capabilities of *Generative Components* (the completion of the first prototype is scheduled for the summer of 2008). The principal idea behind the *SmartMosaic* is to select typical dimensional scraps with standard X and Y dimensions, but variable Z heights (resulting from standard slicing techniques in the limestone industry), and scan and record the shape and dimensional information about these scraps along with color and texture information into a scrap catalogue. These scrap stone pieces are labeled with a barcode for storage. An *Excel* database catalogue is made available to the parametric modeling system (figure 2.18). The parametric model allows the formal design visualization, where the finish of the façade surface is controlled with a *b-spline surface* (figures 2.19 and 2.20) or an image

2.19 and 2.20.
SmartMosaic: parametric façade controls.

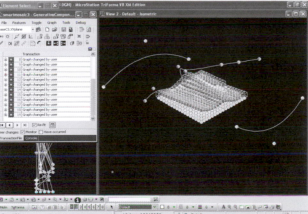

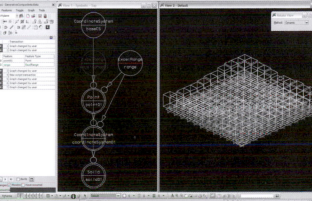

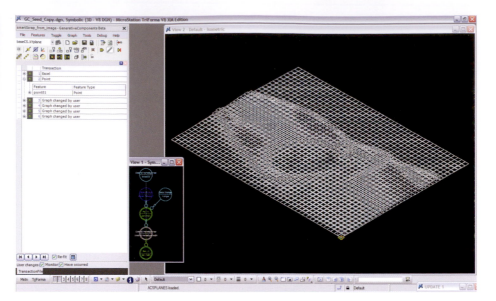

2.22.
SmartMosaic:
image translation
into variable
heights.

2.21.
SmartMosaic:
selected image
for translation
and database
query.

data translation of pixel information is used to drive
the surface condition (figures 2.21 and 2.22). During
the design visualization process, a *VisualBasic* script
queries the database for available pieces that could be
plugged into the matrix based on the next-best-available
technique. Once the finished field conditions with
available stone scraps are established, barcoded pieces
will be selected in the physical catalog and assembled to
produce unique panels in the system.

The most significant outcome of *SmartScrap*
project lies in the direct link between the university-
based research center and the limestone industry that
can lead to mutually beneficial techniques and ultimately
an applicable building component, while simultaneously
reducing the waste generated in fabrication (figure
2.23). The digital exchange of information is central to
the development of this collaboration.

CONCLUSION: DESIGNING AND MAKING RELATIONS IN ARCHITECTURE

As the Machine Age gave way to the Digital Age,[25] key
players have started to collaborate at earlier phases of
the design process. As a result, considerably more time
is devoted to the design phase to incorporate a more
diverse range of considerations than was typically the
case a mere decade ago. It is instructive to examine in
contemporary architectural thinking the discourse –
however positive or negative – during the time period
when architecture debated the merits of returning to
nostalgic notions of the *Arts and Crafts* movement and
when *Art Nouveau* flourished, in light of the potentialities
of realizing an industrialized architecture. Gropius
correctly identified in the late 1940s the slipping role
of the architect resulting from the disconnection with
building practices:

2.23.
*Indiana
Limestone*
scrap yards.

In the great periods of the past the architect was the "master of the crafts" or "master builder" who played a very prominent role within the whole production process of his time. But with the shift from crafts to industry [the architect] is no longer in this governing position.[26]

The implication of this historical position is instructive for our situation today. We must advocate for flexible structural conditions that enable fluid and direct information exchange in architecture, or be destined to repeat the mistakes of the past. We must gravitate towards technologically driven design through greater attention to research, experimentation, and production considerations. Additionally, we must encourage a *total process of design-through-production* approach that engages all those involved in building design and production in a *collaborative evolution* of each project.

Even though invisible in the final built work, *information* is central to the realization of contemporary projects. Effective communication, sharing, manipulation, formation, decoding, recoding, and association of information are the primary transactions of architecture today. We are charged with the stewardship of this information as we develop a new set of architectural strategies and principles that relate to the spirit of our age.

NOTES

1 Ludwig Mies van der Rohe: "A Speech to IIT (1950)", in Philip Johnson, *Mies van der Rohe*, New York: Museum of Modern Art, 1953.

2 Umberto Eco (ed.), *History of Beauty*, New York: Rizzoli International Publications, 2004, p. 50: "Since in Plato's view the body is a dark cavern that imprisons the soul, the sight of the senses must be overcome by intellectual sight, which requires a knowledge of the dialectical arts, in other words philosophy. And so not everyone is able to grasp true Beauty. By way of compensation, art in the proper sense of the term is a false copy of true Beauty and as such is morally harmful to youth: better therefore to ban it from the schools, and substitute it with the Beauty of geometrical forms, based on proportion and a mathematical concept of the universe."

3 Kevin R. Klinger and Joshua Vermillion state: "Digital technology allowed us to design with different formal strategies, requiring new ways of thinking about architectural principles," in A. Angulo, J.R. Kos, and G. Vasquez de Velasco (eds) "Visualizing the Operative and Analytic: Representing the Digital Fabrication Feedback Loop and Managing the Digital Exchange," *International Journal of Architecture and Computing*, vol. 4, no, 3, September 2006, pp. 79–97.

4 The directors of the *Emtech* program at the Architectural Association during this dissertation were Michael Weinstock and Michael Hensel, as well as studio master Achim Menges.

5 Lewis Mumford postulates that "By the sixth century, a new god had captured the Acropolis ... This new god was the polis itself; for the people who built these great temples were seized with an ecstasy of collective self-worship; they never noticed, perhaps, that it was their own image of order and beauty and wisdom that they set high upon a hill." (Lewis Mumford, *The City in History: Its Origins, Its Transformations, and Its Prospects*, New York: Harcourt, 1961, p. 146.

6 Negroponte offers: "I therefore propose that we, architects and computer scientists, take advantage of the professional iconoclasms that exist in our day – a day of evolutionary revolution; that we build machines equipped with at least those devices that humans employ to design. Let us build machines that can learn, can grope, and can fumble, machines that will be architectural partners, architecture machines." (Nicholas Negroponte, *The Architecture Machine*, Cambridge, MA: MIT Press, 1970, p. 121).

7 Ibid., p. 119.

8 Buckminster Fuller: "Man has been lacking in comprehensive disciplines and the developed ability to synthesize, essentially because of the bewildering arrays of complex behavior items of natural phenomena. Man shows synergetic re-genius inferior to Nature's regeneration," in "Total Thinking," in J. Meller (ed.), *The Buckminster Fuller Reader*, Worcester, and London: Trinity Press, 1970, p. 298.

9 Further discussion of digital principles can be found in Kevin R. Klinger: "Digital Futures, Defining Digital Discourse," in S. Carmena and R. Utges (eds), *Digital Culture and Differentiation, Proceedings of the VII Congreso Sociedad Iberoamericana de Gráfica Digital (SIGraDi) 2003 Conference*, Rosario, Argentina, 2003.

10 See the influential essay by Phillip Bernstein entitled: "Integrated Practice: It's Not Just About the Technology," October 2005, available online at http://www.aia.org/aiarchitect/thisweek05/tw0930/tw0930bp_notjusttech.cfm

11 Kevin R. Klinger, "Retooling the Architecture Machine: Innovations of Digitally-Driven Architecture," in *Blueprints: Journal of the National Building Museum*, (published in conjunction with the *Tools of the Imagination* Exhibition, Washington D.C., 2005), vol. XXIII, no. 3, Summer 2005, pp. 8–12.

12 See Walter Gropius, "The Architect Within Our Industrial Society," in *Scope of Total Architecture*, New York: Collier Books, 1962, p. 74. "The architect of the future – if he wants to rise to the top again – will be forced by the trend of events to draw closer once more to the building production." In critique of the AIA 1949 convention addition to the mandatory rules of the Institute, Gropius offers: "I have very great doubts about the wisdom of this rule which would perpetuate the separation of design and construction. Instead we should try to find an organic reunification which would return us to the mastery of the know-how in building."

13 Based on an original plan by Thomas Stedman Whitwell entitled "Design for a Community of 2000 Persons Founded upon a Principle Commended by Plato, Lord Bacon, and Sir Thomas More."

14 For an in-depth discussion of this issue, see the chapter by Branko Kolarevic in this book.

15 For a concise outline of these strategies, see Branko Kolarevic, "Digital Production," in B. Kolarevic (ed.), *Architecture in the Digital Age: Design and Manufacturing*, London: Spon Press, 2003, pp. 29–54.

16 See B. Kolarevic and A. Malkawi (eds), *Performative Architecture: Beyond Instrumentality*, London: Spon Press, 2005.

17 The scale issue is fundamentally important; it has resulted in the creation of new firms, such as *designtoproduction* from Zurich, Switzerland, to provide this "scaling" service.

18 However, we run the risk that much of the process-oriented pragmatic problem-solving strategies get all the attention as we critique contemporary architecture – what end will this serve?

19 Makai Smith demonstrates in his chapter in this book the exacting yet flexible use of associative modeling strategies through his work with *Kreysler and Associates* and now more directly with *Bentley Systems*.

20 Kevin R. Klinger, "The ability to move directly from three-dimensional modeling to real three-dimensional output challenges the need for traditional means of representation such as plan, section, etc. ... This subjugation of traditional forms of representation and fabrication has serious implications for architectural design process and production," in H. Penttilä (ed.), "Making Digital Architecture: Historical, Formal, and Structural Implications of Computer Controlled Fabrication and Expressive Form," in *Architectural Information Management Conference, Proceedings of the Education in Computer Aided Architectural Design in Europe (eCAADe) 2001 Conference*, Helsinki, Finland, 2001.

21 For an in-depth examination of these techniques, refer to Kevin R. Klinger and Joshua Vermillion, "Visualizing the Operative and Analytic: Representing the Digital Fabrication Feedback Loop and Managing the Digital Exchange," *International Journal of Architecture and Computing*, vol. 4, no, 3, September 2006, pp. 79–97.

22 For more on these types of projects, visit http://www.materialsystems.org.

23 Student team: Robert Beach, Austin Durbin, Melissa Funkey, Jorie Garcia, Robert Horner (Project Lead), Anne Jeffs, Katie Marinaro, Christopher Peli, Josh Reitz, Jeremy Richmond, and Chelsea Wait.

24 The project is funded in part by the *Graham Foundation for Advanced Studies in the Fine Arts*.

25 The "digital age" used in this context inherently implies information exchange, more open knowledge sharing, and a new global economy.

26 Gropius goes on to suggest: "Today the architect is not the 'master of the building industry.' Deserted by the best craftsmen (who have gone into industry, toolmaking, testing and researching), he has continued thinking in terms of the old craft methods, pathetically unaware of the colossal impact of industrialization. The architect is in a very real danger of losing his grip in competition with the engineer, the scientist and the builder unless he adjusts his attitude and aims to meet the new situation." (Gropius, op. cit., p. 73)

3
MATERIAL PRACTICE

SHoP ARCHITECTS / CHRIS SHARPLES

3.1. (above)
Carousel House,
Mitchell Park,
Greenport, Long
Island (2001).

3.2a–d. (right)
Carousel House:
model illustrating
construction
sequence.

SHoP interrogates the practice of architecture, and examines how it can evolve to embrace new tools and methods to benefit the built environment. The act of building is not only the physical production of an idea, but a social and cultural process as well. Technology has changed the way that form is generated, rationalized, and realized. But more importantly, technology has allowed a shift away from an individual, style-based approach to a more collaborative, performance-based approach. As building design becomes more sophisticated, with technological advances such as computational fluid dynamics simulation, parametric modeling, lighting analysis, etc., it is critical that we develop this collaborative, performance-based approach. It is useful to look beyond the field of architecture to other models of practice, such as the aeronautics and automotive industries, where design criteria are integrally linked to performance. What is evident in those models is a constant dialogue between design, engineering, and fabrication.

In a way, the practice of architecture is returning to the pre-industrialized state. With industrialization, the process of building changed as the labor force became accustomed to using standardized components, ordering products from catalogs, and working with prefabricated materials. New technology is creating a method of production where there is efficiency in customization – allowing the emergence of individually crafted solutions to problems. This capacity brings us to the crux of the main issue of contemporary practice: how we manage and share information.

A building is a complex undertaking. Traditional two-dimensional representation relies on a reductive

symbol system to communicate intention, which cannot fully or accurately embody the total scope of work. This representational system also relies on manual coordination of autonomous data, often across separate disciplines and disjointed timelines. Three-dimensional visualization tools not only allow physical coordination of multiple building systems, they become a basis of collaboration, and encourage early participation of design disciplines and construction trades. Through this collaborative process, performance-based criteria can be identified, which will direct the development and detailing of the project. When these criteria are parametric, value is placed on maintaining ideal relationships versus ideal entities. This valuation is manifest not only in the physical built work, but also in the cultural environment in which it is created. Further value is added to the system when it embodies live data, which can be extracted by diverse user groups, such as costing information, marketing facts, or direct fabrication instructions.

While the primary goal of many of these value-added initiatives is the reduction of time and waste, and thereby cost, the added benefit is that the architecture becomes richer by engaging multiple forces within the project's sphere of influence. This results in a new, pliant, form of practice stemming from a collaborative attitude, and informed by innovation in the application of new technologies. To illustrate these ideas, the following projects describe, incrementally, the research and development approach taken at *SHoP* in both the implementation of new technology and the transformation of practice, and demonstrate how we would like to develop the two strategies as they inform and drive our design process.

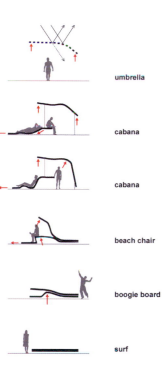

umbrella

cabana

cabana

beach chair

boogie board

surf

GREENPORT CAROUSEL HOUSE: AN INAUGURAL METHODOLOGY

Our first major project was a waterfront park in Greenport, Long Island (2001), which included a house for the village's antique carousel (figure 3.1). The *Carousel House* was a low-bid, public works project, with federal and state funding. The design of the carousel house was fairly simple, but seemed complex in two-dimensional plan and section drawings – being round, it was based on polar (i.e. non-Cartesian) coordinates, and plans and sections could only represent information exactly at the plane of the paper. Separate drawings were therefore required at each plane of every element of the structure, and it was difficult to understand how those elements would come together. Our concern was that the seeming complexity of the structure would add unnecessary cost to the bids, resulting in abandonment or substantial redesign of the project.

3.3. (right)
Dunescape at *P.S.1 Contemporary Art Center*, Long Island City, New York (2000).

3.4. (above)
Dunescape: programmed uses.

3.5. (below)
Dunescape: digital model.

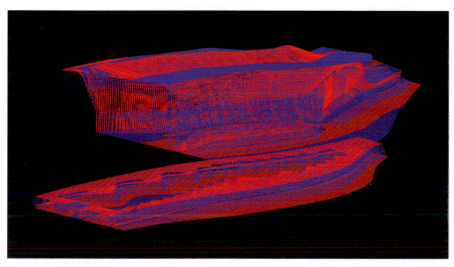

We felt strongly that the actual construction of the structure was much simpler that it appeared in the drawing set. Therefore, in a precursor to Building Information Modeling (BIM), we built a large-scale model and photographed each step of the construction in the order we envisioned it would be built in actuality (figures 3.2a–d). At the pre-bid meeting, we presented the model and the booklet of photos. The booklet was issued as part of the construction document set along with the drawings and specifications. The low bid was within budget, and the project was built substantially as originally designed. So in this case, the model was created not as a representation of what the building would look like, but as a basis for communicating the feasibility and chronology of how the building would be built. As a result of this exercise, we were better informed to assist the contractor with means and methods assessment during the construction phase. The successful outcome of this project confirmed for us that this methodology needed to be the foundation of our practice.

DUNESCAPE AT P.S.1: MEETING A BUDGET

Around the same time we were completing the design for the *Carousel House* in Greenport, we won the competition[1] for a summer installation in the courtyard of the *P.S.1 Contemporary Art Center* in Long Island City, New York (2001, figure 3.3). The idea for the installation named *Dunescape* was to create an urban beach – a place for people to hang out on a hot day in the city. We had a budget of $50,000 and six weeks to build the project. With this limited budget, we could not afford skilled labor. It was also essential to make the most of materials, so we created a composite relationship where program, structure, and skin worked together. This led to a strategy to create an efficient structure where the design could accommodate complexity, but the construction was simple. Working with an animation software that was still relatively untested in architectural applications, we generated a form where a basic prototypical section varied along the length of the structure to accommodate different programmatic uses, including pools, cabanas, benches, and a canopy (figure 3.4).

Using 2″ x 2″ pieces of cedar wood, in 8′–10′ lengths, we created an A–B–A–B relationship and built every frame laterally (figure 3.5). The construction documents (CD) set was actually a series of full-scale templates used to construct the frames in the field. Templates were color-coded and each frame drawing was offset by a few inches so that one sheet of paper could be used for multiple frames (figure 3.6). These frames were pre-assembled in

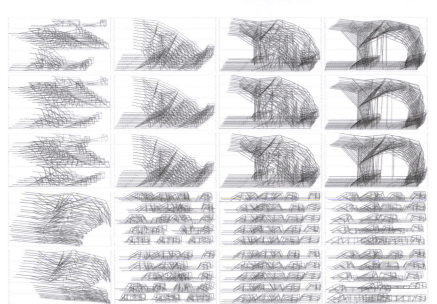

3-ft sections and then assembled into the whole (figures 3.7a–b). Construction tools were limited to a chop saw and a power drill, and the frames were simply screwed together, thus the assembly learning curve was very fast.

The project was built by architecture students headed up by our staff.[2] Understanding our constraints, in this case the budget, and making it a part of the design criteria, we were able to control cost proactively. We had used new technology to generate a form that incorporated structure and was responsive to the program. We deployed a non-traditional form of drawing output to drive the construction, and took on the responsibility for cost and schedule (as opposed to tendering the work out to a bid by a contractor). It proved to us that we could apply this approach to a variety of challenges, and encouraged us to further refine our methods and redefine our role as architects in the building process.

VIRGIN ATLANTIC CLUBHOUSE: THE VALUE OF FEEDBACK

In 2004, *Virgin Atlantic* approached *SHoP* with a project to create a first class lounge in Terminal 4 at *John F. Kennedy* (*JFK*) *Airport* in New York (figure 3.8). The terminal authority required that the design for the *Virgin Atlantic Clubhouse* should not block views from the terminal onto the tarmac. At the same time, Virgin wanted a sense of privacy and exclusivity for their guests. The solution we devised was a series of screen walls that were adapted to suit different programmatic uses (figure 3.9). We again faced a budget constraint related to labor – in this case, the cost of union millworkers pre-qualified for work at JFK. However, since all the elements of the screen were water-jet cut directly from our digital files, we were able to have fabrication done at a non-union shop and treated these customized elements as "parts," which were then delivered to the union millworkers for assembly and installation. The parts were all numerically coded for assembly and put together with a simple screwed-in dowel connection (figure 3.10). Therefore, the most difficult part of the job (cutting thousands of uniquely shaped parts) was automated, and the use of high cost labor was minimized.

3.8.
Virgin Atlantic Clubhouse,
JFK Airport, New York
(2004).

3.9.
Virgin Atlantic Clubhouse: screen assemblies.

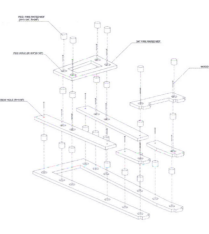

3.10.
Virgin Atlantic Clubhouse: assembly detail from CD set.

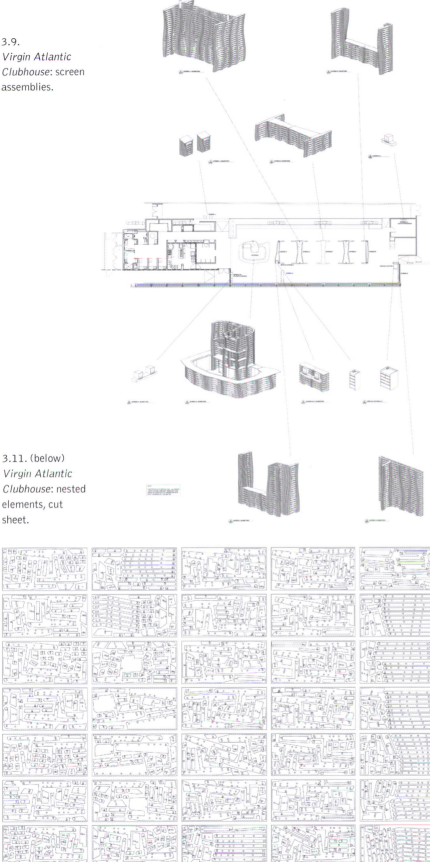

3.11. (below)
Virgin Atlantic Clubhouse: nested elements, cut sheet.

Direct communication is vital to the development of a project as illustrated in the assembly of the *Virgin Atlantic Clubhouse*. The elements of the screen were nested for cutting on 4' x 8' sheets of medium density fiberboard (figure 3.11). Early on, there was a discussion about whether the pieces should be fully cut out of the sheets, or left in place connected by a small tab, similar to the way the parts come in a model airplane kit (figure 3.12). We recommended that they be cut out, since otherwise each tab would have to be individually sanded off once the piece was removed from the sheet. However, the contractor was concerned that the pieces would get mixed up, and a lot of time would be wasted sorting them out. So in the end, we reconfigured the files with tabs. Unfortunately, the representative of the union with whom we were communicating was not the actual person doing the work on site. After pieces started to arrive, the workers on the shop floor found themselves exerting extra energy dealing with the tabs. Because we had approved a sample with a very clean milled edge, they realized that they could not just sand off the tab – they had to re-sand the whole piece to create an even finish. Ironically, they asked us why the pieces were not just cut out and sent in crates, since each piece was numerically coded. The best assembly process was clear to the workers (later runs were then cut without the tab). We discovered that once direct communication started, fabricators began to talk openly about how they would do things and this feedback, in turn, told us more about how to approach a particular problem.

3.12.
Model airplane elements with tabs.

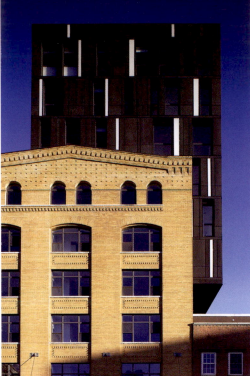

3.13.
The Porter House,
New York (2003).

3.14.
The Porter House: new zinc façade
against existing brick façade.

3.15.
The Porter House:
panel schedules.

Nested Zinc Panel Components

THE PORTER HOUSE: RISK REWARD

We co-developed this 22-unit condominium project in the Meatpacking District of Manhattan (2003, figure 3.13), and leveraged our knowledge of digital fabrication techniques to achieve high design on a minimal budget. Working with a trusted waterproofing contractor as advisor on *The Porter House* project, we designed an easy-to-install zinc rainscreen cladding system, even though initial conversations with zinc panel manufacturers showed the systems were unaffordable, with little chance of creating efficiencies, since the fabrication and installation details of those proprietary systems were fixed.

Historically, elevations have been thought of as compositions, which prioritize the design of singular elements and their proportional relationships to one another. These compositions may take into account material constraints (such as brick coursing), program needs (such as relationships of windows to interior spaces), or structural requirements (such as column spacing). But, generally, elevational compositions are not very flexible once established. The façade of this addition, however, was conceived with the goal of minimizing material waste, while at the same time creating a kinetic sensibility as a counterpoint to the solidity of the existing brick building (figure 3.14). Window locations were not fixed, but could shift within a range based on interior layouts, and the seemingly random pattern allowed a great deal of flexibility with panel sizes.

Open dialogue with the sheet metal fabricator (a company that specialized in laser cutting) established the exact parameters, down to the bending radius of the material. Once all dimensions were determined, we created a family of 50 different pieces based on optimizing nesting configurations on a stock sheet, and produced the digital files for cutting and bending. All pieces were coded, and panel schedules keyed each panel with specific instructions for sequencing of installation, flashing requirements, etc. (figure 3.15). Team meetings with the fabricator and contractor[3] brought to the surface a concern about field tolerances. The team decided to start assembly of the pieces in the middle of the building and work out toward the corners. When installation was complete within 10 feet of the corner, the workers stopped and did as-built checks to see if any adjustments had to be made to the remaining sheets. The adjusted files were then sent out for fabrication, and all of the resulting final pieces fit perfectly. The building skin was achieved and assembled like a fine-tailored suit with major cost efficiencies realized by controlling the fabrication process. Money saved on the façade was spent on upgrades to the interior finishes, and that in turn, along with the unique design of the exterior, led to a higher sales price and profit margin on the project.

PEDESTRIAN BRIDGE(S): MATERIAL INFORMATION

SHoP was called in immediately following the attacks of September 11, 2001, to design a temporary pedestrian bridge, which would reconnect Battery Park City with the rest of lower Manhattan (figure 3.16). The bridge was designed with a largely opaque enclosure to prevent use as a viewing platform for the World Trade Center (WTC). Built in 2002, *Rector Street Bridge* was intended to be taken down in 2004, and has now outlived its intended use.

We are now in the schematic phase of designing its replacement (figure 3.17). The new design criteria called for openness, controlled daylighting, and a more durable walking deck. We also had to reuse the existing structure. So while upgrading the walking surface was critical, we had little room for additional loading of the structure. We were faced with the puzzle of how to construct a weather barrier that simultaneously allowed daylight but minimized its load on the bridge.

Immediately, we started looking at two lightweight materials: ETFE[4] and glass composites. We had been aware of the possibilities of ETFE through many recent projects in Europe and Asia, but we were not convinced that existing steel and aluminum armature systems that structured these surfaces would be light enough for our application. It became increasingly clear that the high strength-to-weight ratio of aerospace composites would be optimal for this application, but the affordability and application seemed to be questionable. When we contacted boat-builders in Portsmouth, RI, about this design problem, we knew instantly that we had found a good fit. As fabricators of high-end custom yachts, their experience and expertise in the design and construction of complex composite structures were exactly what we needed. In the first few minutes of our initial meeting, it was clear that we spoke the same language; we shared a deep passion for structural and design optimization, and we even used the same software packages. Our collaboration with them in these early stages of the design process allowed us to immediately incorporate their expertise, allowing for a fluid dialogue between the design objectives, fabrication constraints, and potentials of the material.

On both the original bridge and its replacement, site constraints during construction factored into the design. The first bridge was built by the same contractors who were doing demolition in that segment of the WTC site, and the bridge was understandably not a priority for them. We had to develop plans for crane location, laydown space, and traffic routing in order to expedite construction. The replacement

3.16.
Rector Street Bridge, Ground Zero, New York (2002).

3.17.
Rector Street Bridge: version two model.

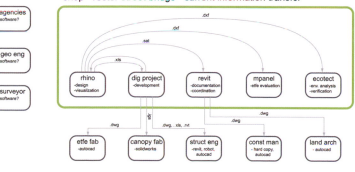

shop - rector street bridge - current information transfer

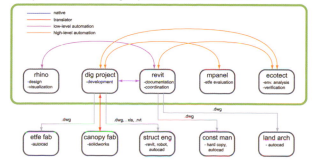

shop - rector street bridge - potential information transfer

3.18.
Software and information transfer chart.

bridge will have many of the same construction issues, as it will be assembled over a busy open highway. There will also be unique considerations as a result of the properties of the materials being used. Therefore, we used multiple virtual and physical modeling tools to assist us with troubleshooting and management of these issues in order to incorporate what we learn into the design as it is developed.

It became clear early in the process that a singular software platform would not be sufficient (figure 3.18). Our imposed performance requirements such as coverage, drainage, weight, and daylighting, combined with the highly specialized constraints imposed by composite and ETFE engineering, required a process that was at once flexible and yet controlled. To address these requirements we developed methods for both high-level and low-level data transfer among multiple software applications for "sketch" level modeling, parametric modeling, structural analysis, environmental analysis, pneumatic modeling and analysis (ETFE), and drawing production. We met our project-specific goals through concept design, detail development, construction and fabrication documentation, and delivered a design that came in about $1m under budget. Just as importantly, however, the lessons learned about information management on this small research-intensive project will continue to inform our process in the future.

290 MULBERRY STREET: PILOT PROJECT

While *SHoP* had been using parametric software for some time to assist with complex or specialized building components, such as millwork or curtain walls, we had yet to apply this technology to the design of the base building. Because it was manageable in scale, with repetitious floor plates, the *290 Mulberry* residential building in New York (expected completion 2008) was chosen as a pilot project to initiate BIM as standard practice in the office. Since the building has a complex façade, it also became a case study for integrating different software platforms.[5]

Located in Manhattan's NoLita District, *290 Mulberry* is bound on the north by Houston Street and on the west by Mulberry Street, and directly across from the historic landmark *Puck Building* (1885) and is defined by its context through a direct response to zoning and building code regulations (figure 3.19). A special zoning district requirement specified the use of masonry on the two street walls. We saw this as an opportunity to respond directly to the *Puck Building*, one of New York's most recognizable masonry structures.

Building code written with classical ornamentation in mind allowed us to project 10% of any given 100 sq ft area of façade up to 10" over the property line. Thus, maximizing the amount of projected area, while minimizing the overall depth of the enclosure (maximizing usable floor area), would become one of ruling criteria of the design (figure 3.20). When coupled with material properties and fabrication constraints, these ruling criteria began to define an approach that was a contemporary

3.19.
290 Mulberry residential building, New York (expected completion 2008).

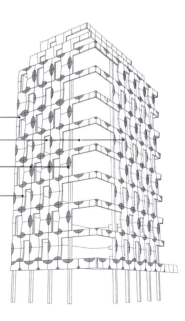

3.20.
290 Mulberry: brick recess/ projection diagram.

CONTINUOUS 'RIPPLED' BRICK SURFACE

WINDOW OPENINGS

BRICK SURFACE PROJECTING FROM 0" TO 3 3/4" (SHOWN IN GREEN - APPROX. 15%)

BRICK SURFACE RECESSED FROM 0" TO 3 3/4" (WHITE AREA - APPROX 85%)

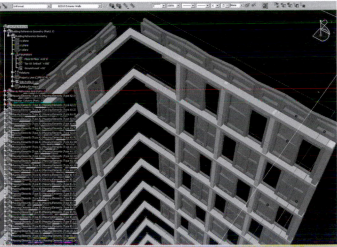

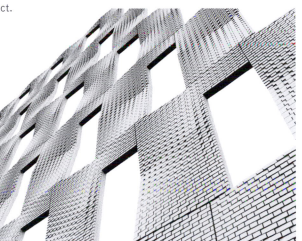

3.21.
290 Mulberry:
the corbelled
material
effect.

3.22.
290 Mulberry:
parametric model.

ick overhang on two axes < 3/4"

3.23. (above)
290 Mulberry:
Flemish bond
pattern.

3.24a–b.
290 Mulberry:
mock-up of formliner
and the resulting
panel.

3.25.
290 Mulberry:
panel variations
from single master
mold.

reinterpretation of brick detailing. The eventual corbelled material effect acknowledges the fact that the brick is panelized, not load-bearing (figure 3.21).

The design team researched fabrication constraints with top panel manufacturers in the US and Canada, in order to understand not only how to correctly detail the panels, but also how to affect the cost structure. For instance, larger panels are more costly to make and transport, but each crane lifting is between $2,000–3,000, so value engineering had to take that into account. Complexity of the panel design, including cost, weight, brick coursing, fabrication, transportation, and installation, reaffirmed the use of parametric modeling as essential in order to be cost effective from a design standpoint. For example, the repeat length of a panel is dependent not only on the standard module of a brick, but also on window and column locations, which themselves were dictated by structural and programmatic concerns (figure 3.22).

To be economical, we worked with a standard brick size, and used a Flemish bond because the alternation of half-bricks allowed more steps over a given panel length (figure 3.23). The manufacture of the panels is fairly standardized. The only custom component of the design is the formliner into which the bricks are set for casting into the concrete panels (figures 3.24a–b). The manufacture of the master form is the most expensive part of the process, and also the slowest. Maximizing the use of this mold – in order to get the most number of different panel shapes from the smallest area of the master mold (figure 3.25) – became the final defining element in the design process. Also, because the formliner is a negative template created from a master form, it was in this master form that coordination and exchange of digital information became critical. Software, in its most basic function, was the interface through which we controlled all the variables and their mutual influence in the feedback loop.

CONCLUSION

SHoP is committed to innovation on many different levels, from the design of projects to the role we take in their planning and execution, by embracing new tools and methods, and in the evolution of the practice as a whole. In order to achieve excellence, we have to collaborate and engage one another in the academy, in the profession, and in the building industry. There is a revolution taking place, thus making this one of the most exciting times ever to be an architect.

ACKNOWLEDGMENT

This chapter is the result of a collaborative effort by *SHoP Architects* partners and staff.

NOTES

1 The *Young Architect's Program* by *Museum of Modern Art* (*MoMA*) in New York.
2 It is important to note that everyone who worked on this tight budget job was paid.
3 The installation was done by rough carpentry crews, not specialty curtain wall installers.
4 ETFE stands for *Ethylene Tetrafluoroethylene*.
5 Multiple software packages are used, depending on the application, as each is purpose-built to prioritize certain values.

4

INNOVATION THROUGH ACCOUNTABILITY IN THE DESIGN AND MANUFACTURING OF MATERIAL EFFECTS

RUBEN SUARE / 3FORM

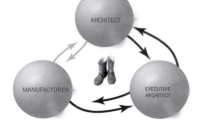

4.1.
The standard tri-partite structure for design and fabrication.

4.2.
Architects at *3form* work with both the architect/designer and the contractor.

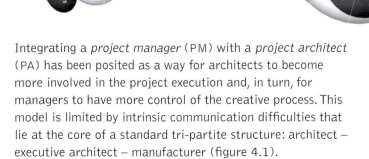

Arguably, one of the most important goals of architectural practice today is to minimize its exposure to liability. Countless design firms are set up in this way, regardless of the broader impact to the profession; as Carl Sapers notes in his article "Toward Architectural Practice in the 21st Century: The Demise (and Rebirth) of Professionalism" in the *Harvard Design Magazine*,[1] "reduced exposure at the same time reduced the architect's authority."[2] Sapers shows how reducing exposure develops a condition that minimizes the architect's role to design only, leaving implementation and execution to others:

> A small group of gifted architects design and a much larger group produce technical work. This split in roles has produced new notions of project delivery and new relationships between the architect and the construction community. These changing relationships have effectively undermined the architect's professional status.[3]

What is crucial to understand is the importance of the relationship between *liability* and *innovation* – without the assumption of risk and liability, there can be no innovation. Avoiding the issue of liability has marginalized the profession of architectural design from its core elements of creativity, execution, and adding value by design. As we moved to a practice driven by liability concerns, we built barriers between creation and execution precisely because execution attracts liability and demands expertise.

The architectural profession needs to *fuse* together the disciplines responsible for creation and execution – it needs to move beyond the ideas of participation or integration. Some propose integrating a *project architect* (PA) with the *executive architect* (EA) as a solution, but I would argue that this position remains inherently limited, because it still excludes many participants: manufacturers, material experts, fabricators, and others. Integrating project architects and executive architects is not sufficient to address the needs of innovation.

Integrating a *project manager* (PM) with a *project architect* (PA) has been posited as a way for architects to become more involved in the project execution and, in turn, for managers to have more control of the creative process. This model is limited by intrinsic communication difficulties that lie at the core of a standard tri-partite structure: architect – executive architect – manufacturer (figure 4.1).

Fusing creation and execution requires a practice with embedded knowledge of working processes that are broadly based on expertise in the following areas: (a) material properties and behavior; (b) material analysis (done prior to design, allowing for a clear definition of cost structures and to address performance); (c) manufacturing; (d) fabrication processes; (e) Design–Led–Build contracting (as opposed to Design–Build); and (f) project evolution from product development through execution. An architectural practice that relies on and engages these processes creatively and productively will be in a prime position to accept liability, and thus return to the center of design innovation.

An architectural practice that includes manufacturing and material expertise is an idea that will take time to develop fully. It is encouraging to see that some offices, such as *SHoP Architects* and *REX*, to name a few, are collaborating closely with manufacturers, becoming more familiar with the manufacturer's processes of production. These offices are making themselves accountable not only for the design, but also for fabrication. Assuming these typically avoided responsibilities has enabled those offices to be highly innovative both in design and in production. Eventually, new models of architectural practice will emerge in which the present distinctions between design, production, and execution will be not only blurred, but also made irrelevant.

OWNING BOTH DESIGN AND EXECUTION

In the traditional architectural practice, architects perform a hand-over after creating a design vision, ironically aware that high-risk, innovative elements of the design will be substantially or entirely eliminated by the executioner (i.e. the contractor). Is it possible to set up a practice that lies between the architect and the contractor that mitigates the risk and offers itself as a conduit to or catalyst to innovation?

Three years ago, I joined *3form*, a manufacturer of resin panels based in Salt Lake City, Utah, with the idea of creating an architectural studio within the manufacturing business structure; the studio would in essence act as the connection point between the manufacturer, the architect, and the contractor. If firms like *SHoP* and *REX* today are successfully connecting with and collaborating closely with manufacturers, the manufacturers could also reach out to architects through an architectural studio that can assist their offices in creating and executing highly complex and innovative projects. This model provides the value-added material, manufacturing, and fabrication knowledge that is inherently absent in architectural offices today. *3form*'s architects work with architects around the world, providing material analysis,

4.3.
Sunset Boutique Façade, Los Angeles (2007), designed by *Patterns*.

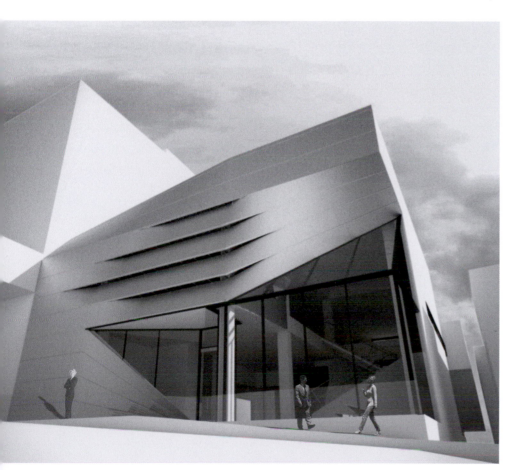

geometry definition, modeling, structural design and analysis, heat-forming, and digital fabrication services, thus creating a working process that begins to erase the boundaries found today between architects, contractors, and manufacturers.

Projects, from panels to hardware and structure, characterized by a high degree of innovation and complexity are digitally fabricated at *3form*. The working process we use is a well-defined, coordinated, and collaborative structure that allows the architects at *3form*, the architect/designer, and the contractor to make "real-time" design decisions. This *Design–Led–Build process* is driven jointly and collaboratively by architects at *3form* and architects outside of *3form* (figure 4.2). The result is an equilibrium that addresses the needs of all parties involved, producing a balance between cost and aesthetics – a cost-effective, highly innovative project.

An architectural studio within a manufacturing facility – as is the case with *3form* – can create opportunities for high levels of material innovation; for example, we have created a *translucent wood panel* for the interior of the *Alice Tully Hall* at the *Lincoln Center* in New York (completion scheduled in 2009), designed by *Diller & Scofidio + Renfro*, a *translucent mirror panel* developed for the *Natural History Museum* at the *Smithsonian Institute* (with *SOM, Skidmore Owings & Merrill*), and a *translucent metal panel* for the façade of a boutique on Sunset Boulevard in Los Angeles (designed by *Patterns*).

TRANSLUCENT METAL PANELS

In the project for a façade of a boutique on Sunset Boulevard in Los Angeles (2007, figure 4.3), designed by *Patterns*, *3form* was engaged in model rationalization and re-definition, panel fabrication and heat forming, and structural design, fabrication, and installation of the support system.

The project was originally designed to be fabricated with monolithic metal panels. This idea became the aesthetic goal we needed to achieve. We considered the possibility of creating a resin panel that had a metallic look, and also studied the various technologies used at *3form* for panel fabrication, such as encapsulation, lamination, printing, etc. Because of a limited budget and the desire to create a real metal panel, the product had to be optimized towards a

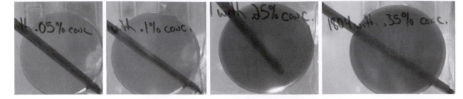

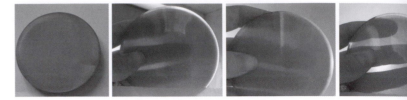

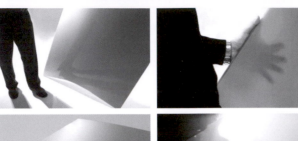

4.4a–b. (above)
Sunset Boutique Façade: material studies, with different amounts of aluminum pigment in the resin sheets.

4.5a–d. (right)
Sunset Boutique Façade: formed panels shown in different light conditions.

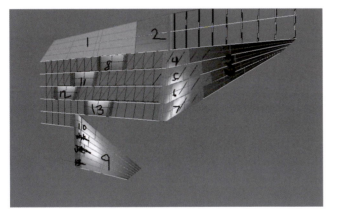

4.6.
Sunset Boutique Façade: rationalizing the geometry of the panels.

minimum amount of steps for fabrication. We started with a process of embedding an aluminum substance into the panels during the extrusion manufacturing process of the raw sheets. The next step was to define the amount of pigmentation in relationship to aesthetics and allowable light transmission required for the panels for the building façade (figures 4.4a–b). We arrived at a panel that achieves a metallic look when non-lit, and becomes almost transparent when lit – a real *translucent* metal solution (figures 4.5a–d).

The next step of the process was to analyze the geometric complexity of the project and find areas where geometry could be rationalized to make the process of fabrication cost effective (figure 4.6). Typically, molds carry a high associated cost; rationalizations are often necessary to minimize the number of molds without impacting the aesthetic intent. Another cost-savings technique is the use of *ruled surfaces* (i.e. single-curved), which allows the fabrication of less expensive molds. Rationalizing geometry is always a collaborative process among the parties involved in the project with the goal of arriving at an ideal balance between aesthetics and cost.

Once the geometry was defined, we worked with structural engineers to design the structural support system for the façade. This process was also highly collaborative; we worked together with the architect and the engineer. The outcome of that collaboration was a design deeply informed by the

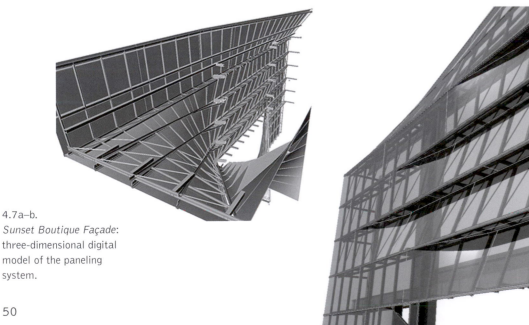

4.7a–b.
Sunset Boutique Façade: three-dimensional digital model of the paneling system.

4.8a–b. (below)
Sunset Boutique
Façade: prototyping
the panels and the
support structure.

4.9a–d.
Sunset Boutique
Façade: the design of
the aluminum support
channels provides for
panel connections at
different angles.

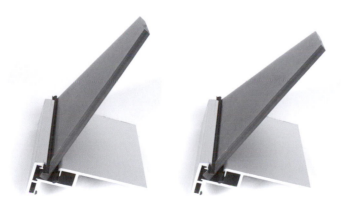

fabrication process. We contracted a steel fabricator for the production and installation of the structural steel. To control the process, we worked with the steel fabricator very closely, approving every detail of the shop drawings and analyzing every connection detail, from extrusion techniques to trusses that connect to the existing building. Such an approach entailed generating an accurate survey of the various points of the existing steel. Once these points were obtained, we could enter them into our three-dimensional digital model and define the actual shape and dimensions of each façade component (figures 4.7a–b).

At this stage we required the production of a *prototype*, which is probably the most important phase of any project that necessitates a relatively high degree of innovation. We see *prototypes* as work-in-progress tests at different levels. In developing the translucent metal panels for this project, it was important to demonstrate the material complied with code requirements for fire resistance and strength, as well as for light transmittance, which was at the 30% level for this project. The ultra-violet (UV) requirements were also met; the performance of the material was defined for a 30-year life span.

Various intermediate tests were conducted and a full prototype was fabricated for review with the entire project team (figures 4.8a–b). To fully enter the fabrication phase, we had to reach decisions on: (a) structural fabrication, tolerances, and finishes; (b) hardware fabrication, including aluminum extrusions and their connection to the steel structure; (c) panel geometry and heat-forming; (d) panel-to-structure connections; (e) panel-to-panel connections; (f) material selection; (g) weatherproofing; and (h) lighting.

Thirteen dies were fabricated to pull aluminum extrusions. The aluminum channels that hold the panels in place have a cavity that allows some movement of the panels within this cavity, thus enabling the angle of each panel to change (figures 4.9a–d). The extrusions were also specifically designed to twist in space, which was provided by brackets located at different intervals (negotiating the desired degree of twisting). The three-dimensional model of the façade allowed the accurate positioning of the bracket connections and the accurate fit between the panels and the channels as they twisted. *Dry-fitting* was conducted at

4.10a–c.
Sunset Boutique Façade:
the dry-fitting on the
shop floor (off-site); the
panels are shown with a
protective cover.

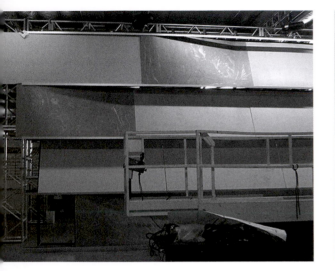

4.11a–c.
*Sunset Boutique
Façade*: on-site
installation of the
twisted aluminum
extrusion that
accepts the panels.

the facilities of the steel fabricator/installer (figures 4.10a–c) to minimize any adjusting or trimming during installation on site (figures 4.11a–c). Through *dry-fitting*, we could further control the cost of the project, as it is more expensive to try to make components fit during on-site installation than it is to anticipate installation problems and take corrective action in advance.

The *Sunset Boutique* is a highly innovative project that was possible through the involvement of an architectural practice at *3form*, capable and willing not only to collaborate in the design process, but also to execute a project where the façade is pre-fabricated digitally, brought to site, and installed, using a process that offers economies of scale where a contractor is no longer involved in sourcing materials, and sizing, fitting, and trimming them on site.

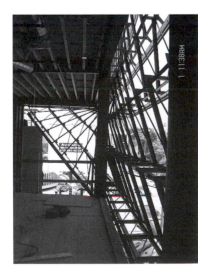

4.12.
The scale model of the *Fidelity Center for Applied Technology* at the headquarters of *Fidelity Finance* in Boston (2006), designed by *Perkins & Will*.

GRADIENT COMPOSITE PANELS

For the *Fidelity Center for Applied Technology* (*FCAT*) at the headquarters of *Fidelity Finance* in Boston (2006), designed by *Perkins & Will* (figure 4.12), we were involved in the definition of the geometry, the development of a comprehensive three-dimensional digital model, panel fabrication and forming, and design and fabrication of the structural support system.

The project started as an investigation of possibilities of fabricating an enclosure for the innovation center made entirely of resin, using the latest technologies available for construction. The idea was to create an exterior wall of curved panels with a single radius, and vary the slope moving in and out of plane. The middle wall was to be constructed out of sheet rock for acoustic purposes. The interior wall was designed with a *double curvature* (a compound geometry), in which about 40% of the wall surface contained embedded monitors, and a counter surface underneath for the placement of media equipment.

The design intent necessitated the manufacture of exterior panels with images representing financial-analysis numerical codes; they were to be done in a gradient from light blue to dark blue (figures 4.13 and 4.14), eliciting a change in the experience of the space as one moved around the *innovation center*. We achieved these material effects by using a fabrication technology that allows for a printed film or fabric to be encapsulated between the panels of resin. The challenge was to create a monolithic composite panel, knowing that the heat and pressure of encapsulation result

4.13.
Fidelity Center for Applied Technology: graphics embedded in the panels showing the gradient.

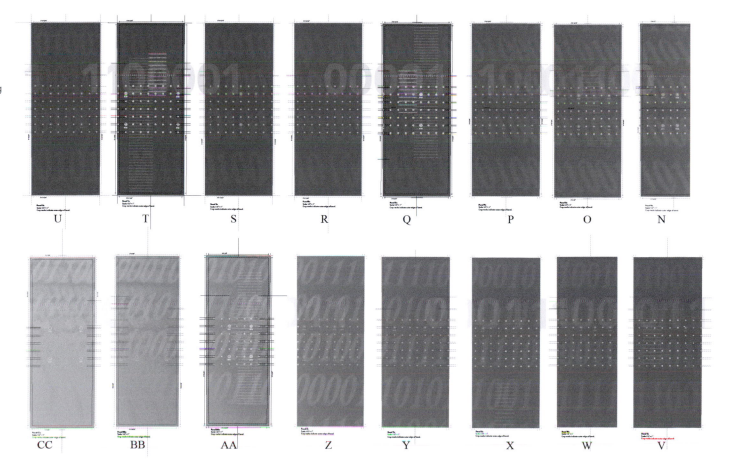

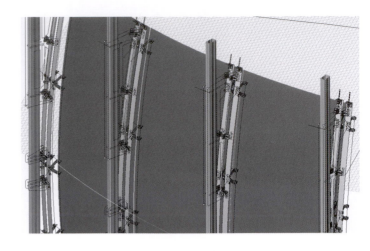

4.15a–d.
Fidelity Center for Applied Technology: the support system for the panels.

4.14.
Fidelity Center for Applied Technology: smooth transitions (indexation) from panel to panel.

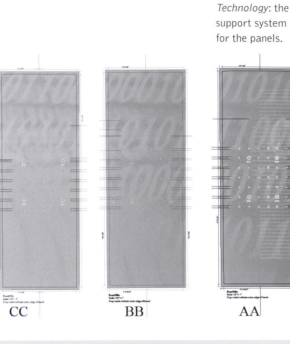

CC   BB   AA

4.16a–g.
Fidelity Center for Applied Technology: all components were digitally modeled and fabricated.

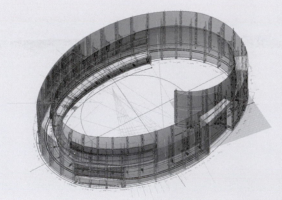

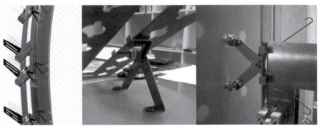

in the expansion of the materials, as they become malleable enough to fuse together. The more materials expand, the more difficult it is to align the edges. To add to the complexity, the composite panels were heat-formed after the encapsulation process to fit the designed curves, thus making the material expand twice. A thorough understanding of the material properties, with extensive prototyping and testing, allowed us to devise a process that was able to accommodate the expansion and maintain tolerances dictated by the model geometry.

The aesthetic intent called for back-lit panels supported by a structural system that would not expose the connection

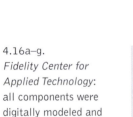

hardware. That meant the panels would have to be back-tapped using a system that allowed their removal for light maintenance and wire management issues. After material analysis, the panels were determined to have a half-inch thickness, providing enough material to embed an insert that could capture a threaded rod. The insert requirements also informed the process, so that the graphics would have to be embedded during manufacturing as near to the front of the panels as possible to avoid damaging the image with the insert.

A custom hardware solution was developed using a torsion spring mechanism design to support panels. The geometry of the panels was controlled by water-jet cut steel trusses, which were attached to the vertical extrusions. The trusses also held in place the perforated steel strips that captured the torsion springs attached to the panels (figures 4.15a–d). This support system is versatile and flexible to compensate for the tolerance discrepancies of the three main elements: the panels, the support structure, and the building. Tectonic versatility and flexibility are necessary requirements for projects that are entirely digitally fabricated and assembled on-site.

The entire project was fabricated digitally using water-jet and laser cutters and 5-axis CNC machines. A cost-effective solution was achieved through careful economic analysis; for example, the shapes were carefully nested prior to fabrication in order to have a minimal ("zero") material waste. Having a minimum amount of waste evolved into an energy-savings exercise made possible by digital fabrication (as Blaine Brownell states, "a 2000 sf home built today with traditional construction methods generates 8000 lbs of waste"[4]). All the support systems were prefabricated and pre-assembled off-site as much as possible prior to shipping to the site (figures 4.16a–g). Through prefabrication, the process of construction was defined by assembly and not by cutting, sizing, and trimming, as is usually the case.

Once the geometry, the materials, and the tectonics were defined, prototyping of the hardware started. After six iterations, the hardware and the panels were prototyped for review with the entire project team, including both architects and contractors (figures 4.17a–c). This review was of critical importance given that the on-site assembly had to be

4.17a–c.
Fidelity Center for Applied Technology: production and review of the prototype.

4.19a–d.
*Fidelity Center for
Applied Technology*:
exterior and interior
views of the innovation
center.

performed by an outside contractor; it was essential that they understood the project in sufficient detail to sign off on the developed assembly process (figures 4.18a–d).

The *Fidelity Center for Applied Technology* (figures 4.19a–d) is a project developed by architects, designers, and installers working together within a highly collaborative structure that allowed all three parties to clearly understand the processes of defining the geometry of the design, its structure, and materials. Resin was chosen as an ideal material, because it could be formed more easily than either metal or glass.

4.18a–d.
*Fidelity Center for
Applied Technology*:
installation process,
showing connection
of the panels to the
support structure.

4.20.
The cross-section of
the *Alice Tully Hall* at
the *Lincoln Center* in
New York, designed
by *Diller & Scofidio +
Renfro*.

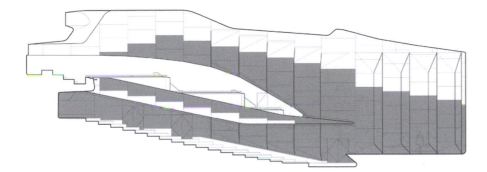

4.21a–d.
*Alice Tully
Hall*: Inventing
a translucent
wood panel.

TRANSLUCENT WOOD PANELS

We started working on the interior of the *Alice Tully Hall*
at the *Lincoln Center* in New York on the day we were
contacted by the architects, *Diller & Scofidio + Renfro*.
We were shown a model of the new design displaying a
beautiful wood finish on the interior, however, some of the
wood panels were solid, and some translucent (figure 4.20).
The design intent called for a *translucent wood panel* to be
fabricated with "real" wood, given that a particular wood
species was going to be used, book-matched, and sequenced
throughout the walls. The interior of the concert hall was
to be finished with a combination of solid and translucent
wood panels that had to meet the following requirements,
most of which related to the city's building-code: one-
inch thickness, a class-A fire rating, approval by MEA
(Materials and Equipment Acceptance) to address toxicity
requirements, formable to various complex geometries
informed by acoustic requirements, no difference between
solid and translucent panels when not lit, and capable of
sequencing the wood throughout the concert hall.

A team effort was essential in the product
development process. *Diller & Sofidio + Renfro* would
define all of the characteristics of the wood veneer to
be used for the project and *3form* would develop a new
technology to encapsulate a 0.2 mm-thick wood veneer
in a 1"-thick resin panel. Since the complex geometry
was defined based on the acoustic requirements for the
concert hall, *Diller & Sofidio + Renfro* performed the
acoustic testing. They also worked very closely with the
wood manufacturer to define the thickness and finish of
the *Moabe* species selected for the project. The panels were
fabricated by first creating a 1"-thick solid resin core,
placing the wood veneer on top of that core panel, and then
encapsulating the veneer with a 1/32"-thick resin panel
(figures 4.21a–d). The wood had to be as close to the front
surface of the panel as possible. The 1/32"-thick resin
layer that protects the wood veneer was given the same
finish as the solid wood panels, ensuring the panels look
identical when the walls were not back-lit. Once the process
and the technology for manufacturing the flat sheets had
been defined, various prototypes with complex shapes were
produced (figures 4.22a–d).

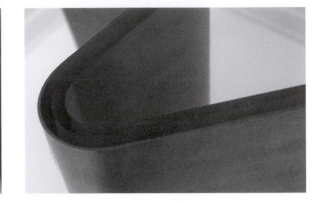

We fabricated a wall section *prototype* of the interior of the concert hall that included a combination of 25 translucent and solid panels (figure 4.23). The purpose of this mock-up was twofold: to further explore the technical issues needed to build the project and to present the wall to the client and other companies involved in the project (including *Turner Construction*). During the fabrication of this mock-up, the following issues were resolved: sequencing of the wood veneer, geometric limits of the wood (with respect to bending), joinery and seaming, hardware development, assembly, and lighting. The wall panels were digitally fabricated at our facilities using high-density foam for the molds, which were fabricated directly from the digital model. The fabrication entailed heat-forming of the panels, and CNC-trimming to control the tolerances. The hardware was defined as a back-taped connection that could support the panels without being exposed on the front surface.

The completed mock-up was a test of material innovation. For the first time in architecture, a translucent wood panel was created that met all of the necessary code requirements for an interior installation in a concert hall. Elizabeth Diller summed up the end results succinctly during the presentation of the mock-up (figure 4.24) at our facilities to the President of the *Lincoln Center* and executives from *Turner Construction*:

> There are intimacy issues, trying to get everything into the hall, and doing it all with one very strong and versatile element, and that is wood. Wood can be steps, wood can do all the sound shaping, and wood can produce the effect of the enveloping quality of light.

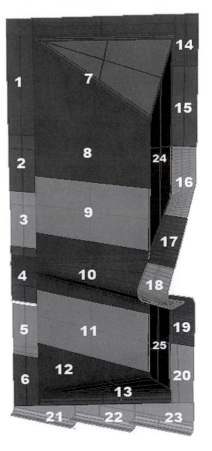

4.23.
Alice Tully Hall: a three-dimensional model of the mock-up surface.

4.24.
Alice Tully Hall: a
mock-up of the wall
section, with non-lit
and lit translucent
wood panels.

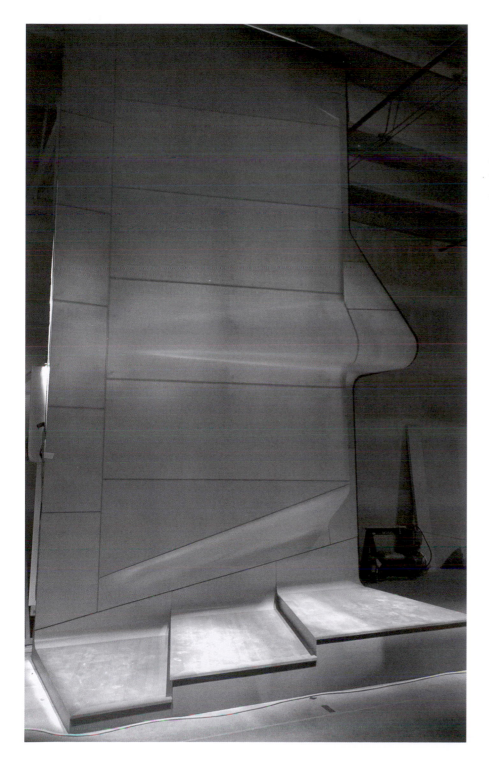

CONCLUSION

Innovative design today requires that the architect
becomes the executioner – and that the executioner and
the manufacturers *become* architects. Some firms have
attempted to adopt this model of working, but remain
limited by traditional strategies of problem solving versus
actual innovation. Innovation can only be attained by
structuring the process to include the manufacturer's
knowledge and material expertise.

The *capacity to prototype* is one of the most
significant competitive advantages that an architectural
group can have at a manufacturing facility. A place that
can manufacture, design, engineer, and prototype – a
"one-stop shop"– is an ideal setting for innovative design
developments. Architects at *3form* have immediate access
to material experts, allowing a very efficient process when
defining a particular material that needs to meet certain
performance requirements.

Several benefits can be seen in this changed business
model:

- Design is informed by the fabrication processes.
- There is a strong potential for material
  innovation.
- Inventions can be patented and intellectual
  property rights protected.
- It results in little value engineering, translating
  into time savings.
- It enables the ability to control the creative
  process.
- It encourages an invaluable learning process that
  accelerates the knowledge curve on all aspects of
  the practice.
- There is greater accountability that is seldom
  found in the traditional architect–client
  relationship.
- It fosters an emotional involvement and genuine
  interest in the highest quality by all parties
  involved in the project.
- A single source or accountability exists for
  the client, resulting in better timing and cost
  predictions.
- There are no surprises at the end due to
  insufficient detailing or specifications on
  construction documents.
- Economies of scale are achievable in digitally
  fabricated projects.

The changed business model addresses directly the existing problematic structure inherent in the relationships between the architect, client, and general contractor. Traditionally, in innovative designs, the clients find themselves in an undefined, amorphous cloud because we, as architects, have not given them proper authorship in the process. That can be attained by clarifying the material definition and performance testing criteria, and through the inclusion in prototypes reviews, where a clearer understanding of the final outcome is attained. The more innovative the project, the more difficult it is to define the inclusions; the problem is augmented by the expectations of a project hand-over to the executioner, knowing that the most innovative and challenging areas will be reduced or substantially changed in the process of construction. The conventional, "muddy" hand-over process will never make innovation attainable (or sustained); architects need to remain involved in the project through all of its phases. At *3form*, we have attempted a highly integrated and collaborative architectural and manufacturing model. Our architects are willing to take the necessary risks that come with innovation; through extensive and intensive collaboration, we are redefining the meaning of authorship to be all-encompassing.

NOTES

1 Carl Sapers, "Toward Architectural Practice in the 21st Century: The Demise (and Rebirth) of Professionalism," *Harvard Design Magazine*, Fall 2003–Winter 2004, no. 19, pp. 80–85.
2 Ibid.
3 Ibid.
4 Blaine Brownell, *Transmaterial: A Catalog of Materials that Redefine our Physical Environment*, New York: Princeton Architectural Press, 2005.

5

THINKING VERSUS MAKING: REMEDIATING DESIGN PRACTICE IN THE AGE OF DIGITAL REPRESENTATION

PHILLIP G. BERNSTEIN
AUTODESK INC. & YALE UNIVERSITY

Designers and constructors in the modern building industry traditionally perform highly specialized and opposed roles of "thinking" and "making." Architects and engineers establish design intent while adhering to professional standards of care; constructors interpret the resulting artifacts to realize a building. This separation, originally anticipated as a mere organizing principle in the early days of modern construction, is now the source of tremendous friction. The resulting oppositional processes typically yield highly unsatisfactory results, and they are unsuited to the challenges of twenty-first-century construction that demands more complex buildings and sustainable outcomes. The separation of design and construction contrasts strongly with current trends in digital form-making, parametric design and fabrication apparent in many innovative schools, firms and projects.

While digital representation tools are remediating the material practice of architecture, technology is only a catalyst, redefining the roles and the responsibilities of the architect. This chapter will outline the resulting tensions apparent in the coming transformation of practice and identify where innovative processes provide promising examples that could be widely adopted.

DIGITAL REPRESENTATIONS: HOW THEY FACILITATE INTEGRATED PRACTICES AND OUTCOME-BASED DESIGN

Digital technology will catalyze significant structural changes in the way the building industry works today, providing a means to address its long-standing failures. Digital modeling connected to fabrication is already impacting the relationship between design and construction. The fundamental tensions that exist between designers and constructors are being somewhat mollified by the presence of technology itself,[1] but digitally derived fabrication is actually part of a larger trend taking place in the world-wide building industry – "integrated practice."

Integrated practice (sometimes called "integrated project delivery" or just "integration") suggests that the building industry should move from traditional ways of doing business to fully collaborative teams that include all the stakeholders in a project's lifecycle. These structural changes create both opportunities and challenges for designers in building delivery. Concepts such as building information modeling (BIM), digitally controlled fabrication, computer-numeric controlled outputs, and sustainability – not to mention the rise of alternative delivery modalities such as design-build, multi-party joint ventures and project alliance models – are evidence of the dramatic changes in the building delivery process as it struggles to define integration.

Why is this change occurring? The fundamental underlying motivation is the desire for the building process to achieve predictable results in an environment plagued by systematically unpredictable outcomes. Everyone in the building process struggles with this dilemma, from designers trying to achieve a certain esthetic goal to clients who are trying to make their projects meet both budgets and schedules. Difficulties abound in accurately predicting construction start and finish times, final costs, building component performance and environmental impacts.

Traditionally, industry participants have used fairly abstract, two-dimensional orthographic projections in the form of drawings to represent the very complex three-dimensional phenomenon of a building. The rapid adoption of new digital tools for building delivery[2] is a clear indication that these traditional orthographic technologies are reaching the end of their useful life in the building industry. Deploying technology to create a digital building information model – a behaviorally correct digital prototype of the design before it is constructed in reality – is a simple attempt to deploy superior project knowledge early in the development process and use those assets to predict the outcome of the final design.

In addition, integrated practices that use digital representation tools are altering the relationship between the craft of building and risk. A craftsman working toward an esthetic end has to assume a certain degree of risk to achieve that goal[3] – and often the most significant artifacts are created when the risk is embraced, not transferred. Current models of design versus product liability do not function in an environment where digital information created collaboratively is the basis for construction and fabrication. This conceptual hurdle will require cooperation between architecture, engineering, and construction (AEC) professionals and clients; yet using predicted outcomes that calibrate potential risk and thereby allow it to be managed more precisely makes this hurdle less daunting. Well-defined goals that identify anticipated outcomes shared by all project participants can drive prototypical design and break the cycle of risk transference and avoidance.

As a further result of the separation of "thinking" and "making" in the twentieth century, the means of production[4] have been fundamentally separated from the act of design. Digital modeling connected to fabrication is redefining the methodologies of production – enabling design innovation as well as driving better outcomes (however one defines them). Technology is being used to explore formal complexity ("blobmeister" architecture), create designs performatively (scripted form generation), or to better predict and control outcomes relating to speed to market, cost, or sustainability. Irrespective of the desired outcome, digital modeling technology can be used to achieve a degree of precision that previous technologies, predicated primarily on digital drawing creation, have been unable to achieve.

Similar transitions have occurred in design technology. The move to three-dimensional parametric models that describe form and drive fabrication is analogous to the transition from two-dimensional computer-aided drafting to building information modeling itself, only now the technology yields a digital prototype that drives production rather than just a set of drawings. Both digital prototyping and fabrication are disruptive innovations capable of unleashing forces with significant effect in the building industry. They will disrupt the esthetic exploration that brings about a finished artifact – resulting in truly unique designs of a kind that have never been built before. They will disrupt building delivery – resulting in changes in the nature of practice and the realignment of the market place, affecting all the players, their interrelationships, and their risks.

PROCESS IMPLICATIONS

The organization of projects and their related rules of engagement are transformed when the definition of design and the transmission of design information are modified, resulting in significant process implications. The movement of project design information has traditionally been linear in nature and is reflected by the classical AIA construct of information flowing, step by step, from program development, to schematic design, etc., all the way to construction administration.

In this traditional information pipeline, two-dimensional orthographic projections of the design are a low-level common denominator that is embedded in the industry's process language and used to continuously determine progress. But in digitally based processes and practices, phase delineations are blurred and the resolution of design information is discontinuous. The standard tasks and outputs associated with traditional AIA phases are shifting and are being inserted into other places, fundamentally altering building delivery processes and the obligations of its participants.[5]

Digital models imbued with construction information appear much earlier in integrated processes: during schematic design to drive form making and to better understand complex geometry; during detailed design and construction documentation in defining materiality, details, and assemblies; during procurement for quantity take-offs and production strategy; and during construction administration to resolve the definitive design and to coordinate production in the field. As a result, design information of varied (and discontinuous) resolution moves fluidly between "design" and "production execution," altering the "DNA" of the entire building process.

PROCESS CHALLENGES

As the traditional roles of designers and contractors are deconstructed and subsequently redefined, deliverables and responsibilities for all constituents in the building delivery process will be transformed. The simplistic explanation of current business practice in our industry might sound like this: designers "think" about buildings and contractors "make" buildings. Designers generally deal in abstractions and building "strategies" and the most detailed things that they create are construction documents. In fact, it might be posited that, in current practice, the architect/engineering team creates a set of construction documents and then "dares" the contractor to build the building from those drawings, with typical exchange of accusations of incompleteness and incompetence, respectively.

Today's industry standard AIA contract documents codify what the American construction industry felt were best practices a century ago, preventing architects and engineers from participating in construction means and methods. Thus, the onus is placed solely on the contractor to determine those means and methods: how to sequence the building and piece it together, based on those documents. Design based on creation of parametric models, however, means more insight into how to create the building must be deployed early in the design process, and the use of these models to facilitate fabrication is, in fact, a proxy for the larger question of the knowledge necessary to put a building together. If your model presages a digitally fabricated building assembly, it is best if you fully understand that assembly in a very concrete way; you can't wait for your contractor to figure it out for you. Conversely, if that model will become the basis for the contractor's construction strategy, perhaps he or she should be at the table while it is created.

The changes anticipated by model-based fabrication in construction include the following business process challenges:

1. **Knowledge.** What needs to be known to deploy technologies that accelerate the resolution of the design early in the design process? What sort of insight is required of designers who digitally "pre-fabricate" the building prior to its actual construction? Under the new construct where construction data move back and forth and throughout the design process, the separation of typical design from the concept of "means and methods" becomes obsolete. For the contractor – who typically arrives at the project after completion of technical documents and was not part

of its implementation strategy – the rules of engagement will have to be changed. Likewise for the designers, who until now have been barred from engaging in construction means and methods. What are the tools needed to complete this vision and how does the process bridge the gap (which was formerly bridged by highly skilled and knowledgeable craftspeople)? Can it be bridged at all, or is there a danger of an irreparable loss of competence?

2. **Scope.** What are the resulting tasks and responsibilities of a changed process, and how do they redefine the normative roles played by each participant? The scope of what designers and builders do suddenly shifts, based upon a new, highly discontinuous information flow, where information is now "hyperlinked" throughout the project. Highly integrated design information evolves in contrast to the former "linear progression" through the traditional delivery process. Under normal circumstances the kind of fabrication information available in today's building information models would not emerge until after the project has been designed. The diagrams and material definitions that are part of a fabricator's routine submittals (keeping in mind that the fabricator is in charge of interpreting those very abstract and likely incomplete construction documents) have been replaced by their digital simulations that presage how to actually get the building built. How does one anticipate what is "integrated" versus traditional? Will the definition of the designer's responsibilities need to be dynamic, depending on the evolution of the design? Does scope move from prescriptive to performative? The question of responsibility, under the aegis of scope of services, becomes paramount, and is directly connected to the question of risk.

3. **Risk.** How are responsibilities redistributed accordingly? What is the meaning of "designer of record" and "responsible control" in such circumstances? In today's world, we can have poorly articulated design paradigms, but we certainly have highly refined methods for assigning fault. Designers are liable for erroneous professional judgment and violations of the standard of care, and contractors face similar risks for product liabilities; all parties are concerned about third-party

lawsuits. After a significant failure, the parties attempt to specify where and when errors were made and assign responsibility accordingly. Was it a failure in judgment on the part of the designer or an error in execution on the part of the constructor? When the designer and the constructor are melded together in an integrated entity (and where it is virtually impossible to determine who made the decision that resulted in the failure), how do we assign that responsibility, particularly in the case where the failed component was created digitally first, then fabricated from those data? Licensing architects is a mechanism designed to protect public health and safety in such circumstances. What does it mean to "design" when processes are integrated?

4. **Reward**. As risks and responsibilities are shifted, how are rewards modified? Does the typical criterion for both selection and success – lowest cost – yield proper rewards to project participants in this new approach? Of course, redefinition of risk requires the same of reward. Perhaps current compensation models will become obsolete and performative or performance-based outcomes will regulate compensation. In lieu of commoditized, "lowest first cost" compensation predicated on "lump sum" fees and lowest "hard bids," what if reward were based on the assumption of risk and that risk was seen as an opportunity to increase profitability? Rather than looking to finish projects for the lowest possible first cost (and suffer unsatisfactory outcomes), would owners consider new risk/reward ratios that reward good or even excellent results?[6]

5. **Structure**. Does the fundamental connectivity of the team – the owner, designers and constructors – change, and if so how? Assuming it is not possible for designers to bring full insight into materiality into their design process, where is that knowledge to be inserted? Since "making" expertise keeps moving forward earlier into building design, suggesting further integration of teams with the necessary know-how and prompting intense building delivery experimentation, the classical architect/contractor/owner construct is constantly remediated. Numerous delivery model experiments

abound – design/build, build/operate, privately financed initiatives – all based on the realization that the separation between thinking and making is crumbling. And ultimately these new structures have to be manifest in the form of contracts and business artifacts that cement the relationship between the players.

6. **Intellectual property**. Who "owns" the design? How is it controlled and how is professional judgment delivered? Does professional certification of the design become less meaningful when designer and constructor collaborate to create a digital model that is the basis for fabricating the building? The building industry is using intellectual property rules devised in 1990 for issues that will roil in 2010. The arcane concept of "Instruments of Service" now defines the means of production. Can this work in an integrated practice? Fluidity, authorship, and responsibility: these all change, so who "owns" an idea in this context? And is that ownership relevant in the increasingly content-rich digital future? If risk allocation can be redefined so that the ownership of ideas in design is not focused primarily on assignment of blame for mistakes but rather on successful outcomes, does the architect's ownership of a set of (digital) documents have meaning beyond the characteristics of the esthetic design?

7. **Education**. How are young designers trained in the increasingly large "footprint" of the design disciplines? For example, the bulk of today's architectural curriculum is still centered on the design studio, following pedagogy conceived in the nineteenth century. Subjects such as structural and mechanical engineering contend with esthetics for attention and care. Digital fabrication, sustainability, community design, building information modeling and redefined professional practice are each trying to find an anchor in the curriculum. The insight necessary to manage the high resolution digital data that permeate the design process requires a different set of skills than what the designer receives in current training. Can the profession of architecture afford to refuse to address the need for these skills without the resulting loss of control of the core design process?

PROGNOSTICATION

It is increasingly clear that the current practices used to build are unsatisfactory. They are not fulfilling the formal objectives of designers. They are not satisfying the performative requirements (such as sustainability, schedule or cost) demanded by owners. There will be a broad process movement towards integrated delivery models mediated by digital design – resulting in a reconnection between the ideas of making things and thinking about things. Fabrication is a component of the integration itself. The resulting changes will blur the distinction between intentional design and production, giving rise to extensive pre-fabrication, mass customization, and factory-produced building components – and eventually factory-produced buildings themselves.

The economics of construction will change as roles, relationships, and the resulting flows of money change. Waste in the construction process is notorious and underscores the importance of creating business processes that maximize efficiency. Digital modeling has the capacity to reduce waste during construction as well as operation – but only integrated delivery models, likely anchored in digital fabrication strategies, will entice stakeholders to share the decisions that inform the building model.

The digital prototype of the building and related models will conflate with the built artifact, and will eventually become all but indistinguishable. The "means and methods" split between design and construction (thinking versus making) will dissolve, yielding projects based on outcome-based models.[7]

CONCLUSION

Like BIM and sustainability, model-based fabrication presents architects with a significant opportunity, but also poses a challenge that cannot be ignored. That opportunity is enormous, because information is power and the key to controlling and delivering superb design outcomes. Architects have the insight and information needed to exert more control over the process than ever before and thus are poised to return design to be the primary driver, and the architect to a role of integrative leadership.

The failure of architects to exert this control will mean a loss of influence, perhaps irrevocably. Within the building industry, whoever controls the means of production will wield the most influence on outcomes. Are architects willing to take up this challenge, or will fabrication be seen as yet another "trend" and relegated to formal exploration only? The future of the profession likely lies in the answer to these questions.

NOTES

1 For example, collaborative tools for digital-based design reviews reduce the amount of construction change orders, according to anecdotal reports from practices based on building-information modeling (BIM).

2 According to recent AIA statistics, 60 percent of large firms have deployed BIM tools on billable projects (AIA Firms Survey 2006, "The Business of Architecture," published by the American Institute of Architects, 2007).

3 Scott Marble, "Risky Business," lecture given at Yale University, New Haven, CT, October 2006.

4 Branko Kolarevic, "The Craft of Digital Making," lecture given at Yale University, New Haven, CT, October 2006.

5 For a particularly provocative example of this, see "Integrated Project Delivery: A Working Definition," a white paper, published by the California Council of the American Institute of Architects, May 2007.

6 In a recent paper on the industry, attorney Pat O'Connor ("Productivity and Innovation in the Construction Industry: The Case for Building Information Modeling," presented to the American College of Construction Lawyers, Fall 2006) describes the consistently low margins in the construction industry as a primary inhibitor to innovation. Relentless commoditization of design services and low bidding methodologies in construction limit process innovation accordingly, and enhanced productivity in design and production yield diminishing returns. New reward schemes might well accelerate innovation that is needed to really redefine new, improved industry processes and procedures.

7 The New York-based practice, Sharples Holden Pasquarelli (SHoP) is an excellent example of a practice that is rapidly integrating design, fabrication, and outcome-based projects. The firm experiments liberally with model-based design, fabrication, and involvement with development, financing, and new planning codes. Each of these efforts is an attempt to redefine the parameters of the architect's control in the service of achieving the design itself.

6
DIGITALLY DEFINED MANUFACTURING

L. WILLIAM ZAHNER / A. ZAHNER COMPANY

6.1.
The *RLDS Temple* in Independence, Missouri (1990).

6.2.
RLDS Temple: the roof consisted of more than 300 uniquely shaped panels.

For more than a century, the *A. Zahner Company* has fabricated intricate metalwork for the built environment. We have participated in the evolution from the tactile contact of the artisan making components ranging from one of a kind cornice shapes to the highly engineered shapely forms of a Frank Gehry design. In this evolution, we have successfully married the ability of fine crafted detail with a *digital definition* of three-dimensional form. The challenge has been to interpret the information conveyed by the designer and instill a *parametric relationship*. The relationship involves not only the interface of the various parts, but also how the machines that cut, shape and pierce these parts interpret the design. This refined definition can be translated into the final product to produce a "machined" appearance and to enhance design intent.

CHALLENGES

I receive a weekly auction notice on manufacturing companies in the United States that are closing their doors and selling their equipment. It is an intriguing idea that US manufacturing could be back on its feet through innovation in industry practice, which is often related to the creative and productive use of digital technologies of design and manufacturing. Some companies seem caught up in digital manufacturing and the digital information aspects of how things are produced, and consequently could be overlooking some larger and potentially more important issues (such as satisfying the requirements of the customer).

The *A. Zahner Company* has been in the manufacturing business for 110 years. Historically, things were made without very elaborate computer-aided systems to develop designs; they were made using templates, patterns, models, and various pieces that craft-workers would produce. The principal questions that emerge are: is there a real need for the use of advanced (and often complex) technologies in manufacturing? Do they benefit the end product and the cost of delivery of the materials that we produce? What are the benefits of the complexities involved?

Products are generated in response to demand (or perceived demand) from a customer. How this demand is fulfilled in a fast, ever-changing environment is where digital manufacturing processes excel. If what is needed is simple repetition, thus creating the same geometric form repeated in basic dimensional parameters, the use of digital manufacturing is less relevant in the profitability of an organization. Many companies still use traditional techniques for repetitive production. However, when competitive forces enter a market, so that customers can order, for example, custom-made, often dimensionally variable products, traditional techniques need to be replaced by more effective and efficient processes of production. Manufacturers must adapt to the changing conditions or they will disappear.

Digital manufacturing processes are situated precisely at the convergence of creative thinking and manufacturing flexibility. At *A. Zahner Company*, we now have a range of additional tools at our disposal to reach solutions to more complex problems. Expressive geometric form or intricate surfaces often employ various generative algorithms, some created by the architects, others provided by the software maker, to arrive at a solution or set of solutions. It is critical that we develop the knowledge to manipulate the forms, surfaces, and algorithmic processes behind their generation. Oliver Wendell Holmes once said, "Man's mind, once stretched by a new idea, never regains its original dimensions."[1] Every time unique solutions are created for particular design applications, the knowledge base expands to conquer problems that previously seemed unsolvable.

RLDS TEMPLE

The *RLDS Temple* in Independence, Missouri, was completed in the early 1990s (figure 6.1). In St Louis, Gyo Obata of *HOK* had asked us to develop a solution for a 300 ft-tall roof, which was to be based on a spiraling conch shell he had selected from a large collection of seashells during a meeting. The solution for that "seashell" roof consisted of more than 300 individual panels of stainless steel – each was tapered and unique in shape (figure 6.2).

6.3.
Hunter Museum of Art in Chattanooga, Tennessee (2006), under construction.

6.4.
Hunter Museum of Art: under construction.

6.5.
Hunter Museum of Art: *ZEPP™ System* installation.

At that time, *HOK* used a proprietary software system for design work, and we were using AutoCAD to augment our drafting. We took field measurements of certain defining points of the roof, and radioed them back to the shop. We had a custom-written AutoCAD script to divide the roof surface into panels. With this technique, we produced a very intricate design, but not using the direct parametric relationships for digital fabrication. Today, this project could be developed and delivered much faster, and probably more economically, mainly because we would first derive the algorithm to convert the surface into smaller panel elements. The algorithm would have "intelligence" about significant parameters, such as the limit of sheet size as defined by our equipment, the tapering relationship as defined by the architecture, and the end laps and edge conditions as defined by water infiltration restrictions.

HUNTER MUSEUM OF ART

Today, our process is much more digitally refined. For the *Hunter Museum of Art* in Chattanooga, Tennessee (2006), designed by Randall Stout, we used digital fabrication techniques based on parametric relationships to define and fabricate the cladding system (figures 6.3 and 6.4). The amount of steel needed to hold the systems and panels for fairly elaborate surfaces was minimized, and the complexities of the design were integrated smoothly into our fabrication processes. As a fabricator and installer, we were involved in the design of the cladding elements, and thus established an early and close relationship with the designer to help develop the project; we provided valuable input to help designers with the decision-making. Thus, we were able to add value to the project, as our knowledge base has expanded significantly through resolving similar types of distinctive solutions for building design applications. Formal complexities, unique systems, and the algorithmic definition are no longer challenges for us; we develop algorithms that process a solid digital model and produce parts that can be assembled on our shop floor (figure 6.5).

DE YOUNG MUSEUM OF ART

We use digital information and parametric modeling to create very intricate surface textures. The *de Young Museum of Art* in San Francisco (2005), designed by *Herzog & de Meuron*, features a textural pattern on its façades (figure 6.6). To achieve this material effect, numerous parameters were considered in the production of the building skin, such as available sheet width, temper of copper, spacing of bump texture, thickness of copper, etc. Textural patterns, inspired by an abstraction of a canopy of trees, were mapped across the surface of this 400 ft-long museum (figures 6.7a–b and 6.8). Also, each copper panel has an edge condition that is folded inward; this edge or seam between two adjacent panels must keep water out of the building. Additionally, *Herzog & de Meuron* wanted all the panels to be tapered to follow the slope of the roof. Thus, fabrication requirements were complex even before adding the texture.

The tapering panels were mapped with the images of the tree canopy. To synchronize the production reality with the design intention, an algorithm was created to interpret and convert the images into a matrix of circles. The circles were of differing diameters that corresponded precisely to a grayscale image of the trees. The position of each circle and its diameter were then directly related to

a machine stamping process – the copper sheets were stamped outward or inward to nine different levels of predetermined depths. The copper surface was selectively perforated as well. This satisfied functional requirements, such as supplying air into the building, and shading the galleries from the direct sunlight coming through the glass. The architects wanted perforation, but not simply standard perforations – the perforations had to emulate the tree canopy abstraction as well, by altering the diameter of each perforation.

After the panels were produced and installed on the building, they produced a very beautiful material effect that combined multiple levels of complexity. The surface, once mapped on the digital model, was reproducible on the plant floor, and was ultimately applied to the project. There are several million bumps of different levels of depth in and out of the surface (figure 6.9). The machines that make bumps in metal are common machines used in many manufacturing facilities around the world; we just made them do things a little differently.

As the panels were installed into precise locations, the panel joints were staggered in a running bond pattern, creating a flowing texture across the entire surface. A "cloud" effect occurs at the absence of bumps in the field; the bumps gradually disappear, so light reflecting off the surface causes an entirely different effect than in the areas where the texture of the bump distorts the reflection. The corners were V-cut and folded; they had to be very precise. The V-cutting removes metal from the reverse side and permits a sharp appearance and a very precise geometry.

The general contractor did not use parametrics in the construction of the building. The contractor worked with our digital model to arrive at the curb cuts, openings in the concrete, and other layout features. We were able to achieve

6.8. (above)
de Young Museum of Art: the textural pattern was based on a tree canopy abstraction.

6.10.
Kansas City Art Institute in Kansas City, Missouri (2006).

6.11.
Kansas City Art Institute: pattern detail.

precise dimensions, allowing accuracy across the surface to a 64th of an inch – for over 6 million bumps! There were no bumps on the corners, i.e. where the panels wrapped the corners. Flashing was not used to cover over the edges in order to better achieve a total machined surface. This did not increase cost, and actually sped up the delivery of fabrication.

We worked closely with *Herzog & de Meuron* to realize a unique surface for the *de Young Museum*. The design team worked together as if in a laboratory. The architects worked in our facility, and we worked in their design offices for a period of several months before the design was completed. We produced several prototype variations on copper sheets to determine the appropriate thickness of metal, and to establish the process of fabrication within the budget constraints. We experimented with several techniques and also mocked up several variations of perforation patterns. The robust nature of the collaborative interaction was key to the success of the unique surface, from both the budget and the execution standpoints. Yet, the best aspect of the finalized building is to see people touching the building and experiencing the surface, and to realize that finely crafted detail through digital definition adds a whole new meaning – a material effect – through surface interaction to those who experience it.

KANSAS CITY ART INSTITUTE

We used similar fabrication techniques in the *Kansas City Art Institute*, an art school in Kansas City (2006, figure 6.10). The architect, Kirk Gastinger, of *Gastinger, Harden Walker Architects*, wanted to enhance the basic flat seam surface with a material effect that would emulate the gesso technique used on a blank canvas (figure 6.11). An image created by the architect was mapped across the copper surface. Our engineers adjusted the image to fit the building surface. The gesso pattern crosses over panels and goes around corners to various surfaces of the building. The intent was to allow nature to slowly "paint" the building, as the copper ages. Water runs down the copper surfaces, across some of the lines, and moves in different directions concentrating in some areas more than others. Over time, the copper will develop a patina with intricate patterns related directly to the water flows. This different definition of the surface did not increase the cost significantly. The patterning was integrated into some of the processes used to make the panel. The equipment screens on this building were selectively perforated first, and then corrugated to create a similar effect. This design and production process illustrates the benefits of innovation by incorporating information into our fabrication and production techniques, and the necessity of establishing good communication with the architect early in the design phases.

71

6.12.

Neiman Marcus Store,
Natick, Massachusetts
(2007), designed by
Elkus Manfreti.

6.13.

Neiman Marcus Store:
Gaussian analysis of
the curvature in the
surfaces.

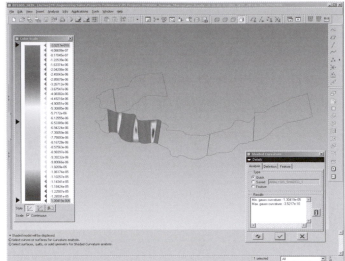

NEIMAN MARCUS STORE

In the *Neiman Marcus Store* in Natick, Massachusetts (2007), designed by Elkus Manfreti, the idea was to create a look on the building of a "woman's scarf draped across a box" (figure 6.12). First, we created a parametric model of the surface using *Pro-Engineer*. We then performed a curvature analysis to find out where we could add more curvature without an increase in cost, or where we could eliminate curvature to decrease cost. Going beyond certain limits requires shaping the corresponding panel using special equipment. If shaping could be done manually, by laying the panel onto the forms, then the costs are decreased. The software allows us to understand these limits: simple *Gaussian analysis* shows areas with different degrees of curvature and how they relate to each other (figure 6.13).

The ribbon of metal that wraps around the building is 410 ft long and 40 ft high. The panels are 9 ft long by 40 ft high, resulting in nearly 70 panels that stack and wrap around the "box." The size parameters were constrained by what we could readily ship from our plant in Kansas City. The panels were manufactured before the building was completed. The support locations were identified in advance, so we could establish where the

panels would interface. A set of standard relationships of the parts of a panel – referred to as the "*Rosetta panel*" – were created, with some parametric relationships to all of the other panels making up the entire surface. The parametric relationships allowed us to "grow" the building. All the fabrication information of the various panels was generated using an algorithm that is based on this "Rosetta" panel's information. The information was shared with the designer to aid in decision-making. Ultimately, that information was used to build the panels.

The behavior of the material was a very important consideration. Metal skins become problematic because of the *anisotropic* nature of metal as it is shaped into curved surfaces. It is very difficult to predict how the shaping will unfold, as metal behaves differently from a sheet of paper: because the sheet metal is *anisotropic*, it cannot be reshaped consistently across the entire surface. Sheet metal has a "grain" direction, as it is produced using hot rolling that is then followed by cold rolling operations. Because the grains are stretched and aligned as the thin sheet metal is produced, it is not always possible to predict how the metal will shape precisely. Curving in one direction will be different than curving in the perpendicular direction across a sheet of metal. This is not easily predictable and adds another layer of complexity to achieving the final form.

For the *Neiman Marcus Store,* the panels were assembled in pairs in house in order to ensure they matched, since the pattern cannot be broken into disjointed segments. We had as many as eight large panels in fabrication simultaneously. These large panels had three colors of stainless steel that were used to create the pattern of the design intent (figure 6.14). The staging devices, used to build the panels, were created with the

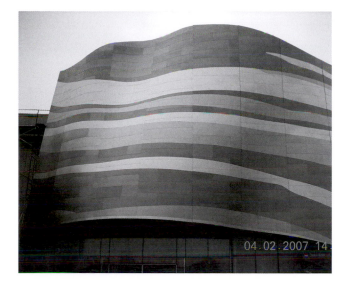

aid of the computer. On the floor, the workmen knew how to set these in place and connect the sides; they knew the fins would go in as predicted by the algorithms. All we had to do manually was to identify where the colors and the patterns change and transfer that information to the next panel. We tried different techniques, and even considered using some laser surveying devices, hoping to pinpoint precise locations on the finished surface using the digital three-dimensional model. X, Y, and Z coordinates for the precise location of the panels relative to steel attachment points were given to the general contractor. This information would reduce adjustment and build in the setting tolerance (figure 6.15). The panels were delivered and installed in about three weeks. The material effects of the different metal surface properties are striking, as light reflects off the undulating surface. The different colors are achieved through light interference: phase changes in the light wave, as it reflects off dual surfaces, generate or

degenerate portions of the wavelength to produce different color tones (figure 6.16).

Not all of our work uses parametric relationships. Earlier work, obviously, was carried out without the value added of *digital definition*. An example is an early project by Frank Gehry, the *Wiesman Art Museum*, in Minneapolis (1992, figure 6.17). At the time, neither Gehry nor Zahner used parametric definition of geometry. Today, we can deploy the parametric techniques with relatively affordable costs. The *A. Zahner Company* is constantly working out ways of making intricate designs affordable. Internally, we seek to improve the interaction of the intricate design with our fabrication techniques to reduce the cost. Some projects are much more straightforward in their geometry, techniques for definition, or fabrication, like the spherical form for the *Museum of Science and Industry* in Tampa (1995, figure 6.18), designed by Antoine Predock. We used AutoCAD to define this geometry and incorporated three-dimensional positioning equipment in the field.

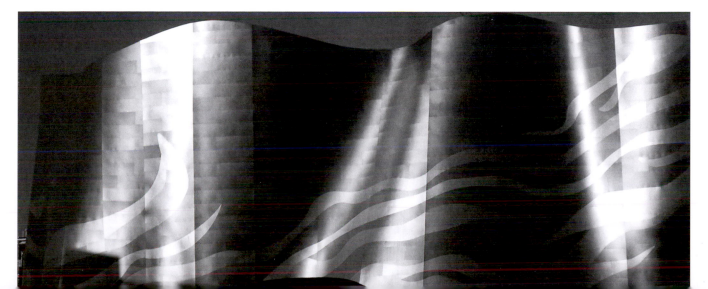

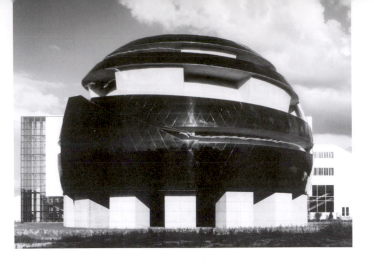

6.17.
Wiesman Art Museum,
Minneapolis, Minnesota
(1992).

6.18.
*Museum of Science and
Industry*, Tampa, Florida
(1995).

FEDERAL COURTHOUSE

A major point of digital definition in manufacturing and design practices is its effect on *how* we design and make buildings. Our collaboration with Tom Mayne and *Morphosis* illustrates this point. We exchanged information at an early stage in order to produce models and samples of what was to be created for the *Federal Courthouse* in Eugene, Oregon (2006, figure 6.19). To begin with, it was necessary for us to clearly understand the design intent for the surface articulation. Initially, the geometry of the building surfaces was provided to us in the form of a solid computer model and a rapid prototype model. Additionally, information about the surface reflectivity, weathering characteristics, and patterning strategies were discussed. In turn, we created various surface samples of stainless steel and zinc with

a range of finishes. Since each surface finish has a cost relationship associated with it, we also created initial budgets to go along with the finishes.

As a collaborative team consisting of the designer, general contractor, and us in the early stages, we established criteria for the paneling of the surface. The medium for exchanging information was generated by creating a matching digital model (figure 6.20) and applying various surface configurations. We integrated parametrics into the metal panel elements that make up the surface, but the final joint system required more development. Thus, we produced a

6.19.
Federal Courthouse
in Eugene, Oregon
(2006), designed by
Morphosis.

series of full-scale physical models showing how various seams would appear as they curved inward and outward across the surface. Once the design team had settled on the surface geometry and finish that provided the greatest value (considering both cost and appearance), a more complete parametric model was created.

It is important to note that the designer resided in Santa Monica, California, the general contractor in Portland, Oregon, the owner in Eugene, Oregon, and we are located in Kansas City, Missouri. The exchange of information via digital file transfer protocols and web-based viewing systems allowed constant and frequent updates of the surface design. The early digital exchange of information was crucial to the success of such a process-oriented, collaborative, complex project. Ultimately, the result of such rigor in the process was

a finely crafted building. The finished building appears as if it were machined almost entirely out of a block of stainless steel. We were able to achieve this "machined surface" effect by developing a parametric model of all parts and surface interfaces, and working closely with the collaborative team.

Many people in the manufacturing industry do not yet have the capability to deal with the digital definition of the geometry. For some reason, they consider it risky. We, on the other hand, are continually improving our approach using digital definition of the geometry and the production processes to increase the value we provide to our customers. We work to get business plans right so that our customers can afford our product, and eliminate redundancy to speed up the delivery, maintain flexibility and operate profitably.

6.20.
Federal Courthouse:
digital model.

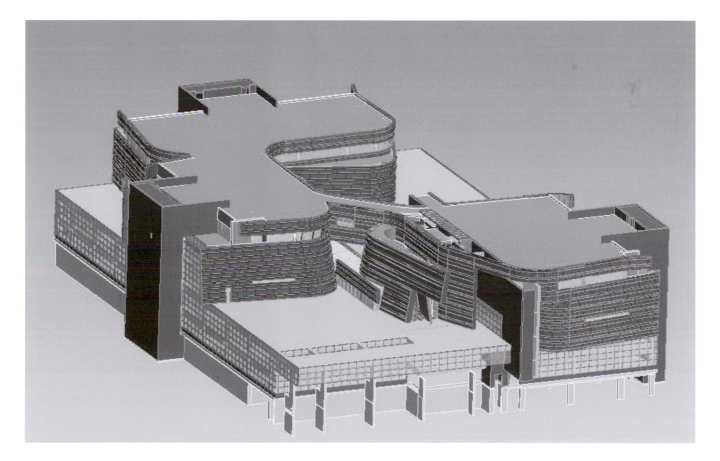

6.21.
Marquee for Philadelphia Theatre Company in Philadelphia, Pennsylvania (2007), designed by *Kieran Timberlake.*

6.22a–b.
Marquee for Philadelphia Theatre Company: Rhino model.

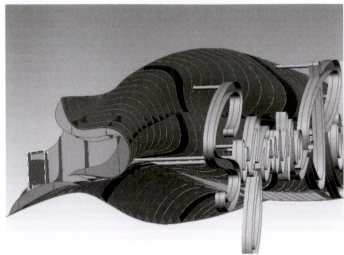

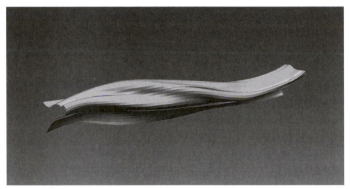

6.23.
Marquee for Philadelphia Theatre Company: ZEPP™ System.

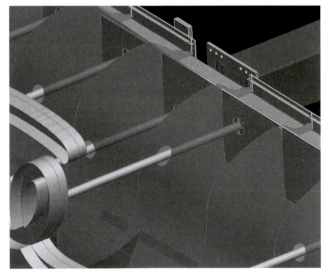

MARQUEE FOR THE PHILADELPHIA THEATRE COMPANY

In 2007, we completed a beautiful marquee (figure 6.21) for the *Philadelphia Theatre Company* that was designed by *Kieran Timberlake*. The design team created and delivered to us a digital solid model in *Rhino* (figures 6.22a–b). From the original model, we established red as interference color on the stainless steel surface, and a texture of small shingles. A small section mock-up was fabricated in full scale to demonstrate the final assembly. We created a *ZEPP™* (*Zahner Engineered Profile Panel*) System using cut cross-sectional fins. This panel system allowed us to incorporate structural steel, an inner skin of aluminum, and cold cathode electrical pathways (figure 6.23). The final marquee was assembled in two large sections, each approximately 45 ft in length. Both sections were completely assembled in the shop, loaded onto two trucks, and delivered to the Philadelphia site for final installation (figure 6.24). The marquee was completely installed in one evening. No paper was used to create the assembly with the exception of the stamped engineering calculations for the internal steel.

6.24.
Marquee for Philadelphia Theatre Company: fabrication in Kansas City.

6.26.
Terrestrial Suture installation, *Indianapolis Art Center*, Broad Ripple, Indianapolis, Indiana (2006).

6.25.
Perimetric Boundary installation, *Minnetrista Cultural Center*, Muncie, Indiana (2006).

6.27.
Federico Negro of *SHoP Architects* discusses *Zahner* production parameters with *Ball State University* students.

Everything else was conveyed digitally. This is the information "reality" of a vast number of design projects today; industry firms with an expanded knowledge base, achieved through innovating techniques in production and collaboration, are well positioned to produce remarkable architectural solutions.

EDUCATING FUTURE INNOVATORS

A. Zahner Company is also committed to partnering with architectural education institutions. Through "immersive learning" opportunities for students, we are able to provide, in a modest way, direct experience with the production realities of digital definition. This knowledge is very important in early design decision-making, and students can only gain this experience through experimentation and applied research through tangible collaborations with industry partners. For example, we produced an installation with *Ball State University* students in the spring of 2006 (figures 6.25 and 6.26). In the seminar at the *Virginia Ball Center for Creative Inquiry*, students developed a delicate metal form in collaboration with *SHoP Architects* in New

6.28.
A. Zahner Company panel production.

York City, based on production parameters related to budget considerations we gave them at the outset. The students optimized their design solutions based on this early design feedback loop; interaction of this kind can directly feed into the development of parameters that drive design development (figure 6.27). These exchanges with students are extremely valuable as they prepare to enter the workforce; they are armed with knowledge about collaborating with industry in much more effective ways (figure 6.28). Students with a collaborative attitude and an expanded knowledge base are well situated to lead architecture into the new realities of digital definition and innovative design and industry partnerships.

NOTE

1 Oliver Wendell Holmes (US author and physician, 1809–1894), *The Autocrat of the Breakfast Table*, Boston: The Atlantic Monthly, 1858.

7

FABRICATING MATERIAL EFFECTS: FROM ROBOTS TO CRAFT-WORKERS

JEANNE GANG / STUDIO GANG ARCHITECTS

7.1.
*Chicago
Architecture Ten
Visions Exhibition*
installation, *Art
Institute of Chicago*
(2005).

7.2.
The installation team.

Can "craft" today truly be performed by an architect and a CNC machine? As early as Frank Lloyd Wright, and his first stained glass window, architects began to visualize a day without reliance on the human craft-worker in order to realize their dreams. Did he and his contemporaries ever succeed in their quest to eliminate the imperfection? What is to be gained by a continued effort to dismiss the work of the craft-worker? Will the machine that spins buildings really liberate architects? This discussion has a direct relationship to other worldwide contemporary issues of labor and sustainability. It will bring forward larger political and economic ideas surrounding fabrication and material in relation to craft and construction. *Studio Gang*'s work experiments in the area between high-tech fabrication and low-tech construction-site realities, while mining the *true* craft still practiced by real people. It attempts to locate the intersection in architecture between architect, robot, fabricator, and craft-worker.

At *Studio Gang*, we are interested in combining digital fabrication technology with rougher, site-built elements. The reason for our focus stems from an effort to find ways to preserve the slightly irregular qualities of material, while also dealing with the physical ways of making things that engage labor – or human effort. It may seem odd to discuss labor and human-made production in the context of manufacturing material effects and digital fabrication, but it is an important counterbalance. It is this unique quality that architecture has been able to maintain, unlike other forms of production. It is greatly satisfying being on a site, being connected to construction, and doing

construction administration aspects of work in addition to design. Architects are no longer required to engage work on that level, since there are so many intermediary professionals today. Many designers would rather stay away from the mess of the construction site, but we think there is a fertile territory to explore stemming from all aspects of "making."

One feature of this interest lies in the emerging importance of engaging the concept of work and labor for sustainability, or put simply: engaging people in the production of architecture. We are especially interested in making the presence of people visible in the physical object. Architecture must explore this critical human involvement if it is to claim a sustainable worldview. Consider that there are already over six billion people in the world; subtract children too young to work, and within the remaining half, 200 million are unemployed, and 550 million make less than $1 a day. Still, these numbers do not represent many people, such as those underemployed or earning very little. The point is that we have a large population that could be contributing and earning a livelihood, but for different reasons, aren't able to do so. Why do we avoid "labor" when there are so many people underemployed? Labor is, in essence, energy – why substitute all of it with machines? We are interested in the implied possibilities that these questions bring forward, while we simultaneously explore the potential of digital means of fabrication. The two are not mutually exclusive.

CHICAGO ARCHITECTURE, TEN VISIONS EXHIBITION

Through our design process, *Studio Gang* has tried to combine human work and digital fabrication in various ways and on different levels. As an introduction to what this approach produces, our installation for the *Chicago Architecture Ten Visions Exhibition* for the *Art Institute of Chicago* and *Illinois Institute of Technology* (IIT) in 2005 offers a concise example (figure 7.1). Constructed entirely of baseball cards, a wall was built for an exhibition. To construct the final installation, with approximately 15,000 baseball cards, required the *Studio Gang*

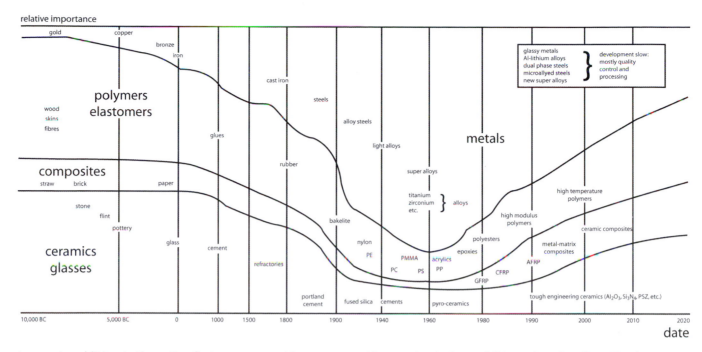

7.3.
Relative historical importance of different substances (from *Lightness* by Adriaan Beukers and Ed van Hinte).

team – in addition to the entire first-year IIT architecture class. The project began with experiments focused on trying to make a structure out of something that was very lightweight and seemingly fragile; by bending the cards and joining them using very basic stapler "technology," we arrived at something striking – a freestanding structural piece that stood 16 ft high. In the case of the design process, fabrication technology played an important role. Special software was used to sort, print, and arrange the images displayed on the wall. Onto each baseball card, we printed a component of research about stadiums and cities, including diagrams and facts we had uncovered about baseball parks in Chicago and other cities.

It took the hands and minds of many people (figure 7.2) to assemble the installation piece by piece, by placing each printed card into a correct location in the matrix. Although the assembly is perhaps possible to achieve with robots, the involvement of the students made the effort *social* and *rewarding* for the shared sense of accomplishment.

MARBLE CURTAIN

We used the same concept of working with individuals on another, larger exhibition installation. With larger-scale work, it is harder to build without the participation of professional trades. In this case, we were lucky to work directly with a master craft-worker from the *International Masonry Institute* (IMI). We were invited by the IMI and the *National Building Museum* to design an entry for the

Masonry Variations exhibition (on view from October 2003 till April 2004). We were asked to imagine new directions for stone. The aim was to get architects interested again in using this incredibly old building material. It was challenging to work with a material that has been in use for so long; where could we go with new directions? To begin the design, we first embarked on material experimentation and research.

Stone is an amazing, mysterious material. It has been used in many awe-inspiring ways, and most typically is used in compression. In light of new tools and new combinations of materials, we wondered if it would be possible to make a lighter construct with this heavy material. A lighter construct was also necessitated by the load level allowed in the *National Building Museum* gallery in Washington, DC, which was barely enough to support visitors to the museum – around 60 lbs per sq ft.

A diagram in Adriaan Beukers and Ed van Hinte's book on the relative importance of different substances, *Lightness*,[1] shows comparisons between different combinations of materials through time (figure 7.3): metals hit their peak in the 1960s; also at that time, the spread of material combinations moved toward composites and polymers (both interesting materials in themselves) with polymers acting just as glue. The *Marble Curtain* installation (figure 7.4) was about answering the question of whether, in light of new composites and polymers, it would be possible to hold stone in tension from the gallery ceiling, as opposed to stacking stone up from the floor.

7.4.
Marble Curtain installation in the *Masonry Variations* exhibition, *National Building Museum*, Washington, DC (2004).

7.5.
Testing marble for the *Marble Curtain* installation in the material testing lab at the Illinois Institute of Technology.

Looking for technical information about stone in tension, we discovered that such information simply doesn't exist. One finds information about stone on "flexure," "absorption," and "compression," but not "tension." The lack of available information led us to collaborate with many different professionals and tradesmen early in the design process; to start with, we approached the *Illinois Institute of Technology* (IIT) *Materials Testing Lab*, Chicago, which is part of the aerospace program at the IIT. They had not worked with architects before, but they agreed to help us.

To make something hang in tension, a joint or a connection between the adjacent pieces of stone that allows the transfer of loads is necessary. Different interlocking joints were assessed (figure 7.5), while the lab tested the strength of stone hung in tension until failure.

It was difficult to determine if the material could provide what was needed for the installation, as most of the design time was spent testing without knowing the outcome of the entire installation. In addition, we had to test backing materials as well. With laminated glass, there needs to be a layer of some laminate sandwiched between two pieces to hold broken glass in place if it shatters. Suspended marble presented the same issue – stone hanging overhead requires lamination. The use of glue (i.e. the polymer) in the *Marble Curtain* was crucial, both as a backing material for redundancy, and as structural silicon in the head joints. Normally, architects are embarrassed about using glue, but since it is so ubiquitous it deserves further consideration and fuller exploration.

The testing process took days to set up in the *IIT Materials Testing Lab*. This brings up a critical point about the process of research-oriented design – experimentation requires considerable time and precise "up-front" work. With the *Marble Curtain* project, only successful tests could be used in the final installation, so many decisions had to be made prior to knowing the final design. To our surprise, and great excitement, the first test succeeded beyond expectation, in spite of being told by one of the lab experts that it would never work, as a tension load of 100 lbs at maximum would break the stone.

Wooden falsework, removed prior to the exhibition, was also designed, fabricated, and constructed to assist with the assembly. The plywood used was cut based on the drawings and assembled off-site first and then transferred to the site by the mason. He used a digital plumb-bob tool that allowed him to locate X, Y and Z dimensions; the plumb was a necessary tool, since the stone courses curved around the shape and were not level with the floor. At the top of the piece, masonry anchors were driven and cemented into the vaulted ceiling. These high strength aluminum anchors held the first course of puzzle pieces, which was bonded using a special kind of silicone to the aluminum. Piece by piece, the stones were hung from the stone above. Structural silicone was used between the vertical head joints to transfer lateral loads around the global structure of the shell. The bottom course was anchored to the floor with flexible masonry anchors. Finally, the falsework was carefully removed and the finished installation hung on its own within the space.

The marble was cut incredibly thin, unlike typical stone applications that are thick and heavy. The stone performed structurally, while also being thin enough to be translucent. It almost seemed as though some inherent beauty in the stone was being unleashed for the first time (figure 7.6). The entire installation weighed about 1,800 lbs and was simply hanging from the ceiling, stone upon stone, without any structural support or frame. The *Marble Curtain* was not only the first time masonry has been hung from the ceiling plane rather than stacked from the floor, but also the first use of the material put into tension to create a structure.

The importance of *craft* is demonstrated in the *Marble Curtain* installation, especially in constructing such an intricate design. Though the stone pieces were not cut by hand, there were many other steps where the craft-worker's judgment and skill were critical. Thus *craft* is very much alive when deploying digital fabrication techniques; the potential of digital fabrication does not eliminate the need of the craft-worker who understands the final product, and from the beginning works with the architect to imagine how to create it. In the end, the design of the *Marble Curtain* was a collaboration to which both experimentation and expertise – essential components of *craft* – were essential.

We reached 750 lbs in the first test, due in part to the knowledge of Matt Redabaugh, the master craft-worker from the *International Masonry Institute*. He narrowed down the material selection to marble instead of granite or limestone. He knew that marble behaves more homogeneously than a sedimentary stone, like limestone, or an igneous stone with crystals inside, like granite. In some of the testing combinations, we achieved up to 1,750 lbs in tension in the material.

The form for the curtain needed to be modeled fully, taking into consideration how it would be fabricated, and analyzing the location of stresses. We also had to consider what would happen to the overall structure if one piece broke. The final design is composed of "chains of stones hanging in tension." There were 622 different shapes cut out of 3/8 inch, or 9.525 mm, thick tile. The tiles were first laminated with fiber resin to provide redundancy in case of breakage, and then each tile was water-jet cut to size, guided by our digital files. At the same time, the tiles were engraved with a number and letter indicating where each piece would be located in the final assembly.

7.7.
*Education Pavilions,
Lincoln Park Zoo,*
Chicago (scheduled
completion 2009).

5. ENERGY

An urban footpath bisects the
new park and pond marked by 7
wind turbines that power site
lighting.

4. EDUCATION

A continous boardwalk
converts pond into an
educational zoo exhibit.

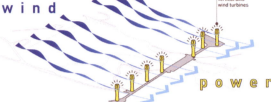

MEMBRANE:
3-dimensional fiberglass
panels fastened together
with single lap joints.

3. WETLAND

Plant shelves filter run-off
water to improve water quality
and to create habitat zones for
animals.

2. HYDROLOGY

Increasing pond depth
oxygenates water. Removal of
concrete edge permits
replenishment from watershed.

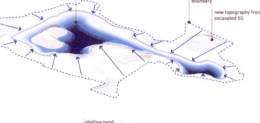

STRUCTURE:
Space-frame assembled
from glue-laminated, CNC-
milled components.

1. EXISTING POND

Dirty, odorous, lifeless, and
dependent on city drinking
water; a problematic
mandmade pond in the city.

7.9.
Landscape and urban pond restoration,
Lincoln Park Zoo, Chicago.

7.8.
Education Pavilions:
exploded axonometric.

7.10.
Elevation, *Walled Garden House*, Chicago (scheduled completion 2008).

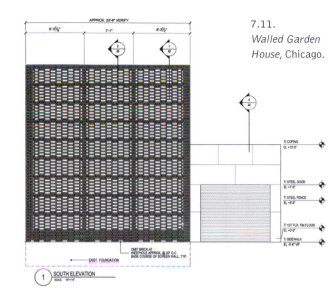

7.11.
Walled Garden House, Chicago.

EDUCATION PAVILIONS

The combination of digital fabrication and site work was a recurrent theme in the conception of two outdoor *Education Pavilions* at the *Lincoln Park Zoo* in Chicago (scheduled completion fall 2009). The goal was to create a space where kids can gather outdoors for class under a roof during their visits to the zoo (figure 7.7). We were searching for a somewhat low-tech solution. In fact, with projects limited in budget or time, we find ourselves often moving toward low-tech solutions. This happens because we imagine how things will be made, how the project will be built, and how it will meet the budget.

For the Lincoln Park Zoo project, we looked to boat-making practices for bending wood. We created pod-like shells that span over a space without the use of columns. By the end of design development, we had devised a simpler approach where a series of bent wood members, fabricated off-site, arrive on the site to be assembled quickly. The bent wood pieces are CNC milled to obtain double curvature. The assembled structures are then topped with fiberglass cladding, filtering light into the space (figure 7.8).

These small-scale pavilions are part of a much larger-scale project that includes the landscape and restoration of an urban pond for the *Lincoln Park Zoo* (figure 7.9). Much of our work is driven by sustainability or doing things that will make sense in the long run. This makes it necessary to collaborate with others who can provide insight from different perspectives on all aspects of a project. In this case, we worked with a hydrologist and a landscape architect in order to try to improve the water quality of the urban pond. The hydrologist suggested making the pond deeper for better oxygenation and temperature control. The landscape architect introduced the idea of a plant shelf in order to clean the run-off water flowing into the pond. Both suggestions helped define the final design.

WALLED GARDEN HOUSE

We employed typical brick technology and modified it from within to offer a new structural solution to a residential project: a 24-ft-high wall made out of a single wythe of brick (figure 7.10). We collaborated early on in design with masons, engineers, and fabricators of small masonry ties. The structure is a garden wall with no roof, so a steel frame inside the wall takes the lateral loads and ties the garden walls back to the house (figure 7.11). The material issue of the project is in marrying the single wythe wall to the frame, and dealing with differences in movement of brick and steel. The combined experience of the team suggested that masonry would move in one direction and steel in another; movement needed to be choreographed to avoid cracks and water infiltration. A solution was found in customization and fabrication of special *masonry ties* – the invisible steel pieces that are found in contemporary masonry. Again, we had to simulate and test the way the pieces would go together, including full-scale mock-ups. However, the most interesting aspect is that the solution was found by exploring the detail of something very small, and ultimately invisible in the final design. Yet, without this piece, the wall would not have been possible.

7.12.
SOS Community Center, Chicago (2007).

7.13.
SOS Community Center under construction.

7.14.
SOS Community Center elevator shaft.

SOS COMMUNITY CENTER

There are three larger *Studio Gang* projects, which also illustrate this ability to engage human contribution while employing digital fabrication technology. The first example re-considers the messiest and least digitally fabricated material: concrete. The *SOS Community Center* in Chicago's Auburn-Gresham neighborhood (2007) functions as a training center for foster parents, a counseling center for foster kids, an after-school classroom, and a daycare center for the greater neighborhood. Its giant meandering staircase connects the building's two floors and doubles as an open classroom and impromptu stage (figure 7.12).

With a small budget, and the potential donation of concrete for the project, we began to explore concrete's interesting and characteristic fluid quality for the building's exterior walls. Concrete, when wet, behaves like molten lava. We wanted the concrete to retain this fluid character even after it had cured. Several physical models were made to understand how this visual fluidity could be achieved. Knowing that we would need a number of separate "pours" to finish the building wall, we experimented with our tiny model to understand how changing the color would work with each pour. We tested the creation of hilly bands of concrete, similar to a geologic section of the earth.

While concrete mix design has been a relatively trial-and-error exercise up until now, computational work in this field is rapidly making the process much more scientific. With the *SOS Community Center*, we were able to tap into the scientific knowledge of mix design to achieve greater control of this variable. Increasing the number of *cold joints* to create the bands required a careful consideration of the overall structure. Cantilevered walls were precisely calculated to accommodate the different strengths of concrete being used. But, while sophisticated engineering was necessary to achieve the banded wall, there was also a need to understand the action of making it. We worked closely with the concrete contractors to understand how the material would behave after pouring, and also how to effectively use vibration inside the formwork. Though concrete contractors are not known for their level of craft, it was clear that they understood their material deeply, and thus brought valuable knowledge to the project. We worked with them to understand the properties of concrete and how we could get each pour of the material to achieve greater variation in elevation — to be hilly (figure 7.13).

Using the elevator shaft in the new building as a 1:1 scale test, the client approved of the banded concrete wall design (figure 7.14). In the final application, it seemed as if the concrete had been liberated from its traditional iconography and had found a new expression as a solidified liquid. The design allowed the material to reflect the way in which it was cast, and as a result, it renders the work of the concrete contractors visible.

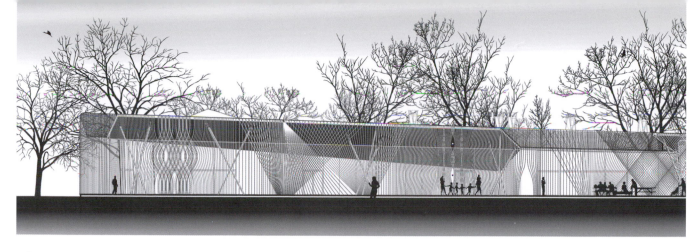

7.15.
*Ford Calumet
Environmental Center,*
Calumet (scheduled
completion 2009).

FORD CALUMET ENVIRONMENTAL CENTER

Another large-scale project exploring materiality is the *Ford Calumet Environmental Center* (scheduled completion 2009), a project won in a competition held by the *City of Chicago* and *State of Illinois* (figure 7.15). What is unique about the center is that the design conceptualizes "making" in a different way – not through digital fabrication, but through making the building out of what is available and on hand – much like the way a bird makes a nest.

The *Ford Calumet Environmental Center* is a place where people will go to learn about the cultural history of the Calumet region, and its role as a natural habitat.

Being situated on the south side of Chicago, the surrounding area has a history deeply rooted in the steel industry (figure 7.16). Calumet is also an incredible natural habitat that has been able to survive, because it has not been covered with single-family houses and monoculture lawns.

The main material, salvaged architectural elements, could be collected within a short distance from the site, saving the energy of shipping materials long distances. Salvaged steel is rejected for non-structural reasons, so it is fine for use in buildings. By using it as is, it saves the energy of reprocessing. Starting with what material is available is a completely different way to conceive of a design. By using reclaimed steel, it will be possible to see the history of Calumet in its

7.16.
*Ford Calumet
Environmental
Center*: industrial
context.

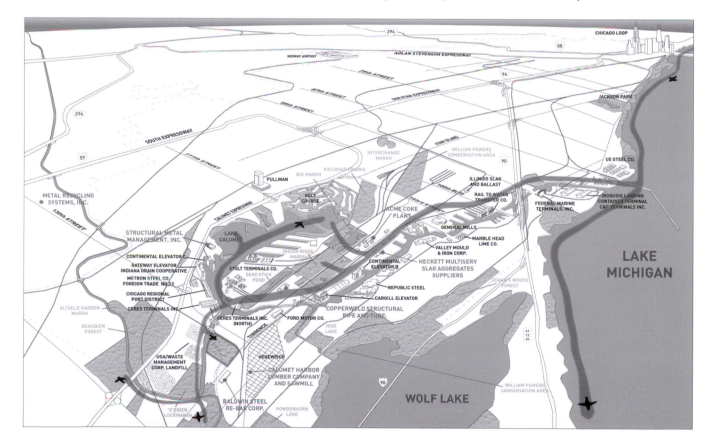

7.17.
*Ford Calumet
Environmental
Center* porch.

7.19.
Aqua Tower,
Chicago (scheduled
completion 2009).

very structure. The steel structure will be made of bundled columns driven at angles into the soil (figure 7.17). The site is also a sensitive bird migratory resting stop. Therefore, preventing bird collisions was another important part of the *Ford Calumet Environmental Center* (figure 7.18). It is important to note that more than 93 million birds die every year in collisions with glass in buildings. In this design, a woven recycled steel basket-like mesh around the building's expansive exterior porch protects birds from glass they cannot see.

Other recycled materials will also be put to use. *Slag*, a byproduct of steel production, will find new purpose in terrazzo floors. Wood from the last remaining mill in Chicago will be used for the formwork. Integrating recycled materials into a building that runs on renewable power, makes use of the earth's temperature, and incorporates the landscape's ability to clean water, will make the building more like a living system; it will be more like a nest.

7.18.
*Ford Calumet
Environmental
Center* bird anti-
collision device.

7.20.
Aqua Tower: the
floor plate effect.

AQUA TOWER

The *Aqua Tower*, an 82-storey high-rise in Chicago (scheduled completion 2009), combines labor and technology in a different way. While digital technology and manufacturing have often been discussed in terms of surface effects, *Aqua Tower* presented a very different scale to consider (figure 7.19). The initial office model started with a very rudimentary mock-up. We were interested in the specific views from the site. The rough model looked similar to a topographic landscape, as the form moved in and out informed by views. With an 82-storey building, it was necessary to consider the topography, not as surface effects, but rather as something more integral to the construction logic of the building. Thus, the *Aqua Tower* design explores what can be achieved by varying the most prevalent element in high-rises: the floor plates (figures 7.20 and 7.21).

7.21.
Aqua Tower: floor
plate diagrams.

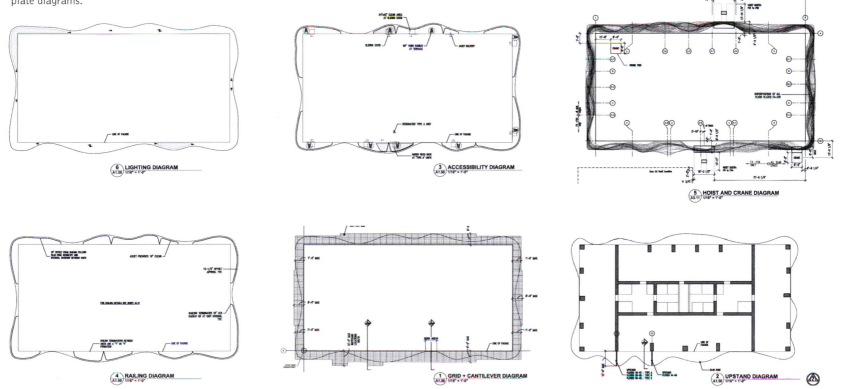

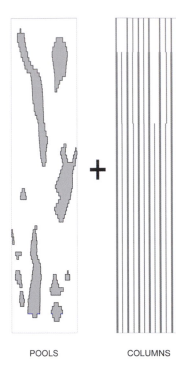

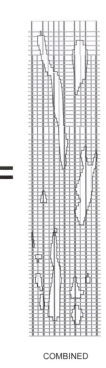

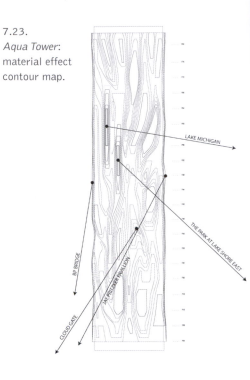

7.23.
Aqua Tower:
material effect
contour map.

CONTOURS   TERRACES   POOLS   COLUMNS   COMBINED

7.22.
Aqua Tower:
successive
zones.

Floor plates are a lot like strata in stone; there are layers upon layers. The expression of those layers creates a material effect – not over a small surface, but rather over the entire length of the building (figures 7.22 and 7.23). In light of available digital technology, we expected that variety and change would be possible on a grand 82-storey scale. Floor slabs or strata were used to achieve both this variety and change while simultaneously optimizing views. The strata were also modified based on the number of units per floor and environmental criteria. Contractors were consulted early on to consider possible construction methods, and to reduce the time it would take to make every floor plate different according to plan.

There were many design repercussions of having changing terraces. Among them, sliding glass doors could not be in the same place in every instance; they had to be placed to relate to both the living room and the terrace. Residents of *Aqua Tower* will be able to take advantage of the outdoors in ways yet unrealized in Chicago high-rise construction. Through the building's large terraces, inhabitants will occupy both the façade of the building and the city at the same time. For pedestrians on the street, the building will present an undulating appearance that changes as one moves around it.

CONSIDERING LABOR

Economist Robert Ayers writes frequently on industrial ecology and material flows. From the economic perspective, he believes that "The fundamental cause of under-employment is that labor has become too productive mostly as a result of substituting machines and energy for human labor."[2] To advance this idea, we must look for ways to engage people again into the building process. Machines and labor are not mutually exclusive; no matter what we design, we engage people. This is an argument for architects to simply begin to think about the physical act of making things, even as digital production continues to evolve. In a certain sense, the idea of using robotic construction is nostalgic for a future that was a future from the Industrial Revolution. This is not the same future that we must think about today. Thinking about the way things are made – not only from a digital fabrication point of view, but also from the point of view of the skills of the people making it – may offer some rich new possibilities.

NOTES

1 Adriaan Beukers and Ed van Hinte, *Lightness*, Rotterdam: 010 Publishers, 1998.
2 Robert Ayers, *Turning Point: The End of the Growth Paradigm*, London: Earthscan, 1998.

8
CUT TO FIT

FRANK BARKOW
BARKOW LEIBINGER ARCHITECTS

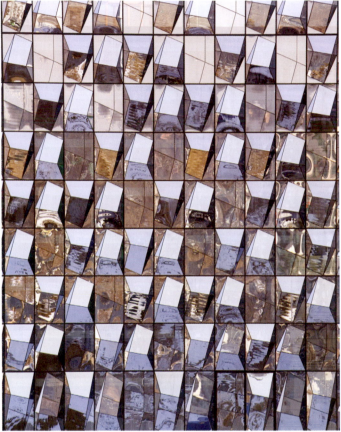

In the early 1990s, the impact of digital technology was starting to become apparent. With a visceral distrust in using that technology to simply produce images, we became interested early on in its potential to have a different bearing on architecture – a more direct and physical one, through fabrication.[1] Our engagement with *machine-tool fabrication* began academically, as a search for an idea for an architectural prototype that would emerge from the control of a technical system. It is now fully embedded within our practice.

Our interest in digital tooling (specifically, laser cutting) began as a peripheral curiosity and evolved into an applied technical ability that now drives and enables most of our projects, both formally and economically. In addition to the conventional CNC cutting, we focus primarily in our research on computer-directed laser welding and cutting machine tools made by the German company *Trumpf*.[2] That research[3] is as an independent, internal effort folded into ongoing building projects within the practice.

We explored tooled sheet metal for its structural potential in architecture, as in the recently designed gatehouse in Stuttgart/Ditzingen, Germany (2007, figure 8.1). A new CNC-cut façade for the *Trutec Building* in Seoul, Korea (2007) marks the digital fabrication technology as globally accessible, economical, and viable (figure 8.2). Applied to the roof of a campus cantina, also in Stuttgart (expected completion 2008), CNC cutting was used to shape sustainable fast-growth wood glue-laminated sections into complex structural forms (figure 8.3). As these projects demonstrate, fabrication components no longer simply "accessorize" construction, they now contribute to essential structural and cladding systems.

8.4.
St. Ivo alla Sapienza, Rome (1643), designed by Francesco Borromini.

8.3.
Trumpf Campus Cantina, Stuttgart (2008).

8.5.
Architectural Association, London, Diploma Unit 8 (1998), Jaqueline Yeo, steel templates for earth-retaining frames.

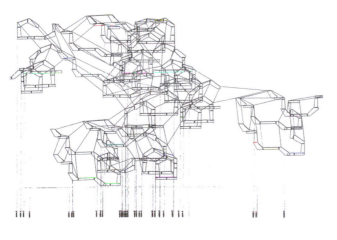

Another important aspect that influences our work is *location* – or *regional specificity*. Despite the alleged leveling of globalization, building cultures are very different, whether in Korea or Switzerland. The economics, skills, available materials, or techniques differ greatly. Our strategy with each project is to discover as quickly as possible the particularities of the local building culture, find out local limits or advantages, and deploy them to produce a singular, locally grounded, autonomous architectural design. Generally, such an approach requires close collaboration with local consultants from the beginning of the project – and not in the middle – as local consultants can often help identify local opportunities with materials, structure, budget, etc.

In the early 1990s, *Joseph Connors* gave a lecture at the American Academy in Rome on *St. Ivo alla Sapienza,* designed by Francesco Borromini in 1643. According to Connors, the spiral tower of that church did not emerge out of a tradition of sculpture or painting, but through the invention of a sixteenth-century tool – the wood lathe – that allowed this form to be realized (figure 8.4). This notion of a design enabled by a production tool was pivotal to our thinking, as our practice began to consider how materials could drive form, rather than render the form materially *post facto*. Several years later, teaching at the *Architectural Association* in London, we asked students to explore how an architectural prototype could emerge from the operation and control of a technical system (figure 8.5). The students used laser cutting to produce a component-based structure that could be added onto a building or a site in Berlin. Such research is now folded into ongoing projects in our practice, with sufficient freedom to develop separately from specific project restraints.

MACHINING RESEARCH

Trumpf, a machine-tool company based in Stuttgart, has sponsored much of our research in the material and tectonic potential of digital tooling. They are pioneers in laser cutting of sheet metal, and have developed a broad range of machine tools that can perform different types of cutting (we initially made an inventory of these machines to understand their capacities). Our first projects were very rudimentary, based on either punching or cutting sheet metal with a laser to

8.7.
"Squiggly" wall
research project
(2006).

8.6.
Moiré-type screens,
laser-fabricated
screen wall
research.

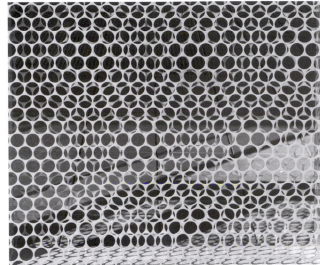

8.8.
Revolving laser
cutting research
project (2006).

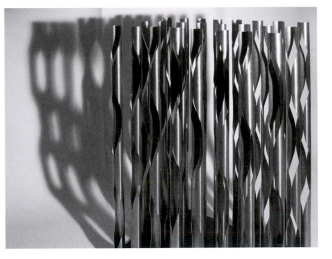

8.9.
Façade study for
*TSE Showroom and
Application Center*
in Alingsås, Sweden
(2004).

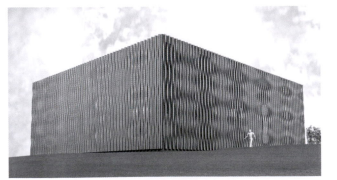

create screen walls. More recently, students joining our firm from the *Massachusetts Institute of Technology* have used their scripting skills to produce fairly simple *Moiré*-type screens (figure 8.6) that can be serially designed and produced, with an almost infinite variation. The scripting skills were also used on bending machines to produce a component that had the greatest number of folds in one piece and could be combined into larger and more complex surfaces. This "unprogrammed" work within our practice sets up a constantly evolving database (or building catalog) that can contribute to ongoing building projects.

In another research project on bending, done in collaboration with the Swiss engineer *Jürg Conzett,* we used *plexi-glass* to produce a wall or structural system. Conzett's idea was to look at structural depth as a space that could be programmed. In this case, a very large perforated box beam could be supported by "squiggly"-shaped walls that are very stiff because of their shape (recalling historical precedents like *Thomas Jefferson*'s very thin serpentine brick walls at the University of Virginia). A full-scale mock-up was manually produced in anticipation of the digital shaping of the formwork for these walls, which would be filled with translucent concrete (figure 8.7).

Revolving laser cutting has been a particular research interest for us, since three-dimensional shapes can be cut from the onset. Instead of just punching sheet metal, a three-dimensional object can be directly cut out of a three-dimensional shape. Multiple parts can be produced from a single tube, using all of the material without waste. We used the tubes to produce a sun protection screen, where the tubes are not fixed onto a frame, but have the potential to rotate, by pivoting on an axis. In this way, a volume of space can be closed or opened up to let in more light and open up the view. This project anticipates the making of a component, which then exists as an available building system within our practice (figures 8.8 and 8.9).

Expanding on the previous project is a research prototype for façade systems. Profiles are multi-tooled: first, we make rolled sections, which are incrementally

8.10a.
X-frame façade
research (2007).

8.10b.
X-frame façade:
component profile.

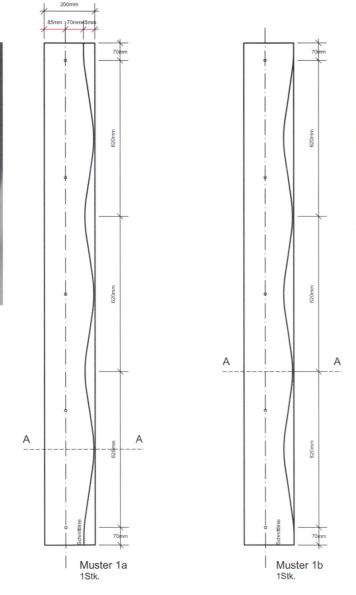

Muster 1a
1Stk.

Muster 1b
1Stk.

8.10c.
*X-frame
façade*:
detail.

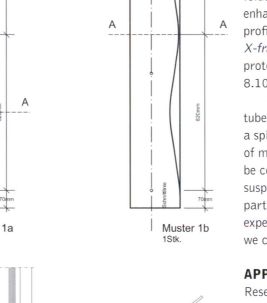

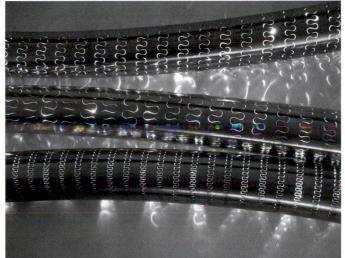

folded to make slightly curved reflective surfaces that enhance daylighting. Second, those surfaces are cut in profile in response to structural loading. The resulting *X-frame façades* are an internally developed façade prototype that we can apply in our own projects (figures 8.10a–c).

We also used scrolled puzzle-like cutting to produce a tube that can be extremely flexible, cut either in bands or as a spiraling cut. Depending on spacing (due to the amount of material that is cut), the flexibility of each tube-cut can be controlled. By inserting LED lighting into these elements, suspending or floor mounting them, they can serve as very particular and intricate lighting elements. Begun as a formal experiment for *Trumpf*, the outcome is now a design element we can produce directly (figure 8.11).

APPLIED KNOWLEDGE

Research aspects of our work have a direct bearing on actual building projects. The following projects for *Trumpf* realized an ongoing ambition: to employ fabrication technologies directly in the design and making of buildings for the company. Since factories are never complete, we have been given the opportunity to continue to build for them, and offer new prototypes as they renovate or add buildings to their campus.

8.12.
Model of the gatehouse
for the *Trumpf* campus,
Stuttgart (2007).

8.14.
Gas station by Jean
Prouvé, now located
at *Vitra* in Weil am
Rhein, Germany
(1951).

8.13.
The completed
gatehouse for
the *Trumpf*
campus,
Stuttgart
(2007).

8.15.
Trumpf
Gatehouse:
material effects.

We designed a gatehouse to create a new public entrance to the *Trumpf* campus that will be a highly visible icon for their technology (figures 8.12 and 8.13). We revisited a gas station project began 50 years ago by Jean Prouvé (1951, figure 8.14). Prouvé's idea was the embodiment of a completely conceived and fabricated piece of architecture, where all systems are integrated and complete, using sheet metal as a primary building material (figure 8.15). It is a system that can be scaled up from furniture to a building. Our aim was to rethink the meaning of this project now with the availability of digital tooling. At *Trumpf*, we discovered tabletops being prototyped and constructed of laser-cut and welded steel sheet metal (figure 8.16). These extremely stiff and light surfaces made us think that a roof structure could work in a similar way, achieving a very large cantilever. For feedback on achieving this complex roof section, we started working with structural engineer Werner Sobek, and quickly changed our plan from a bridging structure to one that could cantilever 22 m out from the core of the building. In order to achieve this large cantilever and begin interpreting the system into a laser-cut roof, we acquired a digital loading diagram from Sobek's office (figure 8.17). It was very important that the structural logic be legible in the roof, and not simply display an arbitrary graphic pattern (figure 8.18). We began cutting prototypes at a scale of 1:50, realizing we could use the same technologies for the cutting of the models as we could for fabricating at the 1:1 scale of building. In a very physical way, this roof rests on four columns of the core, which is anchored by an enormous foundation to resist overturning. This core is then wrapped in a glass double façade that creates a sunscreen by filling in the gap with gradiating plexi-glass tubes.

Lighting systems were integrated into the webbing of the roof, and function on a 24-hour cycle, rendering the

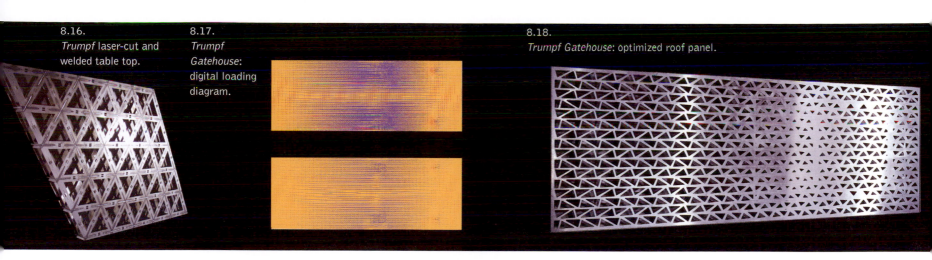

8.16.
Trumpf laser-cut and welded table top.

8.17.
Trumpf Gatehouse: digital loading diagram.

8.18.
Trumpf Gatehouse: optimized roof panel.

8.19.
Trumpf Gatehouse: plexi-glass tube infill sunscreen material effect.

8.20.
Trumpf Gatehouse: plexi-glass tube infill sunscreen installation.

structural system constantly visible. In order to understand the interface between these systems, we created a 1:1 mock-up at the gutter edge, which also explained how all the fastening systems (welding, bolting) would come together. Not only do the laser-cut openings vary, but the vertical chords also change in dimension in relationship to loads. It became apparent that through digital production we could allow each component to be made with a slightly differing geometry, thus completely replacing the old logic of the modular as an efficient and economical building process. At the same time, our original premise of shifting scales from a laser-cut tabletop to a large cantilevered roof was overly simplistic – the roof required pre-assembly into strips, which could be delivered on trucks to the site, bolted together, and lifted up onto columns. We would need both welding and bolting to assemble the roof, and also required a camber in both axes to compensate for structural loading. To achieve this bend, the erected roof was loaded with sandbags to bring it into a level and true horizontal position. The leveling was calculated in advance through collaboration with Sobek's office in order to predict the complexity of how the roof would perform.

The *gatehouse* project was not completely achieved through digital fabrication; rather, it engages a variety of "craft" techniques. A hand-crafted infill of sunscreens – a series of stacked plexi-glass tubes – with a champagne bubble material effect, radiates from a very small size to very large scale in relationship to sun angles for Stuttgart. The tectonic arrangement evokes certain traditions for garden fence building in Germany, which is comprised of stacked wood infill between stakes. Thus, this project is unique in that it embodies both digital-craft possibilities combined with a hand-crafted approach to building (figures 8.19 and 8.20).

8.21.
Trumpf Campus Cantina:
model of the daylighting
effect, *Trumpf* campus,
Stuttgart (2008).

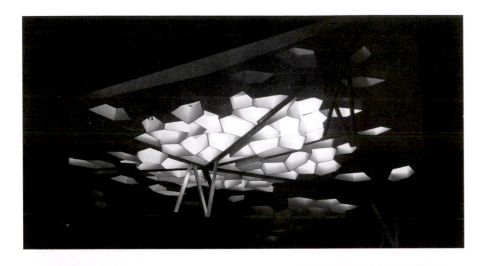

8.22.
Trumpf Campus Cantina
under construction, *Trumpf*
campus, Stuttgart (expected
completion 2008): roof
pattern lighting/material
effect.

A second project for *Trumpf* near the gatehouse is for a campus cantina – an event space. Also engineered with Werner Sobek, this structure is a large polygon-shaped roof with a primary steel structure and a secondary wood webbing infill. The steel is supported by a series of column groups independent of the corner joints, providing spans up to 20 m. Like most of our work, this structure was arrived at through the evolution of a series of very simple study models. Through workshops with Sobek, we selected the model we felt created the most dynamic and flexible space possible. Coincidental with the material idea to use wood glu-lams for the webbing was an interest in developing skylights with an ETFE membrane. Thus, a very lightweight series of pneumatic cells could complement the heavier wood cells of the roof webbing (figures 8.21 and 8.22).

After deciding on a base roof-model, we began to produce larger roof models to test performance with daylighting. We learned that the structural depth of the webbing acts as a filter to allow indirect light into the event space below. This information led to a coding or designating of webbing cells as either skylights, cones for artificial lighting, or acoustical panels (figure 8.23).

The main level of the dining hall is placed at the tunnel -4 level (the entire campus is linked by tunnels). By doing this, the roof hovers over an excavated hollow, which gently ramps up to grade, thereby creating an amphitheater-like space. This means that the mezzanine level is slightly higher than grade, so that the roof is pressed down low over this single height space, and then soars over a double-height space over the lower dining hall. The mezzanine (topographically) is bound to the lower level by two wide stairs, which act as binding or armatures.

During the construction phase, we were invited to a group show at the *Norsk Form* in Oslo entitled "*INDUSTRY.*" Since the exhibition coincided not with a completed project but a project in-construction, we considered architectural exhibition in a different light (figure 8.24). In order to use the exhibition to convey a sense of experience, as well as a research tool for prototyping our roof, we built wood and board portions of the actual planned roof at the scale of 1:3 and 1:1, respectively. By doing this, an audience had the chance to come in contact not with a representation of the project, but with an artifact that evokes its effects much more directly. At the same time, this allowed us to modify and improve the construction, detail

8.24.
*Trumpf Campus
Cantina*: roof mock-
up for *Norsk Form*
"exhibition Industry!"
in Oslo (2006).

8.23.
*Trumpf Campus
Cantina*: base
roof model.

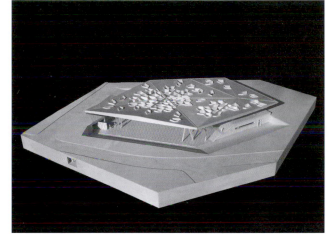

the connections, and refine the geometry of the actual building. After the exhibition, we built an actual construction mock-up at our shop in the Black Forest: a typical Swabian "Werkstätte," only now equipped with millions of Euros worth of hardware, software, and CNC cutting tools.

Glue-lam of fast-growth fir is a sustainable material and one that challenges steel and concrete (figure 8.25). We will continue to work with this material for its aesthetic value and workability. Because of its properties, there was an instinct for immediacy in working with it, that is, a dumbing down of details when it made sense. As with the previous project, this project is enabled only through the direct application of digital technologies. Without them, it would have defied economic calculation.

8.25.
*Trumpf Campus
Cantina*: under
construction.

8.26.
Trutec Building,
Seoul, Korea
(2007).

8.27.
Trutec Building:
the reflection
effect.

REGIONAL VARIATIONS

The recently completed *Trutec Building* in Seoul, Korea (2007) is an interesting demonstration of the potential of a local building culture. We had never worked in Asia. We knew very little about it; all we knew was that we were invited to do an office/showroom building in a city that is quite heterogeneous and very hard to understand (figure 8.26). The given site was extremely anonymous; it existed in a developer master plan next to an unbuilt park, and was surrounded by buildings that had also not yet been built. The reality of site as *tabula-rasa* was a bit of a shock after years of building in Europe, and constantly tripping over layers of history within some context or another. We were used to working in an extremely contextual way with very physical site conditions. In this project, there was no discernible context. At the same time, we became very interested in surface. A history of mirrored American high-rise construction in the 1960s and 1970s could be exemplified by a building like *Pei/Cobb*'s *Hancock Building* in Boston, which used reflective glass. We understood their desire for perfectly flat surfaces, but also the reality that this could not be (technically) achieved – there always exists some amount of distortion from the reflection of an almost perfectly mirrored surface and the surrounding reflected context (figure 8.27). We were interested in understanding this flaw as a virtue.

The *Trutec Building* is a rather standard core and shell office building on the periphery of Seoul. We knew that in some areas of the project we would have certain levels of control, and in other areas our control would be less. As a result, we paid considerable attention to the skin of the building. In the courtyard of our studio in Berlin, we produced mock-ups with a tiling pattern that allowed us to immediately understand its material effects, and how it would both refract and reflect any particular context (figure 8.28). The skin of this building was articulated with very fundamental patterns in the beginning, and with more complex surfaces as the project progressed. We realized that the façade could be the autonomous surface wrapping of an anonymous program type within a 12-storey simple volume. It could operate both visually as an urban public mediator, while giving an identity to the otherwise speculative office

8.28.
Trutec Building:
the conceptual
effect mock-up.

spaces interiors. Another aim was the suppression of the orthogonal façade grid in favor of a surface that could be read on a diagonal and continuously. That strategy offers another scale of reading and complexity to the building. The façade transforms within a 24-hour cycle from reflective surfaces to a lattice-like structure at night, when the façade is transparent. The lattice is formed by a translucent shadow-box façade infill. From the interior, the combination of shadow-box profiles and transparent glass forms a panoramic screened view from the deep loft-like office spaces.

The entrance, close to the park, is the point where the volume of the building punches much deeper than the typical 20-cm façade depth to celebrate the entrance. The core from the center of the building is exposed to the lightless corner and is clad in a black zinc shingle.

Endless studies of how to "get the most for the least" drove the design development strategy for the façades. Other *optimization strategies* were central to evolving the façade. We discovered that by taking one asymmetric complex module and flipping it 180 degrees, and combining it with flat panels, an incredibly complex façade can be created with essentially only two unit types. For the cutting of the façade panel profiles, we found a local fabricator, *Alutek*, who was interested in doing this work (even after their Swiss partners pulled out), although they had little experience of such

a complex façade. With the support of *Arup Hong Kong*, a new CNC saw acquired from Germany, and the requirement for a mock-up (for wind and water testing), we went ahead with *Alutek*. Some of the fabrication decisions were quite ingenious, including the decision to use standard extrusions with somewhat more solid stock material to allow an infinite number of cut angles, while remaining structurally sound. The local-built frames were combined with a reflective *Viacon Glass* (figure 8.29).

The façade acts as an autonomous and phenomenal element that is independent of the interiors. Changes in light, weather, traffic, people, seasons, etc. animate and transform the building. The idea of taking a rather ordinary building type and transforming it through digital technologies can achieve extraordinary results. The trickle-down application of this technology is a particularly compelling aspect of a technology that until recently has been very exclusive and limited to higher-end projects.

What was compelling in Korea was the combination of technological know-how with relatively low building costs, and the ability to learn new techniques allowing construction that would have been unaffordable in Germany. This made us immediately aware of the fact of how one could "exploit" or react to a particular opportunity. This means that in all our work in different regions, there is a period of investigation that facilitates a better understanding of the possibilities within the framework of thinking globally, but acting locally.

CONCLUSION

Our work in relation to digital fabrication has been undertaken in two areas in our studio: first, as an autonomous research project run by student interns and staff within the office, and, second, as embedded in constituting actual building projects in the design and construction phases. Digital fabrication was initially applied to building components as secondary "accessories" to our buildings. Today it constitutes major construction areas for us, including façade systems and structure. Because the research area is separate from building projects, it has the experimental strength and freedom to look at new materials and tooling in a very subjective manner. This means that work produced in this area can be on stand-by to be folded into projects as they arise. What is exciting about applying digital fabrication knowledge in relation to our built works is that it enables projects that formally and phenomenally could not previously be realized due to economic and construction constraints. Digital fabrication is quickly becoming less of an exotic method of construction, and more one that can now reshape the everyday.

With the rising availability of digital capacities in smaller research-driven practices, the practice/research studio challenges the notion that academia is the best place for experimentation. It also begins to close that ever-troublesome gap for architects between representation (the things we draw and model) and realization (the things we build). Prototyping more than merely resembles the construct; it begins to essentially actualize it. This means that now practice is empowered to shape the industry rather than "shopping" for available parts, i.e. practice is at the driving end rather than the receiving end, shaping the purpose of available new technologies. We are at an incredibly dynamic point in our discipline where the vectors of sustainability, digital means, and aesthetics coincide, and are driving new forms and possibilities for architecture.

NOTES

1 Whereas in some respects, areas such as sustainability or structural engineering have progressed quickly in Europe, digital fabrication has been explored with much greater interest in North America.
2 For more information about the company, see www.trumpf.de.
3 Much of this research has been supported by collaboration with a roster of talented and resourceful European engineers, including Werner Sobek, Schlaich Bergermann, Arup, and Jürg Conzett.

9

TOWARDS
A DIGITAL
MATERIALITY

FABIO GRAMAZIO AND MATTHIAS KOHLER
GRAMAZIO & KOHLER AND ETH ZURICH

9.1.
The *mTable*
designed using a
mobile phone and
digitally fabricated.

The digital revolution had an unquestionable impact on contemporary architecture; it has changed the ways in which architecture is conceived, built, mediated, and used. This evolution has only just begun, and it is still too early to predict the long-term consequences for the architectural discipline. Already, a whole spectrum of polemical views on digital technology – ranging from unbridled enthusiasm, at one extreme, to reactionary fear, at the other – have dominated the debate and divided the professional community. Due to its intangible nature, the digital realm is generally misconstrued as being antagonistic to the analogue or physical realm. Our intention is to unite these seemingly opposing realms.

Since its foundation in 2000, *Gramazio & Kohler* has been exploring digital realities within architecture, working with the firm conviction that the digital paradigm will inevitably redefine the discipline. Human intelligence allows architects to take design decisions on complex issues using associative capacities and experience, yet unlike computers, humans are unable to process large amounts of discrete data. By understanding the fundamental concepts of digital logics and mastering its processing techniques, we expand our capacity to integrate information into the design process without losing control over it. The architect is engaged in the selection of relevant architectural parameters and the definition of subsequent rules and processes. The construct is created by a system that is entirely defined by the architect.

One of the most radical consequences of the digital revolution is the computer-controlled fabrication machine. As decades of artificial intelligence research have shown, a physical body is a precondition for every kind of intelligence. Architecture cannot be reduced to a conceptual, geometric, or mathematical phenomenon. Artificial "intelligence" in architecture can only manifest itself through a tectonic logic and a physical, material "body." The application of a fabrication machine in architecture allows a direct coupling between information and construction. In digital fabrication, the production of building parts is directly controlled by the design information. This seamless link between data and material, design and building, dissolves the apparent incongruities

between digital and physical realities and allows a new constructive understanding of the discipline. Thus, these issues are the primary focus of our research in the Department of Architecture at the *Swiss Institute of Technology* (ETH) in Zurich.

ROBOTIC ADDITIVE FABRICATION

In order to investigate the consequences of informing designs with the logic of physical materials and vice versa, we opened a research laboratory at ETH for the digital fabrication of full-scale prototypes and non-standard building parts (DFAB). For our first experiments, we chose a standard industrial robot. Its extreme flexibility, both in terms of the software that controls it and its physical capacities, allows us to program its movements and design the actual construction tools it selects for operations. For us, it is a veritable "personal computer" for construction. With this robot, we investigated the logic of *additive* fabrication, using the most elementary architectural building block – the brick. The resultant projects, described below, confirm that digital logic, both in design and fabrication, will lead to profound changes in architecture, blurring and ultimately dissolving the boundaries between analogue and digital realities. We stand at the very threshold of an exciting development and believe that we should, as architects and authors of design information, actively lead this process towards a new, contemporary, and integral understanding of architecture that is relevant to our age.

MTABLE

The *mTable* table series project, completed in 2002, enabled us to examine the consequences of customer interaction when designing non-standard products. In the process, interesting questions emerged: how much responsibility is the customer

9.2.
mTable:
dimensioning
the table using a
mobile phone.

9.4.
mTable: many
different designs
can be produced
effortlessly.

9.3.
mTable: creating
the deformation
points and holes
in the table's
surface.

able to assume? How much does he or she want to assume? Who ultimately is the author? To what extent does the co-designer identify with the product? What consequences does this development have on architecture?

With *mTable*, we created a table (figure 9.1) that customers can co-design. Modern communications and digital production technologies were used for its customized design and fabrication: we declared the mobile cell phone to be a personal design tool, and examined how it can be utilized to assist the individual to co-design his or her physical environment.

The design principle is simple. Customers choose the size, dimensions, material, and color of the table from their cell phone display (figure 9.2). Next, they place deformation points on the underside of the table and "press" them (figure 9.3); these points then "break through" the surface, creating holes with extremely thin edges, turning the table's top and underside into two distinct "landscapes" (i.e. topographies). The program on the cell phone then verifies that the table with holes is structurally feasible.

Using a mobile phone is an enjoyable and inventive way to control the future physical shape of the table. The phone display's low resolution and a deliberately simplified interface make customers focus on the most essential design features. As soon as the customer is satisfied with the design, he or she transmits the parameters that define the table as a simple series of numbers to the web-based platform at *mshape.com*, where the designed table can be seen in high resolution, and compared with the designs by other customers (figure 9.4). Following the placement of the order, the table is cut by a computer-controlled milling machine (figure 9.5) directly

9.7.
Christmas lighting
on Bahnhofstrasse in
Zurich, Switzerland
(2005).

9.5. (right)
mTable: the CNC
milling machine
produces the table
"landscape" based on
the data transmitted
from a mobile phone.

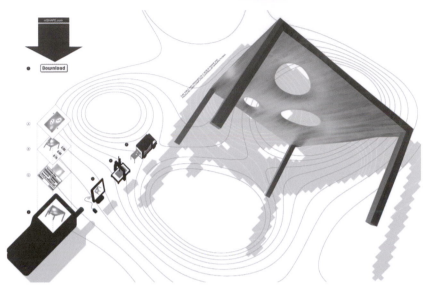

9.6. (above)
mTable: each table
features openings in
the top, curved edges,
and a spectacular
underside.

driven by the data (parameters) transmitted from the mobile phone. The virtual three-dimensional model is transferred to the physical material.

The openings in the table top, the curved edges, and spectacular underside (figure 9.6) lend every table a unique quality. Admittedly, different tables are only unique on the surface, as they all share a common formal and conceptual origin. Still, each table is a result of the customer's decisions and variations on a design pattern. Together, the tables form an entity – the *mTable* design family (figure 9.4).

The *mTable* project changes the task of designing form to defining the *rules of a design system*. The design concept and the formal consequences are carefully embedded in the software that provides a framework within which the customers can develop their own creative strategies, thus giving them control over the ultimate outcome of the design – the form. By deciding for themselves if and where the holes are placed, they assume partial responsibility for the aesthetic appearance, and functional efficiency of the tables. The designer, however, still retains control over which decisions are delegated to the customers and how freely they can intervene. This blurs the distinctions between designer and the customer, as the customer becomes a co-designer.

"THE WORLD'S LARGEST TIMEPIECE"

The project for the *Christmas lighting* on Bahnhofstrasse in Zurich, Switzerland (2005)[1], is based on a winning entry in a competition that called for a contemporary interpretation of the lighting installation designed over thirty years ago by Willi Walter and Charlotte Schmid. Their project was described as "distinctive, generous, unique," and these were qualities the new design was naturally expected to incorporate.

We designed a continuous band of lights with a dynamically changing pattern (figure 9.7). The main premise behind the time-based light installation is that light is not static, but fundamentally dynamic in nature. Light can now be used as a highly flexible and interesting information medium, due to contemporary digital technology that can provide control over its intensity. By changing its appearance during the Advent season, "The World's Largest Timepiece," as the installation is called, accentuates the passing of time and creates a constantly changing "lightscape" on Bahnhofstrasse, and provides every visitor with a truly unique experience.

The installation is conceived as a single illuminated line running from the railway station to the lake, emphasizing the urban "boulevard" atmosphere of the Bahnhofstrasse and accentuating its two slight, yet distinct turns in direction

9.8.
Christmas lighting: a visual backbone of the city.

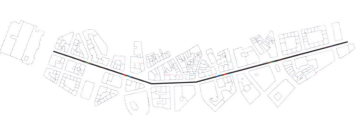

9.9a–b.
Christmas lighting: a section and an elevation drawing.

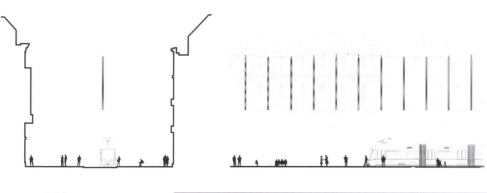

9.10.
Christmas lighting: interface of the *XMAS Generator* software.

9.11.
Christmas lighting: manufacturing of tubes using woven glass fibers.

as it negotiates the heart of downtown Zurich (figure 9.8). Its simple, linear course turns the band of light into a visual backbone of the city. The vertical shaft of light in the middle of the street contrasts with the surrounding building façades and points upward to the night sky. Depending on where the viewer is standing, the *Christmas lighting* can either look like a slick series of individually lit tubes or a glowing, constantly changing curtain of light.

The installation consists of 275 tubes of light, each 7 m high, and placed at 4 m intervals (figure 9.9a–b). Each light tube has 32 small LED bulbs and contains the electronic equipment necessary to regulate 256 brightness levels within each bulb. There are 8,800 LED bulbs in the 1 km-long band of light. The intensity of each bulb can be controlled in real time, using custom-made software written in C++ called *XMAS Generator* (figure 9.10). Approximately 26,000 lines of code were necessary for the creation of this software. Different light patterns were generated and transmitted to the light tubes via an optical databus at the rate of 17 times per second.

The changing patterns of light are generated by an algorithm controlled by the dates associated with the holiday season and the street activities that were recorded using sensors. An increase or decrease in the number of visitors affects the character of the lighting patterns and the frequency of change. Hence, the light patterns not only reflect the passing of time, but also the daily activities on the street itself. In this way, each passer-by can alter the street's ambience by influencing the lighting patterns. In a form of collective interaction the *Christmas lighting* becomes the city's inner timepiece, and creates an unpredictable, dynamic, and immaterial architecture, similar to clouds in the sky.

Each of the 7 m-long tubes had to illuminate in all directions, withstand wind and water, and be lightweight. We had to find a sufficiently rigid material for the shell of the tubes that allowed the transmission of light; a supporting aluminum core would have created unattractive shadows on the outer shell and thus compromised the effect. After several trial and error experiments, we stumbled upon the manufacturing technique for woven glass fibers used in high-tension insulation, in which glass fibers are soaked in resin and spun around a mandrel (figure 9.11). We were fascinated by the additive logic of this process. The winder controls the stacking of the fibers via two computer-coordinated movements. A sliding carriage drives the wound glass fibers back and forth along the spinning mandrel. This creates an extremely stable multi-layered shell. The stacking winder and the number of tiers and overlaps determine the flexural rigidity and torsional stiffness, as well as the transmission of light.

9.13.
Gantenbein Vinery:
interior of the
fermentation hall.

The bands of glass fibers are woven into a rhombus structure: the thick areas are responsible for the stability of the structure, and the slender necks create optical brilliance. In order to optimally join both light diffusion and rigidity, we developed software that simulates the fabrication process, enabling us to test weaving variations with different bandwidths, angles, and tiers. Using more than thirty physical prototypes, we tested effective optical qualities such as brilliance, light transfer, and surface structure for both night and day conditions. We also tested wind resistance. The final tube was 7 m long and 15 cm in diameter; its shell was only 2-mm thick. It weighed less than 23 kg, including lighting and control technology. An intense involvement with the computer-operated production process allowed us to integrate two normally incongruent requirements into one single material, and thus implement for the first time wound glass fibers for lighting on this scale.

9.12.
The new service
building for the
Gantenbein Vinery in
Fläsch, Switzerland
(2006).

GANTENBEIN VINERY FACADE

The new service building for the *Gantenbein Vinery* in Fläsch, Switzerland (2006), was already under construction when *Bearth & Deplazes Architects* invited us to design the façade (figure 9.12).[2] The building had three stories: a cellar for storing the wine barrels, a large fermentation room for processing grapes, and a terrace-like lounge for wine-tasting and receptions. The fermentation hall had to be windowless, because constant temperatures and subdued lighting are required to ferment the grapes properly. To provide natural lighting despite these preconditions, we designed a façade in which the bricks were laid with gaps between them to allow daylight to enter the fermentation hall (figure 9.13). The façade itself has two layers: outside, the masonry layer functions as sun protection, light filter, and temperature buffer; inside, polycarbonate panels protect against wind.

We decided to imbue the façade with a pattern that looked from afar like a basket filled with grapes (figure 9.12). To create this effect, we designed an information generation process that produces an impression of a precisely controlled result by applying purely systematic chance. We interpreted the *Bearth & Deplazes'* concrete frame structure as a massive basket, and filled it with abstract balls (the "grapes") that varied in diameter (figure 9.14). The balls fell into a virtual container via digitally simulated gravity, until a specific density was reached (figure 9.15). The elevation images of the digital "basket" were then used to create the "grape-like" brick wall patterns (with gaps), using an automated layout process (figures 9.16a–b).

9.15.
*Gantenbein
Vinery*:
the falling
"grapes."

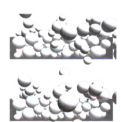

9.14.
Gantenbein Vinery:
a "basket" filled
with "grapes."

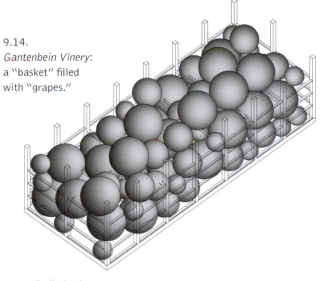

9.16a–b. (below)
Gantenbein Vinery: elevation
images of the digital "basket"
were used to create the "grape-
like" brick wall patterns.

9.18. (right)
Gantenbein Vinery: rotated
bricks function like "pixels"
that form the "grapes" image
pattern on the façade.

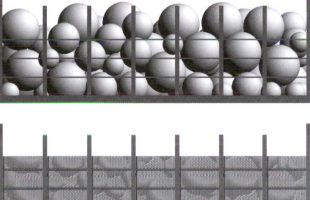

9.17.
Gantenbein Vinery:
the brick wall
patterns are three-
dimensional.

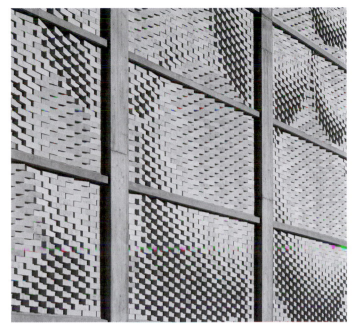

The brick wall patterns are three-dimensional. Bricks are rotated slightly, and thus reflect light differently, resulting in slightly different tonal values on the surfaces (figure 9.17). In this way, bricks function like pixels that form the "grapes" image pattern on the façade, and thus brand the identity of the vineyard. Unlike a two-dimensional image, however, there is a subtle interplay between plasticity, depth, and color in a three-dimensional brick pattern, producing not one but many material effects that constantly shift during the course of the day (figure 9.18). The result is a dynamic surface that possesses a sensual, textile softness.

On closer view, the walls reveal a materiality that resembles stonework, and one is surprised that the soft, round form is actually composed of individual, orthogonal, hard bricks (figure 9.18). The façades appear as solidified dynamic forms, whose shallow three-dimensional depth invites the viewer's eye to wander. Once inside, the transparency of the brick wall surface becomes evident. The daylight creates a mild, yet luminous atmosphere in the fermentation hall (figure 9.13); the design intent becomes manifest through the subtle light modulation by the gaps between the bricks. The superimposed image of the landscape glimmers through in various ways.

A three-dimensional brick façade, therefore, is far more *affective* than a two-dimensional image. To create subtle visual and tactile effects, bricks were rotated in two counter-directions, with a maximum deflection of 17° (figure 9.19). Each façade was balanced, so bricks would progressively rotate as much in one direction, as in the other.[3] Where there

9.19. (above)
Gantenbein Vinery:
the bricks can be
progressively rotated
in two counter-
directions.

9.20a–b.
Gantenbein Vinery: the
bricks were laid in a
layer-by-layer fashion
by an industrial robot.

9.21.
Gantenbein Vinery:
the robot also applied
the bonding agent to
the bricks.

9.22.
Gantenbein Vinery:
the wall panels were
installed on-site by
a crane.

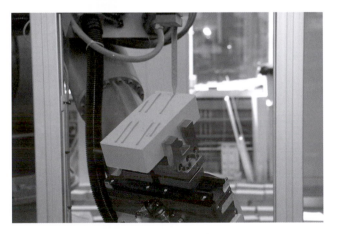

is no visible "grape" (meaning where a gap is created in the virtual "basket"), bricks are in a neutral position and thus form a simple running bond.

The construction technology we developed at the ETH enabled us to lay each brick precisely using an industrial robot[4] (figures 9.20a–b). Not only did the robot lay the bricks, it applied a special bonding agent onto each brick (figure 9.21) rather than traditional mortar. With this new digitally driven, additive production method, we were able to construct each wall differently, so that each would possess the desired light and air permeability,[5] and thus create the overall pattern that covered the entire façade. We designed 72 different brick wall panels using a computer program created expressly for that purpose. The program generated the production data directly from the design data and calculated the exact rotation for each of the 20,000 bricks that comprise the 400 m² façade. The bricks were then laid out automatically by the robot according to programmed parameters, at prescribed angles and at exact intervals.

Because each brick is rotated differently, every single brick has a different and unique overlap with the brick underneath. We had to find a method of applying the bonding agent so that it fits precisely every overlap (all of which were dimensionally unique) and, at the same time, distributes the adhesive evenly. Working closely with an engineer from the brick manufacturer, we devised a strategy whereby four parallel bonding agent paths could be applied at pre-defined intervals to the center axis of the wall panel. This strategy allowed us to attain consistent dimensions. Load tests performed on the first manufactured prototypes revealed that the bonding agent was so structurally effective that the reinforcements normally required for conventional prefabricated walls could be completely eliminated.

Manufacturing 72 façade panels was a big challenge, both technically and in terms of deadlines. Due to the advanced stage of construction, we only had three months to complete the design and production before installation on-site. Because the robot could be directly driven by the design data, we were able to work up to the last minute on the façade design, while developing simultaneously the production method.[6] In the end, the façade panels were produced over just two weeks (with the robot working double shifts!). They were then transported by truck to the construction site and installed by a crane (figure 9.22). The procedure was developed in collaboration with a brick manufacturer who, as an industry partner, was subsequently able to take on the system guarantee on our manufactured panels.

PERFORATIONS

What is the spatial effect and architectural significance of a perforation in a wall, in the form of a diagonal, round hole? Openings regulate the amount of light and air that enters a building. Moreover, by allowing one to look into or out of the building, they also create visual relationships between the interior and exterior. Qualities such as dimension, position, depth of a reveal, and geometry determine their architectural expression. The complexity is heightened if an opening (i.e. a perforation) passes through a wall at a non-orthogonal angle; the reveal's visual presence is emphasized and the wall acquires more depth. Besides formal qualities, the number and arrangement of the holes also affect the architectural effect of a perforation.

Today, complex, perforated architectural components can be created using digital design methods. In contrast to industrially manufactured elements, such as a punched perforated metal sheet, the digitally designed perforations do not need to be based on a repetitive, regular grid. The individual openings can be different in shape or diameter, and the material can be perforated not only orthogonally, but also at different angles through the surface. Moreover, given that each element can have a unique pattern of perforations, larger constructs made of different perforated components, such as façades, can be designed without repetition.

What is the best way to design using a large number of openings? What would it mean if each individual opening was at a different angle to the surface? In several elective courses[7] at the ETH in Zurich, the students were asked to examine the spatial potential of highly perforated wall elements. These wall elements had to be developed using innovative digital tools, which we encouraged to be seen as more than simple technical aids to manage geometric complexities. In each course, students produced full-scale prototypes of perforated wall panels, concentrating on the materialization and development of a self-devised production technique. Designing with large amounts of information – and "informing" the material in the process – required the development of computational tools as an integral element of the design process. The students altered and expanded the digital tools in an agile, creative manner, based on the feedback attained through the iterative processes of design and production.

In the "oblique hole" course (*Das schiefe Loch*), students had to allocate 2,000 holes over an irregular polygonal volume (figure 9.23). The objective was to examine the architectural potential of spatial perforations produced by distributing a large amount of circular openings in an irregularly shaped form. The production tool was a milling spindle mounted on a robot hand; the robot's ability to drill holes at any angle to the surface expanded the design possibilities from merely distributing the holes to also defining their direction. Various algorithmic tools for distributing the holes had to be developed, as it was impractical to process such a large number of perforations with conventional computer-aided design (CAD) technology. The digitally generated design data was translated into production data for the robot by a custom-developed post-processor. The production data for each individual hole consisted of its position in space and a vector that described the tool's drilling path through the material (figure 9.24).

Surprising architectural artifacts were created despite the fact that design options were intentionally limited to a single hole (i.e. drill) size of 10 mm in diameter. It was the thickness of the material, which transformed a supposedly two-dimensional job into a complex three-dimensional design task, that revealed the project's full architectural potential. Orienting fields of holes towards a certain point in space caused the physical depth of the material to collapse into an abstract, almost immaterial surface when seen from a particular vantage point. The openings created new spatial and visual paths between the interior and exterior that were independent of the volume's physical geometry. For the viewer moving about the room, the three-dimensional nature of the perforations changed the effects of the architectural volume.

9.23.
The "oblique hole" project: 2,000 holes were created in an irregular polygonal volume.

9.24.
Simple robotic drilling inscribes the digital architectural information into the material.

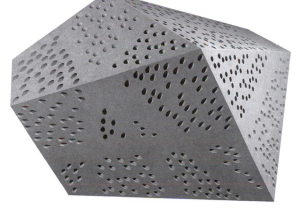

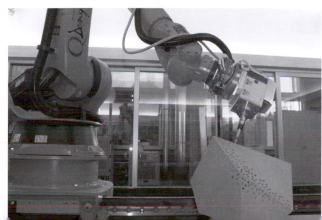

9.25.
The "perforated wall" panels.

9.26.
Cutting of the formwork boards for the perforated wall.

9.27a–b.
Completing the formwork by inserting standard pipes into the holes.

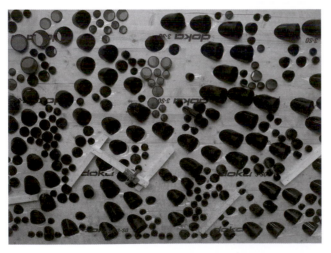

The exploration of perforations continued in the "perforated wall" (*Die perforierte Wand*) course. The students examined the potential of "informing" large Styrofoam panels (1 x 2 m in size) with a large number of round holes; the panels were considered full-scale components of a larger wall or façade design (figure 9.25). As in the previous project, the holes could be defined using five different parameters: the X and Y position on the wall, the "alpha" *directional* ("deflection") *angle vector* into the wall mass, the "beta" *cut-out angle* around the central axis of the hole, and the *radius* of the hole. The holes were distributed using dynamic force fields of attraction and repulsion, in which parameters defining the location and intensity of the forces could be interactively changed. The holes could produce different perforation patterns on two sides with the use of "target" points to define the "deflection" of the holes. We also used the custom-developed "color mapping" tool that translated the red, green, and blue (RGB) values associated with pixels in a chosen image into the "alpha" *directional vector*, the "beta" *cut-out angle*, and the *radius* of the hole, respectively. Working with images provided the students with an intuitive and direct way to "inform" the material.

With another group of students, we worked on developing a method to cast a large (3 x 2 m in size) perforated wall in cement. We used a robot to cut the geometric extensions of the holes into the formwork boards (figure 9.26), in order to transfer the perforation information onto the concrete formwork. After assembling the formwork, standard plastic pipes were inserted into the holes as block-outs (figures 9.27a–b). The design information was thus indirectly transferred to the material via the formwork design.

Manufacturing the formwork presented a particular challenge, because, due to the irregularly distributed holes and the narrow breadth of the web, neither a conventional reinforcement, nor a mechanical re-densification of the concrete was possible.[8] Also, we were unable to use the self-compacting steel-fiber concrete that had recently been developed by the *Institute for Building Materials* (*Institut für Baustoffe*) at the ETH Zurich. After a successful casting, we used various load tests (figure 9.28) to check the structural effectiveness of the wall element. We tested wall elements

9.28.
Perforated panels
were tested for
their load-bearing
capacity.

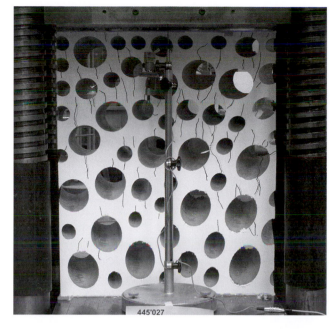

9.29a–b.
Perforated panels
cast in concrete.

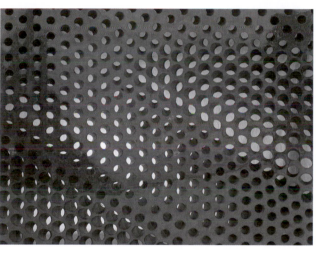

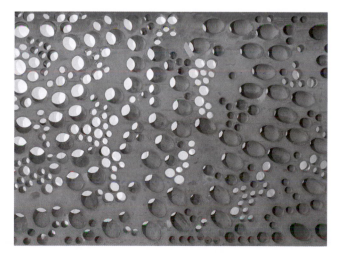

with different densities of perforations and demonstrated that even highly perforated walls could be used as bearing walls in a building structure. We also demonstrated that the load-bearing capacity can be locally controlled with a density of perforations and the deflection of the holes. Our prototypes revealed the multiple architectural potentials of a perforated wall. By moving from Styrofoam to concrete, we created not only complexly "informed" concrete panels with some very interesting potential for light and sight modulation (figures 9.29a–b), but also produced actual load-bearing, structural components.

THE PROGRAMMED WALL

A key assumption underpinning our work is that new digital technologies of design and production will influence the architectural definition of building components. Our research interests are not limited to the technology only. Examining the robotic additive fabrication of brick wall panels, we asked our students to explore social and cultural implications of that technological possibility.[9] What does it mean to digitally fabricate a brick wall using a robot rather than a person? A robot is not only quicker, more precise, and more productive, but it also enables complex designs that are impossible for a human to build with that level of accuracy. The robot does not need an optical reference or an identifiable pattern in order to lay bricks precisely. It also allows complex walls to be built without relying on repetition.

We chose to work with bricks, because a brick is perhaps the most highly developed module in building history. For over 9,000 years, human hands have optimized the brick's dimensions, proportions, weight, and material. The sequencing, the joint detail and the type of bonding agent used determined the specific structural qualities and appearance of the brick wall. Despite the long history and well-established traditions in the building industry, the brick walls today aren't nearly as ubiquitous as they were not long ago; the brick is now mainly used as a single-layered facing on a building. Due to the high cost of labor, walls today are mostly made of large, industrially manufactured blocks or reinforced concrete.

If the brick walls are too expensive because of the high cost of labor, to continue working with this material, the assembly of brick walls could be programmed and automated. A wall made of brick is subject to the rules of mathematics, meaning the relationships (i.e. connections) between the bricks, and can be described by an algorithm and therefore, "programmed." In turn, digital production

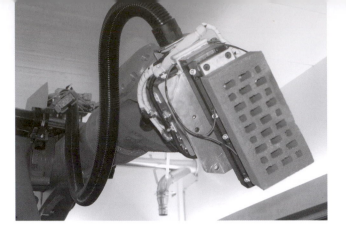

9.30a–c.
The robot
producing one of
the "programmed
walls" brick by
brick.

allows direct translation of computer programs into physical artifacts. A robot can build a wall: it can lay each brick in the exact prescribed position, at the exact angle, and at the exact interval, as described by the author of the program, i.e. the designer. The robot can also position each brick differently with no additional time and effort, which is not possible for humans (figures 9.30a–c).

New spatial and architectural possibilities open up with "programmed" brick walls. Continuous, procedurally controlled variations of the position and rotation of each brick could create flowing transitions between open and closed areas. Some walls can be formed three-dimensionally by bricks receding or projecting out of the surface plane of the wall; even if the bricks are laid on one plane, the wall can still appear three-dimensional. Structural patterns, plasticity, and transparency can change dramatically depending on where the viewer is standing or the angle of light (figure 9.31).

The appearance of the wall is not only affected by a purely surface effect, but by its *depth*. The qualities of this third dimension cannot be designed two-dimensionally or described pictorially. The geometry of the walls has to be programmed, i.e. algorithmically, procedurally defined; it can only be experienced in physical space in time, through movement of the body through space.

9.31.
Different
"programmed
walls."

9.32.
This "programmed wall" is defined by two nested loops, one for the horizontal direction and one for the vertical direction.

9.33.
The concepts were first tested manually.

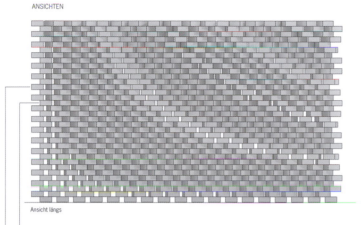

ANSICHTEN

Ansicht längs

Ansicht quer

MAUERWERKSPLAN BEISPIEL

Mauerwerkslage A

Mauerwerkslage B

9.34a–b.
A different kind of a brick wall.

We asked students to design a "different" brick wall and to produce it using the industrial robot in our research lab. The wall had to be 3 m in length and 2 m in height (containing about 400 bricks). Students developed algorithmic design tools to define the spatial disposition of the bricks according to procedural logic. These tools drew upon the knowledge that the layout of a brick wall is based on a system of rules that describe the sequence of operations needed to build a wall. A brick is laid next to another brick, shifted, and perhaps rotated until the end of a row is reached. The next row is then shifted by half of the brick width, and the previous procedure repeated, and so on, until the desired height is reached. When programming, this process can be described with two nested loops, one for the horizontal direction and one for the vertical direction (figure 9.32).

Students examined different brick bonding schemes along with various criteria for brick laying, stability, and overall bonding effect. First, they manually tested the feasibility of the concepts (figure 9.33). Afterwards, they transferred their findings to a simple computer script, which they could expand and redefine through an iterative, step-by-step process. The students did not design a geometric system, but rather constructive logics that created an architectural form by organizing material in space and this directly provided the production data for the robot.

In the end, the walls – products of a digital, highly rationalized, design process and built by a robot – contain both the archaic presence of the material as well as the differentiated qualities of their procedural design. Adding information created a new, different kind of a brick wall, of previously unknown forms coming from a familiar and trusted element of the construction industry (figures 9.34a–b).

9.36a–e.
The different
screens designed
with algorithmic
tools and produced
with robotic
cutting.

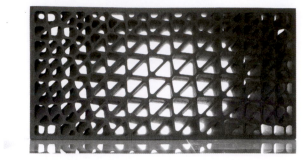

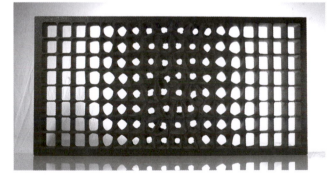

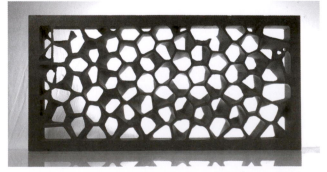

9.35.
The robot cutting
holes to produce a
screen.

SCREENS

The German writer Kurt Tucholsky once said, "A hole is where there is nothing."[10] Around the hole is a material from which it has been carved. If the holes (i.e. perforations) increase in size, a grid structure develops in the material between the holes and the attention shifts from the holes to the resulting mesh-like structure or screen.

Screens are a common and rich architectural device that can separate spaces, while maintaining a certain visual (and often audible) transparency. In contrast to glass, screens have a strong spatial presence and offer great potential for variation in material, color, texture, etc. The architectural definition of the screen mesh, i.e. its width, alignment, and form, can guide the eyes' glance, obstruct it selectively, or allow full views.

Grid-like structures make the structural depth of a building layer tangible. According to where they are positioned, hybrid structures like screens can assume other functions, such as *passive shading* (sun protection) on façades. Screens have been used throughout the history of architecture by very different cultures; they have developed in many different ways due to a wide variety of available technological means. As an example, consider the screens in Islamic religious architecture: highly perforated grid structures separate women from the main room of prayer. Besides a purely ornamental value, these highly sophisticated devices allow observation of the events in the main prayer hall without the viewers being seen.

Our work with screens is in many ways a continuation of the previous experiments with the perforated walls – with a shift in focus from the openings to the material remaining between them (figure 9.35). We asked students to produce full-scale prototypes (2 x 1 m in size) in styrofoam.[11] We also varied the forms of the openings, i.e. we didn't limit the explorations to the round holes only. With the help of algorithmic tools, we were able to manipulate the contours, dimensions, angles, and the sequence of openings, which could take any regular or irregular form (figures 9.36a–e). Moreover, in addition to being at an angle to the surface, the openings could also be distorted three-dimensionally, meaning that the front and the back of the screen-wall element could be different in appearance.

CONCLUSION

The projects presented express our empirical approach to the physical and constructive reality of architecture as well as our understanding of the digital as a tangible and sensual reality. We believe that a truly substantial discussion on "digital architecture" can only arise from built projects that physically manifest the underlying logic of this technology. We want to know how it looks, feels, smells, sounds and how much it costs. To do this, we adopt a strategy of operating in small steps and experiments, finding ways (or creating them if necessary) of integrating this technology into projects we are actually building, testing their architectural potentials as well as their limits in terms of technological and economic feasibility. We work, whenever possible, at full scale, using the real materials and construction methods. This provides us with substantial feedback for our design process, both at a conceptual and technological level and allows us to understand the real consequences of digital technologies on architecture.

The beauty and power of digital technology lies in its universality and its generic quality. Binary data is an abstract entity that can contain anything we want. We consider it a new raw material in our hands that we can creatively manipulate in an infinite variety of ways with a degree of complexity we would not dare attempt by hand. It is like a brick, its generic nature does not impose one given architectural form but rather offers the potential for an infinite variety on a given theme. Programming thus becomes an open and self-evident exploratory technique like sketching and model building.

While the technology necessary to change from mass-produced serial parts to mass-produced custom parts certainly does exist, and is thriving in other industries, it is not yet available to architects. This is largely because architecture-specific interfaces for digital fabrication do not yet exist. If we want to take full and creative advantage of the amazing technological possibilities at our hands and finally fuse the seemingly separate worlds of analog construction and digital design data we have to get involved in the conception of these interfaces and directly link the design data we produce and the machines that are actually able to fabricate architecture in both directions, technically and conceptually. We should be able to "get our hands dirty," so to speak, and proactively develop a technological savoir faire that directly relates to the way architecture is conceived, processed, built, and used today. Technology needs to be demystified and (re)integrated into the architectural discipline, not just as a source of inspiration but as an integral part of the professional vision.

The fundamental architectural potential of the "digital materiality" we have been describing here remains of course to be explored through more built projects and at larger scales. One can still question whether or not the deterministic and rational nature of digital logics really is compatible with the creative and subjective practice of architectural design. Our work attempts to dispel this doubt and we hope that our projects will convince others who will in turn make their own contributions to this effort. Indeed, we feel that our own experience proves that digital technologies do not contradict the architectural process. If we understand its nature and use it as a complementary tool to our intuition and intelligence, digital technology will unleash its systematic, aesthetic, and poetic potential.

NOTES

1 The project's clients were Zurich's Bahnhofstrasse Association and the Electric Utility Company of the City of Zurich.

2 The project's clients were Martha and Daniel Gantenbein. The façade was designed in cooperation with *Bearth & Deplazes Architects*.

3 Despite the relatively slight deviation from linearity, the human eye could detect even the finest rotations with the subtlest light reflection, making them architecturally readable.

4 The wall panels for the Gantenbein vineyard were manufactured within the framework of a pilot project at our research facilities at the ETH in Zurich.

5 While we were testing the interior of the space using prototypes, we realized that it would be difficult to read the design if the openings between the bricks were too large. For this reason, we laid the bricks as close as possible, so that the gap between two bricks at full deflection was nearly closed. The eye reads this as maximal contrast value.

6 The robotic brick-laying production method was initially developed for an elective course entitled "The Programmed Wall." We had to optimize it for the 400m² façade, so that the production time and the quality of the elements could be guaranteed. Besides further developing the picker arm and the feeding chute, this mainly involved developing an automated process to apply the two-component bonding agent. We installed a pneumatic, hand-held, hot glue gun as a fixed external tool onto the robot, linked its activation mechanism with an interface to the robot's control unit, and integrated the application of the bonding agent into the automated process.

7 The courses were: *Das schiefe Loch* (The oblique hole) elective course offered in the winter semester in 2005/2006 academic year, *Die perforierte Wand* (The perforated wall) elective course offered in the summer semester in 2006, and *Die perforierte Wand* (The perforated wall) graduate elective course, also offered in the summer semester in 2006.

8 There were other difficulties too: the forces resulting from the pouring of concrete had to be dealt with by geometrically complex braces in the formwork.

9 These themes were explored in the "programmed wall" (*Die programmierte Wand*) graduate-level elective course, offered in the winter semester in 2005/2006 academic year and also during the seminar week in 2007 at the *Domoterra Swissbau Lounge*.

10 Kurt Tucholsky, *Gesammelte Werke*, edited by Mary Gerold-Tucholsky and Fritz J. Raddatz, vol. 3, Reinbeck bei Hamburg: Rowohlt, 1961, p. 804 (original 1931).

11 The screens were first explored in the "disintegrated wall" (*Die aufgelöste Wand*) elective course offered in the winter semester of the 2006/2007 academic year; the explorations were then continued in an elective course during the summer semester in 2007, when we asked the students to design a safety fence that surrounded the construction site for the new Science City Campus at the ETH Zurich.

10
THE (RISKY) CRAFT OF DIGITAL MAKING

BRANKO KOLAREVIC / UNIVERSITY OF CALGARY

An architect must be a craftsman. Of course any tools will do; these days, the tools might include a computer, an experimental model, and mathematics. However, it is still craftsmanship – the work of someone who does not separate the work of the mind from the work of the hand. It involves a circular process that takes you from the idea to a drawing, from a drawing to a construction, and from a construction back to idea.

(Renzo Piano[1])

Architecture as a material practice implies that making, the close engagement of the material, is intrinsic to design process. Making, however, is increasingly mediated through digital technologies: today, it is the CNC[2] machines and not the hands of the maker that mostly shape materials and their properties. *Digital making* – the use of digital technologies in design and material production – is blurring the sharp discontinuities between conception and production established in the twentieth century. New techniques based on close, cyclical coupling of *parametric design* and *digital fabrication* are restructuring the relationships between design and production, enabling a closer interrogation of materials during the earliest stages of design.

For example, designers today, like resurrected craftsmen of the past, are increasingly using new digital techniques and technologies to explore *surface effects*, such as pattern, texture, relief, or variable properties, as a means through which building surfaces manifest the design intent, at a range of different scales. As surfaces become more complex in form, shape, composition, and appearance, the generation and manufacturing of material and surface effects become a locus of design and production efforts.

As argued later in the chapter, these effects are designed and produced with an *iterative precision*, where the final outcome is carefully *crafted* through cyclical interactions between the conceptual and representational articulation of geometry, its performative dimensions and material manifestation, and the economic and technological realities of manufacturing and assembly. In this context, craft is no longer entrusted to the realm of production, which was its operative domain historically; it

is manifest everywhere – in the definition of geometry and its manipulation, the engagement of the material and its production process, and in the multiple circular feedback loops that these emerging non-linear processes entail.

THE CRAFTSMANSHIP OF RISK

Any discussion of craft in general in a contemporary context requires an apt definition of this, as some would argue, rather obsolete term, and in particular, of what is meant by the notion of craft in architecture. In the book *Abstracting Craft*,[3] Malcolm McCullough provides an excellent examination of contemporary meanings of craft, both as a noun and as a verb, and describes the technological and cultural origins of what he calls "digital craft," an emerging set of material practices based on digital media that engage both the eye and the hand, albeit in an indirect way. He refers to this as "the seeming paradox of intangible craft."[4] McCullough argues that "digital craft" as a term is not an oxymoron, but that today the craft medium need not have a material substance, and the craftsperson need not touch the material directly.

Although McCullough's book offers a seminal examination of the contemporary meanings of craft, it is David Pye who has provided, more than 30 years earlier, in his book entitled *The Nature and Art of Workmanship* (published in 1968), a definition of craftsmanship that is particularly suitable for our contemporary "digital age:"

Craftsmanship ... means simply workmanship using any kind of technique or apparatus, in which the quality of the result is not predetermined, but depends on the judgment, dexterity and care which the maker exercises as he works. The essential idea is that the quality of the result is continually at risk during the process of making.[5]

David Pye distinguishes manufacturing from craftsmanship, defining manufacturing as the *workmanship of certainty* and craftsmanship as the *workmanship of risk*. According to Pye, an artifact is *manufactured* (industrially or by hand) if the risks involved in its creation are minimal; on the other hand, an artifact is *crafted* if there are risks involved in its

10.1.
Parametric
variations by Nia
Garner.[8]

10.2. (far right)
Sampled parametric
variations by Nia
Garner.

creation and production, i.e. if "the quality of the result is not predetermined, but depends on the judgment, dexterity, and care which the maker exercises as he works," as quoted above.

The *craftsmanship of risk* – the notion of craft in which an outcome "is continually at risk" – has particular resonance today. In contemporary practices that have fully adopted digital technologies into the processes of design and production, digital media is often deployed to *discover* a promising formal configuration or spatial organization. In other words, results of a particular design process are not predetermined or anticipated – they are to be discerned among many alternatives and variations produced in carefully articulated, structured investigations, often in a circular, non-linear fashion. As the unanticipated design outcome hinges on discovery – and the discovery is by no means certain – there is an implied element of risk in the entire process. This notion of risk, stemming from the inherent lack of predetermined design outcomes, is how we could interpret Pye's seminal work in a contemporary context. McCullough affirms this essential idea: "In digital production, craft refers to the condition where [we] apply standard technological means to unanticipated or indescribable ends."[6]

CRAFT IN PARAMETRIC DESIGN

In contemporary architectural design, digital media is used not only as a representational tool for visualization, but as a generative tool for the derivation of three-dimensional constructs and their transformation.[7] In a radical departure from centuries-old traditions and norms of architectural design, digitally generated forms are not designed or drawn as the conventional understanding of these terms would have it, but they are calculated by a chosen generative computational method, most of which are based on some form of parametric design.

In parametric design, the parameters of a particular design are initially declared, not its shape or form. By assigning different values to parameters, different geometric configurations emerge. Parametric variation can be automatic (figure 10.1), or can be controlled manually, in discrete, incremental steps; when specific values are

assigned to parameters, particular instances are created from a potentially infinite range of possibilities. Furthermore, equations are used to describe the relationships between objects, thus defining an associative, linked geometry. This way, interdependencies between objects are established, and objects' behaviors under transformations are defined. These interdependences become the structuring, organizing principle for the generation and transformation of the geometry. How these interdependencies are structured and reconfigured depends to considerable extent on abilities of the designer to *craft* these relationships precisely.

In parametric design, the conceptual emphasis shifts from particular forms of expression (geometry) to specific relations (topology) that exist within the context of the project. Using parametrics, designers create an infinite number of similar objects, which are geometric manifestations of a previously articulated schema of variable dimensional, relational or operative dependencies. Shapes and forms become variable, giving rise to new possibilities, i.e. the *emergent form*. Instead of working on a *parti*, the designer constructs a generative, parametric system of formal production, controls its behavior through parametric manipulation, and selects forms that emerge from its operation for further development (figure 10.2). For instance, designers can see forms as a result of reactions to a context of "forces" or actions, as demonstrated by Greg Lynn's work.[9] There is, however, nothing automatic or deterministic in the definition of actions and reactions; they implicitly create "fields of indetermination" from which unexpected and genuinely new forms might emerge; unpredictable variations are generated from the built multiplicities.[10] Structural and formal complexity is also often deliberately sought, and this intentionality oftentimes motivates the processes of construction, operation, and selection in parametric design.

The capacity of parametric computational techniques to generate new design opportunities is highly dependent on the designer's perceptual and cognitive abilities, as continuous, transformative processes ground the emergent form, i.e. its discovery, in qualitative cognition. The designer essentially becomes an "editor" of the generative potentiality of the designed system, where the choice of emergent forms is driven largely by the designer's aesthetic and plastic sensibilities. The designer simultaneously interprets and manipulates a parametric computational construct in a complex design development process that is continuously reconstituting itself. This "self-reflexive" process relies on the visual results of the deployed generative parametric procedure to actively shape the designer's thinking process. The potential for crafting the parametric processes of conceptual production – and the outcomes of those processes – lies precisely in the designer's capacity to effectively edit the *minutiae* of the underlying parametric generative system. This capacity comes with experience and dexterity – knowing intuitively which small quantitative change could potentially produce a qualitatively different outcome (the so-called "threshold" effect). This is precisely how many of the conventional, creative crafts operate.

By stressing the *discovery* of form, the determinism of traditional design practices is abandoned for a directed, precise indeterminacy of innovative digital, parametric processes of conception. There is an explicit recognition that the admittance of risk – the unpredictable and unexpected – paves the way to poetic invention and creative transformation. Non-linearity, indeterminacy, and emergence are intentionally sought, with a considerable degree of risk involved, as the successful outcomes (however determined) are anything but certain.

CRAFT IN DIGITAL FABRICATION

While the digital techniques of parametric design have redefined the relationship between conception and representation, enabling the designers to carefully craft the formal outcomes through iterative processes, the technologies of digital fabrication have facilitated a closer investigation of material outcomes at the earliest stages of design.

The various computationally numerically controlled (CNC) processes of shaping and reshaping, based on cutting, subtractive, additive and formative fabrication,[11] have provided designers with an unprecedented capacity to control the parameters of material production, and to precisely craft desired material outcomes. Knowing the production capabilities and availability of particular digitally driven fabrication equipment enables designers to design specifically for the capabilities of those machines. The consequence is that designers are becoming much more directly involved in the fabrication processes, as they create the information to be translated by fabricators directly into control data that drives the digital fabrication equipment.

For example, using digital fabrication technologies in sheet-metal production, corrugated, flat, and curved profiles can be perforated, drilled, milled, etc. in a wide variety of ways. Virtually any corrugation profile can be produced including variations in frequency and amplitude; perforations of any pattern can be produced by mechanical milling. A very good example of what could be attained with flat sheets is the recently completed *de Young Museum* in San Francisco (2005), designed by *Herzog & de Meuron*. The large surfaces of the rain screen that wraps the building are made from over 7,000 copper panels (12 ft by 2½ ft in size), each of which features unique halftone cut-out and embossing patterns abstracted from images of surrounding tree canopies. The circular perforations and indentations produce abstract patterns and images when seen from a distance, similar to how halftone patterns of dots of varying size fool the eye into seeing different shades of gray in newspaper images. A number of geometric and material alternatives were developed in an iterative fashion (figure 10.3), in early

10.3.
Studies of the perforation and indentation patterning of the rain screen panels in *de Young Museum* in San Francisco (2005), designed by *Herzog & de Meuron*.

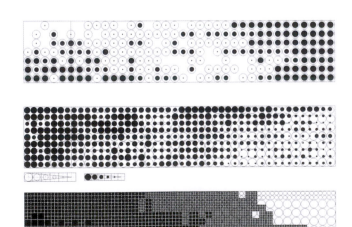

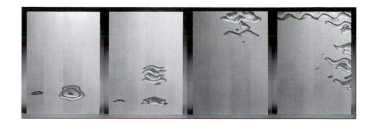

10.4b.
Objectiles: these panels were produced by shallow CNC-milling of laminated wood sheets.

CRAFTING SURFACE EFFECTS

> The properties of a building's surface – whether it is made of concrete, metal, glass, or other materials – are not merely superficial; they construct the spatial effects by which architecture communicates. Through its surfaces a building declares both its autonomy and its participation in its surroundings.
>
> (David Leatherbarrow[12])

and close collaboration with the fabricator, *A. Zahner Company* of Kansas City, until the team arrived at the final double patterning solution.

Working on the smaller scale of a single panel, and using CNC milling (i.e. subtractive fabrication), Bernard Cache developed a parametric production process in which slight variations of parameter values, either incremental and/or random, produce a series of differentiated yet repetitive objects, referred to by Cache as *objectiles*, each of which feature unique decorative relief or cut-out patterns, striated surface configurations, and other surface effects (figure 10.4a). A particularly effective technique was to exploit inherent properties of the material, such as varying coloration of different layers in laminated wood sheets, to produce intricate surface effects by CNC-milling shallow 3D curvilinear forms of a relatively small surface area (figure 10.4b), thus introducing a certain "economy of production" by reducing the amount of machining and the material waste.

Many projects have now been completed in the past decade and a half that have used parametric design techniques and digital fabrication technologies in an innovative fashion. Typically, both the parametric description of the geometry and the resulting CNC code for fabrication are crafted through a series of iterative steps, in which small quantitative changes in the values of certain parameters produce qualitatively different results. Just like the craftsman of the past, the craftsman of the digital age – the designer working with virtual representation of the material artifacts – seeks out unpredictable outcomes by experimenting with what the medium and the tools have to offer.

In a parametric production process, slight variations of parameter values, either incremental or random, can produce a series of differentiated yet repetitive objects. For example, geometric and manufacturing logic can be precisely *crafted* to produce different instances of a parametrically defined variable paneling system, in which size is fixed, but relief or cut-out patterns vary, as shown previously by Bernard Cache's work. Pattern, relief, and texture can be parametrically controlled to produce variable surface effects. Parameters can be related to the geometry of surface intricacies and chosen fabrication processes; they can also be dependent on the properties of the selected material. Furthermore, the produced objects (i.e. panels) can be organized in a grid-like configuration to generate a carefully choreographed *field effect*, resulting in another set of parameters that can influence the final outcome, either at the scale of an individual component (panel in this case) or the entire assembly (the "field").

The following projects[13] investigate figurative expressiveness of architectural surfaces, i.e. their capacity to communicate visually, and the newly attained capacity to digitally design and manufacture highly crafted surface and material effects. The emphasis was placed on parametric calculation of curved and variable shapes and their production using CNC tool paths, which were precisely crafted in software and executed on a CNC-milling machine. Through cyclical, iterative development, parametrically defined geometry was refined based on the feedback attained through digital material production and the *affordances* and *resistances* encountered along the way. Each step required careful crafting of both the parametric geometric description and the subsequent material production.

10.4a.
Objectiles (1995), series of panels designed by Bernard Cache, in which various surface effects were parametrically defined.

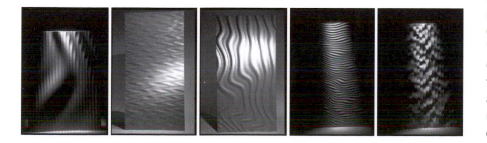

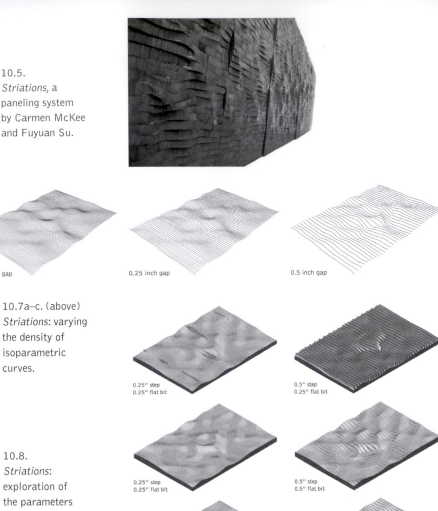

10.5.
Striations, a
paneling system
by Carmen McKee
and Fuyuan Su.

10.6.
Striations:
isoparametric
curves were used
directly as CNC
toolpaths.

0.125 inch gap

0.25 inch gap

0.5 inch gap

10.7a–c. (above)
Striations: varying
the density of
isoparametric
curves.

0.25″ step
0.25″ flat bit

0.5″ step
0.25″ flat bit

0.25″ step
0.25″ flat bit

0.5″ step
0.5″ flat bit

10.8.
Striations:
exploration of
the parameters
related to CNC
milling.

0.25″ step
0.5″ round bit

0.5″ step
0.5″ round bit

10.9.
Striations: one of
the CNC-milled
panels.

In the *Striations* project[14] (figure 10.5), Carmen McKee
and Fuyuan Su modeled a simple time-based parametric
process, based on force physics simulation, using *Maya*
animation software that resulted in different undulations
of a rectilinear surface. Isoparametric curves, used in
visualizing NURBS[15] surfaces, were extracted from selected
frozen frames of the time-based animation and translated
directly into CNC toolpaths for milling (figure 10.6). The
density and number of isoparametric curves were carefully
explored (figures 10.7a–c), as were the sizes of milling bits,
and whether round or flat bits should be used (figure 10.8).
Equally important were the hardness and texture properties
of the wood to be used in production. Thus, the process
was defined by parameters related to designed geometry,
parameters pertaining to production (such as the size and
shape of the milling bit, the feed-rate, etc.) and parameters
related to the material itself, such as wood hardness, grain
size, etc. These parameters were interrelated, thus numerous
design opportunities were explored through several iterations
informed by continuous feedback loops between design and
production. In the end, the panels were manufactured at the
rate of 15 minutes per panel, each of which was 1′ by 2′ in
size (figure 10.9), and assembled in a linear configuration
(figure 10.5).

In the *Field Explorations* project[16] (figure 10.10) by
Jill Desimini and Sarah Weidner, the parameters that defined
the geometry of panels were based on image processing
techniques using *halftoning* and *motion blur* operations.
Selected sequences of images were first halftoned using
Photoshop and then a motion-blur filter was applied to the
halftones, resulting in what appeared as a grayscale image
of an undulating surface (figures 10.11a–b). These bitmap
images were translated into height-deformation maps once
imported into *Rhinoceros* modeling software to define the
extent of deformation of a flat, meshed square surface.[17] The
deformed surface configuration was used to compute milling
paths using *MasterCAM*.

A number of different material studies (figures
10.12a–c) were conducted, involving a plywood panel (found
acceptable because of the intricate surface effects resulting
from the revealed layering of the material), laminated
wood dowels (rejected because the dowels were visually

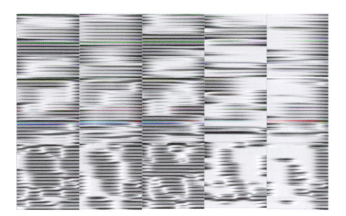

10.10.
Field Explorations,
a paneling system
by Jill Desimini and
Sarah Weidner.

10.11a–b.
Field Explorations:
image processing
using halftone and
motion blur filtering
procedures.

10.12a–c. (below)
Field Explorations:
material studies.

  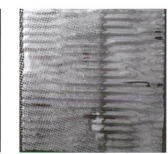

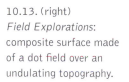

10.13. (right)
Field Explorations:
composite surface made
of a dot field over an
undulating topography.

10.14.
Field Explorations:
an unsuccessful
production run
(parameters of
production and the
inherent material
properties were not
taken into account).

10.15. (far right)
Field Explorations:
the final installation.

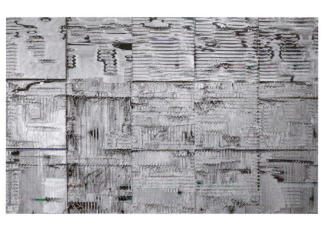

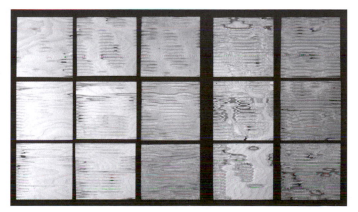

distracting), and a composite made of acrylic over plywood (rejected primarily because of difficulties in production). In the composite configuration, the intent was to superpose halftone patterns over the undulating topography resulting from the motion-blur images (figure 10.13); the halftone pattern was laser-etched in acrylic as a top layer thermally slumped over the topographical surface CNC-milled in plywood.

The final field configuration was achieved using CNC-milled plywood, with the intent of using the material's lamination (its inherent material property) to produce a subtle and intricate surface effect, both locally, within each panel, and globally, over the entire panel assembly. The initial production attempt was unsuccessful (figure 10.14), as the grain of the wood was not taken into account. To further aggravate the production process, the milling feed-rate (the speed with which the milling bit is moved through the material) was too high, resulting in complete destruction of the material. Minor adjustments in the geometry, careful selection and positioning of the laminated sheet of plywood, and careful setting of the production parameters, yielded in the end rather compelling surface effects. As in the previous project, the parameters related to the production (size of the milling bit, etc.) and the properties of the material (texture, hardness, etc.) were crucial to the overall success of the project; the feedback loops between design and production were essential for the success of the project. After several, quick iterations, the final field configuration (figure 10.15) was carefully and quickly produced.

10.16.
Parametric Weave
screen by Virginia
Little and Maggie
McManus.

10.17.
Parametric Weave:
close-up view of
the screen.

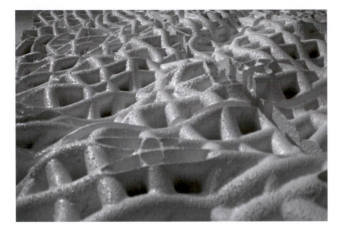

The *Parametric Weave*[18] screen (figure 10.16) by
Virginia Little and Maggie McManus was modeled using
a simple time-based, force-physics simulation process
using *Maya* animation software resulting in slight, ripple-
like undulations of a rectilinear surface. Isoparametric
curves were extracted in both U and V directions from
each surface configuration, and used as sweeping paths
for circular profiles of gradually increasing radii. The
resulting configuration of "tubes" was cut with a flat
plane, revealing the internal voids in the tubes, and
producing an intricate surface effect (figure 10.17). This
subtle effect was produced by accident, due to the fact
that solids were represented in the modeling software
as enclosed voids. The "parametric weave" was then
milled quickly in ordinary insulation foam panels, which
were then coated with a layer of white hi-gloss latex
house paint, resulting in an intricate latticework screen
configuration.

In the *Kinetic Hyposurface*,[19] Dustin Headley and Mickel
Darmawan were interested in carving out a complexly shaped
volume from a stack of layered sheets, with members spaced
apart to reveal an inner void (figure 10.18). The outcome was
quite surprising, i.e. purely incidental: as one's eyes moved
along the side of the resulting construct over time, a subtle,
dynamic effect emerged. This performative aspect of the
resulting "kinetic hyposurface" was fine-tuned by exploring
different values for key parameters, such as the thickness
of the layers, and the size of the spacing between the layers.
As with previous projects, the parametric definition of the
geometry was fairly simple, as well as the production of the
individual panels. After several quick iterations, the (virtually
kinetic) result was more than the sum of the (static) panels,
carefully arranged in a linear sequence.[20]

ECONOMY OF METHOD

An important design and production dimension of the
described projects was a certain "economy of method,"
introduced as "less effort, less machine time, less material,
less waste," and summed up in the end as "less for more"
– a thinly veiled reference to Mies van der Rohe's famous
aphorism, but with an entirely different connotation. This
design/production dimension was an attempt to introduce
resource economy (time-, material-, and energy-wise) into the
design and production processes. Complex effects were to be
achieved through simple means; the underlying ethos being
that complexity need not be synonymous with complicated,
i.e. that conceptual and production simplicity can produce a
perception of complexity in the outcome.

Expanded Topographies[21] (figure 10.19), a project
by Dustin Headley, offers a particularly successful
demonstration of such a resource economy approach to
design and production. It was inspired by research into
expanded metal meshes, which are produced by simultaneous
slitting and stretching of a flat sheet of metal, resulting in a
regular, repetitive pattern of diamond-shaped holes. What is
interesting about this process is its geometric and production
simplicity, and that nearly zero metal waste is generated
during the process; in addition, the final product – the
expanded mesh – is stronger (by kilogram) and lighter (by
meter) than the original sheet.

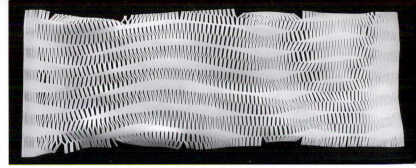

10.19.
Expanded Topographies,
by Dustin Headley.

The project's premise was that variegated surface patterns, i.e. apertures of gradually increasing or decreasing sizes, could be produced by simply varying the values of expansion parameters including the length of cut, aligned spacing between the cuts, and spacing between the successive lines of cuts. Using scripting with *Rhinoceros*, a simple parametric procedure automatically generated different cutting patterns (figure 10.20), which could be directly transmitted to a digitally controlled cutting machine. Various prototypes were produced by laser-cutting flat, rectangular sheets of acrylic, which were then heated and expanded by applying equal force (in opposite directions) to the two shorter sides of the sheet. The sheets would deform in the process, depending on the density and the lengths of the cuts, producing topographic surfaces, with apertures that vary in size across the length of the surface. Precise topographies were produced by controlling the length of each cut and X and Y spacing between the adjacent cuts. In addition, by making non-parallel cuts, i.e. by introducing angle as an additional parameter, further possibilities for surface articulation opened up. The design and production processes were simple and straightforward, with nearly zero material waste, resulting in an artifact with intricate surface effects, subtle undulations and series of apertures that change in size across the length of the panel.[22]

CONCLUSIONS

In design and production processes driven by digital technologies – digital making – craft is understood as a set of deliberate actions based on continuous, iterative experimentations, errors, and modifications that lead to innovative, unexpected, and unpredictable outcomes, discovered in the intertwined processes of conception and production. More precisely, craft in this context is associated with slight adjustments and subtle changes to parameters that define processes of design and production in search of such an outcome. Knowing what, why, and how to adjust requires deep knowledge of the processes, tools, and techniques, just as it did in the pre-digital era.

Designers – contemporary craftspersons – are in continuous control of design and production and rely on iterative, cyclical development based on feedback loops between the parametric definition of the geometry and the digital fabrication of material artifacts. The discoveries are in most cases directly dependent on unanticipated outcomes and are anything but ascertained (and to reiterate, therein is the contemporary understanding of Pye's "workmanship of risk"). Designers are constantly looking for particular *affordances* that a chosen production method can offer, or unexpected *resistances* encountered as they engage a particular tool and a piece of material. This constant, cyclical interaction between the "work of the mind" and the "work of the hand," in the words of Renzo Piano, is what provides a particularly rich and rewarding context for design and production. This highly iterative process is the essence of the contemporary understanding of craft – the craft of digital making.

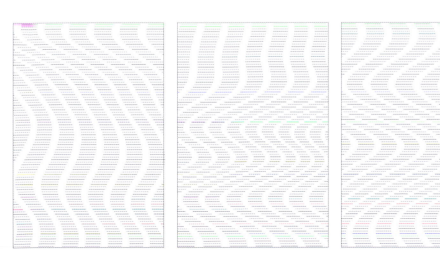

10.20.
Expanded Topographies:
a simple parametric
procedure automatically
generates different
cutting patterns.

NOTES

1 Peter Buchanan, *Renzo Piano Building Workshop: Complete Works,* vol. 4, New York: Phaidon Press, 2003.

2 The abbreviation CNC stands for *computer numerical control* and refers to a computer control unit that reads the digitally encoded instructions and drives a machining tool used in fabrication based on the selective removal of material (as in subtractive fabrication).

3 Malcolm McCullough, *Abstracting Craft: The Practiced Digital Hand*. Cambridge, MA: MIT Press, 1996.

4 Ibid., p. 22.

5 David Pye, *The Nature and Art of Workmanship*, Cambridge: Cambridge University Press, 1968, p. 2.

6 McCullough, op. cit., p. 21.

7 For more information, see Branko Kolarevic (ed.), *Architecture in the Digital Age: Design and Manufacturing*, London: Spon Press, 2003. In particular, refer to Chapter 2, "Digital Morphogenesis."

8 Parametric explorations by Nia Garner; *Performative Architecture* design studio, Branko Kolarevic, University of Pennsylvania, Graduate School of Fine Arts, Philadelphia, fall 2003.

9 See Greg Lynn, *Animate Form*, New York: Princeton Architectural Press, 1999.

10 The underlying computational processes are actually highly deterministic; it is our inability to anticipate the outcomes of these processes that gives them the qualities of unpredictability and indeterminacy.

11 For more information, see Kolarevic, op. cit, Chapter 3, "Digital Fabrication."

12 David Leatherbarrow and Mohsen Mostafavi, *Surface Architecture*, Cambridge, MA: MIT Press, 2002.

13 The different techniques of crafting surface effects using parametrics and digital fabrication technologies were explored in a four-week project within elective courses at the University of Pennsylvania in the spring of 2005 and at Ball State University in the fall of 2005 and the spring of 2007.

14 *Striations*, by Carmen McKee and Fuyuan Su; *Digital Fabrication* course, Branko Kolarevic, University of Pennsylvania, School of Design, Philadelphia, spring 2005.

15 NURBS stands for Non-uniform Rational B-splines.

16 *Field Explorations*, by Jill Desimini and Sarah Weidner; *Digital Fabrication* course, Branko Kolarevic, University of Pennsylvania, School of Design, Philadelphia, spring 2005.

17 The parametric setup was extremely simple: the size of the dots for halftoning, and the angle and distance for the motion blur image transformation in *Photoshop*, and the extent of height deformation in *Rhinoceros*. The point is that complex effects could be produced with simple, parametrically driven tools, that are more or less readily available in every "digital craftsman's" toolkit.

18 *Parametric Weave*, by Virginia Little and Maggie McManus; *Digital Fabrication* course, Branko Kolarevic, University of Pennsylvania, School of Design, Philadelphia, spring 2005.

19 *Kinetic Hyposurface*, by Dustin Headley and Mickel Darmawan, *Contemporary Praxis: From Digital to Material* course, Branko Kolarevic, Ball State University, College of Architecture and Urban Planning, Department of Architecture, Muncie, Indiana, fall 2005.

20 Even though only a simple prototype was produced, this project could be further developed into a shading screen, or a highway acoustic barrier, producing in both cases an intricate, dynamic effect as one moves along.

21 *Expanded Topographies*, by Dustin Headley, *Parametric Constructions* course, Kevin Klinger and Branko Kolarevic, Ball State University, College of Architecture and Urban Planning, Department of Architecture, Muncie, Indiana, spring 2007.

22 As in the *Kinetic Hyposurface* project, only prototypes were produced as a test of the concept. The project could be further developed into a façade rain or shading screen by working with aluminum metal sheets that could be cut and expanded (albeit through a different process from what is currently done in the industry).

11

COMPUTATION AND MATERIALITY

MARTA MALÉ-ALEMANY AND JOSÉ PEDRO SOUSA / ReD

Due to its physical nature, architecture has a strong relationship with the realm of materials. Architects have always been concerned with finding the appropriate material solutions to realize the production of built objects. In ancient times, materials such as stone or wood were used in the same state they were found in nature. Progressively, with the development of tools and processing technologies, humans learned how to adapt materials to better suit constructive solutions. Raw materials could not only be cut, shaped and assembled in more efficient ways, but they could also be combined to produce new materials.

Today, after steel, glass and concrete have notably expanded the building construction possibilities over the past 150 years, we are witnessing the emergence of an immense range of new composite and artificially designed materials, which promises to overcome the limitations of traditional materials. New technologies in engineering and science are defining our present condition, in which architects are consuming more materials, both in quantity and diversification, than in any other period in history. Nowadays, innovation has become a buzzword in the field, and this clearly illustrates the race for novelty that is moving design teams and attracting more clients to architecture.

When Vitruvius, in his influential *The Ten Books of Architecture*, declared the three essential qualities of architecture – *firmitas, utilitas* and *venustas* – there was an implicit understanding of materiality beyond its physical properties and corresponding structural performance. Following these premises, buildings had to stand firmly upright, but they also ought to look firm. Furthermore, they had to fulfill the requirement of beauty, which was an intangible quality. Thus, besides their structural integrity, materials had to address certain additional effects, some of which lay in the realm of poetics and symbolism. This is still true today, as architects continue to build with materials, while constructing intellectual discourses about their application. Perhaps more than in other disciplines, material selection in architecture tends to occur by evaluating a diverse set of performances resulting from physical and mechanical behavior, assembly methods, structural logics, environmental and economic constraints,

aesthetic and symbolic assumptions, or historical and contextual concerns.

During the 1980s, when digital technology started to be widely used in practice, the traditional relationship between architecture and materiality seemed to be threatened. This fact was perceived by many, and was widely discussed both in academic and professional environments. The emergence of a new tool (the computer) and a new medium (the digital) to develop architectural projects prompted a natural resistance from those who were deeply tied to conventional representation techniques. Although this reaction is understandable, the discrepancy between the ability to describe any imaginable geometry in the computer, and the limited building methods of that time to execute complex forms did not help in facilitating the cultural assimilation of digital technologies in practice. As became more evident during the 1990s, architects foresaw the possibility of new material effects emerging from alternative digitally designed forms, but they could not find the means to realize them physically.

Since then, the progressive integration of computer-aided design, engineering, and manufacturing (CAD/CAE/CAM) systems and computer numerically controlled (CNC) production has changed the speculative nature of many digital design explorations. These technologies, transferred from other disciplines, allow the design, analysis, and fabrication of customized material geometries and properties. Besides the possibility of making physical artifacts out of digital information, materiality can also be reverse-engineered into digital media through scanning techniques. Thus, a total cycle of material development in architecture can now occur within a dynamic interplay between digital information and physical prototyping. A material system can be digitally crafted to achieve particular design goals. In that manner, geometric complexity and component variation can be instrumentalized, not solely for aesthetic purposes, but also to achieve more efficient building solutions. Freed from standardization constraints, material innovation may emerge from these processes, revealing surprising effects. As a result, for those architects committed to traditional representation techniques, this new digital condition has changed their perspective on computer technologies.

11.1a–b.
Digital craft: with CAD/CAM technologies, design can be extended into the fabrication process, as in traditional craft-based modes of production.

For *ReD*, with studios in Porto, Portugal, and Barcelona, Spain, the close link to materiality established by CAD/CAM systems has been the key factor in granting computers a central role in the development of architectural projects. For that reason, the office established itself as a research and design practice in architecture and digital technologies. Despite the fascination of the virtual possibilities unveiled by these technologies, we are critical of discourses that radicalize their impact on architectural design. Instead of supporting a vision of rupture, *ReD* sees the influence of these technologies in practice within the logics of extension and expansion (figures 11.1a–b), where re-thinking and re-using become strategies as valid as invention or discovery in a digital design approach. With this understanding, traditional conceptual and material possibilities are simultaneously taken into account with

new digitally enabled ones, thus opening up a wider world of design opportunities.

Being involved in academia, through teaching and research, has been extremely important for the development of our practice. Due to its nature, academia is a privileged space for investigation and information exchange, often transcending the boundaries of the architectural discipline. In the past four years, *ReD* principals have conducted several design studios, seminars, workshops, and advanced research projects to explore alternative design opportunities emerging from the integrated use of CAD/CAM technologies (figures 11.2a–h). Associative and parametric design, scripting and programming, CNC machining and rapid

11.2a–h.
Non-standard structures made out of variable components, conceived and fabricated using CAD/CAM parametric modeling processes (seminar at the *University of Pennsylvania*, Philadelphia, 2005).

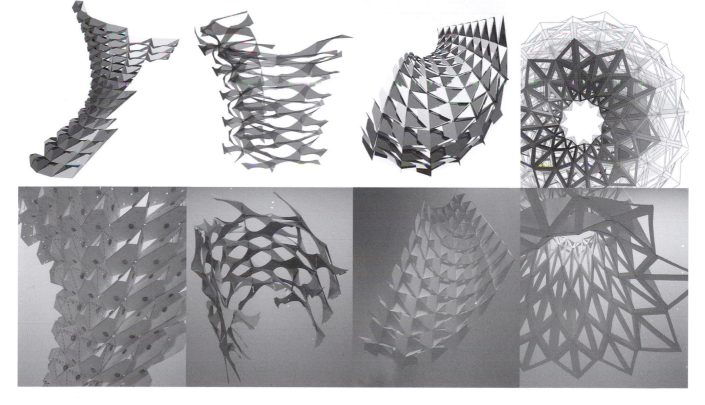

prototyping are some of the techniques that have been used to investigate how computation can influence the development of building materials, components, and structures, in ways that would be difficult to achieve without these enabling technologies (figures 11.3a–p).

These academic projects have natural repercussions in *ReD*'s practice. Without refusing the value of speculative digital explorations, the studio is deeply committed to the physical manifestation of its designs and technological investigations. The ultimate challenge lies in "real" problems and constraints. Understanding production as a creative endeavor, fabrication is engaged in early stages of the design process to avoid losing important creative opportunities. Throughout its working trajectory, *ReD* has interrogated a range of production techniques and materials, such as concrete, acrylic, wood, foam, plastics, and cork.

The following descriptions of four projects illustrate ideas and processes fundamental to our practice. In *XURRET System*, we explored the

production of formally complex and ornamented elements in concrete, while investigating the use of CAD/CAM associative parametric models to address the formal adjustments required by design and industrial partners. *MORSlide*, a project of variable panels fabricated entirely by our office, gave us the possibility to capitalize on the material effects of milled plywood emerging from 1:1 scale tests, thus making the fabrication process central to our design endeavor. In *DRAGORAMA*, we explored similar possibilities to produce textured variable panels in acrylic, and consolidated our mission of collaborating with other architectural practices to engage our digital design and fabrication expertise. Finally, the *M-City* project was an opportunity to expand our digital design methods by incorporating scripting techniques to resolve two large-scale installations in textile that explored variable geometries. Such an approach to the development of the project was necessary in order to address constant programmatic and economic fluctuations and the inevitable necessity of having to deal with several parties.

11.3a–p.
Re-thinking traditional materials using CAD/CAM technologies: experiments with cork (PhD research at *Instituto Superior Tecnico*, Lisbon, with the support of *FCT*, *Amorim*, and *Lasindustria*, 2005).

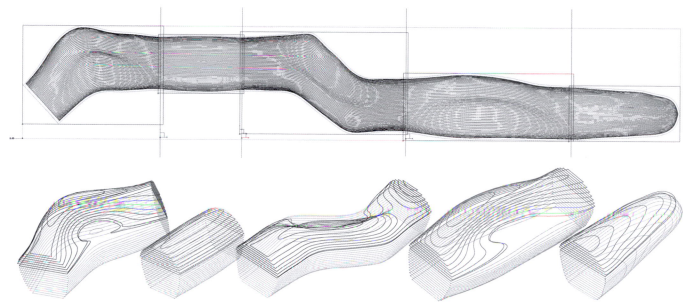

XURRET SYSTEM

XURRET System is a seating structure or bench, originally designed by architects *Ábalos & Herreros* (*A&H*) for the *Barcelona 2004 Forum* and produced by the concrete company *ESCOFET, S.A.* Due to the formal complexity and ornamental intricacy of the design concept, two problems immediately emerged for the designers and the manufacturers. On the design side, there was a need to capture and test the project's intentions with an accurate digital model; yet, on the fabrication side, it became evident that traditional production processes would not be able to address the creative objectives of the project. In this context, *ReD* was hired as a consultancy firm to invent and implement a digital production process linking design, development, and fabrication. In addition to bridging the architect's ideas into mass production, the studio also collaborated in the final design.

As a system, *XURRET* consisted of five parts that had to be connected end-to-end in multiple ways, thus creating an array of seating combinations varying in length, orientation, and overall shape. Given the original information from *A&H*, a series of variable two-dimensional sections and a basic three-dimensional model, we began modeling the bench as a smooth surface, carefully considering its future subdivision and assembly (figures 11.4a–b). The geometry was designed to have the same section at the end of each part, whereas the surface tangency was controlled to match the curvature from part to part. As a result, any combination would always be perfectly continuous with the rest.

Besides the irregular form of the bench, the designers wanted to cover it with a filiform three-dimensional texture, taken from a leaf with extremely visible veins. They had designed this ornamental motif by repeatedly mapping the same leaf image all over the model. Instead, *ReD* proposed an alternative approach based on a system of tubular veins, crossing the end sections at specific controlled points. Form and ornament were engineered so that, regardless of the specific assortment of parts, the ensemble would always look both continuous and differentiated. This second approach seemed much more coherent with the combinatorial and organic nature of the project. Thus, ornamentation became a strategy to blur the boundaries between the parts, highlighting the assembly as a whole. In this process, the digital model was crucial to assure accurate tangency, guarantee the continuity of shape and texture, and extend this precision into fabrication.

Parametric design was used to develop an interactive process, which facilitated the design adjustments requested by either the designers or the concrete company. Based on the filiform ornamental concept, *ReD* developed a

11.5a–d.
XURRET filiform texture: (a) parametric diagram
of the filiform veins; (b) 3D vector mapping of the
splines onto the bench surface; (c) 3D generation
of the veins with swept tubes; (d) final 3D model.

11.6a–b.
XURRET: CNC fabrication of
the final prototype with the
vein texture, in high density
polyurethane foam.

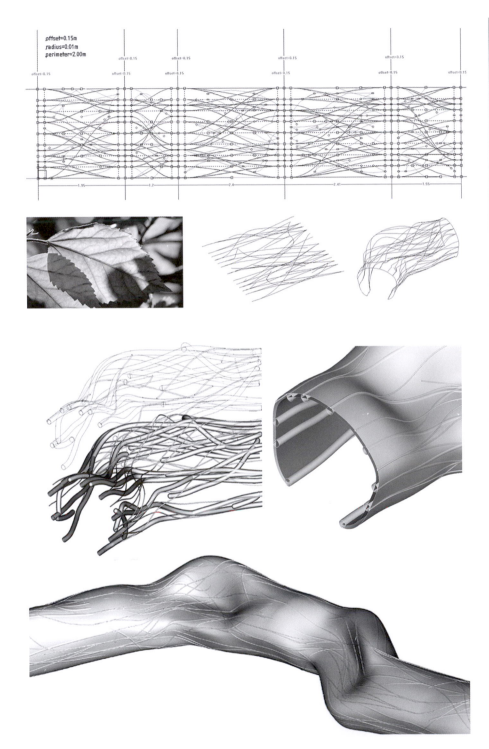

parametric diagram of the veins with spline curves; control
points located at the contact sections were constrained
to ensure the tangency from part to part, while the rest
could be manipulated freely to adjust the curvature and
density of the ensemble. This pattern was then vector-
mapped onto the bench surface, and the resulting three-
dimensional curves were used as extrusion paths to sweep
parametric circular sections. Linking the spline diagram
with the overall topology generated an adjustable model
of the overall bench surface and the extent of the veins
protuberance from the surface (figures 11.5a–d). This
associative definition of the geometry supported the
generation of multiple versions of the project, enabling the
exploration of different solutions and providing immediate
evaluation of the results.

As part of the consultancy, *ReD* took charge of the
CAD/CAM production of two prototypes of the bench.
The first one was required by the concrete company
to understand the scale of the bench and check its
functionality and comfort. Made of *Styrofoam* and purely
volumetric, it was quickly produced by milling only the
top of each part and completing it with simple sections at
the bottom. The second prototype, in high-density foam,
was milled using a 5-axis CNC machine to detail the vein
texture over the entire form (figures 11.6a–b). This final
version, which took much longer to execute, was used to
extract the molds for the mass production of the *XURRET*
parts in concrete (figure 11.7).

11.7.
XURRET: more than 20 benches have been installed in different configurations in the park of the Barcelona Forum.

11.8.
XURRET's organic concrete: the complex curvature and intricate surface veins perfectly match at the contact sections.

For *ReD*, the value of this experience was manifold. Besides its significance as a successful collaboration between architectural practices and manufacturers, the *XURRET* project exemplified a process from virtual data to material product, with a digital methodology for evaluating the design and the capacity to test it at full scale. The possibility to digitally fabricate an early 1:1 scale prototype of the bench was a key moment in the development process. Indeed, it was decisive to instill confidence in all parties in the project, where structure and surface, volume and texture, form and ornament ought to be delicately blended (figure 11.8). Finally, the mass production of large, heavy, and monolithic elements in concrete revealed a much broader interest for *ReD*. The scale of this project (and in particular the weight and dimensions) definitely exceeded the scale of furniture design to achieve that of an architectural building.

11.9.
MORSlide: the surface
pattern takes into account
all possible positions of the
sliding panels to achieve
continuity in any situation.

11.10a–d.
MORSlide: Morse-
coded text was used
as a graphic device to
develop a set of digital
surface manipulations.

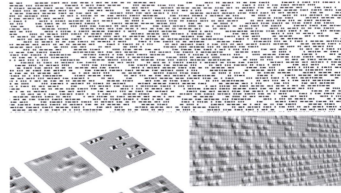

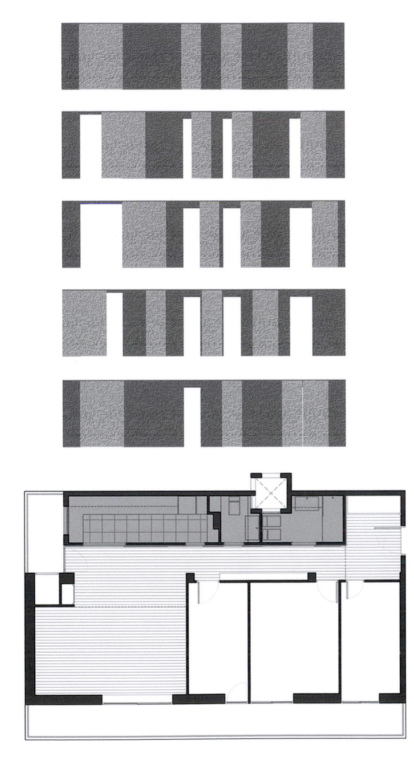

MORSlide

After the *XURRET* system, in 2005 *ReD* did the interior
renovation of an apartment in Barcelona, focusing on
maximizing the common space to stimulate a new living
experience. Reflecting on issues of scale and functionality,
ReD's design proposal focused on wrapping the wet core
(kitchen and bathrooms) with a single material surface.
For this purpose, *MORSlide* was developed as a system of
wall panels and sliding doors in plywood, which, by hiding
the spaces behind it, created a large box with a unique skin
effect. Visible from everywhere, it turned into the most
significant design element, offering a suggestive opportunity
for ornamental exploration (figure 11.9).

To emphasize the overall continuity, the existing doors
were replaced with sliding doors, with the aim of unifying
the plane of ornamentation. The next step was to find a
decorative motif that could blur the vertical joints between
the panels of the box, while taking into account all possible
positions of the sliding doors. Morse code emerged as the
most promising visual pattern, with simple abstract symbols
and few rules of composition. Its three elements – dash,
dot, and space – offered endless combinatorial possibilities.
Beyond the representation of meaning, a Morse-coded text
constructs graphic patterns that are horizontal, generating
a complex, randomly distributed field. Furthermore, the
superimposition of a piece of text over another does not
affect its overall appearance as a motif of dots and dashes,
a crucial aspect when considering the mobility of the sliding
doors.

11.11a–i.
MORSlide: material
exploration.

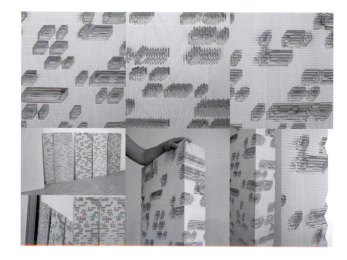

Going beyond the simple mimic of its pattern, Morse code was used as a graphic device to create a three-dimensional surface expression (figures 11.10a–d). Departing from the image of a coded field, the project evolved through several studies of surface curvature manipulations, with simultaneous assessment of their material effects through the CAD/CAM production of physical prototypes. The CNC milling of the plywood panels was fundamental because the machining parameters dramatically influenced the material effects resulting from the same digital source. As different tools and alternative milling trajectories produced very different engravings (figures 11.11a–i), material prototyping became an integral part of the design process. The production of milled samples early in the process suggested various design avenues; the creative process could no longer be detached from the experience of fabrication. In the end, the use of CAD/CAM technologies supported the production of seventeen differentiated textured panels.

A particularly successful aspect of *MORSlide* can be observed in the overall *field effect* that helps to hide the joints between panels. The plywood skin presents a continuity that still exists when displacing the sliding doors (figure 11.12). In addition, its eroded effect produces appealing light reflections that vary during the day. The corner of the box presents what is probably the greatest effect, which is visible from the entrance (figures 11.13a–b). There, the precision attained with digital fabrication tools is unmistakable: the texture perfectly continues despite the 90° angle at which the two surfaces meet; the corner edge – no longer a vertical line – presents an intricate (eroded) intersection curve, resulting from the milling process on both sides. More importantly, *MORSlide* produces a perception of a larger space, enriched by the scenographic quality of its plywood panels, which was its intended material effect.

11.13a–b.
MORSlide: the eroded
corner; view from the
entrance.

11.12.
MORSlide: interior
view of the apartment;
the kitchen is hidden
behind the panels.

MORSlide explores the potential of the interaction between computational design tools and material fabrication qualities to support emergence of additional creative opportunities. Its final material effects can only be understood by recognizing three equally important factors: digital geometry, machining parameters, and material properties. One can identify all three by looking at the panels: the three-dimensional surface from the computer, traces of the milling tool, and the emergent colored rings from the laminated composition of the plywood boards. *MORSlide* shows that traditionally distant poles of design and fabrication can fluidly be merged through extensive use of digital technologies, approximately relating our experience to the crafts production.

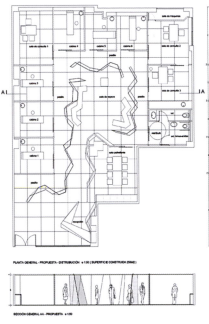

11.14a–b.
DRAGORAMA: plan of
the Chinese medical
center and layout of
the folding screen.

DRAGORAMA

DRAGORAMA was done in collaboration with the firm
Habitat Actual Arquitectura of Barcelona. *ReD* was invited
as a consultancy firm to develop a partition for the interior
renovation of a Chinese medicine center. The designers had
developed a simple scheme, placing the doctor's offices
along the perimeter of the space and leaving an empty
central waiting area, easily accessible from the entrance
reception. A lightweight partition, like a folded origami
screen, separated the offices from the central space, creating
a private corridor to connect all of them. Extending towards
the entrance, this screening surface also conducted the
patients from the reception to the waiting area (figures
11.14a–b).

ReD developed the *DRAGORAMA* partition as a
continuous surface. Its constituent panels, which had
different sizes in accordance to their varied spatial
orientations, were done in acrylic and decorated with a
customized engraved pattern. As a way of contextualizing
the project, *ReD* proposed a pattern that indexed the
distance between the folding screen and the doors of the
offices: by increasing the pattern's density according to
proximity, the final engraving would offer a play between
translucency and opacity. In that manner, the partition would
present not only an interesting material effect, but also act
as a functional screen to hide the doors along the corridor.

11.15.
DRAGORAMA:
examples of patterns
with different degrees
of density and
continuity.

texture 8   texture 9   texture 10   texture 11   texture 11b   texture 20 a1   texture 20 a2   texture 20 b1   texture 20 b2   texture 21

11.16a–g.
DRAGORAMA: CNC
engraving of the patterns on
translucent acrylic panels,
followed by laser-cutting the
panels' contours.

The specific texture of the *DRAGORAMA* screen was generated by determining areas of the partition that were closer to the doctors' offices and finding the intersection between a series of virtual spheres located at the center of each entry door and the surface of the partition. By unfolding the screen, the resulting intersections created an instrumental gradient map of proximities. Using this diagram, *ReD* generated several graphic motifs (figure 11.15), and selected one that presented enough regularity to emphasize the screen's continuity, while including simultaneously the desired performance-based density variations.

To assess the material effects of engraving the patterns on acrylic, full-scale samples were fabricated using a CNC milling machine. For the final production, the *DRAGORAMA* panels were produced by milling the ornamental motif on standard acrylic sheets, followed by a secondary process of laser-cutting the panels' particular contours (figures 11.16a–g).

Once installed on-site, *DRAGORAMA* produces delicate spatial and material effects, as its milled texture becomes visible to different extents under changing light conditions. When someone walks along the corridor, the perception of the continuous ornamental pattern is greatly enhanced (figure 11.17), because the engraved lines are revealed when someone stands right behind the panels, obstructing the light. (figure 11.18).

11.17.
The *DRAGORAMA*
effects: the translucent,
textured screen provides
different levels of
translucency.

11.18.
DRAGORAMA:
a view from the
entrance.

M-City

In 2006, the design of the installation for the *M-City* exhibition at the *Kunsthaus* in Graz, Austria, presented *ReD* with a double challenge, due to the unique singularity of the building and the scale and heterogeneity of the event's program. Unlike traditional museums, the *Kunsthaus* is an art institution that has no permanent collection. The building is an empty container without divisions, in which every venue is built from scratch with a new formal manifestation. Previous exhibitions have either used standard modular walls to subdivide the space and organize visitor circulation, or relied on the construction of completely autonomous installations with an inherent structure and morphology. However, both strategies, whether anonymous or self-referential, lack a direct relationship to the building. By contrast, *ReD*'s intervention sought to activate the singular conditions of the building, creating an interface between the exhibited works, the visitors, and the building's particular context.

The *M-City* exhibition examined emergent urban landscapes in average European cities, and was divided into two main curatorial subjects – *Urban Themes* and *City Portraits*. While the former was broken down into six subsections (*Earthscapes*, *Eurosprawl*, *Mapping*, *Migrations*, *No Vision?*, and *Shopping*), the latter consisted of six video projections based on the European cities of Basel, Krakow, Graz, Ljubljana, Ruhrstadt, and Trieste. *M-City* combines 30 artists in this dense programmatic organization, with works that included models, videos, photographs, paintings, and installations. The list of works changed constantly during the development of the project, thus requiring a design process sufficiently flexible to accommodate such changes without compromising the general design intentions. As in the

11.19.
M-City: *Topographies of Negotiation* concept rendering showing different installations, *FLUOScape* and *CONEplex*, on two floors of the *Kunsthaus* building in Graz, Austria.

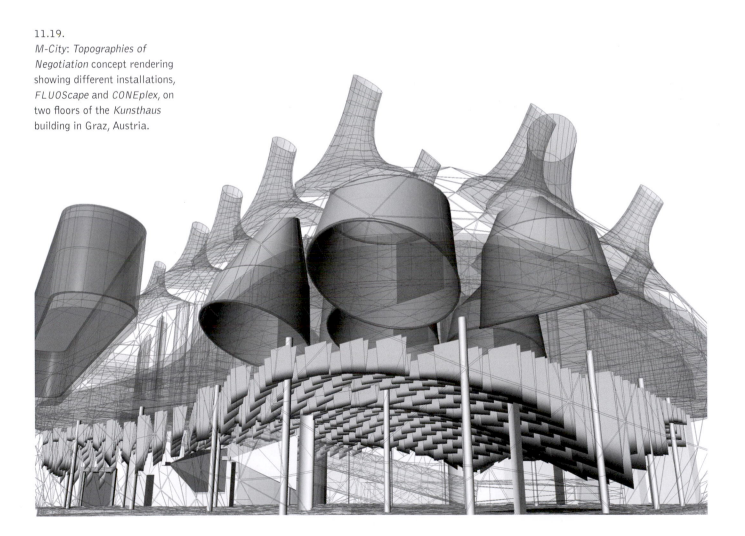

M-City: the *FLUOSoft* script creates a three-dimensional model for each of the 587 different "flags" with labels and surface areas.

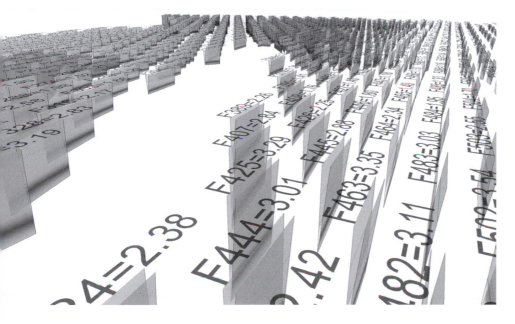

previous projects, *ReD* explored parametric and generative digital processes to assist both design and manufacturing. This digitally integrated approach provided the needed flexibility to deal with program and budget fluctuations, while simultaneously facilitating the negotiations among architects, curators, artists, and fabricators.

ReD's first intention was to interact with the existing building as much as possible. In order to reflect its singular qualities, an intervention in the *Kunsthaus* interior ought to be necessarily different than one inside a conventional museum. At *Kunsthaus*, the lighting systems on both floors were so striking, that they provided a departure point for the project's development. The design concept aimed at generating a "response" from the ceiling to the artwork beneath. By controlling the light and suggesting various circulation paths, the intervention became an interface between the exhibition content and the building. Although this concept was applied to both floors, their spatial differences suggested two formally distinct installations: *FLUOScape* on the first floor and *CONEplex* on the second (figure 11.19).

On the first floor, the excessive, monotonous grid of 587 fluorescent lights provided the basic infrastructure to generate a completely new spatial effect. By fixing a soft cover (a flag) of varying lengths to each fluorescent light, the flatness of the ceiling was transformed into an inverted topography that would flow over the entire space dedicated to the exhibition themes. This topography of flags, with their differing lengths related to the works exhibited below, suggested gathering areas and new circulation paths without using any conventional walls or corridors.

Several modeling techniques and alternative software solutions were tested to generate this topography and were then rejected as insufficiently flexible and precise. We had to develop our own "design tool" to generate and interactively control the ceiling topography: *FLUOSoft* is a customized script written in *AutoLISP*, which merges design, analysis and fabrication. The script was written to manage an infinite number of "flags:" for each light, it calculates the relative distance to the center of each thematic area, evaluates neighboring conditions, and determines the flag length according to curvature parameters. The script constructs a three-dimensional model of each flag, draws a flattened duplicate in the XY plane with a contour line for laser-cutting, computes its surface area to provide an accurate (and immediate) overall material (and cost) calculation, and automatically generates an individual label to be engraved or printed onto the flag for installation (figure 11.20a–b).

11.21a–d.
FLUOScape was fabricated in Germany with a large-scale CNC laser-cutter normally used in the production of boat sails.

11.23.
FLUOScape: the ceiling as a soft response; a cupola-like form is created above each thematic area by progressively varying the flag lengths.

11.22.
FLUOScape: view from the arrival ramp on the first floor of the *Kunsthaus*.

Despite the geometric complexity of the final topography, the flexibility of the design process allowed changes to be incorporated right up to the fabrication deadline. Different alternatives were quickly produced and evaluated, providing immediate aesthetic, functional, and financial feedback, without compromising the overall design intentions. At the end of this entirely digital process, the "flags" were laser-cut in Germany from white translucent voile by directly following the patterns generated by the *FLUOSoft* script (figures 11.21a–d). The scripting-based process enabled a fully non-standard production with full-scale prototyping and on-site material testing. The 587 flags were installed over three days at the *Kunsthaus*, using a simple system for attachment to the support structure for the lights. Despite the large number of elements, the positioning in the space was simplified by the *FLUOSoft*-generated labels, matching each flag to its corresponding fluorescent light (figures 11.22 and 11.23).

The second-floor installation entailed the creation of six "projection environments" displaying video "portraits" of six cities. The curved ceiling and lighting – now large skylights with circular fluorescent lights – were the most striking spatial features for exploration. To avoid conventional enclosed, orthogonal rooms, we designed lightweight, conical elements that were suspended from the existing skylights. These intimate enclosures were gently tilted, without touching the ground, to invite visitors to gather beneath them and view the projections.

11.24a–b.
CONEplex: 3D model
of the six projection
cones at the top level
of the *Kunsthaus*
building.

11.26.
CONEplex in space,
showing the strong
relationship between
the cones and the
building context.

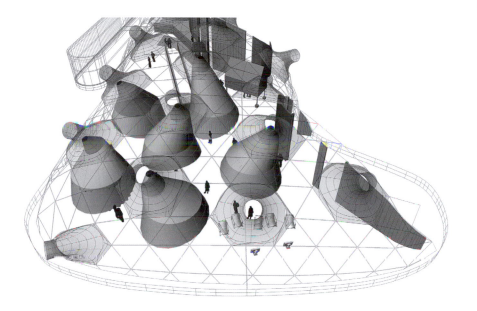

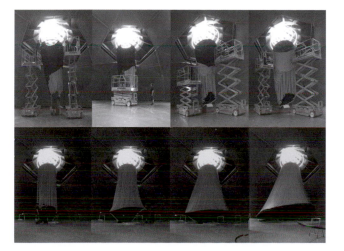

11.25a–h.
CONEplex:
installing the
cones.

As on the first floor, the *CONEplex* installation avoided creating any linear or preconceived trajectory for the visitor. Each of the six cones was assembled from two parts that resulted from connecting three circular rings. While the bottom part was identical for all cones, the length of the top part was adjusted to absorb the variable ceiling height at each specific location. Because the cones were designed to be asymmetrical, the different rotation of each cone in relation to the others produced a formal configuration that gave an impression of six completely different cones (figure 11.24a–b).

The cones were also fabricated in Germany using information extracted directly from the three-dimensional model. The textile skin was CNC-cut, the metal rings were CNC-bent, and a full-scale mock-up was assembled in the factory. The material for the cones – a double-sided stretchable Lycra – provided a double effect: the outer silver layer reflected the ambient light, while the inner black layer created enough darkness for the projections. Structurally, the Lycra layers support the metal rings, which were positioned in space using tension cables to achieve the designed configuration (figures 11.25a–h). The screens and projectors were hung from the middle rings, which were all positioned at 3.5 m above the floor to create a "horizon" that established yet another relationship with the context; perfectly aligned with the fourth-floor viewing balcony, this virtual plane highlighted the changing curvature of the ceiling (figures 11.26 and 11.27).

143

11.27.
CONEplex: suspended rooms;
without touching the ground, the
six cones define dark spaces for
projections while inviting visitors to
enter and stay underneath.

In developing a proposal that negotiates between the particular spatial conditions of the *Kunsthaus* and the specific programmatic requirements of the *M-City* exhibition, the use of digital technologies for design and fabrication was fundamental. The use of programming (scripting) enabled the conceptual and material exploration of customized elements by liberating the project from the standardization that still dominates the construction industry. The direct use of data from the digital models to control CNC fabrication allowed highly precise production in a very short time. Moreover, this twofold condition facilitated the architectural process, allowing (despite many geographical barriers) a more interactive collaboration by all parties involved in the project.

As with the previous projects, the *M-City* exhibition provided a "real" context to test critical interests that the studio has been developing since its creation. Concerned with the exploration of the impact of digital technologies on the discipline of architecture, *ReD*'s research and professional agenda are not tied to a singular digital design method or manufacturing technique. By expanding the design and fabrication know-how, the studio can augment the creative and productive strategies to efficiently fit the particularities of each design challenge. The four projects presented here clearly illustrate this vision. Different materials – concrete, wood, acrylic, textile, and metal – and their inherent potential to create particular *effects* were investigated using various digital modeling and scripting techniques, while interacting simultaneously with diverse CNC fabrication processes. In all cases, the association between computation and materiality allowed the crafting of particular production processes to attain unique design solutions.

12

HOX AESTHETICS: THE RESTRAINED PROFLIGACY OF SECOND-ORDER GENERATIVE PROCESSES

DECOI / MARK GOULTHORPE

An *aesthetic*, in the early twenty-first century, might be characterized as a work, act, or process that offers identity and community through its (social) *salience*: it binds people due to its implicit capture of cultural value. The twentieth-century aesthetics, as discussed by Habermas or Marcuse, for example, shifted emphasis from formal quality to social identity as the essential aesthetic act – to social localization in modernity's delocalized field. Even Walter Benjamin, in announcing the loss of "aura" and the de-pedestal-ing of art in a mechanical age, shifted emphasis to the increasing engagement with everyday life as the new aesthetic condition of the arts, rather than dwelling overtly on mechanically produced art. His seminal essay, "The Work of Art in the Age of Mechanical Reproduction,"[1] illustrates the elusive nature of aesthetic transition occasioned by technical change, evidently a complex realignment of base social value, not simply the formal articulation of new technique.

These thinkers did not mourn the cathected object-hood and inculcated value of more traditional aesthetics, each writer recognizing and celebrating a shifting technical aptitude that often had quite obscure cultural import. At issue here is the possible update of aesthetic concern from a mechanical to a communication age. For in a digital global context, aesthetics seems ever more a de-formalized issue, a *socius* impelled to acts/works/processes that offer implicit, inexpressive, self- and group-identity within a delocalizing information sea. There is, it seems, no explicit formal equivalence to a revolution in networked computation, the immediate calculation and transfer of data, despite the shoal-like or curvilinear forms allowed by the mathematical capacity of CAD software.

Latent in the issue of "material effects" is the question of aesthetics: the *salience* of the effects within contemporary culture. Linkage to "manufacturing" within the thematic framing of this book ("*Manufacturing* Material Effects") then foregrounds the issue as being the pertinence of late-industrial *techniques* in their aesthetic potential, since "manufacture" is deeply imbued with a machinic logic, it being defined as the transformation of raw materials by mechanical process and division of labor into "useful" products. (I use inverted commas to suspend judgment as to the "useful" value of design aesthetics, since writers such as Gianni Vattimo note the role of "design" as undergoing

12.1.
The milled mathematical surface for the *Miran Galerie* in Paris, France (2003), by dECOi (with Alex Scott), leaving trace of the machine-head of the drill-bit, material witness to the brutal dexterity of the tool.

a profound shift from the production of machine-age functional-value to information-age identification-value: design divorced from its proto-functional history.)

Yet the transition to a now-digital machinic protocol, where cutting or milling machines are given a new-found dexterity in their 5-, 6-, or 7-axis aptitude, seems a less than paradigmatic shift: the destructive noise of these machines-at-work is sufficient to establish their brute force "manufacturing" lineage, the tail-end of an industrial logic. Thus one wonders, awed by the undoubted animism of their non-standard agility, as to the actual locus of their supposed "salience"; as to how that might be captured *in form*, except as the marvelous trace of machinic force (figure 12.1).

Yet the equation "available technique = aesthetic" is evidently facile, just as a numeric command milling machine seems somehow suspect in its industrial "lateness." Indeed, the deft 3D printer silently eclipses its mechanical power in its ability to place material in space felicitously, offering far subtler formal progeny, albeit no longer forceful.

Indeed, *Art Nouveau* (1890–1914) developed in large part as a celebration of the technical sophistication of manufacturing processes, its exquisite cast-iron machine-organicism seemingly the zenith of Romantic Formalism, the first ornamental style of the *Machine Age*. Yet, despite a short-lived stylistic brilliance across the plastic and decorative arts, it failed as an *aesthetic* that captivated even a middle-European industrial *socius*, which abandoned its over-wrought formal semantic (the "total art" *Gesamtkunstwerk*) for a far more streamlined *Machine Age logic*. Art Deco (1920–1939) evinced a more pragmatic industrial form-ism, machinic and repetitive in its look; which was itself further reduced by Modernism in its apparent eradication of formal expressivity. This "eradication" one might consider the aesthetic of Modernism – its socio-economic *identity*, its capture of a formal/material "austerity-lightness"; as if forms of stoic nomad-ism, with their erasure of cultural history, were the most salient aspects of modernity's technical advance – architecture as a sort of stripped sanatorium of machinic man. The complex scrollwork of reinforcing bars behind the

"simplicity" of the *piloti*/slab forms, scarcely sufficient to serve as (tacit) witness to the remarkable technical prowess of its time (yet the only complexity there was). Indeed, Modernism's forms were somehow formally at odds with its available speed and power, but seemingly capturing the socio-economic mood of the time.

So what aesthetic "speed" this time, in the instantaneity of digital communication? A high-speed drill-bit in a biotech age seems an unlikely harbinger of aesthetic salience, all too predictably a *nouveau-nouveau* (ground-down) "organicism." Machined surfaces evidencing technical dexterity as forms of digital ornamentalism seem just as aesthetically fateful as their *fin-de-siècle* forebears, unless, perhaps, they stimulate a new speed of mind via alternative generative process.[2]

Indeed, the numeric command machine operators remind me, when I ask them to machine-intricate (ornamental) surfaces, that their machines are bought for *economy*, to re-align the labor needs of extant fabrication processes, to streamline industrial separatism-of-trades into seamless post-industrial process-ing. They complain at the pulverized material logic implicit in such decorative finishes, which for them screams contradiction. Boat hulls, turbine blades, or car bodies are milled from soft synthetic blocks as single one-off molds, then vacu-formed as thin carbon-fiber shells whose curvature is refined and strategic: a minimal, multi-purpose shell nuanced for performance. Yet even these performance aesthetes dream of giant 3D-print machines, liberated from such still-mechanical clumsiness, with the capacity to strategically deposit even, material *property*. Their digital drive being a relentless quest for efficiency: of labor, of material, of embodied energy, of operating energy: a post-machinic attitude driven by the base efficiency imperative of Western economies.

Despite the apparent decadence of this late-industrial period, a return to technicist ornamentalism seems an unlikely generalized trend. Today, the effete tectonics of late-industrial "lite" manufacture (the aluminum sticks/struts hegemony) still utterly dominates the field because of its extruded economic performance. The legacy of the machine age(s) is evermore starkly one of a despoiled planet with an ever-pressing need for technical advance to

12.2a–c.
Bankside Paramorph in London (under development) by dECOi.

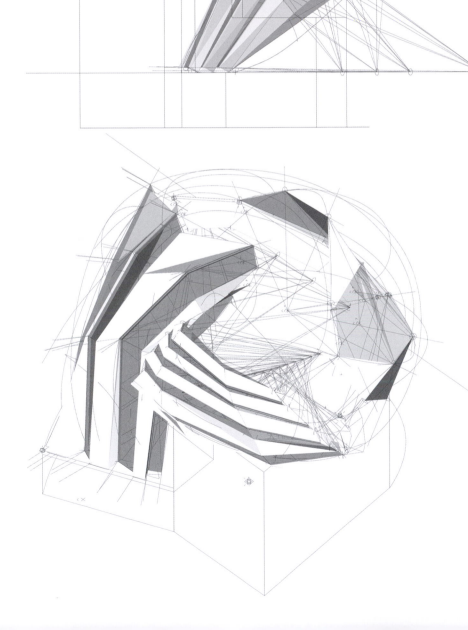

stave off any fall-back of quality of life or life expectancy (the crucial gains of the twentieth century). There is clearly an identity crisis in the after-Modern delocalization and dematerialization that digital communication engenders, expressed by the great surge of "designer" activity (identity production as proliferating forms of heterotopic "fix" that Vattimo persuasively argues offers a contemporary "aesthetic"); which also comes into play as the emollient to capital circulation in a consumer society. Yet my feeling is that the underlying impulsion of architecture will be to remain essentially tacit and background (like Modernism), formally *inexpressive* in respect to function, a backdrop to social and communication flows, and essentially economic as such, at least environmentally. It will, in fact, be mandated as such, and one only has to witness the rapid normalization of international building protocols to realize this.

If there is an *aesthetic* that might legitimately emerge to contest the hegemonic sticks-and-struts bricolage-ism of late-Modern, late-industrial production (from Gehry to Foster), it will be, I conjecture, via second-order logics of architectural *performance*, with an increasing emphasis on energy and environment. This will be coupled with a radical rethinking of fabrication logics, driven by an economic prerogative to streamline its by-now anachronistic machine-age legacy. This is not to say that there is not enormous capacity for formal innovation in architecture (figure 12.2a–c), just that this will be driven by logics other than the manufacturing of "effects"

12.3.
"Our Pre-Cambrian Ancestor" from
"The Plausibility of Life" by Marc
W. Kirschner and John C. Gerhart,
illustrated by John Norton.

as a celebration of technical virtuosity. If organic forms directly influenced the formal development of Art Nouveau designs, a curiously representative logic in an age of mechanical reproduction, then this time it will perhaps be the *organizing* logics of bio-systems about which so much has recently been discovered (digital technology subtending the genome project, for instance). Peter Eisenman once pointed out[3] that Modernism did *not* eradicate a representative legacy in its preference for the "look" of a machine to the "look" of nature, yet I would argue here that it did exhibit a preference for the logic of the machine, for man as suddenly machinic. I would also note that this was remarked upon by Sigmund Freud in his famous "Fort/Da" essay,[4] articulating the self-constitution of a child's repetition-compulsion, which was then extrapolated by Jacques Lacan in his *Seminar 23* analysis of James Joyce,[5] both thinkers marking a decisive change in subjectivity of Modern man from Jean-Jacques Rousseau's earlier man–machine opposition.

HOX LOGIC

The *Hox* gene manifests the controlling logic by which organisms differentiate into basic compartments, the organizing principle of cellular differentiation from egg to adult. The typological worm that biologists conjecture is the common ancestor of all modern bi-lateral animals on earth, would already demonstrate a compartmentalized *hox* logic, with differentiation of body into distinct compartments, a through-gut organism with discernible head and anus (figure 12.3). Within such compartments, there is greater liberty for independent genetic variants of aspects of the 4 trillion-odd cells of a human being. What is most striking is that the basic compartmentalization, or the base organizing logic, has survived virtually intact through 500 million years of evolution (in contrast to individual species that have come and gone).

Such post-genome research has only been permitted by the speed of digital analytical processes, allowing the first factual assessment of the base formative logics of inheritance and variation after 150 years of genetic speculation (from Darwin on). So an ancient biological

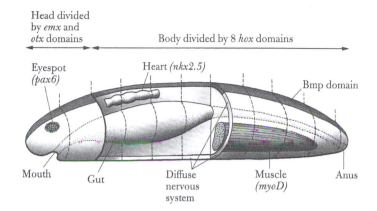

organizational system is somehow inimically linked to digital systems from the outset, allowing organizational logics to be comprehended that were hitherto only guessed at by prescient biologists. Might one venture that such cognitive aptitude, engendered by groping comprehension of genetic organizational systems, constitutes a particular *strain* of digital technology, the shift in cognition engendered by a new technique, a newfound bio-morphism?

Given the propensity for technologies of mind to take hold technically as well as culturally, we might conjecture that it will be the *implicit* logics of organizational discipline that will subtend the aesthetics of post-industrial production. This will emerge not with celebratory late-machinic zeal, but with attempts at processural and environmental sophistication. The politic of constraint that increasingly surrounds the globe via a seething digital normalization, motivated by the spectre of imminent environmental catastrophe, will insist on highly selective and efficient protocols of *formation* in all fabrication domains, whether architects like it or not.

Yet we conjecture that this will offer a radically diverse range of formal possibilities, just as natural systems, all based on robust and quite limited inherited rule-sets, exhibit extraordinary diversity. Yet we doubt, as Roger Callois intuits, that this will be a case of "legendary psychaesthenia," since it will be subject to a stricture that restrains its free expression in merging with or differentiating from the environment.[6] Thermal codes, structural norms, energy-of-production quotas, methane and carbon limitations: these will be the "ethics" imposed on the generative process. Yet such will be the sophistication of (digital) generative protocols, imbued

149

with inherited restraint (such as environmental stricture) and acting as second-order generative engines, that there will be a great diversity of formal variation. The *aesthetic* in biology, as its base logics of constrained variants are slowly revealed, seems less formal than organizational: "even though the detailed structural organization of our brain is very different from that of a fly (*Drosophila*), it is based on the same underlying basic compartment plan, which has been conserved for over half a billion years."[7] Digital systems, crucial to revealing such biological process, are themselves rule-based: mathematics, at the root of computational systems, being fundamentally *relational* in its methodologies.

My concern here is evidently less biological metaphor, much less mimicry, than biological *logic*, the principle of differentiated speciation from restricted ancestry. Or rather, the deep question that will haunt all creative fields: would a *hox* logic, deeply structured yet vividly variant, subtend a somehow salient contemporary *aesthetic*?

NOTES

1 Walter Benjamin, "The Work of Art in the Age of Mechanical Reproduction", in Hannah Arendt (ed.), trans. Harry Zohn, *Illuminations: Essays and Reflections*, New York: Schocken Books, 1969. (The essay was first published in 1936.)

2 Elsewhere I have written extensively on "trauma" as an emergent aesthetic category, where an impalpably complex, yet evidently precise generative process is left as material trace – a post hand–eye formalism offered by digital processes, which we evidently strive for in much of our work. See, for instance, "Autoplastic to Alloplastic," in *The Possibility of (an) Architecture*, Paris: Hyx, 2007.

3 Peter Eisenman, "The End of the Classical: The End of the Beginning, the End of the End," *Perspecta* 21, Summer 1984.

4 Sigmund Freud, *Beyond the Pleasure Principle*, James Strachey (ed.), New York: Norton, 1961.

5 Jacques Lacan, *Le Séminaire, Livre XXIII (1975–1976): Le sinthôme*, Paris: Seuil, 2005.

6 Roger Callois, *Mimicry and Legendary Psychaesthenia*, trans. John Sheply, October 31, 1984.

7 Marc W. Kirschner and John C. Gerhart, "The Plausibility of Life", in *Invisible Anatomy*, New Haven, CT: Yale University Press, 2005, p. 197.

13

DESTINY OF INNOVATION

MICK EEKHOUT
JEANNE GANG
MARK GOULTHORPE
FABIO GRAMAZIO
MATTHIAS KOHLER
MARTA MALÉ-ALEMANY
CHRIS SHARPLES
JOSÉ PEDRO SOUSA
RUBEN SUARE
WILLIAM ZAHNER
KEVIN KLINGER
BRANKO KOLAREVIC

BRANKO KOLAREVIC: We hope to discuss some broader issues that deserve our attention, such as: What is the proper place of "making" in architecture? what do architects make and should they make anything? What is the proper place for material innovation? If architecture is a material practice, different notions of making are pertinent, as are questions of investing effort, both in terms of design and production of material effects (including Mark Goulthorpe's "plea" for decoration).

MICK EEKHOUT: The principal question should be whether we are getting better architecture. Classical architecture had its rules and regulations, including the golden rule. After eighty years of modernism, we know what a good modernist building is and is not. But should we accept all the free-form buildings we have seen so far? How do we define good free-form buildings; is it possible to do so? Which of the free-form buildings would appear on a monument list in twenty years time and will never be demolished, and which could disappear without opposition?

MARK GOULTHORPE: Time will tell which end up on the monument list, what else? But what comes out of this? I think the best of the digital work in architecture is going to radicalize the fabrication industry. This change will not be led by the fabrication industries, but by the prescient architects at the present, imagining spaces and forms.

CHRIS SHARPLES: In an Introduction to a show entitled "Ruskin, Turner and the Pre-Raphaelites" at the old *Tate Gallery* in London, in March 2000, David Hickey wrote about Ruskin and the lack of spirit within the building industry today. He criticized industrialization and how people were losing their souls, wondering if human beings were being de-humanized. Hickey focused on what Ruskin was trying to get at – what makes people excited about architecture. The word "delight" came up; there were three things that Hickey understood from Ruskin: in gothic architecture what made that "delight" possible was that architecture had to embody *variety*, it had to have *irregularity*, as well as *intricacy*.

I would argue that "delight" in space, in the level of intricacy, variety, and irregularity is something that is timeless. In many projects that were presented, the architects who

designed them appear really excited with what they do. I think that is because they take great delight, for example, in how a machine could lay up a brick wall and generate an incredible amount of choice and chance, as shown by Fabio Gramazio and Matthias Kohler. Many of the technologies that have emerged over the past two decades have allowed us to be much more pliant and much more social in terms of the creative process.

Greg Lynn describes how society is quite drawn to the idea of trying to build buildings, or trying to unravel the pattern, and reconstitute the building in their mind as they experience it. A gothic cathedral is a perfect example of that idea; one walks through the space and constantly tries to understand the language of the patterns that are generating the form. That notion is what we at *SHoP Architects* have tried to achieve in the *P.S.1 Dunescape* project. Once everybody understood the basic parameters, we began to modulate the form to take it in a different direction. That is what it is all about – engagement between people and the object, and in the case of the object, taking it beyond its actual physicality to a much higher level of experience and understanding. These notions, I think, are evident in many of the projects that were presented.

MICK EEKHOUT: In gothic times, with bricklayers or stonemasons, there were still good cathedrals and bad ones, to which one would not return a second time. So, which buildings pass the test?

JEANNE GANG: Architecture needs to be judged on how it is put to use; it should not be judged only by the shape, but also by the structural capacity. I would argue that the stronger projects are the ones that are doing multiple things simultaneously. Same with the gothic cathedrals: the ones that went furthest with the structure are the ones that got the largest openings, or the most colorful glass, etc. The project is not being judged on material effect alone. There were many projects shown that had multiple levels of qualities, and need to be observed on all those levels. There is a focus on how some material effects were achieved, but hopefully the projects are not being judged on that alone. We might relate to the way something is made, the way in which material is in its own state, like its fluidity, for example, or its structural state, or imagine how it was put together. That is why

I am less excited about the robot just laying bricks; it seems like something so easy for people to do, so why not just have people do it? I like to relate to things by how they are made. I like to make things. I think the public also has this kind of sensibility and will come to know how these other fabrication methods exist because they will encounter them in their own realms of experience and start to have that relationship with those things. So, it is all of those combined qualities that will make some projects rise to the top, I think.

BRANKO KOLAREVIC: What about the "delight" Chris Sharples referred to, or "pleasure"? Some people are even using the term "elegance" right now as another dominant motif.

AUDIENCE MEMBER: I do not want to paint everybody with broad brush, but many of the presented projects have a very similar continuous curvilinear form. I think that the pleasure is in the potential for multiple reading of the spaces, but when there is much variation in the surface itself, that becomes so dominant spatially, so overwhelming, that the multiple reading of the space seems to be absent.

BRANKO KOLAREVIC: Anybody want to address this question of the absence and the presence of multiple reading?

MARK GOULTHORPE: The complex group projects we have executed have been very few. I recognize a few executed banally, like an impoverished Greek taverna. If the project is executed really well, there is a real bizarre spatial ambiguity that can be attained even in a very small complex curved surface. By introducing an uncertainty of depth, which is almost vertiginous, there is enormous potential in exploring that spatially. I do not think this is impositional or simple out of necessity. I think the play of light in a well-executed complex curved space can be fascinating.

FABIO GRAMAZIO: What intrigues us in the brick walls and even in the perforated walls is not the surface in itself, but the depth in the material. Adding material, for example, by placing every brick in a different position and angle, is a very simple operation. The result is not a hi-tech building element, but one which uses the latent possibilities embedded in this, the oldest material building block of architecture. The bricks' dimensions and proportions have evolved over 9,000 years of construction history. Bricks are this way because the human – the craftsman – has to be able to take one after the other for hours and put them in position. Yet what was not possible until now was to angle every single brick differently. This would have been an unnatural operation for a human to do, similar to remembering 3,000 phone numbers; nobody could do this. You would have to train for years and years to do this. Yet for a robot and a computer, it is so simple, it is so logical – it is normal. Seeing the first digitally fabricated brick walls we felt that something had happened which we had anticipated, but we were never able to see before. The richness of these walls was not happening on the surface, but in the depth of the material, when looking at the walls in different perspectives and when observing their differentiated transparencies. This led to a wonderful moment that gave us the motivation to continue research in that direction.

AUDIENCE MEMBER: The brick wall you did had frames, and then it had effects of the implied spherical parts that overlapped over the frame. The gothic architecture has that singularity of the way the structure was made and the uniformity of forms, but they are related. You can also read planes or layering across from side aisle, to nave, to side aisle, and then even within side aisles, chapels that might be in the depth of the structural wall. That quality is what we do not see so much in the presented projects. We see many individual, singular events, but not an idea about relating those into overlapping systems or multiple events. I wonder if this is inherent ... Is it in the way of this making that we are missing that *multiplicity* or is it that is just not something of interest (as in: because visually I apprehend the rest is uninteresting)?

BRANKO KOLAREVIC: Fabio Gramazio is right to make distinctions between the depth and the surface. One cannot experience depth in a flat projection screen. Seeing and experiencing the spaces would perhaps bring the multiplicities to the fore.

FABIO GRAMAZIO: We are experimenting on a 1:1 scale, and focusing our research on elements that are prefabricated. In the winery project we conceived the entire façade. It is very difficult to appreciate in still images what happens in the winery throughout the day, as it changes completely from inside and outside depending on whether it is morning or evening, whether it is a nice, bright day or a cloudy day, and where one is looking. Until now we had not achieved a level of examination that involved an entire architectural project. This is something we are looking for, but we have to keep in mind that these developments are very new. Everything we describe has been technically possible for only a few years. We have been involved in research with digital fabrication for the past ten years, some others for twenty. Think about what this means. We are at the beginning of an important development, and that is the reason why it is exciting. We believe that this will evolve considerably, not just through technology, but also through culture.

MARK GOULTHORPE: Has this parametric logic developed since the Second World War? Surely that is the case as these technologies have become available. But, then I think absolutely not – it has always been part of architecture. Gaudí's *Sagrada Familia* has through and through a generative parametric intellect behind it: Gaudí has deployed hyperbolic paraboloids at every level of detail. He has mastery of design, so that craftsman can have a template, carve stone on the ground, and lift it into place. Returning to the question, Gaudí was very disliked in his time. He really struggled to get the project built. Now, in a recent survey, 96 percent of people in Barcelona feel Gaudí is the definition of Barcelona. So, first of all, you do it for yourself. The intellectual project is a profound one at its best.

WILLIAM ZAHNER: I am not an architect – I am simply the hands of many architects. We are able to customize things that used to take much longer to do. In making custom surfaces, we have eliminated recreating the process each time. By changing part of the code, you can make the bricks set a little differently. Changing part of the surface in the parametric model changes the surface a little bit. Frank Gehry always wanted to control what happened on my plant floor. We have a certain relationship, so we make the changes without adding cost and time. We

let the computer do the hard stuff. This gives us the ability to customize very rapidly. That intriguing potential is where I see much happening in architecture.

FABIO GRAMAZIO: For us, it is not only a question of the direct value of this new design and fabrication philosophy. A project will be good or bad depending on how such a philosophy is used, felt, understood, or developed by architects. We are sure that it is an enrichment of the discipline. Our profession is much more interesting today than ten years ago, when architects were very largely detached from the actual production process, when they were obliged to do design at shape level, and then rely on product catalogs and rigid construction conventions to realize projects. If we as architects are now being engaged and developing our own techniques, instead of being just observers and consumers, we can redefine processes and reclaim power. This might be a romantic idea, but it is in fact a chance to take charge of an integral design and fabrication process. It is possible to change the power relations that for the past fifty or a hundred years have been dictated by different specialized industries. It is up to the architect's intellect and imagination to define what we want, when we want it, and how we want it.

CHRIS SHARPLES: The shift is a generational issue as well. Young people coming out of school are able to write scripts, model comprehensive conditions, and are smart. They can pick up the phone and call Ruben Suare or Bill Zahner and have an intelligent conversation. I think that is something that one could not necessarily expect ten years ago, unless you have been a project manager and you knew how to put a construction documents set together. That is exciting; it forces the question of how the academy and the profession have to interact much more with each other. In Europe, that interaction is much stronger and faster, but that is critical to the idea of *playtime*. What is encouraging about some of the digital tools is that they are usable on many different levels in many different ways. It is exciting to embrace that potential and play with it. Again, it is also a very social process as it breaks away from compartmentalization and opens up the question of transparency, which also deals with issues of risk. There are just so many interesting things starting to happen because of the way designers are now able to be much more fluid and playful.

VOLKER MUELLER, NBBJ (from audience): I am curious about the socio-economic context and ecological aspects, as nobody explicitly has addressed that. Do any of you see these types of opportunities? I have disjointed images in my head, such as thousands of FEMA trailers sitting somewhere in empty lots rotting. We have mass customization, and there we have the opposite (in a way). There are plenty of people in this world that do not have a decent roof over their heads. I would like to see and hear something optimistic about all those mass-produced dwellings that are so far away from gothic cathedrals and "delight." People will be delighted if they get good answers to their needs. Does anybody see opportunities like that?

CHRIS SHARPLES: It does tie back to the gothic cathedral. It is basically industrialization that gave us the FEMA trailers, by embracing the standardized approach. (I think Kevin Klinger told me when I was in Indiana in the spring of 2006 that many of those FEMA trailers come from within the state.) The fact is nobody is asking how we can be more creative about that.

VOLKER MUELLER (from audience): If we tie back to the gothic cathedral during those times when they were being built, there were a lot of people living in substandard conditions. I think it is great to bring that back in, because that time was also pretty devoid of such socio-economic awareness, wasn't it?

CHRIS SHARPLES: No, no, no. Again, back to Ruskin: wasn't the gothic embodied in the idea that every human being had the capacity to be creative? You do not need much creative capacity to put one of those trailers together. Where you need the creative capacity is to rethink the idea of the trailer, and how it could be changed and modified to deal with different conditions in a very cost-effective and meaningful way. That is not how the U.S. operates, but there is a really good point: in the way some practices are evolving – in terms of how these tools are being used, and dealing with issues of cost and performance – we will start having people say: "Why can't I rethink the FEMA trailer? Why can't I deliver something in a very short period of time that actually is a piece of architecture?" That is the kind of attitude that we are engaging.

MARTA MALÉ-ALEMANY: I would add to the discussion that the use of cutting-edge digital fabrication equipment does not necessarily lead to an elitist project. In Barcelona, we are working with students on a digital fabrication project, collaborating with a company that recycles leftover plastics and produces a new material called *Syntrewood*. Due to its quite unattractive appearance, this material is mostly used in the production of backseats for chairs that get upholstery. The material is not only ugly, but it smells and breaks easily. In short, it has almost everything negative about it ... but we are using digital fabrication to give it wider chances to succeed, increasing its value through design. In particular, the project explores the use of digital fabrication to de-standardize the repetitive parts produced by the company, and obtain differentiated ones to produce variable assemblies. By means of digital production, these recycled plastic parts could potentially turn into the building components of interesting surface constructions, for interior and landscape design applications.

In a similar fashion, my partner José Pedro Sousa is doing a PhD research using the example of cork, a material that is natural, ecological, and not much used in architecture. He is investigating how digital technologies allow us to rethink the use of traditional materials and bring them back to an interesting point for contemporary architecture, in ways that are economically viable and ecologically responsible.

MARK GOULTHORPE: The question of the destiny of innovation is a complex one. In what is often a struggle to do something extreme that appears capricious and aesthetic, the learning curve goes on. That learning then just naturally evolves new processes and outcomes as a pattern across the sciences, and across the arts. A Minister of Technology in France came to MIT recently. Introducing himself, he just said: "Why innovate? Why do we innovate?" and said, as a politician, it was an easy question to answer: "Quality of life." Longevity of life is constantly increasing in the West, and we have an expectation of it, therefore we have to be more efficient. In France, in particular, the working population is dwindling. The West in general should look outside of the West; the West has to innovate like mad for the other areas of the world, which do not have these institutes and research. It is very clear that the whole world requires this, and I do not think we should make any judgment that the pursuit of a curious use of the digital, or something within a research initiative, should be dismissed in any way as capricious, aesthetic, or something else because there is a learning going on.

FABIO GRAMAZIO: I agree, and would like to add that innovation happens anyway. But innovation alone gives us no guarantee of good architecture or of solving social problems. What we have gives us just a new range of possibilities. When things change very fast, if you are part of the game, then maybe at some moments you can influence things in your direction. Perhaps the two questions, about the guarantee of good architecture, or of a better social condition, are wrong. The real question is whether we, as architects, want to be involved in this innovation or not. Innovation will happen whether we take part in it or not. This is what happened fifteen years ago with Computer Aided Design. CAD was a tragedy for architecture, because it was not developed by architects, with architects, and for architects. We were just using tools that were developed for other industries. Fifteen years ago, only a marginal group of architects were trying the possibilities, while the majority said we would not need CAD. Only some years later were all architects obliged to use CAD for productivity reasons. The majority of the digital tools used in offices have nothing to do with design problems; and that is a nightmare. If we do not engage now with the digital fabrication innovation that is going on, we will miss another major opportunity.

VOLKER MUELLER (from audience): Social responsibility is not mutually exclusive to innovation, right? I do not understand why you say that is the wrong question. Yes, of course, to innovate can be perhaps socially responsible.

FABIO GRAMAZIO: We can do that, of course. That is logical. But it is the wrong question: Why should we innovate, if innovation does not give us the guarantee that things will change in the right direction?

VOLKER MUELLER (from audience): But there are opportunities.

FABIO GRAMAZIO: Yes, they are big. But we have to engage in innovative research; if we do not, the change will happen anyway, and in ten years we will use the tools that contractors will tell us to use, but those will not be the tools architects are interested in or tools that follow our logic.

MARK GOULTHORPE: This is all very complex. The boat builders that we are using for the *Tower Top* project, the Danish family, they have five big CNC machines, and they constantly remind me that these machines are not there for aesthetics, they are there for economy. They have invested in these machines because they make money from it; because they can make boats cheaper than they used to, use fewer people, and use the materials more efficiently. There is a deep-down drive for it; they make most of their money at the moment building windmill blades for wind turbines, which are suddenly socially acceptable as a clean form of energy. He confided to me: "Have you any idea how much energy and polluting materials are used in these blades?" So, the image of social responsibility is actually corrupted at the core, and, yet, who judges the morality of that? That is a very, very complex issue.

JEANNE GANG: Machines are used to save time and labor – that is a fact because we all know that labor is extraordinarily expensive, but there is still labor happening in putting things together. It might not be that repetitive, but it is still there – there is hand labor in everything. Over different periods of time, we have acknowledged it more or less. One of the questions that we should try to address is why the labor is so expensive if there are many people that need work. I do not know the answer to it. In this forum, we seem obsessed with the machines, but I think we have to at the same time consider why labor is expensive.

WILLIAM ZAHNER: We were a very hand-craft-based, custom company thirty years ago. Today, we employ about ten times as many people. As we add more machines, there might be a frightening aspect to some: "They are bringing a robot; you know what – they are going to replace me!" The opposite happens: adding more machines actually increases the amount of work that we do, and the number of people we employ. The relation is almost exponential.

JEANNE GANG: And that is invisible, as we focus on the machines, but there are still many people who are working and putting things together.

WILLIAM ZAHNER: And the wages go up. Perhaps one of the less skilled things is having a robot handing something to somebody. But, the wages do improve.

RUBEN SUARE: I am not sure that I would focus so much on the machines, as I would on what they are really doing for us. The level of collaboration that exists in our company with architectural offices is such that the lines are being blurred of who is responsible for what. That is where innovation exists, and that is what really brings about a position where you begin to ask yourself where academia is today, an issue Phil Bernstein addressed. Is the work that we do at *3form* architecture? Should the architect really be focused in academia in a traditional way? The work that was presented is not the norm. The normal is one in which you work with catalogs. One of the main ideas we have at *3form* is to break that style of working and have a very strong participation from all sources, not only the architect, but the client, the lighting designers, etc. Innovation is a very important question, and it is a very, very difficult thing to do. Many different companies, maybe the majority, fail at innovation. Innovation requires a process where everybody is completely and fully focused. What is intriguing about some of these technologies is that they are bringing about a certain level of craftsmanship back to the field of architecture where all the parties are involved in a very focused manner, emotionally and mentally. You no longer have an architect working alone, doing CAD drawings, and developing construction documents, and then the next party comes in and takes it from there. That is really what is most fascinating about this new technology.

STEVEN RAINVILLE (from audience): Do you feel that rapid prototyping has a place today in the architectural practice? Similar to what Fabio Gramazio mentioned about how CAD has been generated from different professions, I think that rapid prototyping coming from the manufacturing world now has opportunities in architecture.

MATTHIAS KOHLER: In our practice, we decided to minimize the number of renderings that we produce. Having gone through architectural education in the 1990s we have experienced an inflation of rendering of images and imagery in architecture. We chose to abandon these modes of architectural production in order to engage with what we now refer to as *Digital Materiality*. Building models and prototypes, and developing digital projects physically in parallel, this allows us to get subtle perceptions of the spaces and their qualities. It also enables us to test construction logics intuitively, especially as we work with complex geometries.

BRANKO KOLAREVIC: I would be surprised if none of them used rapid prototyping. But, I know Mark Goulthorpe referred in his writing to the dream of a giant rapid prototyping machine that does not give you a model, but the entire thing, at full scale.

MATTHIAS KOHLER: Basically, the robot is a step towards that dream. In our research on additive digital fabrication we are building up material from the ground. The robot undertakes a process similar to a rapid prototyping machine, but on an architectural scale with real construction materials. It is important to understand that material performances cannot be scaled up from rapid prototyping models to buildings. Architects are therefore invited to rethink constructive and structural issues, fabrication processes and architectural expressions of robotic fabrication on a 1:1 scale. Adding material lets us place materials where they are needed without producing any waste. Bringing additive processes closer to digital design technology and fusing them conceptually is therefore a central and challenging opportunity. It seems much more promising than milling out tons of foam …

CHRIS SHARPLES: Modeling is very critical to the project. It comes back to what Matthias Kohler said about rendering, the representational processes being quite useless when you start extracting information into reality. What is really great about having the rapid prototyping equipment – we have two laser cutters, a 3D printer, and also a table saw, jig-saw, and all the other stuff – is that it forces people to begin the process of how to extract information from that virtual reality into the real world; that is the beginning process of how to start thinking about putting things together. Problem solving at this level of complexity is something that has been lacking in the way people have been working. When we used to build models, we tended to build them as representational devices. Now, we actually have to think about how to make that model, and at what scale we are making that model, and how that model references other scales. These tools are critical! They are critical to the design process. They are also going down in price. An office with ten people can actually afford a 3D printer. These devices pay for themselves rather quickly, and are also a good public relations tool when the client comes to the office.

KEVIN KLINGER: I should note that the audience clapped when they saw the robot from ETH. What *is* the relevance of the technological approach in the collective work that was presented? I was discussing with Ben Nicholson during the break the significance of the "T," for Technology, found in MI*T*, E*T*H, II*T*, etc. Obviously, there is something very germane to our conversations about that "T." The "T" enables changing our practices through our processes. But, at the same time, to what end? What is the ethical imperative that we are serving? Frank Barkow has in his office a Charles and Ray Eames molded plywood splint on the wall. The splint design was incredibly innovative, while having nothing to do with digital fabrication processes, but rather innovation through interrogating material and technology. How is that approach analogous to what we are doing today?

JOSÉ PEDRO SOUSA: In previous interventions the relevance of digital fabrication technologies has been widely discussed, but I believe their application in architecture has specific limitations. If we compare architecture with other disciplines, such as product design, we realize that even if we work with similar technologies, our design interests and constraints are often very different. In relation to architecture, rapid prototyping technologies work with reduced production sizes and very limited materials; from a representation viewpoint, they imply quite a scalar distance regarding the final building. Moreover, when producing a rapid prototyping model, one often needs to overcome the limitations of this technology by thickening the thinner elements of a model to avoid it breaking, thus keeping architects far from testing real assemblies or the material resistance of things. However, rapid prototyping can be a valuable tool for architects when dealing with complex geometries; while physical models of more traditional buildings can be built from printed sections and plans, those of buildings dealing with complex forms, like the ones that were discussed, are difficult to make using conventional means. In that field, rapid prototyping technologies can be very helpful to quickly evaluate the building geometric articulation in a model scale, and think of other project strategies. However, when dealing with buildings of innovative design and construction, addressing 1:1 scale details and consideration of final materials is crucial for architects. In that sense, the fabrication of prototypes using CNC equipment allows us to test solutions – beyond geometry – that are much closer to the reality of the final architectural building. At another level, Fabio and Mathias' robot launches yet another step in orienting technology towards the reality and specificity of architecture by building with real materials and at 1:1 scale. Finally, I will point out that recent developments in the realm of Rapid Manufacturing can be very promising for architects because – despite the small scale of their production – they work with final building materials like metals, and thus may permit addressing real construction solutions with RP parts.

MARK GOULTHORPE: Referring to the Danish company we are working with, of the five CNC machines they have, one they are experimenting with is the use of paste in additive fashion. It is a sticky resin, and they are working with chemical companies to develop a suitable material, because they think it is going to be cheaper than milling foam. This is sort of cost driven, but also because of these crazy aesthetic architecture projects out there that demand it.

BRANKO KOLAREVIC: We will bring this discussion to a close on this note of crazy architectural projects that demand innovation.

14

DIFFERENT DIFFERENCES

DONALD BATES / LAB ARCHITECTURE STUDIO

14.2.
Thin rock section.

14.3.
Portrait by Alberto Giacometti.

Within the context of limited formal differences, the commercial office tower offers a restricted set of design parameters, wherein the exploitation of the elevational and surface effects presents the greatest opportunity to create a different kind of difference. This implies more than a "wrapping up in a new skin" approach to distinction and image. While there is no doubt that this approach involves "image," it proposes a process whereby "image" contributes to the spatial and experiential engagement where surface is not superficial, but rather uncertain in its depth of influence and involvement. The experiential linkage of proximity to distance can also be manipulated to offer an expanded domain of form-into-surface.

These directions are the consequence of investigations and advances made in the development of the *Federation Square* project in Melbourne, Australia (2002). As a cultural and civic institution, *Federation Square* is the opposite of a commercial tower – specific versus generic, formally expansive versus constrained, multi-faceted versus singular, an assemblage versus a discrete entity. And yet, the pursuit of an "interoperability" of surface-to-form underwrites many of our projects, and was central to the design and development of *Federation Square*.

LAB Architecture Studio emerged from the circumstance of Peter Davidson and I, after having known each other through teaching at the Architectural Association in the early 1980s, deciding in 1994 to start working together. We began by doing 15–20 competitions in the next two or three years. One of these was the open international design competition for the *Federation Square* project, a project in the center of Melbourne, Australia. The project is located at the south-eastern quadrant of the principal intersection in the city (figure 14.1), with the main road that goes south and north through the central business district (CBD). The main train station, Flinders Street Station, is to the west and the historic building of *Young and Jackson's* and the *St Paul's Cathedral* to the north. The project is a heterogeneous mix of art galleries and multimedia spaces, a large public space, commercial activities, restaurants, cafés, and shops, all of it built above the railway lines that are located 8 m below street level. The project was a way of completing this significant intersection, which from the very beginning of Melbourne – and certainly with the introduction of the railways – somehow remained incomplete in its south-western corner. In 1996, the Government of Victoria and the City of Melbourne decided to launch a two-stage competition for this unfulfilled site, and we were fortunate enough to win the project.

We re-examined much of our previous research while working on this project. This approach informed our work methods, re-formulating the issues we thought were relevant to the competition. For instance, we had collected images of thin rock sections, i.e. thin slices through different types of rocks (figure 14.2). These images encouraged us to consider a different kind of organizational strategy, what we might call a "matrix order." We were also inspired by drawings and paintings by Alberto Giacometti (figure 14.3). We wondered what the "architecturalization" of this kind of condition could be, where there is a clear recognition of an image, but

14.5.
The *Federation Square* site plan.

14.6. (bottom)
Federation Square: view from south-west.

14.4.
One of the conceptual drawings developed during the *Federation Square* competition.

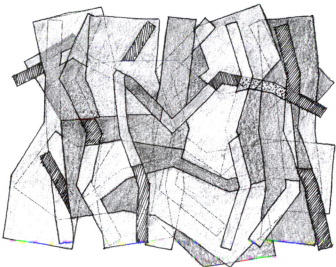

not a single line defining that image – unlike most instances of architectural production where a single line differentiates and makes differences. Giacometti uses a multiplicity of lines, so that there is no singular line that makes the chin, nose, or ear. Nonetheless, there is a clear reading of the face. The question was what it would mean architecturally to produce an indeterminacy of delineation and still have a clear reading of a space, event, or function. From this inquiry, we produced a number of drawings (figure 14.4), working by hand, with some use of *Adobe Illustrator*. The preliminary sketches were another way of envisioning how different ordering and organizational formulations would emerge.

The project privileges an ordering on the site that is quite different from the orthogonal grid structure of the central building district (CBD) in Melbourne. Our analysis revealed a zone of difference south of Flinders Street (the main east–west street before the railways) to the Yarra River – one where this residual zone does not follow the geometric structure of the city grid (figure 14.5). This distinct domain had a different form of organizational structure, which left it open to the new ordering we would develop for the project.

As an overview, *Federation Square* (figures 14.6 and 14.7) involved the design and creation of a large public gathering space, since there was no space in Melbourne where political events, concerts, or celebrations could convene. The building opened officially in November 2002, and in February 2003 the first significant public event happened – the first world-wide anti-war protests against the US invasion of Iraq took place in Melbourne and then spread around the world (figure 14.8). Some 40,000 people descended on the site. It was amazing to see what happens to the complex when so many people converge on a site: the architecture was submerged – overwhelmed even – in

161

14.7.
Federation Square:
view along Flinders
Street.

14.8. (below)
Anti-war protest at
Federation Square.

a sea of people. The aim of the project was the production of contemporary public spaces and outdoor venues capable of sustaining large events, supported by a large video screen on the plaza side of the *Transport Building*. *Federation Square* is now the primary social and public gathering place in Melbourne, and the principal site for the main cultural festivals – the arts festival, the film festival, etc. It is also a major focus for New Year's Eve celebrations and most sporting celebrations (figure 14.9).

Many programmed (and unprogrammed) spaces exist within the *Federation Square* precinct. The *National Gallery of Victoria – Australian Art (NGV_A)*, an art gallery (figures 14.10 and 14.11) and one of the main programmatic components of the project, features "*intra-filament*" spaces that act as the connections or linkages between different gallery spaces on the north and south (figure 14.12). Another institution within Federation Square, the *Australian Centre for the Moving Image (ACMI)* (figure 14.13), includes

14.9.
New Year's Eve
celebrations at
Federation Square.

162

14.10.
Federation Square:
the foyer and the lobby
area of the *National
Gallery of Victoria*.

14.11.
Federation Square:
contemporary gallery
of the *National Gallery
of Victoria*.

14.12. (below)
Federation Square: the
north "intra-filament"
space in the *National
Gallery of Victoria*.

14.13.
Federation Square: the
central arcade of the
*Australian Centre for
the Moving Image*.

cinemas, multimedia galleries, exhibition spaces, electronic workshops and classrooms, and administrative offices. Within the same building (actually two buildings joined by a central arcade) is the Melbourne center for the national broadcaster *Special Broadcasting Service (SBS)*, the national multi-cultural broadcaster for television and radio. *SBS* houses its Melbourne broadcasting and administration offices at *Federation Square*.

One of the major issues in designing the project – a theme that came up both in the overall planning, but also more specifically related to the façades – was the idea of "coherence and difference." Because *Federation Square* is a large complex, involving a number of different institutions and functions, there was a question of maintaining on one hand a certain kind of coherence in this large site (220 m x 110 m, almost 3.6 hectares), and on the other hand, registering the differences within the ensemble. Allowing a discernible registration of these differences, and at the same time providing coherence to the overall planning, was important both across the whole site and in any individual component. Working through that question, and thinking about the consequences, it became very important to consider how this notion of coherence *and* difference might develop relative to the façades. At the same time, it was also a critique of modernist tendencies, not just as a style, but in terms of production techniques, curtain walls, and prefabrication. We knew that the façades could not be handcrafted within the timeframe of the construction schedule. They had to be prefabricated and produced industrially. The disquiet was

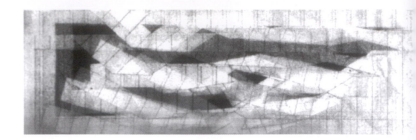

14.14.
Federation Square:
façade concept
drawing.

14.15.
M.C. Escher's
woodblock print:
Swans into Fish.

also about the ways in which modern façades tend to be about repetition. They often result in a lack of difference between the north side and the south side. Environmentally, there is no differentiation; visually, there is very little differentiation. The module of a rectangular, repeating grid starts to impose a logic that is almost always ever-present. We determined organizational strategies for the façades, within the context of a different organizational structure for the overall planning.

We were very fortunate at that time to be surrounded by an amazing concentration of the design and engineering talent in London. Our office was located not too far from the *Architectural Association*, off Goodge Street. Right across the street from our office was one of the great engineering offices in London, *Atelier One.* Down the street was a great environmental engineering services group at *Atelier Ten* (the two firms had previously been associated). For all of the globalization of engineering services, this part of London, *Fitzrovia*, is curious, since within two blocks there is a phenomenal concentration of inventive engineering: *ARUP, Buro Happold,* and *Whitby Bird* are all in the area.

We had worked on 15–20 competitions with *Atelier Ten* and *Atelier One*, and were quite comfortable augmenting our design process through consultation with these engineering firms. At the very beginning of the *Federation Square* design process, we showed a number of fairly abstract drawings to the engineers and asked a series of questions. For example, we asked what a sketch would mean as a façade (figure 14.14), or how we could achieve a façade that is an interpretive condition of the drawings. We wanted to know whether we could interpret certain areas as a degree of transparency or translucency, or solid or not solid. All the questions revolved around devising an innovative way in which the façade could be organized in a profoundly different way than current curtain wall technology. We knew the façade still had to be mechanically produced, pre-fabricated, and erected onto the building.

This interest in enunciating differences in the façade was simultaneous with a desire to blur the demarcation line while it moved and shifted. *M.C. Escher*'s woodblock print of "*Swans into Fish*" (figure 14.15) was a useful inspiration. The fascination was in shifting from one object (or materiality) to another without revealing a clear moment where that transition occurs. In Escher's woodblock, there is no line that separates fish and swans. The shift from one to the other clearly happens, but it does not happen on a line, at a certifiable moment. We wondered how that strategy of blurring might translate into the façade for *Federation Square.* The differentiation between sandstone, zinc, perforated zinc, and glass was not clearly demarcated by an overriding logic, but emerged in a different way. Having worked through many options and abortive directions, and looking at different technologies to think this through, we came across a *triangular tiling system* by Joseph Conway, a mathematician from Princeton, known as the *Conway Pinwheel Grid.* One of the multiple benefits of deploying this tiling system is its *aperiodic* character, meaning that it constantly shifts. The singular triangles are identical, and follow a very simple logic of orientation, placement, and repetition. But, because it is a triangular grid as opposed to a rectangular or quadrilateral grid, alignments are visually more complex. Different figurations were selected within this triangularly gridded array. "*Figurations*" were made by following the lines of the triangular grid, with multiple possibilities across any one section of the surface (figures 14.16a–b). The system was interrogated to create an array of different figural effects on the surface, and to register differences between materials. The grid did not possess an overtly apparent logic – most importantly, it was not a confining logic.

The organizational system for the façade is quite elegant and simple (figure 14.17), as the basic element is a triangle. Together, five triangles make a larger, self-similar triangle. In the system, the singular triangle becomes a "tile." Five "tiles" form a "panel." The "panel" joins four more panels to form a larger "mega-panel." The system operates either from the smallest to the largest component, or from a large element to subdivisions. The same organizational logic was used to define the façades geometrically, materially, and

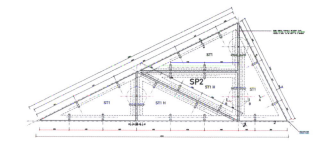

14.16a–b.
Federation Square:
triangular pin-wheel
grid with different
"figurations."

14.17.
Federation Square: the
fractal grid that operates
the same way across
different scales.

14.18.
Federation Square:
working drawing
for a "panel."

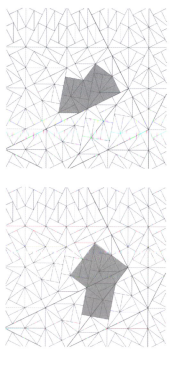

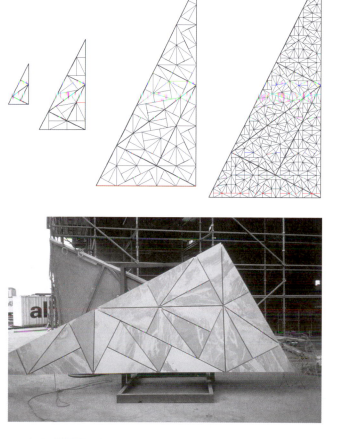

14.19.
Federation Square:
mega-panels ready
for erection.

14.20.
Federation Square:
façade segment.

tectonically: five "tiles" of a singular material (sandstone, zinc, perforated zinc, or glass) came together on an aluminum frame to form a "panel" (figure 14.18); five "panels" were fixed onto a steel frame as a "mega-panel," and then erected onto the building (figure 14.19).

Up to the placement of the "mega-panels," the work was done entirely in the factory. The arrangement of the individual triangles – particularly the sandstone tiles with their variegated coloration – was left up to the workers on the factory floor; there were no drawings that privileged arrangements of one piece of stone to the next. The logic of the system helped organize the material decisions. Each "panel," which is made up of five triangular "tile" pieces, is always in the same material. But the "mega-panel" can be composed of any grouping of the different panels with distinct materiality (figure 14.20).

Although we started working on the system of the façades immediately after winning the competition, it took nearly two and a half years to develop them fully for construction and fabrication. Before and after the project had gone out to tender, when we had a contractor on board, we were still looking at different possibilities of the system's figurations, compositions, and overall arrangement.

Peter Davidson and I each assumed responsibility for different buildings within the project. Peter was responsible for the *National Gallery of Victoria – Australian Art (NGV_A)*. I was responsible for the *Australian Centre for the Moving Image (ACMI)*. The way in which the figuration in the façade became evident depended on the differences in the way the two partners' eyes would work. Some of the differences were intentional in fixing particularities between certain surfaces – having more zinc or less zinc, more sandstone or less sandstone – but many differences resulted from each partner selecting a different logic of figuration within the overall triangular grid (figure 14.21).

One of the developments within the façade system was the accommodation of office functions, where the occupants needed a view to the outside. To provide that within the same system, we added a fourth element: *absence*. We anticipated gaps within the façade that allowed openings or framed views. One intention was to counter the typical stratification within a façade, where floor levels and floor slabs are

165

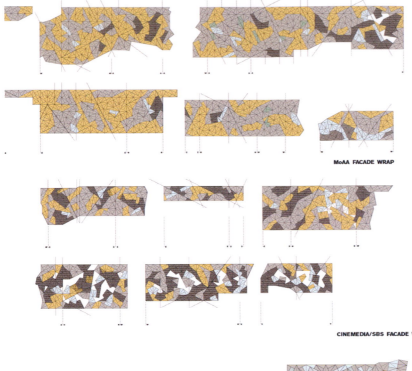

MoAA FACADE WRAP

CINEMEDIA/SBS FACADE WRAP

YARRA BUILDING FACADE WRAP

14.21.
Federation Square:
unfolded façades.

enunciated, by using figuration to deny that articulation of layers. That was more complicated vis-à-vis office building needs (figure 14.22). Thus, in a puzzle-like fashion, openings were made at desk height or head height, by not having the resulting openings read as a band that went across the building.

Given the variety of input considerations, we ended up with a collection of façades with significant differentiation. Within the overall tiling, figuration, and material shift, in a variety of places perforated zinc was used because of the air-handling units placed behind that required ventilation. The perforated zinc offered another layer of depth to the surface, and also acted as a primary screening device for the offices. The difference between the thickness of the sandstone and the thickness of the frame necessary for the zinc enabled shadow lines. That small amount of difference created secondary figurations and groupings.

In sections, the surface is solid due to functional considerations of the gallery and exhibition spaces behind the façades. A secondary grillage in the office section supports

14.22.
View of *Federation Square* along Flinders Street.

14.23.
Federation Square:
SBS offices, view to
outside.

14.24.
Federation Square:
entry to the *Australian
Centre for the Moving
Image (ACMI)*.

14.25.
*Federation
Square*: folding
the façade.

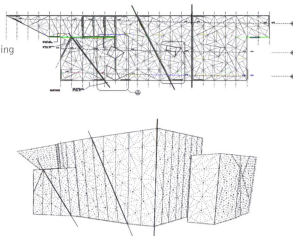

14.26.
*Federation
Square*: NGV-A
south façade.

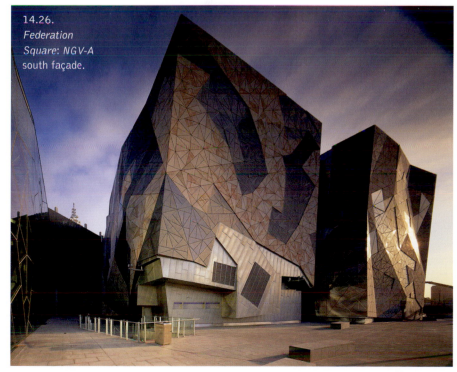

the façade elements, allowing views to the outside (figure 14.23). The façade differences between the cinemas and the offices are registered by having openings and more glazing within the system, with light coming through (figure 14.24). Where the façade faces north towards the sun, it acts as a shading device, with significantly more perforated zinc and translucent glass. Where the façade covers the gallery spaces, the panels are more opaque and solid, since the gallery could not allow natural light in the exhibition spaces.

Within the geometry of the system, alignments of the edges of the panels become fold lines in the façade (figure 14.25). There is no vertical extrusion of the façades. Rather, they fold and bend back and forth. That folding condition was useful, partly because we could not imagine the form and mass of the buildings solely as an extruded envelope. Additionally, the folding accommodates the mechanical air-handling units and ductwork between the façade and the inside of the galleries. We were also able to push and pull the façades in and out relatively easily to accommodate late changes, such as the need for the mechanical equipment to be larger. On one side of the building, a stair runs from the upper level of the galleries down to the main lobby area and pushes the façade out to bulge at that point, allowing the staircase to exist within the fold. The façade facing the river changes quite dramatically over time. At different times of the day, the sun strikes it directly and it looks reasonably flat, but as the sun moves round (figure 14.26), the folding and weaving in and out across its surface become more apparent.

In the office building, the façade acts as a screening and shading device. Looking out, one gazes through the façade – through perforated zinc, translucent glass, or through the openings themselves, with the orthogonal grid of the curtain wall glazing being layered over to contribute to the overall composition.

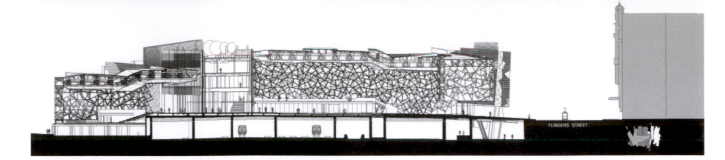

14.28.
Federation Square:
section through the
Atrium.

14.27.
Federation Square:
the "Atrium".

Another significant component of the precinct is known as the "*Atrium*." It is a large, enclosed public space, operating in conjunction with the large, open external space of the plaza. In winter, Melbourne can be quite rainy, windy, and a bit cold, so a second public space, protected from the elements, was desirable. We treated this indoor space as an extension of Russell Street, and as a 24-hour open public space – it had no front door. It had to be less like a contained mall, and more like a large open atrium, such as the *Galleria* in Milan (figure 14.27).

The *Atrium* space starts at Flinders Street (the main east–west street defining the southern edge of the city grid), and continues to the river, above the working railway lines. It is quite a large volume, with a 16-m-high space, that is 18 m across, and extends almost 125 m, coming down to make a transition to the riverside at the southern end (figure 14.28). The *Atrium* is a main entry point to *Federation Square* from Flinders Street, while the southern end houses an amphitheater and performance venue.

For the *Atrium* structure, the triangular grid was deployed three-dimensionally. The *Atrium* grid began as two

14.29a–c.
Federation Square:
fragment and the
overall model of the
three-dimensional
triangular structural
grid.

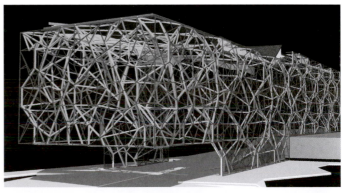

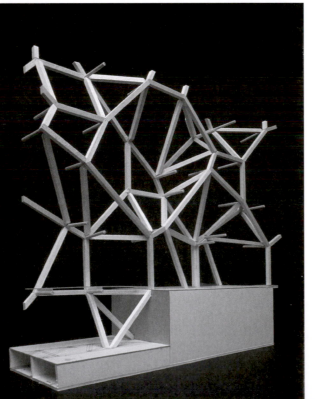

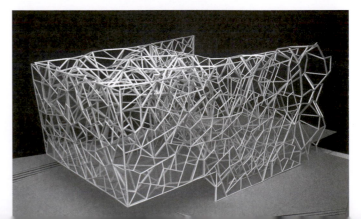

168

14.30.
Federation Square:
primary framing.

14.31.
Federation Square:
structural frame
joint.

14.32.
Federation Square:
Atrium entry.

14.33.
*Federation Square,
North Atrium:*
overlapping framing
and shadow play.

complete regular triangular grid surfaces, separated, and connected by horizontal struts. This configuration was developed into a more integrated structural web, working as an apparently irregular space frame, but based on the aperiodic structure of the *Conway Pinwheel Grid*. Within this three-dimensional framing, redundant structural members were eliminated – elements that were not carrying significant loads. The framing started to either evolve or devolve into another kind of system – still based on the triangular grid – but working three-dimensionally from one side of the structural frame to the other (figures 14.29a–c). There is an outside line of support with the framing, and the forces travel across to the inside line of support. There is a depth to the structural wall in order to create a portal frame, but the support members are not equally dispersed throughout, so the concavities exist.

The primary structural frame is made of 200 x 200 mm galvanized steel sections (figure 14.30). On both sides of the structural wall is a glazing system for the glass. The panelization of the glass follows the triangular grid, so the different shapes are all sub-divided into a set of triangles. Remarkably, given all of the apparent irregularity and the aperiodic nature of the system, there are only nine different panes of glass. The system, created from standardized elements, produces a non-standard arrangement of glazed panels.

The connections and joints were fairly complicated from a fabrication point of view. Three different structural sections come together in one plane, with two more – each in a different plane and at an angle – welded to form an integral joint (figure 14.31). Yet, for all this complexity, the types of joints were limited, all connecting standardized lengths of structural framing.

The entrance area is a 13-m cantilever without a front door, i.e. remaining open 24 hours a day, 7 days a week (figure 14.32). Within the space of the *Atrium* itself, a spider's web of primary structural framing and secondary glass framing is the dominant feature. The aluminum framing creates a more filigree texture, while the primary structure becomes partially self-shading, creating an environmental control as the sun moves round (figure 14.33).

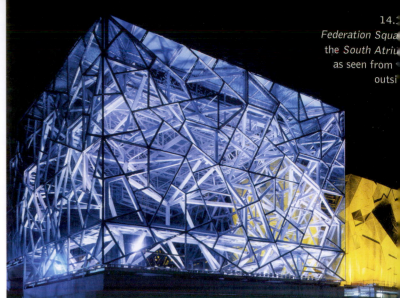

14.34.
*Federation Square:
South Atrium.*

14.36.
The tram ticket
in Melbourne.

14.37.
LABsolute.

The *Atrium* is a large, public space where numerous events take place. Since the space transitions down to the riverside over its length, we imagined the *South Atrium* as an informal meeting or resting place, with background music or lunchtime jazz. However, the acoustic engineers looked at the volume and suggested that if the glass surfaces were to follow the concavities of the primary framing, then the space could be tuned acoustically (figure 14.34). Deviating from the competition brief, as this space had not been prescribed, we considered a possible music venue. Since the space could be reasonably tuned to support chamber orchestra music – with a high quality sound – the *South Atrium* (or *BMW-Edge*) has become one of the major venues for music in Melbourne. Thus, we ended up developing a unique venue to enjoy an event, with visually compelling material effects, an excellent acoustical performance, and views to the river and the parklands beyond.

Just as importantly, for a space that was not part of the original brief, the *BMW-Edge* acts as a significant public venue for lectures, debates, and town-hall discussions. Given it exists as a direct extension of the open and public space of the *Atrium*, it offers a unique site for civic and cultural exchange. Unlike most public venues, the *BMW-Edge* is not secluded or behind-closed-doors, but readily accessible in both a physical and social sense (figure 14.35).

Finally, the *Federation Square* project illustrates a different kind of material effect – the effect of the project serving as the center point for the city, both geographically and through iconography. The façades and their unique qualities are used in many promotions of the city. Tickets for the tram and the train systems use representations of the surfaces, with the Pinwheel grid symbolizing the city image (figure 14.36). Celebrities have their pictures taken in front of the project. Even *Absolut Vodka* produced a big ad featuring the building skin wrapping a vodka bottle on a signboard near *Federation Square*, for which we produced our own version (figure 14.37).

BEYOND FEDERATION SQUARE

After having completed this major cultural project in Melbourne, we have yet to find more work in Australia. *Federation Square* was the first project we had built. We expected that, after completing an art gallery, multimedia, commercial, and public spaces, we would be eligible for a range of new projects, but nothing happened for the next two years. We found, however, opportunities in other countries. The first project following *Federation Square* was the *SOHO Shangdu* project in Beijing. We were invited to enter a competition for a high-rise residential tower, a second high-rise office tower, and a 5-storey L-shaped commercial and retail podium (figure 14.38).

The project provided an opportunity to examine the typology of the tower. At the very basic level, there is very little room for innovation in high-rise tower construction. Strategies outlined at the beginning of this chapter, where surface attention can offer an expanded domain of form-into-surface, were also deployed in this project. Surface and elevational techniques were incorporated to alter the sense of how the tower is imagined – and for that matter, how it operates as a speculative real estate development – across a very small band of space from column grid to external surface. Due to the limited budgets for these kinds of projects in China, the design essentially happens

14.38.
SOHO Shangdu,
Beijing, China
(2007).

14.39.
SOHO Shangdu:
floor plans
stacked.

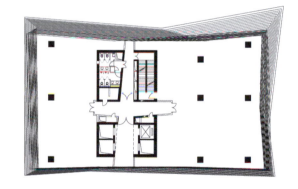

14.40.
SOHO Shangdu:
night-time
rendering.

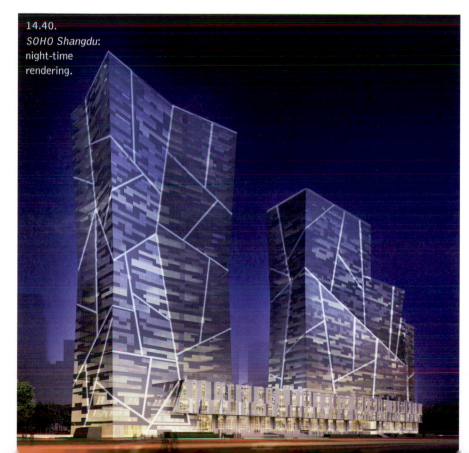

in the cantilever. The project is about having a simple core, a straightforward set of columns and supports, and a significant amount of formal and spatial play that happens in the shifting of the cantilever (figure 14.39).

From the socio-economic point of view in China, the cost of the apartments is defined almost to the square millimeter. With our strategy for developing the project, we achieved an almost infinite array of slightly different floor plans. The plans are all basically the same in configuration, but their GFAs – Gross Floor Areas (or sellable areas) – are different. No two apartments have exactly the same amount of sellable area, which offered a great number of options to potential buyers and affected the kinds of loans they could obtain. For instance, if someone cannot afford a 79 sq m apartment, there is another one that is 76 sq m somewhere in the building. In a construction environment where variation at the level of the plan (such as the framing of the concrete slabs) can be managed by the availability of many hands, this supports a degree of variation for the benefit of greater variety of sellable product. There is a play between upper-level apartments, which have higher rates because of the views, and the lower-level apartments. We looked at how the upper levels might be larger and more expansive, and therefore the towers are tapered in the "waist" area, before again expanding at the lower levels.

The façades have a series of "*ice-ray*" patterns, breaking up the massing and acting as fairly graphic lines of light (figure 14.40). The actual curtain wall is a combination of glazed panels, operable windows, solid metal panels, and perforated panels over AC units, modulated by a reaction against the repetition of elements (figure 14.41). This project was recently completed and opened in August 2007.

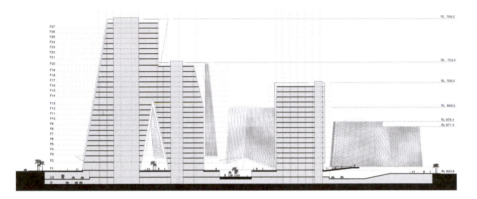

14.42. (top left)
Riyadh Business Centre Complex, Riyadh, Saudi Arabia (project realization uncertain).

14.43. (above)
Section through the *Riyadh Business Centre Complex*.

14.44. (top right)
Omniyat Tower project at *Business Bay*, Dubai, the United Arab Emirates (project – not to be realized).

The *Riyadh Business Centre Complex*, won as a competition in 2006, uses the façade as a screening device. A perforated aluminum skin acts as a shading mechanism, dealing with the major impact of solar gain in Riyadh. This perforated skin envelopes the curtain wall. The project is a collection of six towers, each slightly beveled and shaped; they are tilting, and two of the larger buildings are actually leaning against each other (figure 14.42). There is a secondary framing grillage structure outside the curtain-walled tower, and a mesh veil that fits over the top of each beveled tower.

Again, as in the project in China, the design strategy involves keeping the cores and the structural columns vertical, but having the building and the overall massing tilted to different degrees. Two of the towers lean to the point that they support each other (figure 14.43). Other towers lean much less as a result of examining efficiencies; they are quite tall and the cores with excessive tilting would not remain within the building volume. Shorter towers can lean more.

The latest projects are in Dubai, in the United Arab Emirates. The *Omniyat Tower* project at *Business Bay* is a fairly simple 23-storey building. Again, we resisted designing a box that has been extruded upwards. The project investigates the offset – the shifting planar surfaces operating across different floor levels – by trying to break up the mass. The design strategy keeps a vertical core, with vertical columns, for a simple construction methodology, while breaking up the massing of the form (figure 14.44).

In *The Quartz Tower*, also at *Business Bay* in Dubai, the formal exploration aims at non-recurring building elevations, so that there is no repetition between the sides. The façade system is the same across all surfaces; each side, however, has a different proportion and massing, with beveled corners, cuts, and shifts. The façades are clad in glass laminated with a dichroic or radiant film (figure 14.45) – the same material that *Ben Van Berkel* used on the *La Défense Building* in Almere, the Netherlands. The film, being made of very thin polyester, changes chromatically as one moves around it, or as the sun shifts.

The project for the *Jumeirah Village Cultural Center*, also in Dubai, was a competition for a new central space, as part of a new commercial and residential development. Beyond the formal development of the torqued form (the "Snake in the Lake"), we looked at possible patterns resulting from Islamic geometries, and pattern systems that derive from negotiating the twisted geometries (figure 14.46). The building has two main programmed areas: a children's museum and a performance venue. The project is situated in the middle of the central lake, so that the lake is above as well as underneath the building. The two sides are connected where parking and the main foyer form an interface underneath the water, and this serves as the main entry sequence leading into either the performance venue or the museum.

The most recent project in Dubai is the *Museum of the Creek – Culture Village*, situated on an artificial, constructed island (figures 14.47a–b). The project has museums and exhibition spaces, an amphitheater, the Islamic Institute, various other public spaces and external gardens, and creek-side promenade. The project investigates the possible pattern and surface modulation across interlacing forms. These woven filaments shift orientation across the site and within the internal organizational and exhibition structure.

14.45.
The Quartz Tower, Dubai, United Arab Emirates (expected completion in 2010).

14.47a–b.
Culture Village, Dubai, United Arab Emirates (expected completion in 2012).

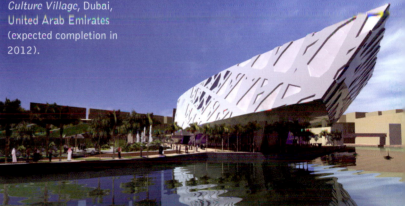

14.46.
Jumeirah Village Cultural Center, Dubai, the United Arab Emirates (competition decision not yet announced).

CONCLUSION

As the work of *LAB Architecture Studio* has changed from cultural/institutional projects to more commercially determined office and residential towers, we have faced the limited arena of formal and organizational manipulations inherent in such projects. *LAB* has sought to maintain an investigative approach to its work, looking closely at the legacies of repetition, standardization, and the tower as a geometrically pure object. Research into façade systems and various types of surface effects has been complemented by challenging the limits of regular column and slab framing.

The attempt in many of these cases has been to develop a different use of how surface and material effects can shift the perception and recognition of form and shape. This has not been an attempt to produce pictorial effects, but rather effects that alter the reading and comprehension of the logic of a form. Still using industrially produced components and modular elements, our focus has been on the production of non-repeating experiences, or apprehensions, where a logic and comprehension are constructed through a process of multiple encounters and engagements with the buildings. The main challenges that underwrite our recent projects lie in seeing each surface, each face, and each side of a building as having a certain generative autonomy, as a response to different environmental, functional, and/or contextual inputs – while addressing the commercial exigencies of a speculative tower.

15
OPPORTUNITIES OF HYBRID OPERATIONS

DAVID J. LEWIS / LEWIS.TSURUMAKI.LEWIS

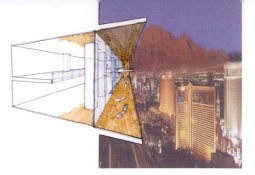

15.2.
Vegas 888, Las Vegas (2006): transformation of the building's curtain wall.

15.3.
Vegas 888: a photorealistic rendering created by *dbox*.

In the discourse surrounding the intersection of digital technology and architectural practice, there has been a profound and welcome shift in the past twenty years from image construction to material production. This change has been mapped and chronicled in a few publications, often accompanied by a near-utopian promise of the immanent reclamation of the role of the master builder to the discipline of architecture, thus short-circuiting the current gap between design and production embedded in conventional practice. There is little question that this shift is a welcome change, and one that has profound implications for the culture of architecture.

As a supplement to this expanding and rapidly evolving discourse, I would like to offer a few overlapping observations concerning the intersection of digital technology and material production. Despite the emphasis upon cultural shifts and epistemological upheavals, there is paradoxically a relentless, yet consistent assumption of technological determinism — where quality of work is defined by the purity and newness of the process. For architectural practices that pursue such work, value is attributed to a project based on the autonomy of its digital form generation, especially to the extent that it is seen to be removed from historical influences and traditional methods of drawing and design. This is in obvious contrast to firms and practitioners who decry the influence of digital technology as detrimental to human knowledge and lament the intrusion of interface screens and mediating devices.

SEEKING OPPORTUNISTIC OVERLAPS

In the work of our firm, *Lewis.Tsurumaki.Lewis*, we directly question the supposed split between digital and traditional means of representation and their translation into and through material conditions. Rather, we seek to find opportunistic overlaps and cross-wirings that exist in the contested middle ground. Recognizing the simultaneous potential and limitation of both sides, we strive to create truly complex architectural representation and built projects, work that learns from both sides, borrows selectively, and pays little heed to zealots on either side. This requires inventing drawing, representational, and production tactics that short-circuit traditional protocols and expected patterns of work embedded in programming constraints. It calls for a rapid and agile exchange between delineation and immersion, between constructing drawings and executing production, and between hand and digital means of working in order to circumvent expected frames of thinking.

In the case of representational drawings, we build these through a method that relies equally on complex modeling software and 4H lead pencils on *Mylar*, tactically using aspects of each.[1] The speed and fluidity of one method of design are augmented and counterbalanced by the slowness and accuracy of the other. Complex shapes, forms and spaces can quickly be studied and tested through an iterative sequence enabled by modeling software, while overdrawing renderings allows a layered approach, constructing the work through attention to detail, scale and delineation. Contrary to popular assumption, we often find that digital technology is not always as fast or as efficient, and traditional forms are not inherently meaningful or immediate. Working in this way requires a much more selective and conscious approach to work than the binary of the digital/traditional would presume, and gives an exceptional range of possibilities and variations that exceed conventions and codes built into the programming structures of one or another software, or the rules of *prismacolor*. As such, standard and often over-determining linear processes are avoided, with the approach to each project tailored to specific constraints in play.

Our work on the project *Vegas 888* in Las Vegas (2006) exemplifies the opportunities of this method of work at the level of representation, especially given that the value of the project was coincident with its value as image. At the suggestion of the marketing company, *dbox*, we were hired by the client mid-way through the design development phase to re-examine the façade, design a large spa on the 38th and 39th floors, and revise selected public areas. Effectively limited to the transformation and thickening of the building's curtain wall – appropriately doing a skin job in Las Vegas – and given a very tight deadline, required us to work quickly at first through line work and hand sketches to tease out options and alternatives (figure 15.1). As the project developed, initial studies were fleshed out through hybrid representations, with digitally generated color studies serving as a critical means of work (figure 15.2). Ultimately, our final drawings, constructed through overdrawing economical digital models were the necessary vehicle for translating design ideas to *dbox*, who executed the necessary photorealistic renderings for the marketing and branding campaign of this luxury 50-storey condominium in the desert (figure 15.3).

This ecumenical approach to building representation using hybrid processes is not limited to images alone, but is carried over into the construction processes of our projects, where the layering of methods translates into a more expansive and engaged role of the architect than is typically assumed. For reasons of efficiency and control, we have often peeled off select aspects or layers of construction and executed them directly as independent installations to an overall contract. The ceiling for the *Tides* restaurant in New York (2005) is a case in point of this "peeling" (figure 15.4). The ceiling was made of 110,000 bamboo skewers – identical to the ones used in the kitchen. Each skewer was individually dipped in glue and carefully placed in the translucent thick foam with the depth, orientation, and tilt all calibrated to

15.4.
Tides restaurant in New York (2005).

15.5a–c.
Tides: the ceiling was constructed from 110,000 bamboo skewers.

form a continuous pattern across the ceiling resembling tidal flows and eddies (figures 15.5a–c). While initial patterns for the flows were generated through modeling software, the final pattern was checked and modified in the process of construction to adhere to optical and cultural expectations of what a marsh should look like, paradoxically meaning that computationally accurate fluid dynamic software had to be manually corrected to look more believable as a tidal flow (figure 15.6).

THE PIXEL-ZOOM EFFECTS

Another observation on the intersection of material and digital practices in the service of manufacturing effects revolves around the cultural and architectural implications of proliferating imaging and production software that can efficiently map and render visible *synecdochical relationships*, i.e. pixel-zoom effects. Whether through high-end parametric modeling software, or domesticated image-manipulating software that breaks whole images into visible pixels, the primary impact is the same in exposing and enabling an alteration of the whole through control of constituent parts. These technologies have fundamentally changed our practice in two primary ways. On an obvious level, it has given greater ability to architects to tweak, modify, or alter projects, working not from top-down plans, but from the individual parts up to the whole, thus enabling mass customization of projects or components with speed and economy. On a more subtle and culturally dispersed level, the ubiquity of breaking images into pixels has made such synecdochical processes and their resulting designs more acceptable and comprehensible to clients who are ultimately asked to approve and finance the work. One need only look at the major change that has occurred in the

15.6.
Tides: the tidal flow topography of the ceiling plane.

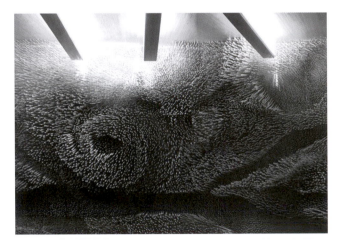

15.7.
Vegas 888: pattern and color studies.

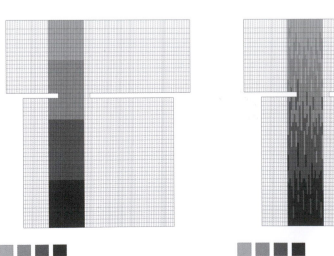

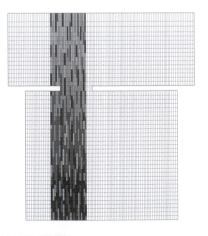

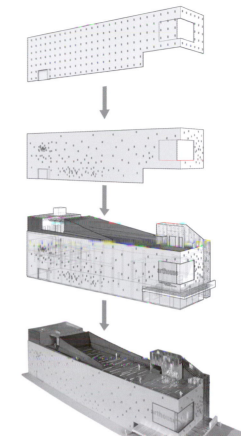

15.9.
Arthouse:
transformation of
the building shell.

developer-driven and risk-averse sector of speculative condominiums over the past five years to witness the change from homogeneous, standardized, and repetitive elevations to complex façades, involving pattern and variation, and the seeming desire to achieve distinction through controlled randomness. Not only would such work be difficult to execute in the absence of recent technologies, but shared reference points permeate Western culture in conceptualizing such designs.

Our experience in working on the redesign of the façades of *Vegas 888* and *Arthouse at the Jones Center* testifies to this change. The initial design for the façade of *Vegas 888* (that we were asked to rework) had deployed a single standardized blue glass for the curtain wall. Using software to quickly test patterns and variations, we were able not only to produce quick studies and images, but also facilitate communication with multiple glass manufacturers in short order (figure 15.7). At *Arthouse*, a museum located in Austin, Texas

(expected to be completed in 2009), we have designed 14,000 sq ft of new program space and transformed the public façade of the existing building (figure 15.8). In order to meet the complex lighting requirements of a contemporary art gallery, and the need for a new public image, we approached the transformation of the existing building's shell through the insertion of 162 laminated glass blocks that penetrate the thick existing walls. The blocks are aggregated on the south and east walls to correspond to interior programs, providing greater density and thus light for the offices and work areas, and reducing light for the galleries and multipurpose rooms (figure 15.9). By working with the distribution of light-emanating blocks rather than the frame, proportion, or size of punched windows, we could effectively take advantage of the light, but not the radiant heat of the intense Texas sun. At night, the programmable LED lights embedded in each block animate the façade, creating a new public surface appropriate for an experimental art venue (figure 15.10).

15.11.
Fluff Bakery in
New York (2004):
creating an illusion
of expansive space.

This ability to work simultaneously on the level of the individual component, while testing the overall effect has been instrumental in the way our firm has approached both the execution and the presentation of projects, especially projects where the greatest impact comes through the orchestration and construction of developed surfaces and materials. We refer to this work as "alchemical assemblages," where repetition and variation of parts create spaces and environments, which operate at divergent optical and haptic levels depending on proximity. Up close, the constituent elements and materials are clearly legible and recognizable for their expected properties, yet from a distance the overall impact shifts the reading of the parts, often to paradoxically opposite readings. In *Tides*, the hard and spiky bamboo skewers form a soft and luxurious surface. When seen from a distance, the individual characteristics are subsumed by the overall assemblage. For the surface-wrapper that forms the interior volume of *Fluff Bakery* in New York (2004), the 18,500 linear ft of ¾" strips of felt shift from a soft absorptive industrial material to a dynamic and crisp linear effect, thus optically blurring the distinction between wall and ceiling to create the illusion of expansive space in a small storefront space (figures 15.11 and 15.12).

15.12. (left)
Fluff Bakery: the
distinctions between
wall and ceiling were
blurred.

15.13. (right)
Fluff Bakery: one
of the full-scale
mock-ups.

15.14.
Fluff Bakery: the pattern is composed of various densities of felt and painted plywood.

15.15.
Lobby wall sculpture for the *Memorial Sloan-Kettering* building design by SOM in New York (anticipated installation in 2009).

Early in the design process, the ability to demonstrate to the client through full-scale, inexpensive print mock-ups was invaluable in testing the impact of changes in the color, pattern, and size of the parts to the overall optical effects of the whole (figure 15.13). Ultimately, the final pattern, composed of distinct mixes of various densities of felt, and colors of painted plywood, was determined to create an overall gradient that moved from darker near the seats where there was greater chance of dirt and wear, to lighter and more luminous at the ceiling (figure 15.14).

PARAMETRIC DESIGN

This use of synecdochical structures of design is not limited in our office to image-based or pixel-based transformation, but operates efficiently in parametrically driven designs, where the computational ability of modeling software is put to best use. Since 2006, we have been involved in the development and fabrication of a new lobby wall sculpture project (figure 15.15) for *Memorial Sloan-Kettering*, within a new building design by *SOM* (*Skidmore Owings & Merrill*) in New York (expected installation in 2009). The design for this art-designated location in the lobby of the new building makes physical a sequence of visual cones drawn through the entry space. Each cone originates in a specific location, mapped according to the areas in plan of greatest traffic and a bell-curve of average eye heights in section (figure 15.16). Each cone is then projected onto the front face of the lobby wall according to a standard grid. The resulting angle and distance of the cone are registered on the front through legible conical distortions (figure 15.17). The back of the wall, however, entirely loses the legibility of the grid, becoming a seemingly random and illogical set of intersecting figures, the visible demonstration of an excess of rationality.

15.16.
Lobby wall sculpture: the design is based on a sequence of visual cones drawn through the entry space.

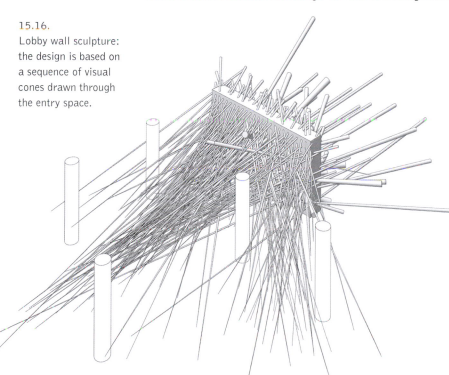

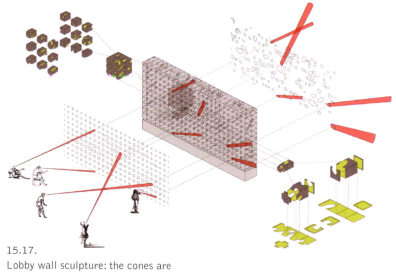

15.17.
Lobby wall sculpture: the cones are registered on a standard grid through legible conical distortions.

15.18.
Lobby wall
sculpture is made
of 480 stainless
steel boxes.

The wall is 3'6" deep, 30' wide, and 12'6" tall, and is made
of 480 individual stainless steel boxes (figure 15.18). The
exterior of the wall is finished to minimize maintenance
and to contrast with an optically intense fluorescent green
interior, a color chosen to reveal the Piranesi-like complexity
of the interior. Each of the 1'3" x 1'3" x 1'9" boxes is
custom-made using unfolded patterns from the digital model
to drive the CNC cutting machine. However, with 275 view-
cones mapped through this thick wall, hitting at the corners
of the first row of boxes and then carving oblique cuts
through the depth of the wall, inevitably parts of certain
boxes are cut free and float independently (figure 15.19).
This has required a constant recalibration of the relationship
between the impact of the optical cones and the coherence of
the boxes – a complex process only enabled through recent
technology, where select parts can be subjected to subtle
independent modification in the production of the whole.

CONCLUSION

From the standpoint of *Lewis.Tsurumaki.Lewis*, it is critical
to approach the manufacture of material conditions through
an open-ended approach to technologies of production and
design, rather than presume a this-will-kill-that deterministic
framework, unfortunately perpetuated by capitalist
economies built on necessary technological obsolescence.
To do so means working opportunistically, and without
preconceived expectations of process. This means being open
to the opportunities presented by technological innovation,
and being innovative about the unitization of technologies
available through the broad spectrum of architectural
discourse: past, present, and future.

NOTE

1 For additional information, see Paul Lewis, Marc Tsurumaki, and
David J. Lewis, *Lewis.Tsurumaki.Lewis: Opportunistic Architecture*,
New York: Princeton Architectural Press, 2008, pp. 176–177.

15.19.
Lobby wall
sculpture: the back
side of the wall
features a distinctly
different pattern
from the front.

16 TRANSLUCENCIES

DAVID ERDMAN

16.1.
Nike Genealogy of Speed, Venice, California (2004).

The title of this book suggests two trajectories. The first trajectory follows developments in manufacturing techniques, from CNC milling to BIM software. This trajectory emphasizes the "how" as a means of increasing efficiency and formal complexity. The second trajectory emphasizes the perceptual aspects of the design work that results from the use of this technology. It shifts the focus from the literal application of techniques onto material to the examination of possible types of experiential effects that may be unique to their use. My design practice, by engaging the various and variegated material effects of translucency, follows this second trajectory. Translucency is a discrete effect that allows different orders of material to mutate, shift, and change over time – resulting in both superficial and spatial conditions that embody differing degrees of mysteriousness (figure 16.1).

While the first trajectory has informed many practices and curricula, it does not answer two critical questions: what is the role of manufacturing technology in design? What distinguishes practices that use the same technology? This book might suggest that effects are the hinge. So let me distinguish what I understand this to be and how it has influenced my work.

TRANSLUCENCY

This work is associated with material effects, which is different from special effects. Many of us are uncomfortable with a discussion that is solely based on the relationship between effect and technology, because one often associates effects with special effects – trickery. *Material effects* and their manufacturing

are much more nuanced and entangled and lie somewhere between *formal effects* and *perceptual effects*. The conceptual shift away from the transparency of material to the transparency of form is central in this respect. It notably distinguishes the quality of a material (glass) as a possible formal characteristic of architecture – which may not even be seen! It is not transparent, but embodies a degree of transparency. As Rowe and Slutzky clearly articulate, this distinction opens the door to issues that move beyond craft and efficiency – beyond what one can see – and place other value systems on architecture.[1] Thus, Gropius' *Bauhaus*, in their opinion, is short-sighted. It makes use of transparency as an optical and literal effect compared to the *formal effects* of transparency in Le Corbusier's *The League of Nations*, which cannot be seen and are driven through a mostly opaque architecture. Noting this as "a transformation of contemporary architecture from the sensual to the intellectual," Jeffrey Kipnis' article "P-TR's Progress" points out that transparency engages a particular model of perception: "It is not seen, but read, it belongs not to the senses but the mind."[2]

Transparency is important in my work, to the extent that the form of architecture is used to produce discrete qualities. However, it also insinuates a degree of legibility, lucidity and understanding. There is an "Aha!" moment in *The League of Nations*, as Rowe and Slutzky so aptly pointed out. Kipnis' article adds a critical dimension to the Rowe and Slutzky notion of transparency describing Peter Eiseman's *Aronoff Center for Design* as embodying "phenomenal translucency, pheromonal translucency and finally pheromonal translunacy."[3] According to Kipnis, at the Aronoff, "formal textuality and process (noted in Eisenman's earlier works) stopped being ends in themselves and became the techniques by which unusual sensibilities were achieved"[4] – a condition Eisenman calls "affect."[5] Formal effect as a result shifts from "a technique of using process to coordinate ensembles of formal effects into increasingly complex texts"[6] to an architecture where the formal effect is so saturated that "the possibility of a correct reading – the sheer number of devices, repeated at several scales made legibility a practical impossibility."[7] However, the article is inconclusive regarding Eisenman's literal use of material, a promise of a direction not yet undertaken, which Kipnis notes may add other types of form and dimension to the work. For me, this missed opportunity is important. It is where both form and matter can be coordinated to produce discrete experiential qualities – where translucency becomes an attribute of mysteriousness.

MYSTERIOUSNESS

Translucency is a subset of mysteriousness. The primary distinction is that mysteriousness adds material into the equation. Mysteriousness places emphasis on its "ness." The formal effects of translucency and the perceptual qualities related to different kinds of matter produce mysteriousness. It layers material orders into a design process, which require a back and forth between full-scale prototyping and intricate formal and geometrical work. If Eisenman's translucency is saturated without material, or still seeking material, mysteriousness ups that ante.

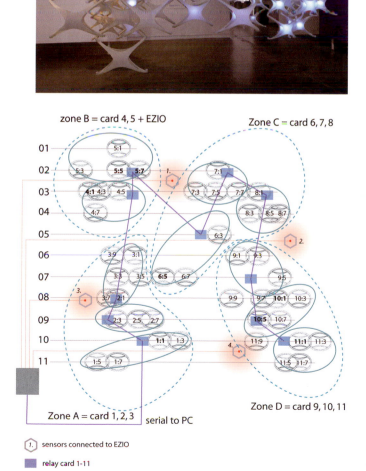

zone B = card 4, 5 + EZIO

Zone C = card 6, 7, 8

Zone A = card 1, 2, 3

serial to PC

Zone D = card 9, 10, 11

1. sensors connected to EZIO

relay card 1-11

PC

circulation

The stakes of the game concerning mysteriousness transcend technological know-how or proprietary knowledge. Malcolm Gladwell, the author of *The Tipping Point*,[8] captured the essence of mysteriousness by drawing a distinction between mysteries and puzzles in an article in *The New Yorker*.[9] Describing a strategic change in the CIA's method of data analysis, Gladwell outlines the fact that historical techniques for information gathering (based upon puzzle logics) are inadequate and that a number of new models are being explored to counter terrorism – the most promising of which analyzes information as mysteries. Gladwell notes: "Puzzles withhold information and are transmitter dependent. As more information becomes available, they become more simple."[10] They require "the application of energy and persistence,"[11] which he regards as "the virtues of youth."[12] One could infer from this that puzzles are about the difficulty of encryption and the complexity of decoding. Mysteries, on the other hand, "require judgments and the assessment of uncertainty. It's not that we have too little information, but in fact that we have too much."[13] Mysteries are "murkier," they are "receiver dependent," they "turn on the skills of the listener," and they "demand experiencing and insight."[14] What is of importance in relation to these works is that mysteries engage the viewer, they draw one in and one may never find the answers. Their seduction lies in their endlessness, vagueness, and degrees of continuous motion.

TRANSLUCENCY OF MATERIAL ORDERS

Mysteriousness defines how technologies are engaged and deployed. While technology is often used to solve specific problems or to increase efficiency, the desire for mysteriousness compels a more exploratory approach towards using technology. As such, technology is used to explore and uncover possibilities and let them feed back through different modes of representation and output. Critical to this design methodology is the development of discrete strategies that allow one to simultaneously manage large quantities and different types of information – graphic, geometrical, sensory, material, tectonic, structural, programmatic, and formal. The goal is to identify and manage different orders and develop the best ways in which to study them – ways that allow the perceptual aspects of their interaction to emerge (figures 16.2 and 16.3).

The majority of these projects are either temporary installations commissioned for group exhibitions or temporary interiors commissioned by arts institutions and corporations for exhibitions. From the earliest prototypes for installations to more recent works, there is an extensive use of modular fabrication (largely using vacuum forming), a consistent use of plastics, and a persistent development of a number of effects.

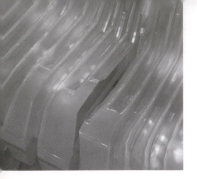

16.4.
Detail of
Thermocline
(2002).

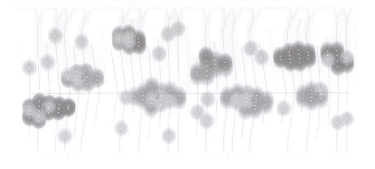

16.5.
Thermocline
informational
network.

These projects do not stop at explorations of material, form, or a fabrication. At every opportunity, there is a compulsion to experiment with a wider range of input, such as lighting, sensors, and sound. Despite the constrained quantity of media embedded in projects such as *Thermocline* and *Lattice Archipelogics*, it was difficult to fully understand their complex relationships and effects until the designs were fabricated and tested at full scale. Both projects examine the relationship and interplay of different sensory inputs – sound is transformed into light in *Thermocline*, while motion is transformed into light in *Lattice Archipelogics*.

In *Lattice Archipelogics*, the depth and boundary of the field appear and disappear as one moves through it. This is a result of using the geometry and form of the modules to manipulate the illumination of the space. *Thermocline* captures the ambient sound of people moving through its surroundings and releases the sound as people approach or sit on it (figures 16.4 and 16.5). As more people inhabit and interact with *Thermocline*, sound and light are activated more intensely – pushing

media back into the space and eroding its object-like quality.

Both *Thermocline* and *Lattice Archipelogics* contributed to the development of subsequent work. They formed the basis of a matrix for the evaluation of how different media interact with matter, space, and form. In different ways, the two projects demonstrated how invisible media and invisible material orders can be formed and manipulated. These invisible material orders have discrete geometries, which can be harnessed, incorporated into the form, and designed to transform geometrically over time. In projects like *Dark Places*, *Nike Genealogy of Speed* and *Diplo_id*, these orders begin to infuse into and transform across one another.

Dark Places, an exhibit installation (figure 16.6) at the Santa Monica Museum of Art, confronts the display of the artwork. Each piece of artwork is formatted digitally, and montaged into a film together with other art pieces. These films are either projected or displayed on touch-screen monitors. The design of *Dark Places* focuses on the interaction between information that is converted into light (projection) and the architecture of the space that light inhabits.

16.6.
Dark Places at
the Santa Monica
Museum of Art
(2006).

16.9.
Nike Genealogy of Speed, Venice, California (2004).

16.7.
Dark Places rear projection prototype at *servo L.A.*

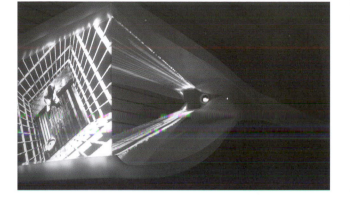

16.8.
Dark Places rear projection prototype detail.

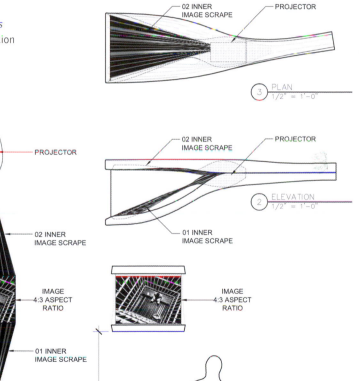

The exchange of the orders that was initiated in earlier projects is intensified in *Dark Places.* Sensory inputs such as light and sound are not only worked with as materials with particular geometries, but also worked with in a translucent manner – a manner which privileges their ambient influence on the space versus their legibility. These relationships become more perceptual and less indexical. Different orders shift from being concealed to being revealed, or vice versa, blurring their tectonic hierarchies and relationships.

The projected image (artwork) is operated on directly and physically – like a substance being pumped through the veins of the architectural display infrastructure (figures 16.7 and 16.8). At the ends of each strand – where it finally emerges and presents an artist's work – orders shift and invert. The illumination heats up at the end of the strand, pries open the architectural housing, and emerges as a three-dimensional object where the cone of light is precisely captured in a series of plastic rear projection screens. The role of illumination and content shifts in relation to the role of the display housing. What was once one-dimensional, immaterial, and internal now becomes three-dimensional, physical, and external – introducing a new material order into the system – a hybrid of light and matter. Design studies were conducted using full-scale prototypes that operated in tandem with schematic design, where both modes of working informed each other. This dialogue between the different modes of investigation, drawing, and prototyping, was crucial in developing the overall design, offering an understanding of the perceptual dimensions operating on the geometries.

In *Nike Genealogy of Speed* (figure 16.9), the sneakers take on multiple roles and are treated as a material – a curatorial substance – one of many orders within the design. Designed and completed before *Dark Places, Nike Genealogy of Speed* sets a precedent for the idea that content and its organization could be treated as matter. This project established that matter could be infused and absorbed into the architecture, both literally and physically. Instead of providing

187

16.11.
Diplo_id detail
of partial
section.

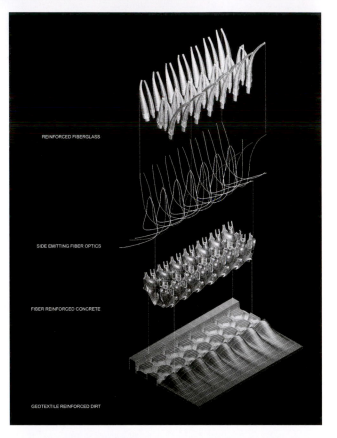

REINFORCED FIBERGLASS

SIDE EMITTING FIBER OPTICS

FIBER REINFORCED CONCRETE

GEOTEXTILE REINFORCED DIRT

16.12.
Detail model of
Diplo_id – LED
network, wood,
plaster, and
resin.

a setting for the sneakers, the architecture facilitates and follows the co-mingling of the different orders, often in close proximity to one another. Placed inside plastic tubes that are part of the suspended ceiling, the sneakers become obstacles in the space. They aggregate, creating moments of illumination that take on dimensional attributes that exceed the literal size of the sneaker.

Translucency is not limited to the use of plastics or other translucent materials. Translucency is intended to be both a perceptual phenomenon and a more aggressively material approach in the use of technology. It places emphasis on "cy" as one possible state of matter in space. More recent projects make use of opaque materials and substances such as water. *Diplo_id* – a proposal for a permanent installation at the MAK Center in Los Angeles – intentionally extends the material palette beyond materials that are inherently transparent or translucent (figures 16.10 and 16.11).

The design explores the interaction between less robust material substances such as data, light, and water with more traditionally material substances such as concrete, fiberglass, and dirt. Working with tight dimensional constraints determined by zoning regulations, the project examines how the material substances can shift roles or fluctuate at a small scale to create a larger-scale effect. A series of fiberglass spouts are used to organize and emit different substances: light, fog, and water (figures 16.12 and 16.13). These substances are laced through the spouts and unleashed at different moments to provide illumination, irrigation, and fogging to the site. The form and geometry of each material order are different, but are designed to influence one another.

To maintain the identity of each substance, diversity in their spectral quality and fall-off is maintained, offering additional opportunities for them to juxtapose and interplay – as the base fills with water, it becomes more reflective, as the illumination intensifies and more fog and water spouts are activated, the fiberglass spouts become more concealed. Seams, edges, and formal work tie them back together, blurring their distinctions.

A translucency of material orders establishes hierarchies between different types of material. At the same time, these orders are managed, mined, and undertaken in the design process as a means of shifting their hierarchy, making them appear and disappear – increasing their degree of mysteriousness.

16.14.
Nike Genealogy of Speed, Venice, California.

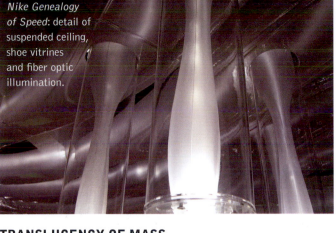

16.17.
Nike Genealogy of Speed: detail of suspended ceiling, shoe vitrines and fiber optic illumination.

TRANSLUCENCY OF MASS

As the projects gain in scale and complexity, the perceptual experience of material effects becomes increasing critical. Translucency, we discovered, not only operates on the geometry and form of a surface, but can also operate as a principle of mass – working with densities, gradients and aggregations between surfaces. *Nike Genealogy of Speed* provided an opportunity to explore this (figure 16.14).

The existing building that *Nike Genealogy of Speed* occupies is subdivided into five discrete rooms. While the client expected the design to transform the spatial quality of the existing building as much as possible, the curators decided to compress eight exhibitions into one. These parameters required the sneakers to move between otherwise stable, defined categories and change locations throughout the exhibit. This fluid shuffling of the sneakers forms a particular set of possible geometries that is coordinated with a suspended ceiling (figure 16.15).

The exhibition organization, along with the existing organization of the building (its walls, beams and sprinklers), acts as a form of resistance to the suspended ceiling (figure 16.16). Interacting with the existing walls of the space, the areas where the sneakers are attached to the ceiling multiplies and redistributes existing boundaries (figure 16.17). As autonomous objects and as agglomerated objects, the sneakers disturb the through-flowing, suspended ceiling, making it quiver,

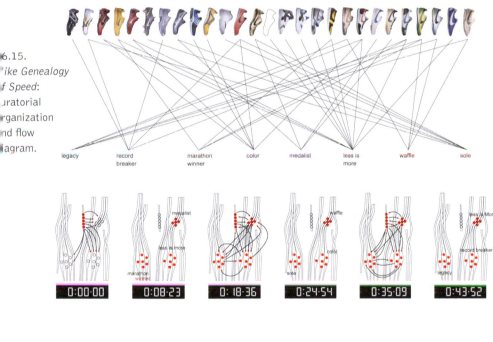

16.15.
Nike Genealogy of Speed: curatorial organization and flow diagram.

legacy   record breaker   marathon winner   color   medalist   less is more   waffle   sole

0:00:00   0:08:23   0:18:36   0:24:54   0:35:09   0:43:52

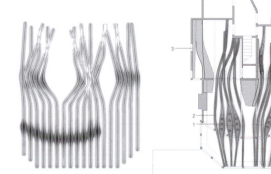

16.16.
Nike Genealogy of Speed: suspended ceiling studies and exhibition plan layout.

1-SUSPENDED SHOE VITRINES
2-SUSPENDED PLASTIC CEILING SYSTEM
3-FURNITURE SYSTEM
4-CARTS

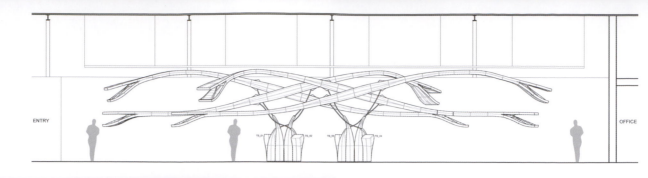

16.19.
Section of *Dark Places*.

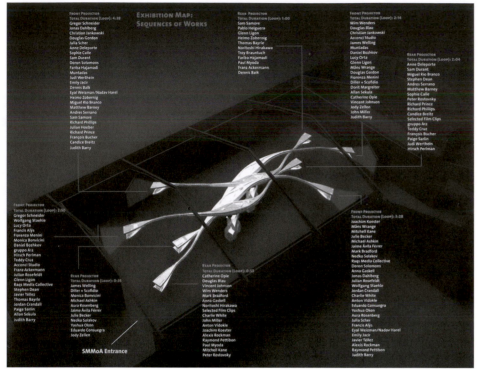

16.18.
Dark Places
curatorial map

Many of these ideas and principles were further developed in *Dark Places*. In this project, the number of material orders increased while the existing context was more limiting – a generic white cube gallery in an industrial "Butler Shed" building. Working with 76 artists selected by curator Joshua Decter, the design paired up the exhibition display infrastructure with the curator's intentions to produce a new group show with a new format (figure 16.18), one that allows varying degrees of contamination and is clearly opposed to the conventional model of a white cube gallery.[15]

Instead of using rooms to organize artwork, the project works with strands that are slightly altered to deal with projection heights, structural loads and storage. These constraints are indexed in the form of individual strands that trace input from computers on the ground to output (projectors) at the end of each strand. Hovering overhead, the strands make legible the organization of the information network (figures 16.19 and 16.20).

Constructed with a set of seven repeated components, the woven strands operate at multiple scales. At the component scale, the number of seams and amount of texture are adjusted based on structural requirements and desired amount of illumination. The formation of the strands seeks to intensify and diffuse different orders of mass illumination, content, material, and human.

The strands are designed and organized to percolate three zones, whose boundaries and modes of occupation are subtly distinct. In the region where strands connect together towards their centers, illumination is the most intense and all-surrounding, information is the most dense and deep, and material is the most diverse and textured. In this zone, where there is no audio accompaniment, visitors use touch-screen monitors to access the artists' biographical information. As visitors browse through information on the monitors, illumination is activated. The illumination is designed to pulse in a breath-like manner, establishing a temporal rhythm in the space that plays off the rhythm of the artwork videos. The pulsing illumination is peripheral and ambient to the visitor, whose interaction is controlling the amount and speed of illumination. This interaction, illumination, and tempo are designed to amplify spatial textures surrounding the visitor.

and rendering its boundaries blurry and vague. Dripping down from the ceiling, the sneakers create a fluid spatial rhythm that is juxtaposed with the compartmentalization of the existing building's organization.

The distribution and texture of each modular component within the project are designed to produce a larger-scale perceptual effect. The repetition of elements and seams are more concerned with producing varying degrees of spatial texture than with articulating discernible patterns and formations. The circulation and use of space contribute to this even further. The clusters of sneakers act as obstacles between rooms, slowing people down and speeding up the architecture. The illumination provides another level of texturing, giving the ceiling an ambient glow and clustering around the sneakers as a cloud of lights. This condensation and dispersion of material orders – sneakers, manufactured components, seams, texture and illumination – operate as masses in the space that fluctuate in density and vagueness.

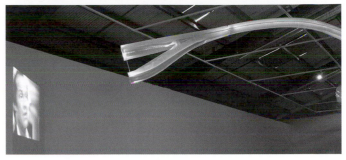

16.21.
Detail of front
projected terminals.

16.20.
Hovering strands
in *Dark Places*.

The eight ends of the strands operate differently from the bodies of the strands. Four of the eight ends house rear projected images and have sound built into them (figure 16.7). These terminals are held closely together and make no attempt to produce a relationship with the existing gallery-container. They operate as cinematic objects, whose role is to aggressively shift the material order of the artwork. Here, artists' works are experienced visually and sonically in close proximity to one another. Their work has been transformed from a plane to an object that embodies a more discrete form of sound. These terminals condense many orders of material and texture tightly (as opposed to dispersing them like the center of the strand), allowing the visitor to look behind, under, and in front of the artwork.

The remaining four ends of the strands are used for frontal projection. These terminals lob light over the visitor's head and throw artwork onto surfaces that peel off from the existing container (figure 16.21). These surfaces not only capture the image, but also torque and

re-work the existing space. The strands move subtly away from each other in these locations, allowing for autonomous large-scale projections of the artist's work. The height and angles allow for better sound, throwing a cone directly over one's head. This is where the objecthood of the strands dissolve and the artwork is brought to the foreground.

What started as singular and separate orders of material and design are engaged and entangled with one another in multiple ways and through various zones. This dialogue between the orders extends towards the surrounding context, contaminating the white cube of the existing gallery.

While both *Nike Genealogy of Speed* and *Dark Places* worked within the constraints of existing structures, *NOLA Filigree* (figure 16.22) is a ground-up building proposal for a developer in New Orleans. Part of the redevelopment effort in post-Katrina New Orleans, this project is situated in the Garden District – renowned and adored for its outdoor spaces and abundance of ornamental porch filigree.

Consisting of six condominium units, the project takes its cue from the existing urban context and contemporary development models for the area. With a higher density than the surrounding neighborhood, the project absorbs open spaces by infusing them into the building mass as opposed to framing open spaces between or around the mass.

A minimum of three open areas is designed into each unit. The interiorized open spaces are highly textured environments that are two or three stories high (figure 16.23). The open spaces work diagonally off of the floor plates, pinching the space in between. The texture of the open spaces takes their cue from traditional iron filigree found on front porches of houses. This filigree is monstrous in scale, one that neither the developer nor the city ever imagined. However, instead of being applied ornamentation, the filigree becomes architecturally active and constitutes 50 percent of the bulk of the project, infiltrating and invading the solid mass.

Consisting of an assortment of modular wood components, the filigree operates at multiple scales (figures 16.24a–c). At the smallest scale, the nests absorb infrastructure such as skylights, lighting, railings, and stairs. They brace-frame floor plates, allowing the plates to be structurally independent of the parti walls. Most importantly, they establish an interior rhythm and distribute space within each unit. As one moves vertically

191

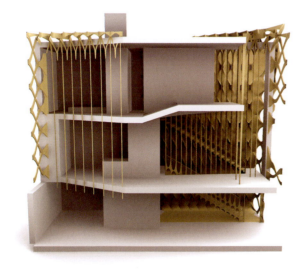

16.22.
Overview of the
NOLA Filigree
proposal, New
Orleans.

16.23.
NOLA Filigree:
Perspectival
section of single
unit showing
three areas of
filigree.

between floors, one is surrounded by intense puffs of texture – above, below, beside and under. The intensity of the texture dissipates beyond the filigree, but its influence continues to resonate across the unit.

At the scale of the unit, the filigree absorbs a number of orders – lighting, circulation, structure, texture, and color (figures 16.25 and 16.26). They are coordinated vertically and horizontally to make a murkier overall unit-space reading, producing cross-programmatic spatial experiences. Boundaries between units are pulled deeper into the mass or pushed to the foreground, oscillating between being revealed and being concealed.

At the urban scale, the filigree intensifies the experience of the building mass (figure 16.27). They emit a rhythm of light, texture, and color, dissolving not only the boundaries between units, but also the edges of the urban mass. As such, the design mines the scalar potentials of material effect that operate both internally and externally. Operating at scales both within and outside of the project itself, the filigree overcomes the compact footprint of the site by amplifying the material effects.

MYSTERIOUSNESS OF DIFFICULTY

A discussion of fabrication today not only addresses the technological aspect of manufacturing, but must also confront its impact on architecture culture. In order to do so, not only does a clearer distinction between technique and technology need to be drawn, but a post-technique set of interests needs to be discussed. Terms such as "digital," "rigor," and "intelligence" are prosaic and should no longer form the basis of a discussion about the production of architecture.

Admittedly, part of this attitude comes from working in Los Angeles, where the computer is aggressively on the ground to the extent that it is blue collar – your carpenter

16.24a–c.
NOLA Filigree:
detail of skylight,
stair, and floor
articulating
different
construction
systems.

D01>SKYLIGHT

01>CNC GLUE LAM BEAM
02>CNC GLUE LAM TENSION RODS
03>LAMINATED, P.RESIN PANELS

D02>STAIR

01>CNC GLUE LAM TENSION RODS
02>LAMINATED WOOD
03>LAMINATED P. RESIN CAP-JOINT
04>LAMINATED P. RESIN PLATES

D03>FLOOR

01>LAMINATED P. RESIN PANELS
02>LAMINATED P.RESIN FLOOR PANELS

16.27.
NOLA Filigree: view of the proposal in the Garden District.

16.25. (right)
NOLA Filigree: detail of single filigree nest.

16.26. (far right)
NOLA Filigree: interior of filigree nest between floors.

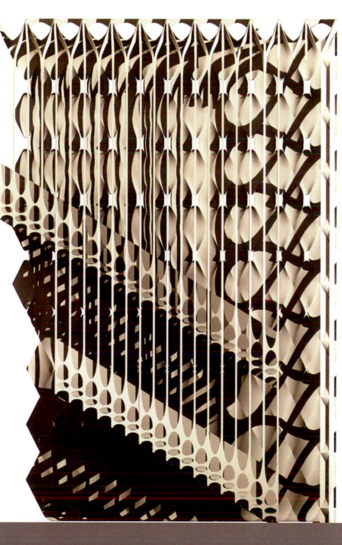

is working with *Maya* and your contractor is working with *Digital Project*. The software is not special, the technologies are not unique; they are as ubiquitous as cell phones and jump drives. Nonetheless, the pervasiveness of technology does not make it mundane or dumb. As Steven Johnson, the author of *Emergence*,[16] noted in his recent book *Everything Bad Is Good for You*, pop culture is actually making us smarter.[17] He argues that television audiences like difficult problems. They are not dumb and they crave cognitive challenges. An acute example (one that ties in nicely with the book in hand) is the difference between the structure of television shows such as *The West Wing* and *The Sopranos* with the structure of shows such as *Dragnet* and *Starsky and Hutch*. *Dragnet* is legible and encapsulated. All the plot lines and characters are introduced and terminated neatly within the scope of a single episode. *The Sopranos* and *The West Wing*, on the other hand, are entirely different. They immerse the viewer in an ongoing stream of characters and plots, none of which are resolved within a single episode. In some cases, an entire season or the entire show is left unresolved. There is too much information in these shows to construct a careful reading, marking a concerted change in both the writer and the viewer. Instead, focus is placed on constructing a full experience and a particular atmosphere.

193

Even extensive DVD viewing – the premiere technology used to deliver these shows – does not resolve issues or make them more legible. They allow the viewer to retrieve more information without necessarily reaching resolution.

It is difficult to imagine Aaron Sorkin and other Hollywood writers of this caliber sitting around talking about emerging DVD technology features, despite Johnson's claim that DVD viewing has enabled this format of writing to undertake more complex relationships. These relationships rely on an ambient perceptual engagement versus an intellectual reading of the material – one does not have to be a presidential staff member who understands the litany of political language and history in order to enjoy watching *The West Wing*. This is a generation that has a different set of cognitive thinking and media receptive skills. These abilities open up new possibilities in the manufacturing of effects in contemporary architectural design.

My preoccupations do not reside in producing technologically based forms that have singular discernible answers – "It appears this way because it results from X, Y, and Z" – or are the result of models of efficiency. Instead my interest lies in mysteriousness – a recipient-based model of design, which is not reliant on disciplinary autonomy, but responds to broader-based cultural appeal. Concerned with the manufacturing of mysteriousness, this work makes use of technologies to explore how singular material and design orders quiver and drift across one another, producing translucency. Translucency is not about being immediately clear or understandable, but is murky and elusive. It is not about endurance, but about duration and intensification. It is not about saturation, but about the solicitation and orchestration of various material orders in the manufacturing of mysteriousness.

Every project presented here contains both mysteries and puzzles. Mysteriousness resides in their reception, perception, and experience, with regards to both audience and method of design of each project. Mysteriousness is not about showcasing technical difficulty or complexity. It is difficult and complex because it absorbs too much information, too much input, and does not embody a singular reading. It is difficult and complex because it engages both designer and occupant. The peripheral action of the form, its phenomenal characteristics, its haptic effect, its temporal components, and its misalignments are as important as the literal aspects. This attitude shifts the focus from objects of desire to environments of desire. The environment is not only shaped by the multiplicity of effects, objects, and design orders contained within it, but also by the variegated relationships between them.

The environments of desire represented in this article have a very strange architectural appetite. Instead of obsessing about enclosure and structure, they obsess about rhythm and texture. They reflect a desire to work with small-scale environments versus large-scale, object buildings. They consume and absorb cinema, light, sound, and sensors in manufacturing translucency and mysteriousness. Surely, translucency can be more robustly explored with the use of contemporary technology. In the case of this work, explorations in technology are pointedly undertaken with mysteriousness in mind. Translucency is superficial, yet it embodies depth and influence – after all, something bad might actually be good for you.

ACKNOWLEDGMENTS

Dark Places, Lattice Archipelogics, Nike Genealogy of Speed and *Thermocline* were designed and completed by *servo*, a design collaboration between Marcelyn Gow, Ulrika Karlsson, Chris Perry and myself. *Diplo_id* and *NOLA Filigree* were developed independently. Many ideas presented here started with *servo* – owing a lot to our collaborative thinking as well as reflecting my personal observations and ideas about the work. Special thanks are due to Sylvia Lavin, under whose guidance these explorations were developed during my teaching at *UCLA Department of Architecture and Urban Design*.

NOTES

1 Colin Rowe and Robert Slutzky, "Transparency: Literal and Phenomenal," in *The Mathematics of the Ideal Villa and Other Essays*, Cambridge, MA: MIT Press, 1976, pp. 159–183.
2 Jeffrey Kipnis, "P-TR's Progress," in *Eleven Authors in Search of a Building*, New York: Monacelli Press, 1996, pp. 170–181.
3 Ibid., pp. 172–181.
4 Ibid., p. 176.
5 Ibid.
6 Ibid., p. 173.
7 Ibid., pp. 173–174.
8 Malcolm Gladwell, *The Tipping Point: How Little Things Can Make a Big Difference*, London: Little, Brown and Company, 2000.
9 Malcolm Gladwell, "Open Secrets," *The New Yorker*, January 8, 2007; see www.gladwell.com/2007/2007_01_08_a_secrets.html.
10 Ibid.
11 Ibid.
12 Ibid.
13 Ibid.
14 Ibid.
15 Joshua Decter, "A Phantasmagoria of Multiple, Simultaneous, Looped Curatorial Scripts," *Dark Places*, Santa Monica Museum of Art, 2006, pp. 4–9.
16 Steven Johnson, *Emergence: The Connected Lives of Ants, Brains, Cities and Software*, New York: Touchstone, 2002.
17 Steven Johnson, "Part One," in S. Johnson, *Everything Bad Is Good for You*, New York: The Berkley Publishing Group, 2005, pp. 62–137.

17

INTEGRAL FORMATION AND MATERIALIZATION: COMPUTATIONAL FORM AND MATERIAL GESTALT

ACHIM MENGES / ARCHITECTURAL ASSOCIATION AND UNIVERSITÄT STUTTGART

Architecture, as a material practice, attains social, cultural, and ecological relevance through the articulation of material arrangements and structures. Thus, the way we conceptualize these material interventions – and particularly the technology that enables their construction – presents a fundamental aspect in how we (re)think architecture.

In many ways, the progress over decades of computer-aided design and manufacturing (CAD/CAM), or rather the greater availability and affordability of these technologies, can be seen in the lineage of other technical advancements. In the history of architecture and construction ground-breaking technologies have often been employed initially to facilitate projects that were conceived – and indeed embraced – through well-established design concepts and construction logics. There is ample evidence of this inertia in design thinking in the context of technological progress. For example, the design of the structure and connection details of the first cast-iron bridges of late eighteenth-century England were modeled on timber constructions. Similarly, the early reinforced concrete structures of the late nineteenth century mimicked previous iron and steel frame buildings. In fact, almost half a century had to pass between the first patent for reinforced concrete and its significant influence on design through the conceptualization of its innate material capacities as manifested in Robert Maillart's bridges and the shell structures of various twentieth-century pioneers such as Franz Dischinger.

While these examples of deferred impact refer mainly to advances in material technology, one can still trace an interesting parallel with the current employment of computer-aided design and manufacturing technologies. The by-now-ubiquitous use of CAD/CAM technologies in architecture serves, more often than not, as the facilitative and affordable means to indulge in so-called free-form architecture as conceived at the end of the last century. Although this may lead occasionally to innovative structures and spatial qualities, it is important to recognize that the technology used in this way provides a mere extension of well-rehearsed and established design processes.

Particularly emblematic is the one-dimensional reference to the notion of *digital morphogenesis*. By now almost a cliché, this term refers to various processes of form generation resulting in shapes that remain elusive to material and construction logics. In foregrounding the geometry of the eventual outcome as the key feature, these techniques are quintessentially not dissimilar to more conventional and long-established representational techniques for explicit, scalar geometric descriptions. As these notational systems cannot integrate means of materialization, production and construction, these crucial aspects need to be subsequently pursued as top-down engineered material solutions. Being essentially about appearance, digital morphogenesis dismisses both the capacity of computational morphogenesis to encode logic, structure, and behavior, as well as the underlying principles of natural morphogenesis.

INTEGRATING FORMATION AND MATERIALIZATION

Natural morphogenesis, the process of growth and evolutionary development, generates systems that derive complex articulation, specific gestalt and performative capacity through the interaction of system-intrinsic material characteristics, as well as external stimuli of environmental forces and influences. Thus, formation and materialization are always inherently and inseparably related in natural morphogenesis. Such integral processes of unfolding material gestalt are particularly striking when one considers architecture which, as a material practice, is (by contrast) still mainly based on design approaches characterized by a hierarchical relationship that prioritizes the definition and generation of form over its subsequent materialization. This suggests the latent potential of the technology at stake may unfold from an alternative approach to design, one that derives morphological complexity and performative capacity without differentiating between form generation and materialization processes.

The underlying logic of computation strongly suggests such an alternative, in which the geometric rigor and simulation capability of computational modeling can be deployed to integrate manufacturing constraints, assembly logics and material characteristics in the definition of material and construction systems. Furthermore, the development of versatile analysis tools for structure, thermodynamics, light and acoustics provides for integrating feedback loops of evaluating the system's behavior in interaction with a simulated environment as generative drivers in the design process. Far beyond the aptitude of representational digital models, which mainly focus on geometry, such computational models describe *behavior* rather than shape. This enables the designer to conceive of material and construction systems as the synergetic result of computationally mediating and instrumentalizing the system's intrinsic logics and constraints of making, the system's behavior and interaction with external forces and environmental influences, as well as the performative effects resulting from these interactions. Thus, the understanding of material effects, the theme of this book, extends far beyond the visible effect towards the thermodynamic, acoustic, and luminous modulation of the (built) environment. As these modulations, in relation to the material interventions and their construction process, can now be anticipated as actual behavior rather than textbook principles, the design of space, structure, and climate becomes inseparable.

Crossing a number of disciplinary boundaries, the design approach presented here demands that structural and environmental engineering, which has tended to be a question of post-design optimization, becomes an essential factor in the setup of the design process itself. Therefore realizing the potential of computational design and computer controlled fabrication is twofold: first, it enables (re)establishing a far more immediate relation to the processes of making and constructing by unfolding innate material capacity and behavior, and, second, understanding this behavior as a means of creating not only space and structure but also micro-climatic conditions. While the latter may have a profound impact on our conception of spatial organization,[1] which can now be thought of as differentiated macro- and micro-climatic conditions, providing a heterogeneous habitat for human activities, the former will be the main focus, especially as the research on integral processes of computational morphogenesis and performance evaluation is a substantial field by its own. This basic research entails developing and exploring new modes of integrating design techniques, production technologies, and system performance. These modes are by no means similar when developed for different systems, but rather differentiate into a wide range of possible material articulations and computational methods. So, while sharing a common objective, a rich palette of different approaches has been explored over the past five years through various research projects. What follows is a cross-section of these approaches.

DIFFERENTIATED MATERIAL SYSTEMS

The research projects presented here seek to develop and deploy computational techniques and digital fabrication technologies to unfold innate material capacity and specific latent gestalt. They commence from extensive investigations and tests of what we define as *material systems*. Material systems are considered, not so much as derivatives of standardized building systems and elements, but rather as generative drivers in the design process.

Extending the concept of material systems by embedding their material characteristics, geometric behavior, manufacturing constraints, and assembly logics within an integral computational model promotes an understanding of form, material, structure, and behavior not as separate elements, but rather as complex interrelations. This initially requires disentangling a number of aspects that later form part of the integral computational setup in which the system evolves.

First of all, the geometric description of material systems, or rather the notation of particular features of the system's morphology, needs to be established. The geometric definition of the system has to overcome the primacy of shape and related metric, descriptive characteristics. Therefore, the designer has to facilitate the setup of a computational model, not as a particular gestalt specified through a number of coordinates and dimensions, but as a framework for possible formations affording further differentiation that remains coherent with the behavior observed and extracted from physical experiments and explorations of the relevant system. This computational framework, which essentially constitutes an open model (referred to as "framework" here due to the ambiguous meaning of "model" in a design context), is then step-by-step informed by a series of additional parameters, restrictions, and characteristics inferred from material, fabrication, and assembly logics and constraints. Principally, this includes the specific material and geometric behavior in formative processes, the size and shape constraints of involved machinery, the procedural logistics of assembly, and the sequences of construction. As these aspects vary greatly depending on the setup and construction of the material system, more detailed explanations follow describing specific projects. However, it is interesting to note the significant shift in the way computer-aided manufacturing (CAM) processes are employed in this context.

Whereas the nature of CAM enables difference to be achieved, it is currently used mainly as a means of increasing speed and precision in the production of variation. Symptomatic for preserving the facilitative character of manufacturing and its related protocols is the term "mass customization." Flourishing due to the reintroduction of affordable variation, "mass customization" nevertheless remains an extension of well-known and long-established design processes embracing the still dominant hierarchy of prioritized shape-definition and subsequent, purely facilitative manufacturing. One needs to be aware that the accomplishment of economically feasible variation through computer-controlled production and fabrication, by manufacturers and designers alike, does not by itself lead to strategies of instrumentalizing the versatility of differentiated material systems. Nonetheless, the far-reaching potential of CAM technologies is evident once they turn into one of the defining factors of a design approach seeking the synthesis of form-generation and materialization processes. At this point, the highly specific restrictions and possibilities of manufacturing hardware and controlling software can become generative drivers embedded in the setup and development of the computational framework.

COMPUTATIONAL MORPHOGENESIS

Generally, it can be said that the inclusion of what may be referred to as system-intrinsic characteristics and constraints comprises the first crucial constituent of the computational setup defined through a series of parameters. The definition of the range in which these parameters can be operated upon, and yet remain coherent with the material, fabrication, and construction constraints, is the critical task for the designer at this stage.

The second crucial constituents of the generative computational framework are recurring evaluation cycles that expose the system to embedded analysis tools. Analysis plays a critical role during the entire morphogenetic process, not only in establishing and assessing fitness criteria related to structural and environmental capacity, but also in revealing the system's material and geometric behavioral tendencies. The conditioning relation between constraint and capacity, in concert with the feedback between stimuli and response, is consequently an operative element within the computational framework. In this way, evaluation protocols serve to track both the coherency of the generative process with the aforementioned system-intrinsic constraints, as well as the system's interaction with a simulated environment. Depending on the system's intended environmental modulation capacity, the morphogenetic development process needs to recurrently interface with appropriate analysis applications, such as multi-physics computational fluid dynamics (CFD) for the investigation of thermodynamic relations, or light and acoustic analyses. It seems important to mention that a CFD analysis provides only a partial insight, as the thermodynamic complexity of the actual environment is far greater than any computational model can handle at this moment in time. Nonetheless, as the main objective here lies not solely in the prediction of precise data, but mainly in the recognition of behavioral tendencies and patterns, the instrumental contributions of such tools are significant.

In parallel with the environmental factors, continual structural evaluation informs the development process, or even directly interacts with the generation of the system's morphology through processes of evolutionary structural optimization. Yet, in general, the notion of single-criteria optimization is opposed to the underlying principles of morphogenesis. It is imperative to recognize that computational morphogenesis does not at all reproduce a technocratic attitude towards an understanding of efficiency based on a minimal material weight to structural capacity ratio. Nor does it embrace the rationale of what twentieth-century engineers called "building correctly." Structural behavior in this sense becomes one agent within the multifaceted integration process. Overall, this necessitates a shift in conceptualizing multi-criteria evaluation rather than an efficiency model. Biologists, for example, refer to effectiveness as the result of a developmental process comprising of a wide range of criteria. Accordingly, the robustness of the resulting systems is as much due to the persistent negotiation of divergent and conflicting requirements as their consequential redundancies.

As of yet, two essential elements of a computational framework for morphogenetic processes have been introduced: the parametric setup based on the material system's intrinsic constraints, and the evaluation cycles through which the interaction of individual system instances with external influences and forces are frequently analyzed. In other words, the possibility of manipulating the system's articulation in direct relation to understanding the consequential modulation of structural or environmental effects has been established. Therefore, the processes that trigger and drive the advancing development of the system are the third critical constituents of the computational framework. The framework through these processes is able to operate, as they provide the variable input to the defining parameters. This input generates a specific output – one individual instance of the system – leading to the registration and analysis of instance specific structural and environmental effects. Through these effects – basically the way the system modulates the environment – the system's performative capacity unfolds from feedback cycles of manipulation and evaluation.

These processes of driving the development of the system through continual differentiation of its instances can be envisioned in different ways. The most immediate possibility is the direct, top-down intervention of the designer in the parametric manipulation and related assessment cycle. More coherent with the overall concept though are processes based on similar principles as natural morphogenesis. In this respect, two kinds of development processes are of interest here: the growth of the individual instance and the evolution of the system across generations of populations of individual instances. In order to facilitate the former, there are different computational growth models that can be implemented, which are all based on two critical factors: on the one hand, the internal dataset or growth rules – the *genotype* – and on the other, the variable gestalt that results from the interaction of the genotype with the environment – the *phenotype*. The critical task for the designer is defining the genotype through the aforementioned system-intrinsic constraints. The generation of phenotypic system instances, enabled through seed configurations and repeatedly applied genotypic rewriting rules, happens in direct interaction with the environment. One critical aspect to be considered here, and captured in the computational process, is the profound influence of goal-oriented physiological regulation mechanisms, such as, for example, homeostasis on the growth process.

Each derived instance then forms part of a population and is evaluated with the aforementioned analytical tools. Driven by fitness criteria, evolutionary computation (through the implementation of genetic algorithms, for example) can then be employed to evolve various generations based on the confluent dynamics of mutation, variation, selection, and inheritance.

A continuous mediation of the stochastic evolutionary processes and goal-oriented physiological developments at play, or more generally the skillful negotiation between bottom-up and top-down processes, is a central task for the designer. Furthermore, in order to enable genuine morphological differentiation (that is, changes in kind and not just in degree), it is of critical importance that the initially established fitness criteria, as well as the defining parameter ranges – in fact, the entire computational framework – is capable of evolving alongside with the system's development.

Before discussing the deployment of computational morphogenetic processes in the context of different research projects, two trite, yet common misconceptions may need to be addressed. First, employing such a computational framework challenges the nature of currently established design approaches, yet it does not invoke the retirement of the architect in favor of computation. On the contrary, it highlights the importance of the designer in an alternative role, one that is central to enabling, moderating, and influencing truly integral design processes and requires novel abilities and sensitivities. Second, despite the fact that the presented design approach requires a serious engagement with technology, as may have become clear from the above description of the involved computational framework, its use is not limited to exotic materials and manufacturing processes. Quite the opposite is demonstrated through the following projects, which are all, in one way or another, based on the above-explained computational framework yet use mundane materials and commonplace fabrication and manufacturing technology. In effect, as the main expenditure consists of the intellectual investment in an alternative conceptualization of material systems and related computational processes, this design approach flourishes in contexts of limited resources. Here, complexity and related performative capacity unfolds from the continuous evolution and differentiation of initially simple material elements and fabrication procedures. All the projects described below have been conducted in studios I have taught in the past few years at different academic institutions and with different colleagues, most notably Michael Hensel and Michael Weinstock.

17.1.
Metapatch:
the basic unit
(patch).

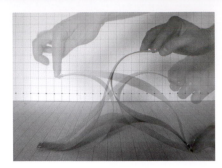

17.4.
*Strip
Morphologies*:
the component.

17.2.
Metapatch: an
array of basic
timber patches.

17.3.
Metapatch:
the assembled
material system.

METAPATCH [2]

An interesting example of a project that starts from a strikingly straightforward element is the *Metapatch* project by Joseph Kellner and Dave Newton. Initial experiments indicated the possibility of inducing geometric changes to an element consisting of two rectangular timber patches, which are attached to one another in two opposite corners by the basic actuation of increasing the distance between the two loose corners through a spacer element (figure 17.1). If a larger panel is covered with arrays of these small patches, each equipped with two adjustable spacers (in this case, simple bolts), the incremental actuation and consequential bending of each individual element led to a cumulative induction of curvature in the larger panel (figure 17.2). Elaborate physical tests then established the relation of element and patch variables such as size, thickness, fiber orientation, spacer locations, actuation distance and torque, which were encoded in the system's parametric definition. The computational setup then provided a specific assembly and actuation protocol from which all relevant information for constructing a full-scale prototype could be obtained. Consisting of 48 identical patches, 1920 equal elements and 7680 bolts, the structure remains entirely flat and flexible after the initial assembly. Only through the subsequent actuation of each spacer bolt, guided by the computationally derived data, does the structure rise into a stable, self-supporting state that gains considerable stiffness and structural capacity through the resulting convex and concave curvature (figure 17.3). This demonstrates how integral techniques can derive a variable, complex material system made up of amazingly simple, uniform elements.

STRIP MORPHOLOGIES [3]

The *Strip Morphologies* project by Daniel Coll I Capdevila explores another approach to an element assembly. Instead of capacitating the material system through differential actuation of geometrically identical elements, here the system's constituents differ geometrically, yet maintain the same fabrication and assembly logic throughout. Again the starting point of the system's development is a simple component of three sheet metal strips connected at the short edges (figure 17.4). The bending behavior of the component resulting from the displacement or rotation of one or two edges was examined in a large number of physical tests. Together with the constraints of fabrication through laser cutting from sheet steel, the observed behavior and related material and geometric limitations were encoded in a computational component defined by parametric relationships (figures 17.5a–c). Subsequent processes of algorithmic proliferation evolve a larger system in which each individual component is geometrically differentiated (figure 17.6). Successive evaluation cycles of testing the system's structural behavior (figures 17.7a–b) and its interaction with light (figure 17.8) trigger further differentiation on the "local" level of the individual component, the "regional" level of component collectives, and the "global" overall system and related distribution algorithm. In this process of enhancing the system's performative capacities, the computational framework ensures that all components are coherent with the underlying fabrication and assembly logic of the basic sheet metal strip. This allows for the immediate manufacturing (figures 17.9a–c) and construction of a system prototype (figure 17.10).

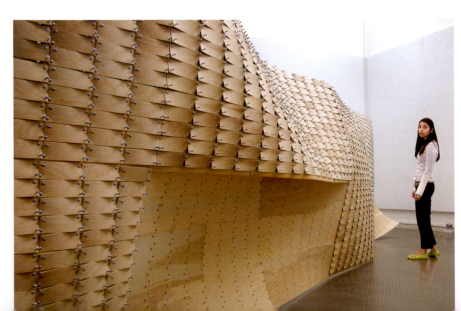

17.5a–c.
Strip Morphologies: (a) control framework, (b) parametric model, and (c) analysis model (top to bottom).

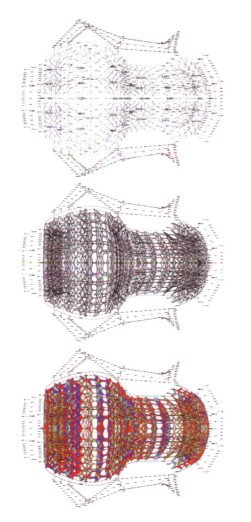

17.8.
Strip Morphologies: light analysis on register surface showing shadow cast, illuminance, and luminance.

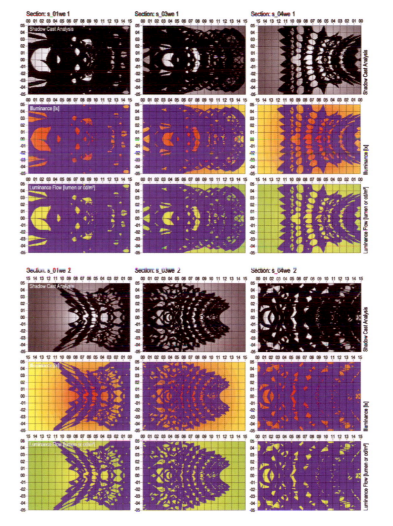

17.9a–c.
Strip Morphologies: fabrication of the full-scale system prototype using laser-cut steel strips.

17.6. (left)
Laser-sintered study model.

17.7a–b. (right)
Structural analysis showing (a) force concentrations, and (b) displacement.

17.10. (far right)
Strip Morphologies: an assembled prototype.

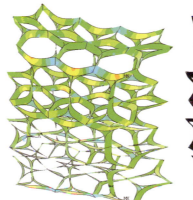

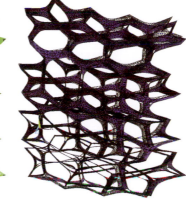

17.11. (right)
Honeycomb Morphologies: the performative component – a honeycomb cell.

HONEYCOMB MORPHOLOGIES[4]

An interesting variant of strip-based material systems is explored in the *Honeycomb Morphologies* project by Andrew Kudless, which aimed at advancing honeycomb structures by developing a double layered system in which each cell size, shape, direction and orientation can be different. Unlike in the previous project, the performative component – a honeycomb cell – does not directly match the actual material element – a folded strip of cardboard (figure 17.11). Starting again from a simple element of two folded cardboard strips, a series of linked physical and digital morphological experiments were conducted in order to investigate the interrelation between surface curvature and honeycomb cell structures, the characteristics of the material (such as the maximum fold angles of the specific cardboard), and the constraints of the laser-cutting process being limited to sheet material of a certain size. These constraints informed the development of a honeycomb deriving growth algorithm that defines the morphology as folded overlapping strips in response to other given design input. The resultant material system, of which a fully differentiated prototype was constructed, shows clearly that innovation in this research does not depend on high-tech material or manufacturing technology (figures 17.12a–c). Here, novelty arises not from singular aspects of the design and construction process, but rather from an integral approach that directly relates modes of production and making with computational form generation.

17.12a–c.
Honeycomb Morphologies: the constructed prototype (above, right, and upper right).

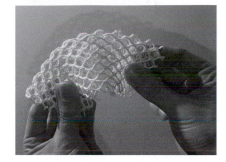

17.13. (right)
3D Gewirke-Verbund: a manipulation-component.

17.14. (above)
3D Gewirke-Verbund: an interdependent manipulation array.

17.15. (right)
3D Gewirke-Verbund: a prototype of the material system.

17.16. (far right)
3D Gewirke-Verbund: another prototype of the material system.

3D GEWIRKE-VERBUND[5]

Whereas the previous projects focused on systems assembled from a large number of elements, the *3D Gewirke-Verbund* project by Nico Reinhardt investigated ways of utilizing local form-finding processes to differentiate a larger, continuous material system. Form-finding, as pioneered by Frei Otto, is a design technique that utilizes the self-organization of material systems under the influence of extrinsic forces or manipulations. In other words, material form can be found as the state of equilibrium of internal resistances and external forces.

Contrary to most form-finding processes, which are concerned with the global morphology of a system, this project aimed at exploring local manipulations. Therefore the notion of component, and the related computational setup, had to be extended as it does not correspond directly to a material element as in the previous projects. Here, component refers to a specific area undergoing parametric manipulation (figure 17.13). The specific manipulation-component defines the vectors and distances of gathering particular points on a three-dimensional spacer textile. Numerous experiments were conducted exploring the behavior of local manipulation areas, interdependent manipulation arrays and the resulting overall morphology (figure 17.14). This led to a catalogue of local articulations, applied through simple procedures of point gathering following computationally derived protocols, which enable overall double curvature and considerably increase the structural depth and bending stiffness of the system. In subsequent steps, the local manipulations were correlated with a larger guiding formwork and a number of full-scale prototypes were constructed (figure 17.15) in order to test the possibility of integrating a similarly form-found glass fiber-reinforced skin (figure 17.16).

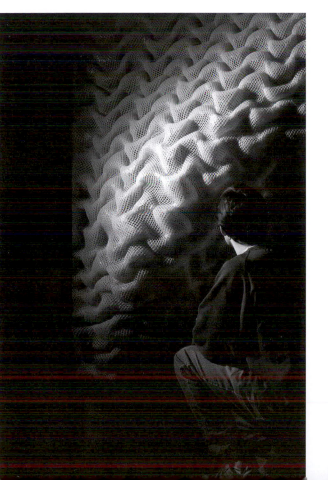

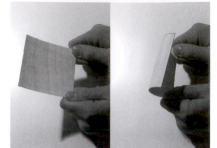

17.17a–b. (right)
*Responsive
Surface Structure*:
the moisture-
responsive
component.

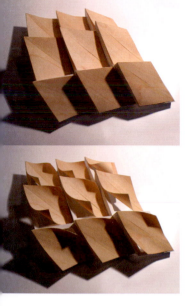

17.18a–b. (above)
*Responsive
Surface Structure*:
an array of
composite
elements.

RESPONSIVE SURFACE STRUCTURE [6]

The performative capacity of the material systems explained above is revealed and instrumentalized through feedback processes of evolving an increasingly articulated morphology, while continually registering and evaluating its interaction with the environment. Due to the inherent dynamics of the environment, the modulations effected by a differentiated system are equally dynamic even though the actual structure remains static. A further intensification of the system–environment relation is suggested by another category of material systems, one in which the system actively reacts to environmental changes.

One example of such material systems is the *Responsive Surface Structure* project by Steffen Reichert, which aimed at developing a skin structure capable of adapting its porosity in response to changes in ambient humidity. The project utilizes timber's inherent moisture-absorbing properties, and particularly the related differential surface expansion, as a means of embedding humidity sensor, actuator, and regulating element into a single, very simple component (figures 17.17a–b). This component consists of a moisture-responsive veneer composite element attached to a load-bearing, folded substructure (figure 17.18a–b). Once exposed to a higher level of humidity, the veneer composite swells and the consequent expansion triggers a deformation that opens a gap between the substructure and the veneer scales resulting in different degrees of porosity. The local component shape and orientation, as well as the mathematically defined surface undulation, evolve in continuous feedback with structural evaluation and thermodynamic analysis of the volume, speed and direction of passing air in relation to the system's response time. As the logics of fabrication and assembly had also been encoded in the initial computational setup, the evolved morphology of geometrically variant components could be directly constructed (figures 17.19a–b). The resultant material system, which is both the structure and a performative skin, provides different degrees of porosity due to local responses innate to the material with no need for other electronic or mechanical devices.

17.19a–b. (right)
*Responsive
Surface Structure*:
the constructed
material system.

17.20.
AA Component Membrane: the canopy structure for the AA terrace.

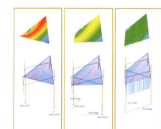

17.24a–c.
Parametric model adjusted according to computational precipitation analysis and drainage models.

17.21.
Stress analysis of the regular membrane component field.

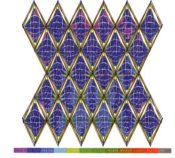

17.22.
Environmental analysis of the average light intensities over one year.

17.23.
Computational fluid dynamics (CFD) analysis of the wind flow and velocity.

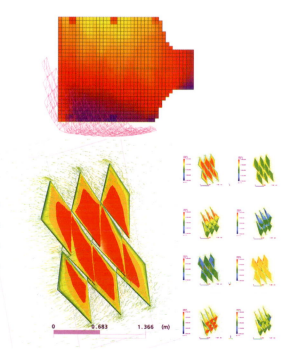

AA COMPONENT MEMBRANE [7]

As evident in the above research projects, a design approach based on material systems promotes a high level of integration of both manufacturing and construction logics as well as performative capacities. Consequently, the setup of a computational framework for developing a specific design is quite an involved operation. Thus, one critical aspect, mainly to inform further research endeavors and directions, is the viability of this approach beyond a mere research context. This was tested in the *AA Component Membrane* project (figure 17.20). Starting from scratch, this canopy structure for the Architectural Association's (AA) terrace had to be designed, manufactured, and constructed in less than seven weeks within an extremely limited budget. This required a versatile computational setup providing for rapid design evolution and performative evaluation, automated extraction of all relevant data for fabricating more than 600 different steel components and 150 membranes, detailed planning of the assembly and construction sequence, as well as continuous exchange with engineering and technology consultants. This project began with the definition of a component that deploys a hyper-parabolic membrane as a load-bearing tensile element within a framework of steel members. The proliferation of the component was evolved in feedback with structural evaluation (figure 17.21), as well as environmental analysis of sunlight (figure 17.22), wind (figure 17.23), and precipitation (figures 17.24a–c). The resulting overlapping membrane articulation protects from rain, while at the same time remaining porous

17.25a.
*AA Component
Membrane*:
close-up of the
canopy's material
system.

enough to avoid excessive wind pressure or blocking views across London's roofscape. Furthermore, the membranes contribute considerably to the stiffness of the overall structure, which acts as a cantilever resting on just three points (figures 17.25a–b).

RAFFUNGSKOMPONENTEN-VERBUND [8]

Two main lineages of material systems have been introduced thus far: one that assumes a specific gestalt through local manipulations of a continuous overall system, as in the *3D Gewirke-Verbund* project, and another based on element assemblies. What is common to all variants of the latter kind is the high level of geometric precision required in defining each element and, in particular, the relation between elements due to the system's morphological differentiation. While the necessary accuracy is afforded by, or rather inherent to, computational processes, it still demands additional effort in terms of fabrication and assembly logistics.

An alternative to the geometric precision of highly defined component assemblies is the topological exactitude of systems consisting of elements that "find"

17.25b.
*AA Component
Membrane*: the
differentiated
canopy system.

17.26. (right) *Raffungs-komponenten-Verbund*: the glass-fiber band as a basic element.

17.27. (above) Structural analysis of the system showing principal forces.

their position and alignments. For example, in the *Raffungskomponenten-Verbund* project by Elena Burggraf, the basic element is a glass-fiber band. By pulling a thread stitched through the band at defined distances, a specific loop pattern emerges due to the gathering action (figure 17.26). In numerous physical tests, the related parameters of band width, length and cut pattern, stitch distance, as well as tensile force induced in the gathering process, were explored in relation to the resultant component's behavior of adapting to formwork curvature and, once hardened by resin, structural capacity. As soon as the taxonomy of the observed component behavior was established, this could be related to the principal stress analyses of specific formwork geometry within a computational setup (figure 17.27). The relation between local

curvature and structural requirements then defines the specific distribution of parametrically varied components. The specific component layout is transferred from the computational realm to the actual formwork via a specially developed projection technique. As the components are laid out in the soft state, the alignment of adjacent components providing for subsequent connections happens by itself. Although the initial distribution focuses only on component type and spacing, the application of resin and related adhesive forces, combined with the self-forming capacity of the strips, produces a highly defined material system (figures 17.28a–b). Material systems consisting of initially loose assemblies pose a considerable challenge not only in developing more advanced computational techniques, but especially in rethinking the notion of geometric precision in the design and planning process.

17.28a–b. *Raffungs-komponenten-Verbund*: the constructed material system.

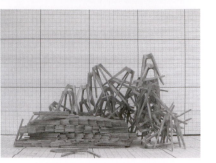

17.29. (right) *Aggregates*: the particle element.

17.30a–c. *Aggregates*: the aggregated material system.

AGGREGATES [9]

An even more radical departure from established design and construction strategies is suggested by a fourth lineage of research projects investigating aggregates, loosely compacted masses of particles or granules. While an abundance of construction applications of bound aggregates exists, such as concrete and asphalt, research on loose aggregates requires a fundamental rethinking of architectural design and its preoccupation with element assemblies, as aggregates are formed not through the connection of elements by joints or a binding matrix, but through loose accumulation of discrete elements.

Aggregates is a research project by Anne Hawkins and Catie Newell, exploring the related space-making potential and performative capacity. This project started by designing a range of simple-to-manufacture particle elements (figure 17.29). A wide range of computational and physical tests were conducted to understand the critical parameters, such as the number of elements, element geometry, pouring speed, pouring height, and the degree of friction provided by boundary surface. Subsequently, liquefaction, an interesting property of granular systems to display liquid-like behavior despite being composed of solid grains, was employed to test the formation of larger structures utilizing both conventional and inflatable formwork (figures 17.30a–c). Through the adjustment of the aforementioned parameters, the aggregation tendencies and behavior can be utilized to create cavernous spaces with multiple stable states, transient spatial conditions, and granular, differentially porous thresholds and boundaries. As no aggregate structure can ever be conceived of as finished, this necessitates a critical shift from the precise design of static assemblies towards the recognition of behavioral tendencies and patterns of self-organizing and reconfigurable structures.

CONCLUSION

Due to the nature of basic research, the projects and related material systems presented here remain in a proto-architectural state still awaiting their context-specific architectural implementation. Nevertheless, they challenge the nature and hierarchies of currently established design processes and promote an alternative approach, one that enables architects to exploit the resources of computational design and manufacturing far beyond the creation of exotic shapes subsequently rationalized for constructability and superimposed functions. This research promotes the unfolding of performative capacities and spatial qualities inherent in the material systems we construct, while at the same time encouraging a fundamental revision of still prevailing functionalist and mechanical approaches towards sustainable design.

NOTES

1 For an elaboration on the spatial and organizational potential of the design approach presented here, refer to M. Hensel and A. Menges, *Morpho-Ecologies: Towards a Discourse of Heterogeneous Space in Architecture*, London: AA Publications, 2006.

2 Metapatch project by Joseph Kellner and Dave Newton, *Generative Proto-Architecture Studio*, Michael Hensel and Achim Menges, School of Architecture, Rice University, Houston, Texas, 2004.

3 *Strip Morphologies* project by Daniel Coll I Capdevila, Diploma Unit 4, Morpho-Ecologies II Program, Michael Hensel and Achim Menges, Architectural Association School of Architecture, London, 2004–2005.

4 *Manifold – Honeycomb Morphologies* project by Andrew Kudless, MA Dissertation Project, Emergent Technologies and Design Master Program, Michael Hensel, Michael Weinstock, Achim Menges, Architectural Association School of Architecture, London, 2004.

5 *3D Gewirke-Verbund* project by Nico Reinhardt, Research Project, Department for Form Generation and Materialisation, Prof. Achim Menges, University of Art and Design, Offenbach, Germany, 2006–2007.

6 *Responsive Surface Structure* project by Steffen Reichert, Research Project, Department for Form Generation and Materialisation, Prof. Achim Menges, University of Art and Design, Offenbach, Germany, 2006–2007.

7 *AA Component Membrane Construction Project*, Emergent Technologies and Design Master Program, Michael Hensel, Michael Weinstock, and Achim Menges, Architectural Association School of Architecture, London, 2007.

8 *Raffungskomponenten-Verbund* project by Elena Burggraf, Research Project, Department for Form Generation and Materialisation, Prof. Achim Menges, University of Art and Design, Offenbach, Germany, 2006–2007.

9 *Aggregates* project by Anne Hawkins and Catie Newell, *Generative Proto-Architectures* Studio, Michael Hensel and Achim Menges, School of Architecture, Rice University, Houston, Texas, 2004.

18

ARCHITECTURAL CAD/CAM: PUSHING THE BOUNDARIES OF CNC FABRICATION IN BUILDING

FABIAN SCHEURER / DESIGNTOPRODUCTION

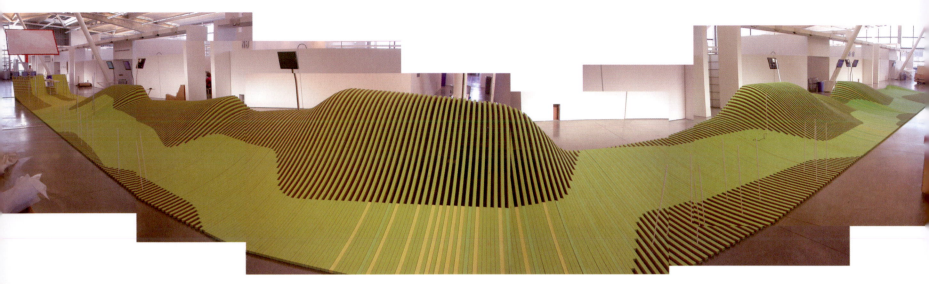

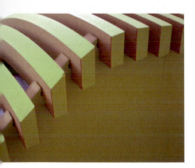

18.2a–b.
Inventioneering Architecture: the upper side of each rafter is a ruled surface, produced using a five-axis CNC router.

The development of "consumer CNC" — small routers, 3D-printers, and laser cutters that are as easy to operate as office printers — opened the doors to rapid prototyping for a wide audience at universities and design practices. Unfortunately, scaling up the results to real-size architecture is not that easy. In a production environment, things are considerably more complex. The methods are not scalable, as quantity, logistics, and integration into the building process become an issue, and the complexity shifts from the machining of material to the processing of information. The limitations are no longer defined by the hardware, but mostly by the software that creates the machining data. When the methods predefined in the computer-aided manufacturing (CAM) systems are not applicable, it is sometimes more efficient to create custom solutions that exactly map the necessities of a specific design to the capabilities of the production environment. Custom-building systems and tailor-made fabrication processes are often the most economic way to translate an idea into reality, especially in architecture, where complex shapes are usually built from large numbers of individual components. The descriptions of five recent projects that follow illustrate this approach.

The first three of the following projects are of rather small scale: an exhibition platform, a trade-fair pavilion, and a sculpture, all realized in a half-academic, half-professional context by the *caad.designtoproduction*

research group at the *Swiss Institute of Technology* (ETH) in Zurich. The main advantage of these projects is the transparency of their underlying concepts, making it very easy to illustrate some fundamental conclusions drawn later in this chapter. However, the fourth project shows that the examined concepts are fully portable to real-scale architecture, though of course additional challenges arise in a professional environment. The fifth project eventually shows where the re-introduction of those professional approaches into academic education can lead.

INVENTIONEERING ARCHITECTURE

Inventioneering Architecture is a traveling exhibition of the four Swiss architecture schools (Zurich, Lausanne, Geneva and Mendrisio) that so far has been shown in San Francisco, Boston, Berlin, Dubai, Shanghai, Tokyo and Singapore. The double curved exhibition platform (figure 18.1) designed by the Zurich practice *Instant Architekten* measures 40 by 3 meters with varying heights up to 1.5 meters. A footpath meanders along the surface, passing the exhibits.

Confronted with a 3D model of the platform, we proposed to chop up the geometry into 1,000 sections, each of them 40mm wide. Each section defines an individually curved "rafter," which follows the upper edge of the platform, supported by a vertical board at the back. Interdigitating from both sides of the platform,

18.3a–b.
*Swissbau
Pavilion* structure
assembled from
320 frames.

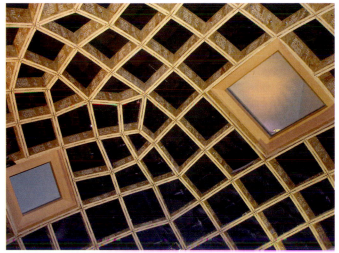

18.4a–e.
Different
intermediate
configurations
generated by the
growth/optimization
script.

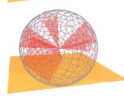

the overlapping sections indicate the closed surface of the path, while the exhibition area is marked by gaps. The components are cut out of 40mm medium density fiberboard (MDF) on a five-axis CNC router. By rotating the cutting tool around its axis of movement, the upper side of each component becomes a ruled surface, following the curvature of the platform along both directions. Carefully placed dowel holes ensure the exact placement of adjacent components (figures 18.2a–b).

Key to the efficient production of 1,000 individual parts was the implementation of a continuously digital production chain from design through manufacturing. This was accomplished by a set of scripts – small programs – within a standard computer-aided design (CAD) system. The first script imports the NURBS-surface defined by the designers, generates a cross-section every 40mm, reads the coordinates for every rafter, and determines the angles of bank for the upper surface. A second script translates this information into the tool paths for cutting and the drilling locations for the dowels. A third script finally arranges and optimizes the rafters on the MDF-boards (nesting) and generates the G-Code programs that control the movement of the five-axis CNC-router. Those machine codes are then passed on to the manufacturing experts who can directly run them on their equipment and produce the parts without further fabrication planning.

SWISSBAU PAVILION

This pavilion was designed and built to exhibit the results of research done by the *Computer-aided Architectural Design* (CAAD) group at *ETH Zurich* during the *Swissbau* 2005 building fair in Basel, Switzerland. It takes the form of a sphere of 4 meters diameter and consists of 320 frames, each constructed from four wooden boards standing perpendicular on the surface of the sphere (figures 18.3a–b). The shape of the frames adapts to the geometry of five arbitrarily placed quadratic openings – in deliberate contrast to a traditional coffered dome where the regular structure dictates the placement of openings.

To generate this adaptive geometry, a custom-built optimization software simulates the growth of a quad-mesh on a sphere following simple rules: the edges try to align with the positions of the openings and the floor level, while at the same time every frame attempts to optimize its size and corner angles in regard to constructive constraints. The simulation is running in real-time, and the user can directly influence the structure by displacing nodes on the sphere (figures 18.4a–e). Under certain circumstances nodes are automatically inserted or deleted from the mesh until it reaches a stable state.

For production, the generated geometry is imported into a parametric CAD model, where a script generates the exact geometries of all frames and their parts, including the connection details. All components are automatically numbered, laid out flat and nested on the OSB (*Oriented Strand Board*, an engineered wood product) used for milling. The G-Code to control a CNC-router that fabricates the parts is generated for every board. It already includes information for drilling the holes and milling the unique part identification into the boards.

18.5. (right)
Libeskind's *Futuropolis*
in the St. Gallen
concert hall.

18.6. (below)
Futuropolis: CNC-cut
boards connected with
aluminum dovetails.

LIBESKIND'S FUTUROPOLIS

Futuropolis is a wooden sculpture (figure 18.5) designed by
Daniel Libeskind for a workshop he held at the *University
of St. Gallen* (HSG) in October 2005. The design is based on
a triangular grid, where 98 tightly packed towers form an
ascending volume up to 3.8 meters in height. The complex
geometry is algorithmically described by the intersection of
two similar sets of extruded profiles, which cut each other at an
angle of 25 degrees.

The first challenge was to find an appropriate construction
method to materialize this geometric idea. We proposed a
structure of wooden boards. In order to guarantee maximum
structural integrity at minimum production and assembly costs,
the detail for connecting the different parts was crucial for the
whole project. By using aluminum dovetail-connectors (figure
18.6) and cutting the necessary miters and notches with a
CNC-router, it was possible to reduce the number of connection
variants to only ten different types (figure 18.7) and completely
automate the fabrication of the connection detail.

18.7. (left)
Futuropolis:
connection
variants.

18.8. (below)
Futuropolis:
detail of the
3D parametric
model.

18.9. (right)
Futuropolis:
the geometry of
592 boards and
the associated
connections was
automatically
generated.

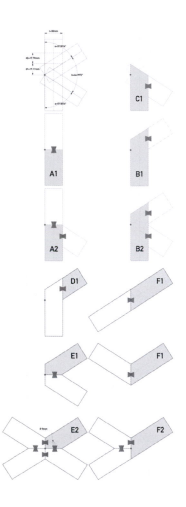

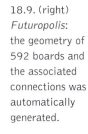

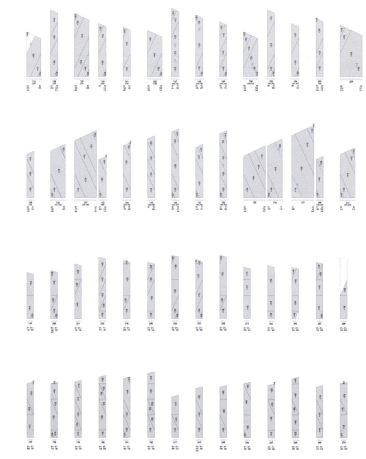

The second challenge was to generate the exact geometry of all 2,164 parts resulting from the intersection of 592 boards with 98 towers. A completely parametric CAD model of the sculpture was developed (figure 18.8), which calculated the outline of all parts by closely following the algorithmic design rules given by the architect. The appropriate connection details were automatically assigned to the edges, the parts were numbered and arranged on boards (figure 18.9).

The third step was to translate this exact geometry information into the machine code for the CNC-router. Since the boards had to be turned around in the middle of the production process, two G-Code programs per board had to be generated by a script. Also, the exact widths and lengths for calculating the material costs and for preparing the raw boards were automatically exported as spreadsheets. The sculpture consists of 360 square meters of 32mm thick boards; altogether, almost 12 cubic meters of birch wood.

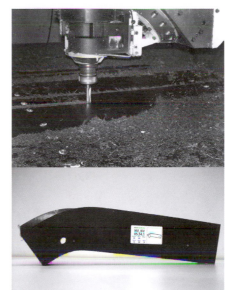

18.12a.
Hungerburg Funicular Stations: CNC-cutting.

18.12b.
Hungerburg Funicular Stations: one of the 2,500 components.

18.10a–d.
Hungerburg Funicular Stations in Innsbruck, Austria (2007), designed by Zaha Hadid.

18.11a–d. (right)
Hungerburg Funicular Stations: custom-cut connection profiles of all four stations (renderings).

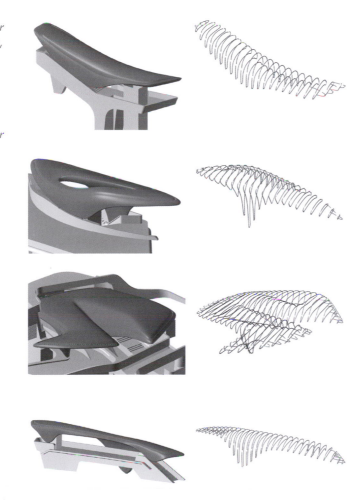

HUNGERBURG FUNICULAR STATIONS

Four free-form roofs with double curved glass panels shelter the new stations (figures 18.10a–d) of the *Hungerburg Funicular* in Innsbruck, Austria (2007), designed by Zaha Hadid. More than two kilometers of custom-cut polyethylene (PE) profiles (figures 18.11a–d) connect the glass cladding of the roof to the steel ribs of the support structure. Since the roof surface is double curved, the profiles constantly change their angle of bank while following the ribs. Very similar to the rafters in the *Inventioneering Architecture* project, the profiles are cut from PE boards with a five-axis router.

But here, the prefabrication had to be integrated seamlessly into a large-scale architectural project. The geometry of the profiles was provided by the engineering partner *Bollinger+Grohmann* in the form of spline-curves in a CAD model. Our firm, *designtoproduction*, automated the segmentation of the profiles, the placement of drillings, the nesting on boards, and the generation of the G-Code for the five-axis CNC-router fabricating the parts. The production documents were also automatically generated, including stickers with the unique part identification codes and information for subsequent production steps of every part. Production was executed just-in-time for every station, following the pace of the construction process and enabling last-minute changes to the geometry. With more than 2,500 individually shaped parts (figures 18.12a–b), the Hungerburg project resulted in the highest number of prefabricated parts so far.

18.13.
The *Camera
Obscura* in
Trondheim,
Norway.

18.14.
*Camera
Obscura*: the
3D model of
the geometry.

TRONDHEIM CAMERA OBSCURA

During the autumn term of 2006, 15 graduate students (13 from architecture and 2 from civil engineering) designed, produced, and built a small pavilion called *Camera Obscura* (figure 18.13) in Trondheim, Norway. The project was part of a full semester course at the *Faculty of Architecture and Fine Art* at the *Norwegian University of Science and Technology* (NTNU). The main aim of the course was to explore the possibilities of prefabrication and file-to-factory processes in timber construction.

With the support of local firms, we were able to use two different types of industrial-strength CNC joinery machines; we carefully studied their characteristics by designing and manufacturing small samples in a three-day workshop with the students. After having learned how to exploit the tools' capabilities for the design, the students developed the final building project as a twisted cube (figure 18.14) with a side length of 4 meters, actually taking the machines' production capacities far beyond their normal use. To our knowledge, this is the first attempt by architecture students to explore and exploit the design potential gained by using automated joinery machines.

18.15.
3D model of the
*Inventioneering
Architecture*
platform.

SIZE MATTERS

Manufacturing methods are not scalable. To illustrate this, let us look at the *Inventioneering Architecture* project. The design of this exhibition platform follows an abstract cross-cut through Swiss topography, forming a double curved landscape (figure 18.15). Manufacturing a landscape model from wood or rigid foam is a straightforward task if you have a common three-axis CNC router at hand: generate a 3D model of the surface and export it to a CAM software; adjust a few parameters depending on the tool and the material used; let the CAM system generate the tool paths, which a post-processor then translates into the G-Code controlling the CNC-router; turn on the machine, and wait until the excess material has been removed layer by layer by the rotating milling bit. For a 1:10 scale model of the platform, a rough cut would take maybe an hour, depending on the material and tool used.

Would it be possible to mill the whole platform from foam and coat it with fiberglass to make it durable? It would. However, to produce the full-scale platform at ten times the size of the model would require a thousand times (10 × 10 × 10) the material volume. And even if there was enough foam around, one would have to find a larger CNC-router moving a ten times bigger tool at ten times the speed; otherwise, it will take 1,000 hours (42 days) to perform the same operation – provided the machine did not break down.

The same effects appear when using additive fabrication methods, such as 3D printing: material cost and manufacturing time do not grow in direct proportion to the scale of an object but to its volume, thus resulting in cubic growth; the only way to speed up production is to reduce resolution and precision (by using larger tools at higher speed); weight is also proportional to volume, bringing the structural integrity into question.

In short, methods that create complex form from homogeneous materials are very convenient and simple to use on a model scale, but when naïvely applied at full architectural scale, they inevitably and very quickly reach a point where they lead to both very inefficient production processes and overly massive structures.

QUANTITY MATTERS

Architecture is built from components. Generations of builders have developed numerous types of building components and successfully used them to assemble large structures from small heterogeneous elements. Since the time of industrialization, those elements have been standardized and general building systems have evolved, which allow prefabrication and very efficient planning and construction processes. However, those systems only work when the shape of the building stays within the rigid boundaries defined by its standardized components. In other words: form follows system. The so-called "free-form architecture" of our times challenges this approach, because it constantly tries to break those rules. Non-standard architecture needs non-standard components.

Fortunately, the progress from industrial age to information age provides the necessary tools to deal with this problem. With computer numerically-controlled (CNC) manufacturing equipment, there is little difference between fabricating a hundred similar or a hundred different parts, as long as the differences stay within the parameter range. With these new tools, building systems become adaptive, in that they follow the shape of the building instead of forcing the building to fit the system. The most important issue, however, is that such adaptive building systems can consist of very few, carefully parameterized types of components. For example, the 40-meter-long *Inventioneering Architecture* platform is built from 1,000 instances of the same element type: a 40mm-wide curved rafter cut from a simple MDF board (figure 18.16a). Placed side by side, they form the double curved surface. The *Swissbau Pavilion* is constructed from 320 quadrilateral wooden frames, each one consisting of four wooden boards that all share the same parametric geometry, but no two of more than 1,200 pieces look alike. The 98 towers of Libeskind's *Futuropolis* are assembled from 2,164 wooden pieces cut with a five-axis CNC circular saw (figure 18.16b). In the *Hungerburg Funicular Stations* more than 2,500 individually cut profiles connect the glass panels to the steel frame, all of them defined by the same parameters (figure 18.16c).

Here, the economies of scale begin to matter, albeit in a different way from what is currently the case. If it does

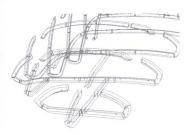

not make much difference whether you produce equal or different parts, the initial investment to develop an adaptive building system and the price for detailing and planning an individual component become the defining cost factor. The development cost is shared among all the produced components, and the planning cost per part becomes negligible when thoroughly rationalized and automated. In the *Hungerburg Funicular Stations* project, for example, those costs were significantly lower than the raw material worth (i.e. the inexpensive polyethylene).

Because architectural structures are large and need huge quantities of components, economically reasonable lot sizes can be achieved within a single project. Instead of developing standard components and aiming to produce cost-effective quantities by using them in different projects, it now makes sense to develop an adaptive building system with a few parametric components especially for a project. It is no longer the system that defines the building – now the building defines its own system.

AUTOMATION AND EFFICIENCY

As stated above, adaptive building systems make sense economically only when the cost for individually planning every component can be lowered significantly. This usually includes two steps: for construction purposes, the component geometry including all details is defined in a CAD system; for production planning, fabrication-specific information is added and the machine-code (the G-Code) for controlling the CNC tool is generated in a CAM software. Depending on the project-specific division of labor, those steps are distributed between a designer, an engineer and a fabrication expert.

The first step can be automated by carefully implementing a parametric CAD model that derives the component geometry from a given overall shape and some additional parameters and rules. In the *Inventioneering Architecture* project, this was done by automatically slicing the platform into 1,000 slivers, each of which defined one rafter. In the case of Libeskind's *Futuropolis*, the algorithmic concept of the

sculpture's geometry laid the base for a CAD script that generated the outline for every board. The complex geometry of the *Swissbau Pavilion* actually organized itself based on the placement of the openings in the sphere. The detailed shape of every board was then constructed automatically by a CAD script. For the roofs of *Hungerburg Funicular Stations*, the engineering partner provided a normal and three curves defining the inner and outer edges for each profile; a CAD script then segmented the profiles and added the details such as holes and notches (figures 18.17a–d).

The second step is usually done by fabrication experts because it requires significant knowledge of the production process. A computer-aided manufacturing (CAM) system is used to add the fabrication-specific information, optimally arrange the parts on the sheet of raw material (nesting), define the tool paths and generate the machine-code for the CNC tools (figures 18.18a–c).

The main challenge for the automated planning and production of adaptive building systems lies in the transfer of information (data exchange) from design to fabrication stage. At present, this data exchange is mostly based on workshop drawings in common CAD formats such as DXF, DWG or IGES, which only transfer geometric information. When using CNC-tools such as laser- or waterjet-cutters, this is generally sufficient because the processing information can be derived unambiguously from the geometry. But with machines that have additional degrees of freedom, the translation of geometries into tooling sequences becomes ambiguous and has to be resolved manually – for every single component in the worst case.

CUSTOM CAM

One way to overcome the gap between CAD and CAM data is to implement not only the generation of the detailed component geometry, but also the automated fabrication planning through custom scripts or plug-ins within CAD system. The language usually used to communicate with CNC machines is a rather straightforward ASCII format (ISO G-Code or XML) that mainly contains coordinate values for the various axes of the machine and a few control sequences to change tools, adjust feed rate, spindle speed, and other (machine-dependent) parameters.

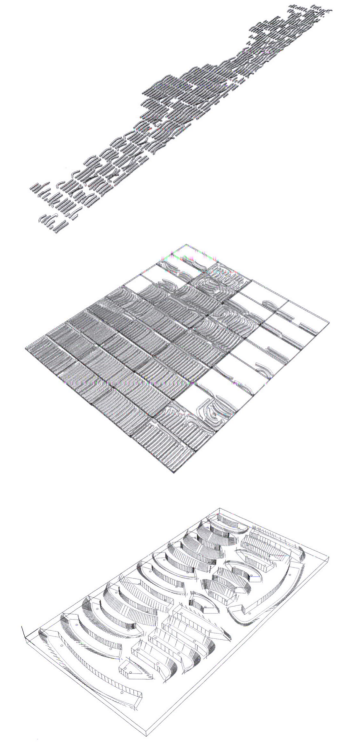

18.18a–c.
Hungerburg Funicular Stations: automated fabrication planning for the roof components: (a) flat layout of one station, (b) nesting, and (c) tool paths.

The coordinate information can be derived directly from the CAD models of the components. Since we know exactly how those were derived from the overall shape, there is no uncertainty in determining how to generate the tool paths. Additional fabrication parameters are either fixed for all components or dependent on some geometric property. For example, two different tools are used for the profiles in the *Hungerburg Funicular Stations* project, depending on the maximum angle of bank in the component. An easy way to create the G-Code is to let the fabrication experts generate it for some sample components and then "reverse-engineer" that code to find the parts that can be replaced by the individual component data.

Another way (which we have only recently started to explore) is to build a custom import function for a given CAM system instead of replacing the CAM system as such. This has the big advantage, in that some useful function of the CAM software could be exploited, such as the nesting function or the generation of the G-Code for different types of machines. This would also allow simulation of the fabrication process within the CAM software, and thus provide another quality check before the CNC machine is switched on. This is very useful since the equipment is expensive and a wrong coordinate that drives the tool into the machine instead of the material could ruin it very quickly.

INTEGRATION MATTERS

Once a continuous digital production chain has been established, information should flow smoothly from the 3D model of the overall shape through the generation of the component geometry, the optimization for production, and the generation of the machine code for the CNC fabrication at the end (figure 18.19).

18.19.
CAD/CAM-process with shop-drawings in standard format.

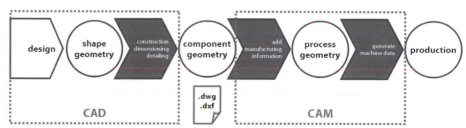

18.20.
Real-world
CAD/CAM
process.

18.21.
Assembly
documents for the
Futuropolis project.

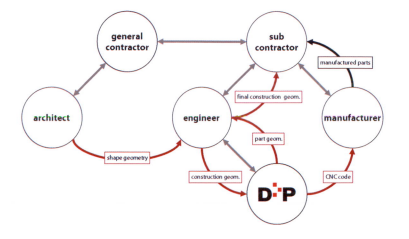

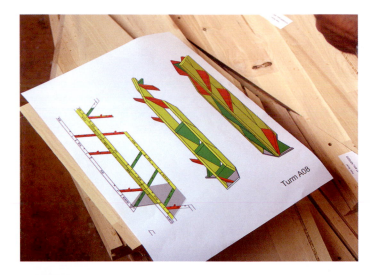

18.22.
Futuropolis:
aluminum
dovetail
connectors.

18.23.
Futuropolis:
detail of the
assembled
structure.

In the real world of building projects, this is hardly ever a linear process. There is likely to be a general contractor and a number of subcontractors and engineers for different trades. Information has to take numerous detours and loops (figure 18.20) and, since all parties have their own CAD systems, interfacing problems are likely to emerge. In addition to that, contractual and legal issues have to be considered, which sometimes take longer to resolve than the actual planning tasks.

The choice of a particular CAD system for the implementation of the digital production chain therefore not only depends on the functionality of the system (it has to be scriptable), but also on the range of systems that are already in use within the project. If 3D data has to be exchanged back and forth – as in the *Hungerburg Funicular Stations* project, where the detailed geometry of the profile segments had to flow back to the engineers and the steel contractor – it makes perfect sense to avoid interfacing problems by agreeing on a common CAD standard.

Also, the production chain does not end at the CNC machine. When dealing with a couple of thousand unique parts, logistics become a crucial issue. The components have to be numbered and labeled, either by milling the part code directly into the material, as in the *Swissbau Pavilion* project, or by providing printed stickers. Fabricators need lists and plans when preparing the material and scheduling their workflow. When parts are finally delivered on site, assembly plans are needed to locate every single component in the overall structure (figure 18.21). Most of this information can be derived directly from the CAD model, but this adds to the development cost of the building system.

One of the hardest problems when trying to integrate all of these into a building process is tender regulations. To develop a custom-building system requires a thorough knowledge of the manufacturing process, which usually only the fabrication experts have. Unfortunately, they are the last to join the team and, as a result, it is difficult to tap their know-how at the very beginning of the design phase and project development.

DETAILS MATTER

Why is it so important to talk to fabrication specialists early in the project? When building with components, the connections between them become an important issue. In rapid prototyping with scale models, connections are often neglected. Either the whole piece is 3D-printed at once, or a drop of glue solves the problem. In contrast, on a full, 1:1 scale, connection details become the most important thing: forces are carried from one component to the other at the joints, so they have to be strong and durable; in a structure of some thousand components there are quite a few connections that have to be established during assembly, which makes details the most labor-intensive part.

When working in wood, as in four of the five projects shown here, there is a multitude of possible connection details. Many forgotten details are now appearing again, because the accuracy and speed of CNC fabrication makes them very efficient. For example, in the *Futuropolis* project, more than 2,000 components had to be joined in a durable and stable way. The fabrication partner (a carpenter) proposed the use of aluminum dovetail connectors (figure 18.22), which had a few intriguing advantages: *stability* – the joints proved to be extremely solid; *CNC fabrication* – the notches that hold the dovetail profiles are milled directly on the five-axis router at very high precision; *self-positioning* – since the notches are fabricated exactly, adjacent boards also match exactly when connected with the dovetails; *speed* – it is fine to glue the contact faces and drive in the dovetail profiles from both ends, instead of having to clamp each connection during assembly and unclamp them when the glue has dried, which saves a few seconds at every connection and adds up to a few hours for the whole structure (figure 18.23).

Another issue that becomes especially important when working on a building together with other trades is *tolerances*. The precision of CNC machines is usually far higher than needed on a full architectural scale, which must be taken into account or otherwise unfortunate surprises could emerge on site. For example, the notches in the components for the *Hungerburg Funicular Stations* had to be 5mm wider than the steel profiles they were sitting on (figures 18.24a–b), because steel tends to buckle when welded on site.

18.24a–b.
*Hungerburg
Funicular Stations*:
components after
fabrication and on
site.

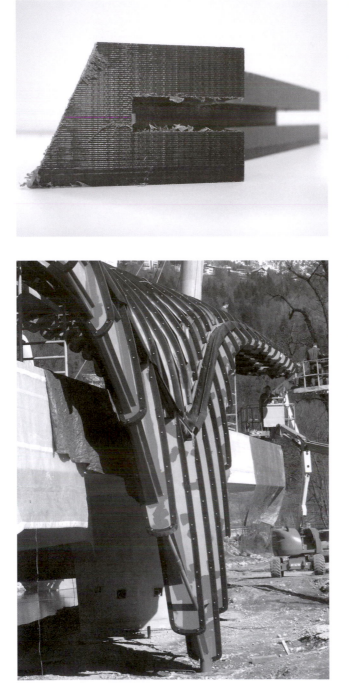

On the other hand, tolerances can be exploited sometimes in the fabrication process. Since wood is a "living material," it was not possible to build the towers of *Futuropolis* perfectly straight. To compensate, they stand 4mm apart, which happens to be the width of the saw blade used to cut the boards. If the towers had had to stand precisely side by side, it would have been necessary to compensate for the thickness of the cut, thus increasing the complexity of the process significantly.

In general, as happened more than once in these projects, the seemingly difficult problems were solved by a simple fabrication solution. On the other hand, a slight change in the design can save many hours in production. Therefore, it is absolutely necessary to know the fabrication in detail and discuss both the details and the process with the experts.

EDUCATION MATTERS

This last point is the reason why *designtoproduction* engages in educational projects. We had the chance to gain experience during our close collaborations with fabricators and building experts on actual building projects, done mostly while we were at the university. After we left the university as a spin-off company, we considered it absolutely necessary to establish close contact between education and practice. Unfortunately, architectural education at universities does not always provide opportunities to engage the "real world" and all the little obstacles it presents. We are especially proud of the last project in this chapter – the *Camera Obscura* – which was designed, fabricated, and built by 15 students from NTNU over one semester in Trondheim, Norway. Here, the process was deliberately started at the back end by introducing students to the capabilities of the CNC equipment and then instigating a design contest. The resulting design is admittedly the least complex out of five proposals that were developed, but it still drove the machinery used far beyond its normal scope of work; it is an excellent example of what would be possible if we could fully use the capabilities of CAD/CAM fabrication in architecture.

19

ASSOCIATIVE DESIGN IN FABRICATION

MAKAI SMITH / BENTLEY

19.1.
Lantern for the Bloom residence, near Los Angeles (2008), designed by *Greg Lynn/FORM*.

19.2.
Lantern: original ribbed construction strategy.

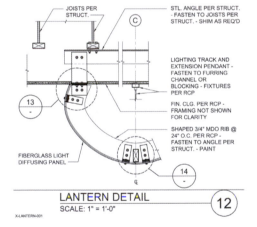

19.3.
Lantern: revised fiberglass flange construction strategy.

The term "*digital fabrication*" is a useful catchall for a number of different technologies, but it implies a manufacturing procedure carried out solely by machines and not by human hands. In practice, the distinction is not so clear – *digital fabrication* processes tend to mix computer-enabled and manual methods, each with their own limitations and potentials, and often occurring together in a construction process.

I have been immersed professionally in digital fabrication, as well as the software industry. Most examples here are from *Kreysler and Associates,* an architectural composites manufacturer located near San Francisco, California. I headed the digital pattern-making activities, where we worked mostly from three-dimensional computer models to make molds and patterns using very large custom-built CNC milling machines. All this work was the result of consultation with designers and architects needing digital fabrication expertise to realize and construct their ideas. Most recently, I have been working directly with the *GenerativeComponents* associative parametric design software from *Bentley,* and will demonstrate how associative modeling techniques are essential for digital fabrication.

AMALGAMATING FABRICATION

Projects by *Kreysler and Associates* clearly demonstrate the amalgamated nature of digital fabrication. We worked with *Greg Lynn/FORM* to design and fabricate a translucent *Lantern* for the Bloom residence (2008). The form is a cocoon-like shape (figure 19.1), about 10 ft at its widest and about 40 ft long, attached to the ceiling of a living space. The drawings that came from the architect's office showed fiberglass panels supported by a series of marine-grade plywood ribs fixed to the structure above by steel clip angles (figure 19.2). Ribbed construction is very strong; it is a good way to construct a boat, but it is far over-designed to support a fiberglass skin, which weighs at most 2 lbs per sq ft. The architect was open to re-evaluating the connection details after being shown examples of typical keyed bolting flanges for fiberglass panels (figure 19.3). Early, open collaboration such as this between the fabricator and the architect is a key ingredient to a successful custom fabrication project.

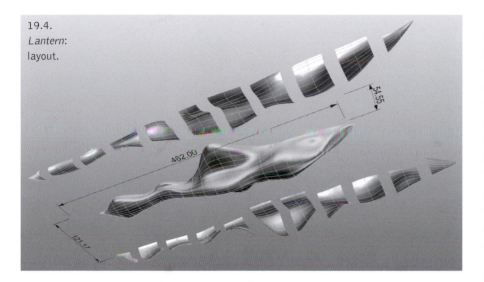

19.4.
Lantern:
layout.

19.5.
Lantern:
translucent
panels and CNC
milled molds.

19.6.
Lantern:
translucent
scrap.

The geometry came from *Greg Lynn's* office in the form of a three-dimensional computer model made of B-spline surfaces (figure 19.4). While the inherent isoparametric lines of the geometry infer a structural performance, the actual constructional logic required much more development and often did not correspond to the computational representation of the form. When we had to take the fabrication into account, the form changed. This critical point underscores the necessity for open channels of communication during the design process. In this project, the dimensions of the raw material stock and the structural action of the form required different segmenting of the overall shape. Detail features, such as flanges, required that molding and assembly also be considered.

A pair of translucent panels (figure 19.5) was deployed to test the laminate specifications and mockup the assembly process. The manufacturing process is made more expensive than opaque panels because translucent fiberglass requires very exacting fabrication to maintain the consistency necessary for even light transmission and coloration.

When it comes to fabrication, it is paramount to know where to set limits for material characteristics, especially for fit and finish. During prototyping, it happened that a scrap piece of a laminate, rejected from an architectural restoration project, was on the other side of the wall from the mock-up. This laminate, which never received its finishing coat, was in a raw state – naturally translucent, yellow-brown, and beautifully mottled (figure 19.6). The translucent laminate for the lantern had to be precisely constructed to maintain the even translucency specified, and was made out of very clear and costly resin. The scrap material, however, was made of regular polyester laminating resin and common fiberglass, and was produced very quickly. Both materials have similar qualities and structural performance, but are different in cost by at least a factor of four. Because of how it was made, the scrap material has visible striation of the fiberglass; it was an artifact of the lamination production process. Assuming the appearance of the scrap laminate was acceptable, circumstances such as this could lead to significant advantages. This example demonstrates that a clear understanding of the production processes, and effective communication with the fabricator, can help control costs.

19.8.
Diderot's Encyclopédie, the process of weaving a net, circa 1751–1776.

19.7.
Lantern: the *GenerativeComponents* associative model of the geometry.

19.8.
Diderot's Encyclopédie, the process of weaving a net, circa 1751–1776.

19.7.
Lantern: the *GenerativeComponents* associative model of the geometry.

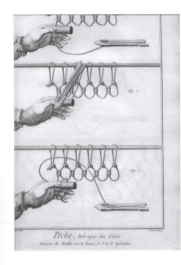

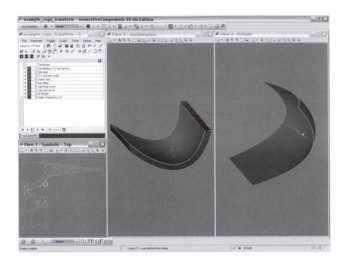

How could a designer make such a financially beneficial decision without an intimate knowledge of the production facility or substantial experience in fabricating fiber-reinforced polymer materials? Early communication, willing participants, and teamwork are paramount to these processes.

EMBEDDING KNOWLEDGE

In an era when computation is pervasive, we can use our software tools for useful information exchanges during the design and production processes. One idea is to put knowledge about how something is fabricated into a persistent form that can be shared and reused: embedding fabrication knowledge into an algorithm, which can be re-executed.

The *GenerativeComponents* model illustrates two views of a panel from the *Lantern* project (figure 19.7). On the right is the source geometry, and on the left is a copy of that geometry in a separate linked model. The copy operation is controlled by a reference point, which can be freely moved about the surface. The flanges are modeled as extrusions of the surface edges, projected with respect to the vertical direction (plus the required approach angle of the milling machine). The geometric copy and the flanging operation are associative relationships, so that when the source geometry is moved, the copied geometry and its flanges are recomputed to reflect the new orientation. This precise flexibility allows a range of possible panel orientations to be explored without having to remodel the flanges for each scenario.

Capturing the execution of a process is not new; consider the plate from *Diderot's Encyclopédie*[1] (figure 19.8), which shows the process of weaving a net. A modern example, the steps of a digital fabrication process, explained in a section of computer programming language (figure 19.9), stands in seemingly direct contrast to the net weaving illustration. One is a graphical representation, the other is text-based code, yet both of them are algorithms describing a fabrication process.

If we go to the root of the process situated between digital design and fabrication, we arrive at *tool making*; we are not making instruction sets, but instead creating the *mechanisms* that write them. An example is a program, often referred to as a *G-code* file, which generates the tool paths

19.9.
Programming code, written in *GCScript*, describing a surface development process.

```
//SNIP...
transaction modelBased "Create 3D Rule Lines"
{
    feature fabricationPlanning01 GC.FabricationPlanning
    {
        CoordinateSystem        = baseCS;
        LeftCurve               = circle01;
        RightCurve              = circle02;
        SampleCount             = 50;
        OutputOption            = DevelopableOptions.RuleLines;
    }
}

transaction modelBased "Create Separate Model for Developed Planar Lines"
{
    feature fabricationPlanningModelBaseCS GC.CoordinateSystem
    {
        Model                   = "fabricationPlanningModel";
    }
}

transaction modelBased "Create Planar Rule Lines"
{
    feature fabricationPlanning02 GC.FabricationPlanning
    {
        CoordinateSystem        = fabricationPlanningModelBaseCS;
        LeftCurve               = circle01;
        RightCurve              = circle02;
        SampleCount             = 50;
        OutputOption            = DevelopableOptions.PlanarRuleLines;
    }
}

transaction modelBased "Create Flattened Rail Curves"
{
    feature bsplineCurve01 GC.BsplineCurve
    {
        FitPoints               = fabricationPlanning02.StartPoint;
    }
    feature bsplineCurve02 GC.BsplineCurve
    {
        FitPoints               = fabricationPlanning02.EndPoint;
    }
}
//...
```

19.10.
The *Sandpainter*
CNC machine,
presented at
SIGGRAPH 2004.

19.11.
The *Pinnacle* in
London (expected
completion in 2010),
designed by *Kohn
Pedersen Fox
Architects*.

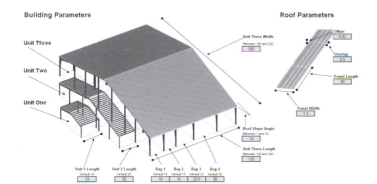

19.12.
A prototype
building for
*Butler Building
Systems* (2006),
designed by Henry
Farnarier.

19.13.
Pinnacle: glazing
detail.

for the CNC milling machine – in this case the *Sandpainter*, a repurposed CNC machine that I helped to construct, prints 12' x 18' raster images in silica sand (figure 19.10). To control it, we wrote a program that took images and generated machine instructions.

Making tools is an order of magnitude more powerful than making the end object itself; it can also be that much more difficult. As architects, engineers, and fabricators, we have always encountered the need to become toolmakers. Historically these tools were physical; today, they are often digital, allowing us to conceive of things not limited by the tools at hand, but requiring a great deal of skill. This means that if the tools do not suit us, we can change them, or in the case of catastrophic failure, we can build them again.

ASSOCIATIVE PARAMETRIC DESIGN

Associative parametric design software affords manipulation of both geometry and relationships. It allows us to create design tools without having to start from scratch. Specifically, *GenerativeComponents* offers the opportunity to efficiently model and represent both the objects to be produced as well as their processes of production.

Compare the *Pinnacle* (figure 19.11) in London (expected completion in 2010) by *Kohn Pedersen Fox Architects* and a prototype building for *Butler Building Systems* (figure 19.12) designed by Henry Farnarier of *Bentley*. They actually share a common approach: both designs take advantage of computation to solve a design problem. Using an algorithm running within *GenerativeComponents*, Stylianos Dritsas of KPF optimized in an iterative fashion the glazing for the *Pinnacle* (figure 19.13). The metal *Butler Building Systems* building was designed and documented by embedding information about the constraints of the manufacturing process and capturing it in a digital form. In both these examples, the inputs, or higher-level controls, were reduced to the necessary minimum, and the problems had to have a computable answer. While minimum representation is elegant, it also requires a rigor, which is rather difficult and unfamiliar to many design practices.

19.14.
The *Lorenz Attractor* visualization in *GenerativeComponents* by Chris Lasch and Steve Sanderson (2007).

Designing using *associative parametric design software* requires a very specific approach and a thorough recording of the choices that are made in the process of evolving a design solution. One can capture different aspects of the design process. First, there are *creation attributes* of the objects. For instance, a cube has an edge-length dimension. The dimension *parameter* is important to record, since having a parametric model means that if we alter a dimension, the geometry updates automatically to reflect the change. Another example of a *parameter* is the thickness of a building's wall, or any other attribute of an object's creation that can be edited later and updated in the geometric model. Second, in the design process there is a set of steps to go through to make something — a narrative or history of an object. This is known as a *transactional model* and can be represented in text form in a computer programming language such as *GCScript*. Finally, there are relationships among objects — properties of an object can drive or be driven by properties of another object. These relationships, or *associations,* are the key to creating models with complex, useful behavior. The relationships themselves are just an exchange of data, thus they do not have explicit geometry that can be seen in a model view. So, they must be represented graphically using a *symbolic model.*

Different representations of the model — *geometric, transactional, symbolic,* and others — support parallel ways of design. We can manipulate objects graphically; we are very good with our hands and eyes in the sense of traditional craft, so design software must support this method. On the other hand, there are things that are by nature non-physical and can only be represented as mathematical expressions or computer programs (which can vary from a simple, one-line script to full-fledged programs). So, we must also support purely abstract representations. One example of such a mathematical object is the *Lorenz Attractor* (figure 19.14), which results from the three-dimensional structure of chaotic flow that can only be visualized through a recursive mathematical approach.

Computational design tools give us ways to create systems of mind-numbing complexity, so they must also offer ways to understand and manage them. *GenerativeComponents* allows us to see multiple models. These may show differently filtered views of the same geometry, or they may be different derivations of the geometry, such as a view of a three-dimensional form alongside a view of the unfolded, flattened geometry of that same form. We can see a *symbolic model*, which makes visible the associative relationships between objects. We can also see the text-based or code-based representations of objects, such as *transactions* and *script editors*. Object dependencies can be also shown as a hierarchical tree, and the objects can be displayed as a list sorted by a chosen category. These different views (windows) represent different ways to understand particularities of the system.

Many core concepts in *GenerativeComponents* are not new; the innovation comes from how they are used and implemented. For example, borrowing concepts from object-oriented systems and information design, there are *hierarchies of inheritance* — objects can have children who inherit properties, which can then be overwritten to produce unique behavior. There are also concepts that apply specifically to the design disciplines, but are not found generally in computer science or software design, such as "*replication*." For example, when designing a building column, instead of having one sectional detail drawing for every column that will be built, we choose to have a whole family of columns represented by a single drawing. The drawing represents either a single column or as many columns as specified. *GenerativeComponents* allows objects to be replicated in a similar way — an object can be singular or can replicate to become a collection of objects. This means that we can have a very highly "geared" system, which can produce a large amount of design geometry from sparse data.

Associative parametric design, however, is not a panacea; it is a tool that is applicable to a specific kind of design approach in certain kinds of projects. If you sit down at the boards knowing what you will draw, with a pre-conceived notion of what the form should look like, then there is likely a more direct way to model it directly using conventional CAD software. *Associative parametric design* requires fluency

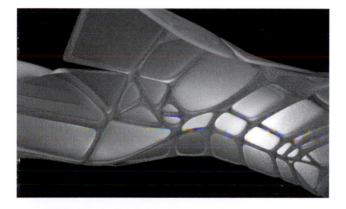

19.15.
UniBodies
rendering, Artists
Space, New York
(2006).

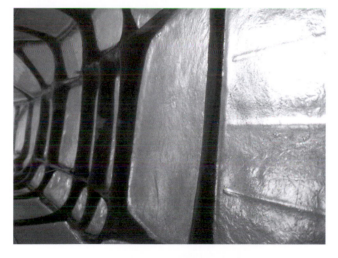

19.16.
UniBodies:
interior view
of the finished
piece.

19.17.
UniBodies: resin
was applied by
hand during
fabrication.

in computational media, three-dimensional geometric modeling, and in managing data and interdependencies. To paraphrase Mark Burry, it requires that you "design the design,"[2] or think upfront about the logic of the design as explicit choices are made about things, which can be left unseen and unexplored in conventional modeling or CAD processes.

DIGITAL AND HANDCRAFTED FABRICATION

In collaboration with *Marcelo Spina/PATTERNS*, *Kreysler and Associates* created a series of pieces, called *UniBodies* (figures 19.15 and 19.16), for the *A+D Series* at *Artists Space* in New York (2006). The produced pieces explored the potential of monocoque structures and fiberglass composite materials in the context of a proto-architecture.

The starting point of the forms for the exhibition was the *Monocoque House*, an existing design that Marcelo Spina brought to *Kreysler and Associates*. In a general sense, form was a given; we received visualizations such as a grainy black and white "photograph" taken with animation software. (It was interesting to compare that image with the fabricated piece. The material effect was very close.)

Digital fabricators model geometry extensively, although the modeling work is not to be confused with authorship; it is very derivative, comprised of *manipulative operations*, *segmentations*, and *indexical relationships*, which are very secondary. Extensive geometric development is almost always necessary, especially in deciding where to place parting lines for fabrication. The forms of the *UniBodies* series were complex, so most of the molds could not be milled in one piece even using a 5-axis CNC machine, because they formed a cavity that could not accommodate the cutter head. Instead, the form had to be broken into pieces, and milled using a 3-axis approach.

Pieces were laid up using translucent laminating resin (figure 19.17). Because the resin hardens very quickly, the work had to proceed quickly too. Depending on the temperature, there is only about 20 minutes to finish the piece before it sets.

Faced with many choices and with limited time, the skilled craftsman must act without hesitation and be prepared to work with the results. The opaque gray ribs,

19.19.
UniBodies: sculptor
Scott Van Note hand
finishes the surface of
a metalic fiberglass
composite.

19.18. (below)
UniBodies:
five-axis CNC
milled mold.

19.20.
Folded Water traveling
installation (2005),
smooth-shaded
rendering.

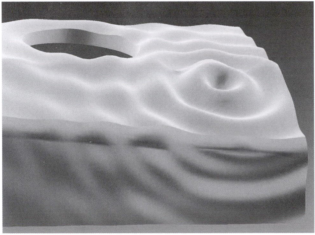

19.21.
Folded Water:
flat-shaded
rendering.

visible in the finished piece, look as if they are of rigid pieces molded separately and then joined. That would have been very difficult to do, involving a tremendous amount of detailed trimming to fit the pieces together. Instead, we decided to apply a thickened, metal-filled resin, using a trowel to fill in depressions, and then finish the surface flush afterwards. Because of the secondary finishing operation, which seemed so easy at first, it took nearly twice as long as having done the ribs as a separately molded piece. The end result was fairly close to what was intended, but only through ample use of abrasives and pneumatic tools.

Accompanying the large model were a series of studies of individual bays of the building and a set of material studies. Even though we milled these parts using a five-axis CNC machine, they still needed to be segmented into a set of piece molds (figure 19.18). Most of the individual components had a post-applied, integrally pigmented, polymer finish. One was made using an aluminum-filled resin, sometimes referred to as a cold cast metal. It is made from roughly equal amounts of atomized aluminum powder and polyester resin. This unique material feels like metal, is cold to the touch, and can develop a patina, but has the light weight of a fiberglass composite. Looking at the crisp interior edge profile of this piece, seeing the dye grinders and rasps used to capture the form, it is evident that digital fabrication does not imply that handcrafting is no longer necessary (figure 19.19).

RISKS AND REWARDS

One of the risks inherent in digital fabrication is illustrated by a project called *Folded Water* that *Kreysler and Associates* produced with the designers at *Tronic Studio* in New York. This piece for *General Electric* served as a backdrop for the announcement of their *Ecomagination* marketing campaign (2005). The project is a mix of corporate branding, sculpture, and spatial enclosure.

Two images illustrate the complexity in exchanging information: the first image (figure 19.20) is what presumably the designers saw on their computer screens when they sent us the data. The second image (figure 19.21) is what I saw when I viewed the data on my computer. The difference is in the triangles – the first image only looks

230

19.22.
Folded Water: hand sanding during fabrication.

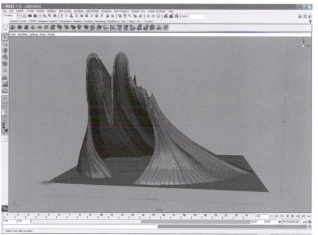

19.23.
Illumination No. 1: model view.

19.25.
Illumination No. 1: model triangulation.

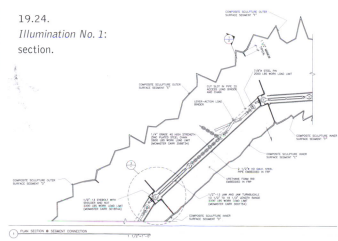

19.24.
Illumination No. 1: section.

smooth because of the *display-shading* mode, but in fact it is comprised of large triangles that are nearly an inch-long on a side!

The schedule lapsed, and after much pleading for a refined dataset, we were forced to mill what we had. We then had to apply the smooth shading ourselves. Roberto Ambriz manually applied the smoothing, also known as sanding (figure 19.22). The lesson learned is that working directly from digital files requires that everyone involved must treat the digital geometry as a real, physical object. Digital objects have interesting properties of their own, but in the fabrication process, the digital representation is a stand-in for the physical object. We cannot lose sight of the relationship between the model and the physical object. It is easy to have things in the computer float free from reality; to forget that geometry is not unit-less, that data is to scale, and that triangulation has a size that matters.

DIGITAL AND HANDCRAFTED FABRICATION (REVISITED)

Sculptor Michael Somoroff created *Illumination No. 1* for installation at the *Rothko Chapel* in Houston, Texas (2006). The form draws inspiration from a concretization of light, and is a shell-like shape about 20' tall and 30' wide at its base (figure 19.23). The sculptor came to us with a rough, three-dimensional polygon model, which more or less served as the construction document. "Here, can you make one of these?" he queried.

Digital fabrication can still require that drawings be done. For example, we needed drawings to work out and document a series of post-tensioning chains, which lock the seven pieces together for assembly after shipping to the building site. However, a mere section detail (figure 19.24) does not describe the overall form. Not even a series of sections could describe this complex freeform shape. In order to effectively make the whole piece, we needed the entire dataset – each and every triangle.

Every triangle is important, even the ones that were left in the model by accident. The image of the digital model (figure 19.25) illustrates some of the stray geometry left over from the sculptor's extensive manipulation of the form. These patches of leftover polygons – and there were

19.26a–b.
Illumination No. 1:
the nesting set-up.

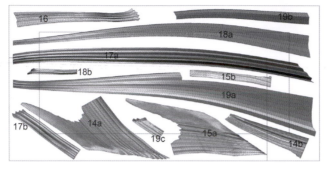

19.27.
Illumination No. 1:
CNC production.

set-up ready for milling, which then takes upwards of two days to complete (figure 19.27). The nesting problem (as described by computer scientists) is an unbounded problem, which can take an infinite amount of time to solve perfectly. The practical way out is to find a solution with an acceptable minimization of waste. For us, the time spent searching for a solution is more expensive than the material it saves. Since the human mind is very good at solving the problem quickly enough to a satisfactory degree (and because we did not have computer scientists on our staff), we solved it "manually."

The flanges form a skirt around each piece in the set-up meant to create a smooth transition from one piece to the next. This avoids a collision with the milling head or collet and the adjoining piece. It is a fairly simple to model one of them, but repeated over hundreds of pieces, there are a couple of weeks of modeling time in that operation alone.

Designing and modeling flanges is even more time-consuming than nesting. Unlike the nesting operation, creating the flanges is a repeatable operation with fairly simple rules, which can be expressed algorithmically. *Associative parametric modeling* is particularly useful at this stage (figure 19.28). A flexible range box defines a region in which the geometry from the source file is automatically imported into *GenerativeComponents* and the edge curves extracted. Another digital component adds the flanges to the pieces: it just needs to be given the angle to draw them and information on how far to project them. The range box can be moved to exclude different parts of the geometry and the

very many like them – seem miniscule in a model on a computer screen. If left, they would have created a divot in the form a few inches wide by about one foot long. It is difficult and very labor-intensive to go over every triangle in the model to verify that the data actually describes the object to be built. It must be done, so the agreement between designer and fabricator has to make clear who is responsible to do it. To avoid problems, there is no substitute for good communication early on and open collaboration throughout the project. The responsibility may be shared, but it requires skill and judgment to check the veracity of the data and examine the entire dataset to find buried problems.

After the geometry was repaired, the overall complex form was decomposed into simpler, manufacturable components (figures 19.26a–b). It can take a day for even a very experienced craftsperson to select pieces and nest them together into a composed

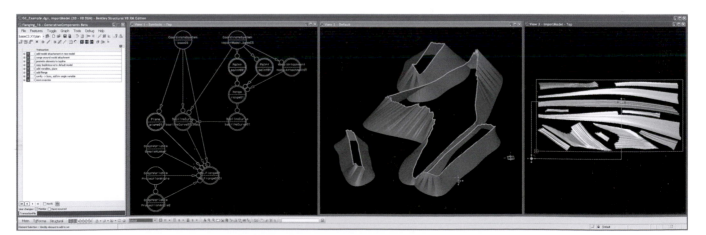

19.28.
Illumination No. 1: the
GenerativeComponents
model.

19.31.
*Illumination
No. 1*: partial
assembly.

19.29.
Illumination No. 1: one
of the 12' tall molds
milled from expanded
polystyrene foam.

19.30.
Illumination No. 1:
finished pieces, ready
to be demolded and
trimmed.

19.32.
Illumination No. 1:
partial assembly.

flange parameters can be edited. What this demonstrates is that there are many practical ways for fabricators to express something we intuitively know about a process in an algorithmic, re-executable form. We can build our own digital tools that embody the skills we master. In this example, the benefit is mostly labor-saving. However, the implication is much broader, as well illustrated by *designtoproduction*'s work, and points to doing things which were not possible otherwise, or at least not practical without the use of computational media to enable the fabricator.

The molds (figure 19.29) were milled from expanded polystyrene foam, on a very large CNC milling machine, which we built ourselves for this purpose. The pieces were fabricated using fiberglass composite lamination (figure 19.30). The trimmed pieces are indexed to each other because of their unique shapes, but since the fiberglass is very flexible, they must be pinned together until they are permanently joined with more layers of fiberglass and resin (figure 19.31). The many ropes, which hang the pieces during assembly (figure 19.32), show that the ancient craft of setting out and drawing lines on the site with strings is very much alive.

The pieces were assembled together around a set of internal connections and structural ribs. They were finished with stucco made from an acrylic modified gypsum and marble dust applied in many coats. Attention to the fairness of the form, continuity of the lines, and lavish handwork erased any sense that it was conceived and originated through digital means (figure 19.33).

Achieving a fair form is particularly difficult when working with extensively manipulated polygonal models. While we spent many hours editing individual vertices in the computer model, in the end, it was necessary to finish the job manually. It is instructive to compare what "looks right" with what "feels right," because in the computer, without a physical object, you can only have the former but not the latter. Fairness on a form is easy to spot in sharp sunlight, and easy to feel with hand, but exceedingly difficult to fully visualize and even harder to correct within a computer. Hand sanding with a block or a long board becomes the appropriate means to achieve fair surfaces.

19.33.
Illumination No. 1,
Houston, Texas
(2006).

CONCLUSION

Digital working methods, such as CNC machines and associative parametric modeling, have entered the shop floor, but they are not a wholesale replacement for what came before them. Digital fabrication and traditional techniques are compatible and complementary. Even more, they are interrelated and enable us to build a new hybrid toolset.

Knowing the right tool for the job is one hallmark of a skilled craftsman. On the workbench today, we find computer-controlled tools, conventional power tools, and we will always, I believe, find many hand tools. Similarly, with the advent of associative parametric modeling, we have to choose between an advanced computational approach, a drawing-based computer-aided design approach, or hand drawing – moreover, we need to know how to smoothly move between them or combine them as need arises. Work from both *Illumination No. 1* and the *Unibodies* series shows the fluid interplay of the digital and the manual in custom fabrication.

Having taken hold in the early 1950s, computer-controlled milling machines are by now a very mature technology. They may be relatively new to the architectural design practice, but they are well established broadly in manufacturing. While the technology itself is unlikely to change quickly, how it is applied in bringing buildings to market is still rapidly evolving. The maturity of the CNC technology suggests that we are ready to move beyond examining the means of production, the machines and techniques themselves, to unlock changes in how we conceive of and realize our designs.

Likewise, associative parametric modeling is well rooted in some manufacturing and engineering disciplines, but it has been largely dormant in architectural design. As the computer-aided drafting paradigm is exhausted, software such as *GenerativeComponents* comes to the forefront because of the tremendous creative and practical advantage it offers. To take full advantage of the new software tools requires using computer models as the communication medium. This has ramifications for the legal responsibility of the correctness of the data, such as discussed in the *Folded Water* project, and for the skill set required to work in the design and fabrication disciplines. As a result, the *culture of use* in these fields is still growing as we explore the questions surrounding how digital fabrication methods are developed, taught, and applied.

NOTES

1 http://www.vobam.se/bilder-raritetskat/diderot-nat.jpg, accessed on 19 November 2007. Reprinted in *L'Encyclopédie ou Dictionnaire Raisonné des Sciences, des Arts et des métiers Diderot et D'Alembert*, Oxford: Pergamon Press, 1969. (Original Paris, circa 1751 to 1776.)

2 From a keynote lecture given by Mark Burry at *Fabrication*, the Association for Computer Aided Design in Architecture (ACADIA) conference, 13 November 2004, Cambridge, Ontario, Canada.

20

MATERIAL EXPERIMENTS IN DESIGN AND BUILD

MICK EEKHOUT / OCTATUBE INTERNATIONAL BV
AND DELFT UNIVERSITY OF TECHNOLOGY

The starting points for our work at *Octatube* are the design, development, and research of new products and systems; the synergy of architectural, structural, and industrial design; and the integration of design, engineering, production, and building. In all our projects, the early and close relationships between design, engineering, and construction are critical. Simultaneously, final production techniques and building methods are indispensable. Experimentation is greatly stimulated by this "design and build" approach, in which design, engineering, prototyping, testing, production, and realization are performed by a single company. In this way, knowledge, experience, and insight are acquired and exchanged faster and in a more transparent way than in more conventional project organizations that typically separate design and engineering parties on one side and the fabrication and construction parties on the other. This split is often counterproductive. Innovation and "design and build" attitude stimulate each other in the tolerant Dutch building climate. It is also important to note that this "design and build" attitude is not new – it was typical of the pioneers of building technology such as Gustave Eiffel, Felix Candela, Pier Luigi Nervi, and Heinz Isler.

The new "design and build" *modus operandi* of the "digital" generation will have an important influence on the future of building design and production through new, highly integrated and innovative processes from computer to production machines. Innovations in building technology often start with architectonic "dreams" with bold imaginative ideas that lead, via sound engineering procedures, to new experimental technologies, techniques, and solutions. At *Octatube*, we have been experimenting for more than 25 years with innovative techniques for direct application on built designs: we have lately bent (cold) glass panels to adapt them to desired curved or twisted forms in projects by Erick van Egeraat (figure 20.1), *Asymptote Architects*, and others. We have deformed flat aluminum panels into double curved forms using an explosion process for a pavilion designed by *Asymptote Architects* (figure 20.6). We have created new composite sandwich roof shells in the *Yitzhak Rabin Center* (figure 20.19) by Moshe Safdie, and are experimenting with new possibilities in the *Mediatheque* at Pau designed by Zaha Hadid (figure 20.20). We see these experimental product developments as positioned between two poles: on the one hand is the *technological and technical*, i.e. the necessary research and design of a general solution for a specific category of technical problems, and on the other is the *practical*, a specific project application that demands a particular solution through thoughtful design and engineering.

THE TOWN HALL IN ALPHEN AAN DEN RIJN

For the *Town Hall* in Alphen aan den Rijn (2003), in the Netherlands, architect Erick van Egeraat designed a fluid building form (figure 20.1). All components in this semi-blobby building design have complex geometry. The building features frameless glass façades with a permanent decorative screening, for which the architect's studio developed three different designs: the first was a mixture of trees and bamboo, based on a large number of silkscreen matrices; the second was composed of letters; and the third was based on tree leaves and petals. In all three designs, each individual glass panel featured a different screen pattern, which required a highly individual industrial production – customization in "lots of one."

Geometrically, the building is quite complex (figure 20.2); only the floors are flat. All columns are oblique and at different angles. The frameless façade is a combination of cylindrical, conical, and arbitrary surfaces. There were 850 glass panels produced in small series with various dimensions. Because of the patterning of the silver screening, each panel had to be separately engineered, printed, produced, and assembled (figure 20.3). With extensive engineering and numerous tests, a precise, well-defined, albeit fairly complex (and complicated) production and assembly process was developed in four different, successive production locations in Belgium and the Netherlands.[1]

The project's complex geometry presented even more challenges with current glass technology. The original design for the back façade of the main building volume consisted of a number of rows of wooden window frames with non-parallel upper and lower sides. The façade surface onto

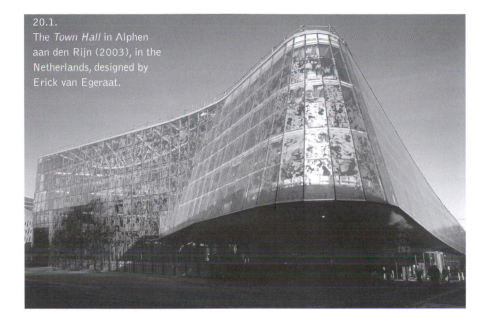

20.1.
The *Town Hall* in Alphen
aan den Rijn (2003), in the
Netherlands, designed by
Erick van Egeraat.

20.3.
Town Hall: each glass
panel was separately
engineered, produced,
and assembled.

20.2.
Town Hall: the building
has a complex, fluid
geometric form.

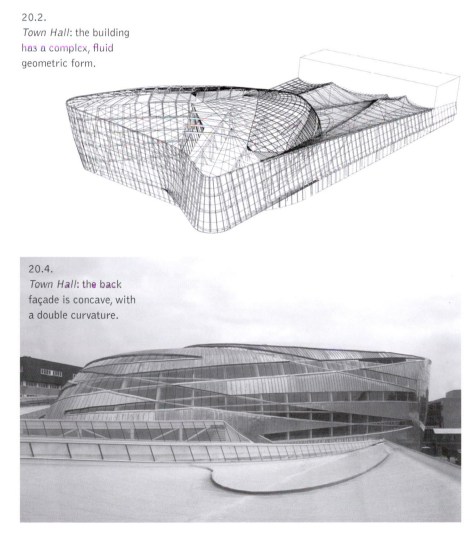

20.4.
Town Hall: the back
façade is concave, with
a double curvature.

which these façade rows had to be placed was concave, and
had a double curvature (figure 20.4). As a result, many of the
wooden frames, which had a maximum width of 900 mm
and maximum height of 1800 mm, had to cant to each
other, and some of the rows had to be designed with torsion.
The first development cycle of the wooden window frames
did not lead to a technically feasible solution; the wooden
frames were inflexible, not properly watertight, and produced
unattractive indentations in the window rows. As a result, the
timber subcontractor pulled out. At the request of the general
contractor, we suggested abandoning the wooden window
frames and devised a solution based on cold twisting of the
insulated and laminated glass panels alone.

The final solution was developed based on a doctoral
research by Dr Karel Vollers at the *Delft University of
Technology* (*TU Delft*),[2] which I had supervised. In this
PhD thesis, Dr Vollers explored hot-twisted glass façades,
and concluded that cold torsion could be used for smaller
surface deformations. This proposal was developed further in
this project. The principal idea was to place the top and the
bottom of each double glass panel into continuous, U-shaped
stainless steel profiles, and use only cold torsion (i.e. twisting)
during assembly to meet the shape requirements. The two
U-shaped profiles were not parallel and were also not in the
same plane. The deformation, however, could easily be done
through manual power and manually operated tools. A series
of mock-ups were constructed and tested in the factory. As
expected, flat glass panels behaved like any other flat panel
when bending: the plate buckling occurred along the shortest
diagonal in a rectangular panel.[3] The maximum deflection

was 50 mm per panel, over the width of 900 mm. The double glass panels were made from a 5 mm-thick outer layer of thermal pre-stressed glass, and an inner layer of 5.5.1 (2 layers of 5 mm glass and a single PVB bonding layer in between) laminated, thermally pre-stressed glass with a low emission coating.[4] The structural analysis showed that only 25% of the maximum bending tension was consumed by the cold torsion of the glass (the remaining 75% was related to the absorption of snow and wind loads, as is common). Although, during the assembly we had more breakage than usual, there were no major setbacks. It is interesting to note that while the European regulations do not allow these kinds of experiments, in the Netherlands they are possible, with the proviso that the risks and responsibilities for such a "design and build" approach remain with the enterprising component designer and producer.

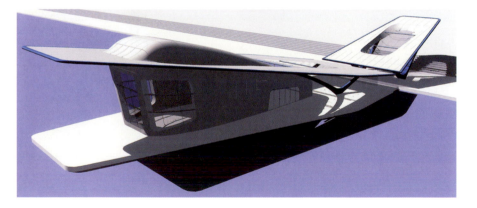

HYDRA PIER IN HAARLEMMERMEER
After a limited design competition in early 2001 for a pavilion for the *Dutch Floriade 2002*, the municipality of Haarlemmermeer in the Netherlands chose the design (figure 20.5) by Asymptote Architects from New York, led by architects Hani Rashid and Lise-Anne Couture[5]. The building was built on an artificial peninsula in the Haarlemmermeer, on the shore of a lake ("Haarlemmerlake"). The building was used as an information pavilion for the first six months, and after that, was converted to a café and a restaurant (figure 20.6), which is its present use.

The building's roof consists of two sloping surfaces. The larger roof surface covers the main building volume, which contains the entrance, exhibition space, and service spaces. The smaller roof surface is a freestanding canopy oriented towards the side of a dike. A continuous stream of water flows from the top of both sloping roofs, fills the 1.4 m-deep glass pond, and flows into two gutters on both sides of the entrance (figure 20.7). The water streams are visible and tangible on the inner sides of two glass walls that define the entrance to the building.[6]

The pavilion was built by several "co-builders:" *Smulders* for the steel structure, *Van Dam* for ceiling and façade elements (who unfortunately went bankrupt several weeks before completion), and *Octatube* for the frameless glazing and roof panels. Apart from these co-builders, there were approximately 30 subcontractors under the direct supervision of the general contractor *Nijhuis*.

Asymptote set up a "virtual office" that consisted of shared storage on the Internet where the project participants could exchange project information, such as models and drawings. Unfortunately, the information exchange did not work, because of a lack of regular communication between participants and a lack of interoperability between different software used by different parties.[7] As became evident during the design and engineering process, no one was assigned to verify and coordinate the dimensions and details in the drawings created by different parties. The outcome was to be expected: for example, there was a dimensional, positioning difference of 125 mm (!) between the glass panels produced by *Octatube* and the end position of panels made by *Van Dam*. Given a short construction schedule, it was unfortunate that insufficient time was spent in setting up a

20.7.
Hydra Pier: a continuous stream
of water flows from the top of
both slopping roofs, fills the glass
pond, and flows into two gutters
on both sides of the entrance.

proper communication and data exchange system among the
different parties to complete the engineering, fabrication, and
construction successfully. The first built "blobby" building in
the Netherlands showed the inadequacies of the traditional
infrastructure of preparation and execution of normative,
orthogonal designs: the traditional general contractor was
unable to coordinate and integrate the co-builders' work and
read the information provided by them; the "adventurous"
architect did not lead the engineering process as the "spider
in the web." The digital information was not coordinated and
integrated. It also became clear on this project that "uniform"
engineering software is an absolute necessity for feasible
"*collaborative engineering*." The alternative to this approach
is "*concurrent engineering*;" the difference being that in
"collaborative engineering," there is real cooperation and
exchange of information, while in "concurrent engineering"
there is only simultaneous and duplicitous labor, with possible
errors in absence of central coordination.

One of the technological innovations on this project was in
the production of aluminum roof panels[8] with complex double
curved forms (figures 20.8a–b). A three-dimensional model
of panel geometry was used in the CNC-milling of polystyrene
foam blocks to produce molds that were subsequently hardened
with epoxy-resin glass. An inverted mold was created by
pouring integral concrete with short fiber reinforcement into
each glass-covered foam mold. The concrete molds were then
used in the custom-developed *explosion process* to deform flat
sheets of aluminum into three-dimensional forms. An aluminum
panel was placed on top of the mold and vacuum deflated. With
the help of a water basin with a small TNT ring, an explosion
was generated that pushed and deformed a 5 mm-thick
aluminum panel with radial, even pressure into the concrete
mold (figure 20.9). The force of the explosion also launched
water (and the plastic gasket) up into the air. As expected, this
highly experimental production method provided the desired
accuracy in production. The panels, however, had marks left by
imperfections in the surface of the molds, and had to be filled
before they could be coated. In *Octatube's* production facility,
a full-scale (1:1) wooden fitting mold was created, in which all
adjacent panels were fitted with aluminum edges, sawn, welded,
and ground into complete panel components (figure 20.10),
before filling and paint spraying.

20.8a–b. (right)
Hydra Pier: some
of the aluminum
roof panels have
complex, double
curved forms.

20.9.
Hydra Pier: the complexly shaped aluminum panels were explosion formed in water basins using concrete molds.

20.11a–b.
Hydra Pier: the glazing panels on the side have bent geometry.

20.10. (below)
Hydra Pier: the panels were fitted, sawn, welded, and grinded over wooden molds.

Another innovation in the *Hydra Pier* is the hanging glass pond (figure 20.7), developed to take the weight of 1.4 m of water, which translates into a load of 1,400 kg/m², i.e. 14 times larger than an average roof or wall load. The depth of the water in the pond increased from the initial 300 to 600 mm, to 840 mm, and finally 1,410 mm. The glass can clearly carry such a large load; the sizing of the laminated glass panels was just a matter of analysis. Normal frameless glazing has a surface area of 2 x 2 m, but in this case, the size was reduced to 1 x 1 m, resulting in a quarter of the bending moment. Such a heavy load caused the dot-shaped suspension (as envisioned by the architect) to be transformed into a "dotted line" structural support, i.e. a series of node-shaped suspensions with an internal distance of 3,000 mm across the width of the pond.

Another innovative aspect of the building technology in this project is the glazing on the south façade. The south façade consists of three surface areas, approximately 6 x 6 m², each divided into 3 x 3 panels, each of which had the maximum surface area of 2 x 2 m². The central surface area is flat, and consists of 9 flat panels of monolithic 12 mm pre-stressed glass. The surfaces areas on the sides are bent (figures 20.11a–b). The original design consisted of a conical and a cylindrical part. While it was possible to make the conical mould, it would have created problems for the glass panel fabricators in Spain and England, who were specialists in hot bending. This is the reason why the architect altered the conical shape into a smaller cylindrical one. The three stacked corner panels were manufactured as

12 mm-thick, monolithic, thermal pre-stressed glass. In addition, two rows of six non-orthogonal panels, each with a surface area of 2 x 2 m², also made from laminated pre-stressed glass, were produced as simple flat panels and were cold bent on site. *Cold bending*[9] was performed on site by pressing two points of the horizontal sides downwards, with a camber of 80 mm over 2 m. The bending stress was calculated as being maximum 50% of the total stress of 50N/mm². The other half of acceptable load tension (50%) was reserved for the wind load. The laminated build-up of these cold bent panels was chosen because of the danger of fracture during assembly.

20.12.
The design model of the *Yitzhak Rabin Center* in Tel Aviv, Israel (1997), designed by Moshe Safdie.

20.13.
Plan of the *Yitzhak Rabin Center*.

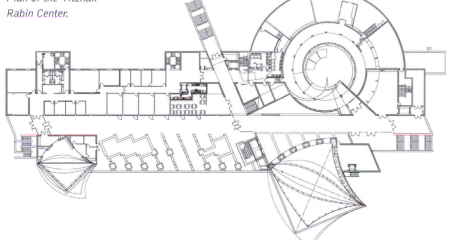

YITZHAK RABIN CENTER

The *Yitzhak Rabin Center* in Tel Aviv, Israel (1997), was designed by Moshe Safdie as a memorial building (figure 20.12) for the late Prime Minister Yitzhak Rabin. The design of the building was an adaptation and extension of a former auxiliary electricity plant near the Tel Aviv University campus. The building features two large spaces – the "Great Hall" and the "Library" – with south-oriented glass façades facing the Ayalon valley below (figure 20.13). Both hall designs have remarkable and plastically designed roofs that resemble dove wings – as a tribute to Yitzhak Rabin the peacemaker.

The roofs were subdivided into five shell "wings;" the maximum size of each wing was 30 m x 20 m. The tender specification called for a profiled steel structure with a non-described skin. With collaborators and co-builders (i.e. other members of the tender consortium), a revolutionary new composite sandwich shell system was proposed as an alternative (figure 20.14). The proposal was to make the roofs like giant surfboards of foam with stressed glass-fiber reinforced polyester (GRP) skins on both sides.

The consortium was awarded a pre-engineering contract to develop a prototype of a composite sandwich shell structure. In the design development of the first prototype, we recreated, using *Maya*, the three-dimensional model of the roof wings based on the *Rhino* model provided by the architect's office, which was inadequate for further engineering. *Holland Composites Industrials*, based in Lelystad, the Netherlands,

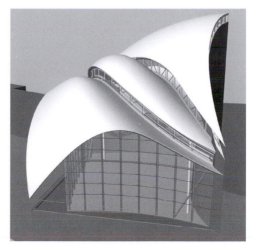

20.14.
Yitzhak Rabin Center: composite sandwich shells were proposed for the roof "wings."

20.15.
Yitzhak Rabin Center: structural analyses of the roof "wings."

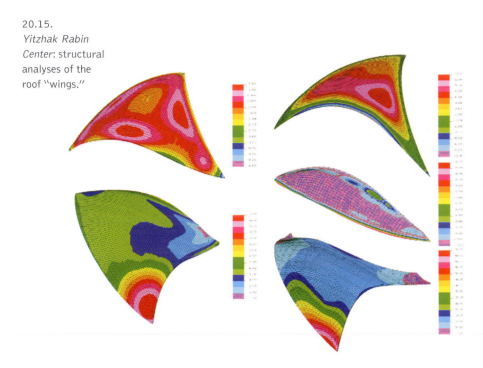

20.16.
Yitzhak Rabin Center: the prototype of the composite sandwich shell for the roof wings.

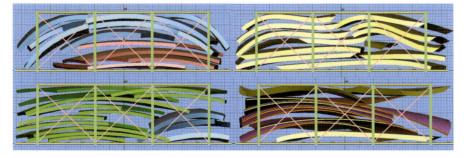

20.17a–b.
Yitzhak Rabin Center: the shell segments were stacked and transported in open containers.

was invited to be the polyester co-builder. They had previously built hulls of motor and sailing yachts, up to 30 m long, in glass fiber-reinforced polyester using *vacuum injection*. The structural behavior of the GRP wings and the steelwork was analyzed by *Octatube Engineering* and *Solico Engineering*, based in Oosterhout, the Netherlands (figure 20.15).

Prototypes of both the originally specified tubular steel structure with a light composite sandwich polyester covering, and the proposed composite sandwich shells were developed (figure 20.16). The pre-engineering work[10] resulted in a dramatic reduction of the cost price of the composite sandwich shells. As a consequence, our composite sandwich shell structure proposal was selected for the roofs instead of the original tubular structure with thin concrete or sandwich cladding. Unlike previous projects in which we were involved, the engineering team at *Octatube* managed the data integration and exchange with various parties quite effectively. We were able to offer an innovative structural and material solution by integrating architectonic, structural, and industrial design, by being responsible for the "design and build" phases of the project, and by exchanging useful data with all parties.

After a year of an initial contract for experimental work and prototyping and the award of the contract that followed, we explored various production methods for the GRP wings, tested the connections of the sandwich panels for possible delamination, analyzed loading deformations of the assembly connections, examined fire resistance of the roof shells,

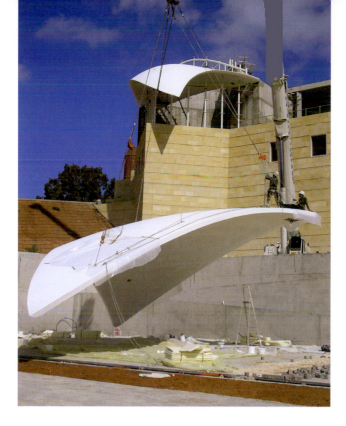

20.18.
Yitzhak Rabin Center: installation of a "wing" shell after it was assembled on site.

20.19.
Yitzhak Rabin Center: the roof shells after installation.

analyzed logistics in the Netherlands and the transport of the shell segments in special open containers (figures 20.17a–b), and studied the assembly of the segments on special molds on the building site, jointing and finishing of the wings, and hoisting of the completed wings into position. We then faced a complex approval process stemming from the change of government in Israel. Finally, after two years of engineering and development, the go-ahead was given for production.

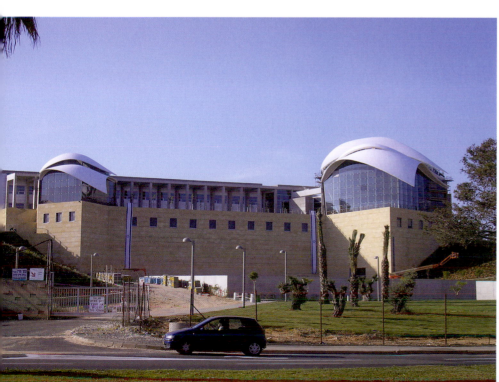

The production process was based on the standard techniques at *Holland Composites* to produce integral *monocoque* ship hulls using *vacuum injection*. The wings had to be produced in rectangular segments, because of the large dimensions (30 m x 20 m as opposed to 30 m x 5 m for the entire boat hull) and the transport constraints. Each segment form was different. The shrinking of each segment after curing was mostly asymmetrical, which was an unforeseen setback. The distortions resulting from shrinking were measured, analyzed, and a solution for a smooth-looking finished surface was developed (figure 20.18). The final result was a combination of structural design with a strong architectural expression (figure 20.19), incorporating the technologies of aeronautics, ship-building, industrial design, and geodetic surveying,[11] and involving numerous innovations in the development and production processes.

CARBON FIBER FREEFORM SHELLS

Some contemporary architects design like sculptors, directly in models (like Frank Gehry); others design entirely on the computer by manipulating complexly shaped three-dimensional models (like Zaha Hadid). Dramatic three-dimensional effects dominate architectural thinking today. The structural designer, however, does not have an equal position and is often asked to turn the sculptural whims in the design of an architect into a trustworthy architectonic structure that is safe. Many shapes of the new generation of freeform shells are much more arbitrary in a structural sense, and hence often adopt an unfavorable structural behavior.

Freeform shells are governed by bending moments rather than by normal and shear forces in the plane of the shell. The structural solution for the new generation of composite shells is in principle the one developed for the *Yitzhak Rabin Center*: a double surface-stressed, composite skin sandwich with a structural core. The two skins take care of the stresses derived from the bending moments, caused by unfavorable loading conditions, unfavorable column or support positions, and sculptural and hence arbitrary shell forms (from a structural point of view). We still call these roof forms "shells," as they resemble and perform structurally similar to the thin-walled concrete shells of the 1960s, but mathematicians and methodologists are suggesting that we need to invent a new name (which could be "*blob-shells*" or "*freeform shells*").

A possible material alternative to the use of glass-fiber reinforced polyester for freeform shells is *carbon-fiber reinforced epoxy*, which is often used in the production of high-tech sailing yachts (such as the *ABN-AMRO* sailing boats in the *Volvo* ocean race in 2005–2006). This material is much

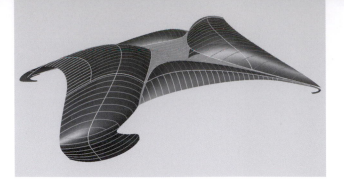

20.20.
The proposed geometry of the roof shells for the *Mediatheque* in Pau, France, designed by Zaha Hadid.

more rigid; it hardly expands, as its thermal expansion factor is very small.[12] Zaha Hadid has proposed the use of carbon-fiber reinforced epoxy in her design for the *Mediatheque* in Pau, France, near the Pyrénées (figure 20.20). Working with her office in London and a co-builder in England, we proposed producing segments of the carbon-fiber reinforced epoxy shell locally in a temporary factory shed, with a re-assembled curing oven next to the site. The tendering process, however, did not allow for prototyping. This extremely experimental project did not advance beyond the tendering stage, as its champion, Pau's mayor André Labarrère, died the day before the tender date.

CONCLUSION

The "design and build" approach is popular among general contractors, because it enables them to shift all responsibilities and liabilities to subcontractors lower in the hierarchic pyramid of the building industry. The existing hierarchical relationships favor established materials and techniques, leaving little or no room for innovation and inventions. This explains the traditional hesitation in the U.S. building industry to accept new technologies (which is also related to its highly litigious nature).

For a Dutch engineer, there are intrinsic possibilities hidden away in the "design and build" approach. For designers, who want to prove that their bold new ideas and complex forms are buildable, the "design and build" approach provides ample opportunities to develop fully the overall scheme, articulate materialization and the details of the design, and take responsibility for the entire project. In the Netherlands, with its more moderate legal climate, the possibilities for experimentation can be pursued in the "design and build" approach through sound engineering knowledge and insight, accompanied by prototyping and testing. The "design and build" approach is the surest way to acquire new knowledge and gain insights into the entire production process, with immediate and clear feedback in a relatively short time.

NOTES

1 After all, Gustave Eiffel built the tower in Paris using 15,000 hand-made drawings, with metal elements made in various workplaces.
2 Karel Vollers, "Twist & Build: Creating Non-orthogonal Architecture," PhD thesis, Technical University of Delft, 2001; the edited version is published as Karel Vollers, "Twist & Build" Rotterdam: 010 Publishers, 2001.
3 Dries Staaks, a graduate student at TU Delft, described the regularities, and the dos and don'ts of cold bending of flat glass panels in a paper entitled "Theory of Staaks" that was published in 2007 (Mick Eekhout, Dries Staaks, "Cold Deformation of Glass," in *Glass Performance Days*, Tampere, Finland, 2007).
4 For heat-transformed glass, such a low emission coating is not yet possible, but in cold bent glass the low emission coating can be integrated.
5 For *Asymptote*, this was the first building to be built in their 15-year careers as architects; their premiere in world architecture.
6 In several pavilions for the *World Exhibition* in 1992 in Seville, Spain, streaming water on façades was used as a cooling system. In this project, however, it is used only as a symbol of the "land of water."
7 The architect used *Microstation*, the engineers used *X-Steel*, and *Octatube* and *Van Dam* worked with different versions of *AutoCAD*.
8 The aluminum panel roof was developed under the supervision of Dr Karel Vollers, who assembled the project task force: Dominique Timmerman of *Octatube* defined the overall geometry, Ernst Janssen Groesbeek created the drawings of the components, Haiko Drachstra produced the CNC-machined foam molds, and Hugo Groenendijk used *Exploform* for the aluminum panels. The assembly, fitting, sawing, welding, filling, spraying, installing, and waterproofing were done by *Octatube*.
9 Cold bending of glass is often avoided.
10 Similar pre-engineering prototype contracts are often proposed for experimental projects in the Netherlands, but are hardly ever rewarded out of fear of monopolization by the involved contractor. An alternative would be to have the architect undertake an experimental prototype development instead of the contractor.
11 Tolerances in the different stages from design and engineering to prototyping, production and building on site govern the success of each prototypical freeform project. As a consequence, geodetic supervision, the measuring of position points during the fixing components in space in assemblies and erection work, has grown in importance.
12 These advantages, however, are countered by a much stricter production process, including curing in a tempering oven, which limits the sizes of components.

21
OMAterial

SHOHEI SHIGEMATSU / OMA–AMO

21.2.
Urban Landscape
installation by Chinese
artist Zhan Wang in
Chicago (2005).

21.1.
The *¥€$ Regime*
—the world governed
and driven by the
market economy.

The *Office for Metropolitan Architecture* (OMA) has
no defined palette of materials, just as it defies a fixed
architectural style. Our office is perhaps not that advanced,
and probably fairly old-fashioned when it comes to
mobilizing the latest digital technologies into the design
and production processes. There is an underlying coherence,
however, in material thinking and use – a palette of strategic
opportunism. It is often based on an almost analytical
approach to specific conditions: local, functional, economic,
literal, etc., or based on intentions that are detached from,
or even at odds with the givens: playful, experimental,
raw, colorful, graphic. This chapter reveals the processes
of material thinking at OMA in various projects designed
over the past decade for *Prada*, *Casa da Musica*, *Cordoba
Congress Center*, plus some more recent projects.

21.3.
The *Skyline of
Egos.*

21.4a–b.
The alternating
identities of the
proposed Dubai
building.

DESIGNING FOR THE ICON AGE

OMA was asked to design a high-rise building in Dubai, in the United Arab Emirates, a location which has had an incredible rate of growth over the past two decades and is one of the fastest growing cities in the world. The incredible modernization of the Middle East, of which Dubai is perhaps the most extreme example, should be considered in the context of an ever-growing relationship between commercialism and iconic buildings. At OMA, we refer to it as the ¥€$ Regime – Yen, Euro and Dollar, i.e. the world that is governed and driven by the market economy (figure 21.1). In this regime, there is not only the usual pressure of budget control and fast-track scheduling, but also enormous pressure to design *iconic* buildings, resulting in the current condition we refer to as the *Icon Age*. (The *Guggenheim Museum in Bilbao*, completed in 1997, represents its starting point.)

Zhan Wang, a Chinese artist, visualized a future city in an installation made of kitchen pots and utensils (figure 21.2), shown in Chicago in 2005. We think it shows the future city, or the current condition in Dubai under the ¥€$ *Regime*, quite accurately. In a similar vein, we created a composite image (figure 21.3) – the *Skyline of Egos* – as a collection of buildings designed over the past ten years by the so-called *starchitects*. Basically, the end result is a collection of "genius" forms that lead to a meaningless overdose of themes and extremes. We at OMA, as part of the *starchitect* enterprise, wondered how to avoid this situation when we took part in a competition that potentially offered Dubai a chance to be the first twenty-first-century metropolis with a "new credibility."

We thought we should mark a point of the "new beginning" for Dubai by embarking on the "rediscovery of architecture." We proposed a monolithic slab in the middle of the Dubai Business Bay – a 900 ft-tall, 600 ft-long, and only 36 ft-wide slab made out of white concrete. From one direction, it manifests its massive presence like a canvas (figure 21.4a), and from the other direction, it reveals exceptional slenderness (figure 21.4b). As such, this scheme is a radical experiment in alternating identities. We were interested in having a basic building with "substance" along its entire height, from bottom to top, as opposed to the surrounding towers that have no substance, especially

at the top, because of their vertical "greed." The proposed building is basically an elevator core, without internal columns, and no curtain wall, which allows the construction process to be reduced to one single effort, where finishes, skin, floors, and core are completed all at once. The section is a very rational vertical organization, being interrupted by four vertically distributed thematic lobbies: (1) art; (2) business forum; (3) wellness center; and (4) panorama.

As if that weren't enough, in order to reinforce the reintegration of architecture and engineering, we proposed to rotate the building on a 24-hour cycle, so that it becomes the first major structure in the world to turn around its vertical axis (figures 21.5a–d). Rotating the building, so that its narrow side always faces the sun, means the main façades receive no direct sunlight. This would minimize any solar gain, and therefore reduce the cooling demand of the building. Whether the proposed rotation is right or not, this extreme engineering was quite interesting, in that the most advanced technologies were deliberately merged with the architecture itself, and were not limited to particular elements of architecture like façades, which is usually the case. In the end, we lost the competition to Zaha Hadid's proposal, which shows that the Icon Age is still alive and thriving.

21.5a–d.
The Dubai building would rotate around its vertical axis, so that main façades would receive no direct sunlight.

21.7.
The program analysis for
the mixed-use project in
Jersey City.

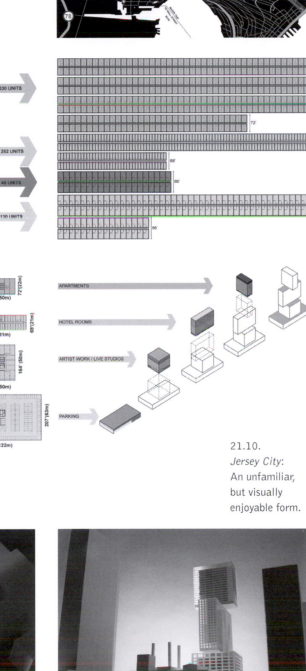

FAR : 14.7

APARTMENTS 357,320 sf — 330 UNITS

RESIDENTIAL PUBLIC 4,896 sf

HOTEL ROOMS 126,140 sf

HOTEL PUBLIC 65,916 sf
HOTEL SERVICE 21,652 sf
LOFTS 53,750 sf — 252 UNITS

ARTIST WORK / LIVE STUDIO 161,375 sf
UTILITY 46,768 sf — 40 UNITS
PARKING 239,205 sf

CABARET 7,572 sf — 130 UNITS
RETAIL 86,940 sf
GALLERY 19,024 sf
LOBBIES 18,314 sf

SITE
1,209,115 sf GROSS

21.8.
Jersey City:
The vertical
stacking of the
programmatic
elements.

164' (50m) 72'(22m)
265'(81m) 65'(21m)
164' (50m)
164' (50m)
401' (122m) 207'(63m)

APARTMENTS
HOTEL ROOMS
ARTIST WORK / LIVE STUDIOS
PARKING

21.9.
Jersey City:
Vertically
distributed
public spaces.

21.10.
Jersey City:
An unfamiliar,
but visually
enjoyable form.

CHALLENGING THE FACIAL EFFECTS

OMA was approached in 2006 by a developer to design a
mixed-use high-rise building in Jersey City. Ironically, the
development of Jersey City was accelerated in the aftermath
of the "9/11" attacks on the *World Trade Center* in New
York, when the financial district essentially moved across
the Hudson River. For many New Yorkers, New Jersey might
mentally be a remote place, but after looking at the well-
connected infrastructure network that surrounds our site, we
quickly discovered that Jersey City and Downtown Manhattan
are virtually part of the same neighborhood (figure 21.6).

We also looked at the "designer-condo wave," and
concluded that in Manhattan, all the design effort is spent on
creating a credible skin and a sleek lobby, mainly because of
the zoning constraints. Surrounded by an incredible amount
of empty lots, and having almost no zoning envelope, our site
was a fertile ground to experiment with how to redefine the
"condo-couture." The program we were given was a typical
mix (the mixed-use is a new generic: condominiums, lofts,
hotel, retail, gallery, and parking). So the first step was to
investigate the typological development optimum for each
part of the program (figure 21.7), such as the normative
dimensions of different areas, circulation, etc. One could say
that we deliberately yielded to the market logic from the
beginning, and tried to make something unknown from the
known ingredients.

We analyzed each component of the program for an
optimum layout, and then concentrated on individual blocks:
a cube of artist work/live studios, a slab that combines hotel
rooms and apartments, and a wider slab that accommodates
deeper apartment units. Those blocks were stacked on top
of and rotated perpendicular to each other (figure 21.8) to
create a series of external public spaces that are vertically
distributed (figure 21.9) and also facilitate and articulate
the mix of two different programs. With these manipulations,
we maintained the familiar features of the typical interior
organizations of each program, but also created an unfamiliar,
but visually enjoyable form that is different from every angle
(figure 21.10). We optimized the structural system, almost
to the level of the conventional flat slab structure, in order
to meet the financial goals of the project. The cantilevered
span was larger when it was conceived, but it became shorter

21.13.
The lumber-
clad columns
in the *Kunsthal*
in Rotterdam
(1992).

21.11. (above)
Jersey City: making a
mark in the skyline by
being unfamiliar.

21.12.
Jersey City: blending
into the surroundings
by being familiar.

and shorter, as the cost analysis became more precise; in the end, the cantilevers became more representative of the economic logic than gravity. The external public spaces became more private towards the top: the public sculptural garden, the hotel terrace, and the private terrace for the residents.

Designing the façade, we wanted to emphasize the simplicity of the manipulation by using a standard window wall system, which is completely the opposite of all "designer condos." With its unfamiliar vertical organization, the building effortlessly makes its mark in the skyline from both Manhattan (figure 21.11) and the New Jersey Turnpike, but because it is made out of familiar ingredients, it is able to blend into the surrounding towers (figure 21.12). We successfully avoided participating in the game of manufacturing "facial effects" by accepting the logics of the market economy, and consequently creating a robust design that could sustain its conceptual clarity through the process.

"MORE AND MORE"

In Japan, where I come from, *reductivism* is encouraged as if it is the ultimate virtue of cultural expression. *Muji*'s brand is the perfect example of capitalizing on this reductivism and its prescribed cultural identity. Today, *Muji* not only produces stationery, but also clothing, furniture, soda drinks, and even cars and houses. The brand has increased its revenue since the 1980s, in the opposite direction from the downward curve of the Japanese economy. Even more striking are the similarities of the *Muji* houses and the current architectural trend in Japan that I refer to as "foam-core architecture" – where both the white color and anonymity are sacred. This is not an attempt to criticize contemporary Japanese architecture, but merely to provide a description of the background from which I came when I started working at OMA.

When I studied architecture, the famous words by Mies van der Rohe – "God is in the detail" – were considered the ultimate truth, even though the methods employed by architects dealing with architecture and urbanism have fluctuated drastically in the twentieth century. At OMA, I came across another maxim by Rem Koolhaas – "No money, no detail." Although the detailing is considered an important factor of architecture at OMA, Rem's words imply that we should always re-examine the state of architecture and the application of materials within the financial context of the project. In other words, there is no default condition in architecture – we must always be cautious in applying our ultimate theories and experiences in order to effectively respond to various conditions.

Rem's response to another famous Mies' maxim, "Less is More," was "More and More," meaning we should permanently cultivate the *unknowns* – deny having a style, accept no defaults. This attitude consequently produces an overwhelming diversity of approaches and applications where we are freer in thinking about architecture and technology as opposed to the example I had given of Japan, where everything is very pristine and fixed. For example, the lumber cladding for the columns in the *Kunsthal* in Rotterdam (1992) expresses the continuity of the trees from the outside (the park) to the inside (the gallery), and also works as the fire protection for the columns (figure 21.13), a counter-intuitive use of wood as a fire barrier, but a possibility because its thickness gives the necessary rating.

21.16.
Sponge: some
of the test
studies of
the "sponge"
material.

21.14. (above)
The "sponge" material
developed with *Prada*
for its stores.

DESIGNING (AND MANUFACTURING) EFFECTS

In the *Prada* stores, we used a material referred to as "sponge" (figure 21.14), which we have developed jointly with *Prada*. This material emerged by accident, as we were investigating the various possibilities: in one study model, the walls were clad with sponge (figure 21.15) to suggest a material condition that would provide optimum natural light for the store environment, and be used simultaneously for the display of the collection. We had investigated a ready-made material that could achieve the effects of the sponge, but in the end decided bravely to *replicate* the sponge at 1:1 (full) scale. We conducted a series of test studies (figure 21.16) that included casting resin inside the mold with silicon-covered, water-filled balloons (figures 21.17a–e), which were later exploded. In the end, we used a Computer Numerically Controlled (CNC) machine to make a mold, but with an extensive *manual* refinement afterwards (figures 21.18a–d). The process wasn't particularly sophisticated from the technological or technical point of view, but the resulting material effects were very beautiful. In the end, the *intention* to accomplish a certain effect is more important than the technical sophistication of the process to achieve a complex shape.

21.15.
Sponge: using sponge
in one of the study
models.

21.17a–e.
Sponge: one of
the test studies
consisted of casting
resin in the mold
filled with silicon-
covered, water-filled
balloons.

21.18a–d.
Sponge: the CNC-
milled molds were
manually finished.

21.19.
The *Prada* store
in Los Angeles
(2004).

21.20a–b.
Prada: the
display windows
are embedded
into the ground.

For the *Prada* store in Los Angeles (2004, figure 21.19), we developed a display-window embedded into the ground (figures 21.20a–b). The concept of the store was a lifted solid box with an open ground level without any façade, which takes advantage of the climate in Los Angeles. The basic idea of the ground floor area is to blur the threshold between public and commercial space. The store doesn't have a vertical display-window or the logo of the brand visible on the façade. This was done in order to distinguish the store from the relentless "screams" of luxury brands all around. The embedded display windows were designed to correspond to the viewing cones of the pedestrian window shoppers, enhancing our intention to have more interaction between the store and the street. Fiberglass was the perfect material for the cones – freeform, lightweight, and light-permeable, permitting varying lighting concepts for different collections (figures 21.21a–b).

21.21a–b.
Prada: the cones
for the embedded
display windows
were made from
fiberglass.

21.22.
The *Guggenheim Hermitage* gallery in Las Vegas (2001), within the *Venetian Hotel*.

21.23a–b.
Guggenheim Hermitage: *Cor-Ten* steel was used on all vertical surfaces.

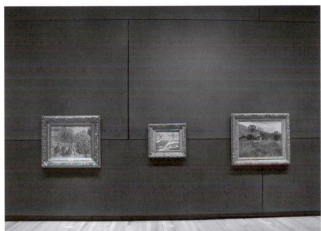

In the *Guggenheim Hermitage* gallery in Las Vegas (2001), an inserted gallery box within the *Venetian Hotel*, the *Cor-Ten* steel was used to distinguish the box from the surrounding gypsum world (figure 21.22). All vertical surfaces were covered with *Cor-Ten* steel (figures 21.23a–b), and we used magnets to display the paintings (figures 21.24a–b). Even though the magnets are so strong that a special device is required to remove them from the steel, quite a few people were very nervous about using them as mounting devices for the paintings.

21.24a–b.
Guggenheim Hermitage: magnets are used as mounting devices for the paintings.

21.25. (above)
Casa da Musica,
the concert hall in
Oporto, Portugal
(2006).

21.26. (right)
A "window" into
the city (and into
the hall).

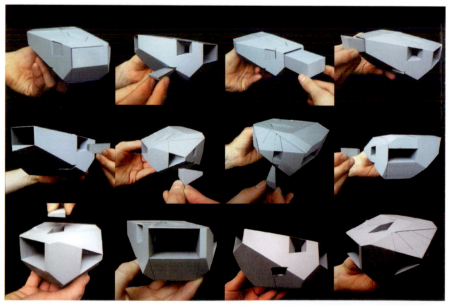

21.27a–b.
All publicly
accessible functions
are attached to the
sides of the main
auditorium.

Casa da Musica, the concert hall (figure 21.25) recently completed in Oporto, Portugal (2006), is the first concert hall that has two large windows, at both ends of the "shoe box" of the main auditorium, one behind the stage facing the historical center (figure 21.26), and the other facing the Atlantic Ocean. Typically, concert halls never expose their main activity, but this building, through these large windows, broadcasts its internal activities to both the public and the city. Also, a typical concert hall doesn't allow the public to see the main auditorium unless there is an actual performance taking place. In this concert hall, all other publicly accessible functions are attached to the sides of the main auditorium (figures 21.27a–b), and have a window into it, thus enabling visitors to peek into the main auditorium and follow the performance indirectly (figure 21.28).

The main auditorium is clad with plywood, which is one of the cheapest materials one can imagine for such a cultural venue. An enlarged gold-leaf pattern of the plywood is applied on top of the plywood cladding (figure 21.29). The gold-leaf layer catches the light sensitively and creates a moment of interesting conflict – a luxurious substance over a very banal material. It turned out that the best way to achieve this finish was to use manual labor, as the cheapest and most effective solution. The entire application of the gold-leaf finish was done by one person over the course of four months (figure 21.30).

White concrete was used for the building skin. Corrugated glass was applied for the large windows (figure 21.31). Because of the corrugation, each glazing is self-supporting without any mullions. The corrugated glass also contributes to the acoustical performance of the auditorium, and creates interesting distortions to the views (figure 21.32). We used locally available material, as much as possible, to make this building symbolic of Portuguese culture in a more profound way. For example, one room was covered with blue *azulejo* tiles (figures 21.33), which are characteristic of this region of Portugal (figure 21.34).

21.28. (above)
All auxiliary functions have a window into the main auditorium.

21.30. (right)
Applying the gold-leaf layer manually.

21.29. (upper right)
An enlarged gold-leaf pattern of the plywood was applied on top of the plywood cladding in the main auditorium.

21.31. (right)
The corrugated glass on the building's exterior.

21.32. (right)
The corrugated glass distorts the views in interesting ways.

21.34. (below)
The blue *azulejo* tiles are used locally in Porto.

21.33. (lower right)
Blue *azulejo* tiles are used in one of the spaces.

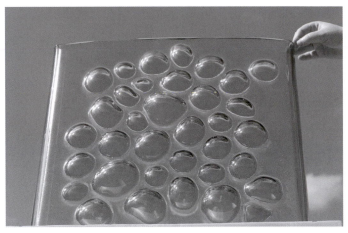

21.35.
The Cultural Center in Cordoba, Spain (in the design phase).

21.38.
The building appears in a permanent state of water condensation in a very dry climate.

In Cordoba, Spain, we are designing a congress center and hotel that are horizontally joined into a 300 m-long building along the river (figure 21.35). For the façade, we investigated the use of local Arabic-influenced patterns. We discovered, however, an interesting glass experiment done in Los Angeles, where recycled glass was used to create glass panels with water bubble patterns (figure 21.36). Based on that experiment, a U-shaped glass panel was developed with "bubbles" (figures 21.37a–c) so that the building would appear in a permanent state of water condensation in a very dry climate (figure 21.38).

WAIST DOWN

The following project could appear somewhat frivolous, but is an interesting example of inter-disciplinary collaboration with a very creative enterprise – *Prada*. The project consisted of curating and designing a worldwide traveling exhibition of their collection – skirts only – from 1988 to the present. After examining thousands of unique skirts, it was surprising to see such a huge (and very inventive) variety in thinking for a single clothing typology. It quickly became apparent that having one or two display devices for the exhibition would be inappropriate, since every collection and every skirt had a very distinctive focus.

The exhibition was designed to celebrate the invention of skirts. We thought we could consciously distinguish the exhibition from the current trend of blockbuster fashion exhibitions in museums by reducing the focus to the product itself. Our goal was to provide an opportunity to view and reappraise the skirt in general as a "product" – as the best device to reveal the movement of the body (i.e. skirt as a vehicle of movement) – not attached to the brand name or price values.

21.40.
Waist Down: mirrors were applied to the backside of the two-dimensional cutouts.

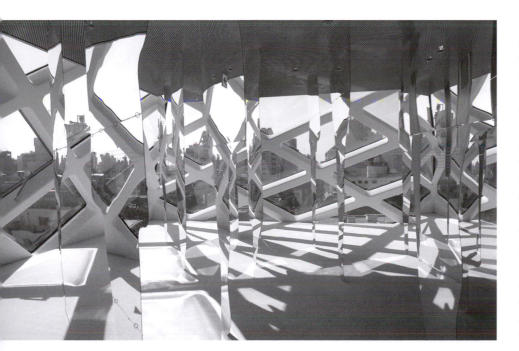

Conventionally, the display systems for skirts are limited to either a hanger or a mannequin. We wanted to make displays that instantly tell the stories behind each skirt – an act closer to a communication design than exhibition design. The principal challenge was to show the movement of skirts. The first inspiration was a photo; we were intrigued by the catwalk pictures that revealed the dramatic motions inherent to skirts – the frozen moment of the movement. Also, by using the photo, the scale could be blown up, and the skirts would be in-your-face, at eye level. The two-dimensional cut-out mannequins were scaled to 250% of the life-size (figure 21.39), so that the upper torso disappeared into the ceiling. This also went well with the title of the exhibition – "Waist Down." A mirror was applied to the backside of the two-dimensional cut-out to show its pure outline (figure 21.40); it acted as homage to the vanity associated with fashion. A total of 56 cut-outs were hung chronologically in space as an installation. People wandered around the dense forest of skirts and legs with intense reflections of the surroundings (figure 21.41).

21.41.
Waist Down: the
dense forest of skirts
and legs with intense
reflections of the
surroundings.

21.42.
Waist Down:
some skirts were
vacuum-packed in
vinyl and shown
in "plan."

21.43.
Waist Down:
some skirts were
shown on pedestals
as if they were
sculptures.

21.44.
Waist Down: the spinning
displays revealed the
structure of the pleats or
the reflection within the
embroideries.

We are used to looking at the elevation of skirts, but not their plan. By vacuum packing the skirts in vinyl, we created a plan-like display that reveals an interesting and not often seen dimension of skirts (figure 21.42). Some skirts had a three-dimensional cut, or a very stiff fabric that allowed them to stand on their own without any support. This produced displays where the skirts were simply placed on pedestals, as if they were sculptures (figure 21.43). The spinning displays revealed the structure of the pleats or the reflection within the embroideries (figure 21.44). The exhibition design was an example of how architectural thinking can be creatively applied to various other fields.

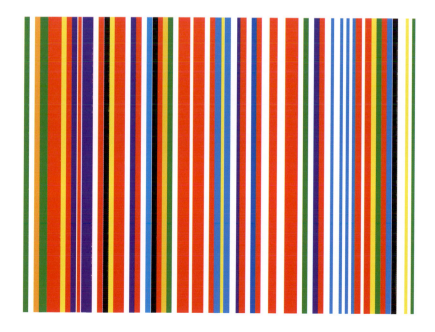

21.45.
The redesigned flag
of the European
Union.

OMA – AMO

OMA has a think-tank called AMO – a mirror image of OMA that focuses on research, branding, consultancy, etc., i.e. basically everything but the architectural commissions. AMO, however, relies on architectural thinking; it is an example of a different kind of initiative that architects can take other than gain control over the building or fabrication processes. We have learned through AMO that the level of social engagement and output can sometimes be considerably more rewarding than that of architecture. AMO creates a dialectic condition within the office, where architectural design can be influenced by the work of AMO and vice versa.

An interesting example of the work of AMO is a project from the *European Union* (EU) to rethink their identity. Until the end of World War II, many nations in Europe were subject to armed conflict. Europe itself also has many definitions and there are varying understandings of its extent and what should be called Europe. Actually, "Europe" is a strategic form of unification for the countries on the Continent that enables them to maintain individual identities as clearly as possible. The flag of the EU, however, is very misleading, since it is shown as a single and stable identity, with a fixed number of yellow stars on a blue background. As the EU gains more members, the number of stars cannot be increased. In addition, some countries are becoming increasingly subdivided, as in the case of the former Yugoslavia and the former USSR (or perhaps the United Kingdom or Belgium in the future). To reflect this ever-changing reality, we vertically extruded all the colors from the flags of the EU member countries, and created a color barcode (figure 21.45) to express simultaneously the EU's diversity and the unity. In this way, each nation can manage to keep its identity but this creates a single abstract image of the EU, which is more true to the actual condition. In any case, it is far more cheerful than the current dull flag. As more countries join the EU, the colors get more and more intense, and also grow more abstract, while maintaining a recognizable whole.

It is inspiring to see how architects are mobilizing intelligence and the latest technological advancements in the design and production of the built environments. At the same time, the goal of all those efforts is still unclear. If architects are too self-indulgent in the processes of achieving "genius forms," in the end, they risk becoming disconnected from society. As the work of AMO shows, architectural thinking could be widened to deal with more issues, producing an *aggressive social engagement* to ultimately create a role for architects in the society. To be more effective in engaging and stimulating public discourse, architects have to be flexible in reaching out and be conscious of the diversity of approaches. What can be more exciting than to see the multidimensional influence of architecture on the public domain?

MATERIAL COLLABORATIONS

FRONT INC. / MARC SIMMONS

22.1.
SCL Glass Headquarters and Showroom (unbuilt), Brisbane, Australia (2002).

Our firm, *Front Inc.*, is a multidisciplinary collaborative design practice focused on the creative development of façade systems and engaged generally in the activities of architecture, fabrication, procurement, construction, and development. Façade design and development is our "Trojan Horse" into an emerging flexible, vertically integrated practice paradigm. Our team comprises architects, structural engineers, mechanical engineers from the aeronautical, automotive, and furniture sectors, environmental engineers, product designers, and computer scientists. We presently employ 25 people in total – a diverse group of nine nationalities, and speaking nine languages – within a small-to-medium organization. *Front Inc.* is a non-hierarchical and self-organizing office based in New York City.

We graft ourselves into a project team and define our own role in light of the aspirations and values of the building project. Collaboratively, as circumstances change, different activities and responses are required to move a project forward. A given project may be characterized by a need for specific engineering innovation and testing, another by material research and creative processing, and many by the need for different and new organizational configurations. Very often, the challenge is in economic constraints, where creative sourcing, process innovation, and optimization are simultaneously required to generate value, while preserving a certain set of intentions.

Performance-driven parameters are established and developed through iterative evolution of a design in a rising spiral process. In this process, information accumulates and reconciles towards a design solution that is often the result of a synthesis or compromise of contradictory requirements pertaining to aesthetics, structure, movement, temperature gradients, air pressure, water infiltration, vapor migration, longevity, maintenance, security, information and media, conductance, solar control, dynamic systems, integrated sensors, power generation, constructability, liability, insurability, cost, software logic controls, embodied energy, carbon emissions and carbon sinks, passive optimization, green walls, and so on. Needless to say, very quickly the design issues become increasingly complex.

The following project specific narratives are presented as vignettes, structured to convey our experience of moving between projects, fertilizing each through the accumulation of ideas and experiments. For each project, we focus on one material, one process, and one effect, which, while not defining the architecture, are often central to its identity. While the following project descriptions are focused primarily on a development sequence related to materiality, it should be made clear that actual projects unfold in a much more random and organic fashion.

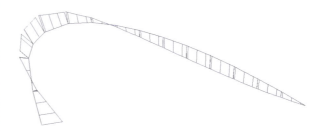

22.2.
SCL Glass Showroom: structural form.

22.3.
SCL Glass Showroom: the structural diagram for one of the ribs.

22.4a–c.
SCL Glass Showroom: the tectonic definition of the pavilion's enclosure.

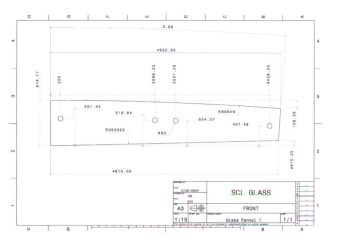

Single pin support from bracket attached to factory gable wall

External 2x12mm fully toughened laminated glass beams

Internal 3x12mm fully toughened laminated glass beams

100mm diameter pins connecting overlapping internal and external laminated glass beams

Triple leaf beam end grouted into base shoe to provide fixed base condition

22.5. (right)
SCL Glass Showroom: a rule-based, associative parametric model was developed in CATIA.

22.6. (below)
SCL Glass Showroom: each component was fully defined in the parametric model.

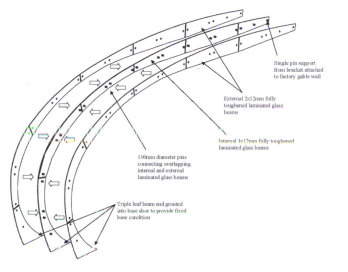

22.7. (right)
SCL Glass Showroom: automatically extracted fabrication drawings.

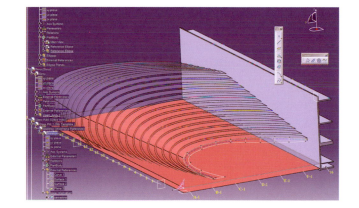

STRUCTURAL GLASS: SCL GLASS HEADQUARTERS AND SHOWROOM

The glass pavilion (figure 22.1) designed as a headquarters and showroom for *SCL*, a glass-manufacturing company in Brisbane, Australia, was our first project starting the practice in 2002. The pavilion was meant to showcase the glass production, fabrication, and installation capabilities of the new manufacturing facility. It was designed as an enclosure made entirely of structural laminated glass with a 21 m clear span (figure 22.2). The ribbed enclosure had to resist thermal variation, wind and induced seismic loadings, with a built-in redundancy for fail-safe operation. All these parameters required the close relationship between geometry and structural performance (figures 22.3 and 22.4a–c). The goal was to maximize efficiency by expressing the forces through the form, which required an iterative design process incorporating required structural performance into each rib form.

The design of the complex organic shape of the pavilion required control through a parametric approach to the definition of the geometry. In addition, stress concentration behavior associated with glass required detailed computer analysis. The project's complexity afforded us an opportunity to engage Eduardo Giuliani-Luzzotto (who was with *IBM* and *Dassault Systèmes* at the time, and is now with *Gehry Technologies*) to help us build a *rule-based*, associative parametric model using *CATIA* (figure 22.5). Full engineering content and a capacity to deliver fabrication drawings, all of which was successfully accomplished, were embedded within and fundamental to this parametric process. The geometry of every component was fully defined parametrically (figure 22.6) with inherent associativity between key features and dimensional values. By manipulating the parametric model, we could change edge distances, maximum and minimum heights, etc. The final, automated outcome was a very simple set of fabrication drawings (figure 22.7), which could be given to the glass manufacturer to automatically create nested drawings for CNC cutting.

22.8.
Interior of the *Glass Pavilion*
(2006) at the *Toledo Museum of
Art* in Toledo, Ohio, designed by
architects *Sejima and Nishizawa
and Associates* (*SANAA*).

BENT GLASS:
TOLEDO MUSEUM OF ART GLASS PAVILION

In the *Glass Pavilion* (2006, figure 22.8) at the *Toledo
Museum of Art* in Toledo, Ohio, designed by architects
Sejima and Nishizawa and Associates (*SANAA*), the glass
was conceptually rendered as an uninterrupted, continuous
band (figures 22.9, 22.10, and 22.11), as if it were cast-in-
place. That aesthetic condition, of course, was not practically
possible, so we searched around the world for companies
that could manufacture the largest piece of slumped, curved,
annealed, laminated, low-iron glass. We discovered four
manufacturers (none in the USA), with the least expensive
of these companies (offering glass of equal quality) located
in Shenzhen, China. The float glass was procured from
a company called *Pilkington*, manufactured in Austria,
and shipped to China for cutting, polishing, curving, and
laminating. On the site, the manufactured glass panels were
set into recessed channels ("railway tracks"), which also
served as the casting channel for the concrete floors (with no
additional finish) – it was very brave of us to put the tracks
down first, cast the concrete floor, and then install the glass
into the channels afterwards (figures 22.12a–c).

The joint between the glass panels was a significant
element throughout the building – an index line, which had to
be as thin as possible. The joint gap is filled with translucent

22.9. (above)
*Toledo Glass
Pavilion*:
conceptual
rendering of
the interior.

22.10.
*Toledo Glass
Pavilion*:
conceptual
model.

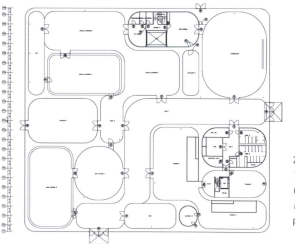

22.11.
*Toledo
Glass
Pavilion*:
plan.

22.12a–c.
Toledo Glass Pavilion: installing the glass panels into the recessed channels.

22.13. (left)
Toledo Glass Pavilion: the translucent silicone joint between the panels.

22.14.
Toledo Glass Pavilion: seamless interior.

22.15.
Toledo Glass Pavilion: installation of the oculus skylight.

22.16. (above)
Toledo Glass Pavilion: the oculus skylight.

silicone, with an extruded, translucent silicone backer gasket (figure 22.13). If the panels were to be conventionally supported on two points, the joints would have to be an inch-and-a-half wide, given the large panel size. Such a large joint, however, was not possible, due to the deflection, settlement, and movement of the concrete, which over time would have caused the silicone joints to open and close. The solution was to place each glass panel within the interior of the building on a "rocker" – a machined bar of steel that was pre-bonded to the bottom of the glass. The inclusion of the rocker detail allowed the panels to move vertically in shear instead of racking. The joints ended up being approximately three-eights of an inch, which was deemed acceptable, creating almost a seamless series of glass surfaces (figure 22.14).

A particularly interesting element of this project was the single oculus skylight, with a 9' 6" diameter, made from double-laminated, insulated low-emission (*low-e*) glass, slumped into a perfect lens perfectly flush with its perimeter condition (figure 22.15). In developing the skylight, it was obvious that a large, flat piece of glass would slump in the middle, requiring a pitch for proper drainage. To further control deflection, the glass thickness would have to increase, which required special interlayers. With the weight increase would come a cost increase, making the flat panel solution no longer viable. Instead, the glass was slumped into a shallow shell, and this result proved to be both viable and conceptually exquisite (figure 22.16).

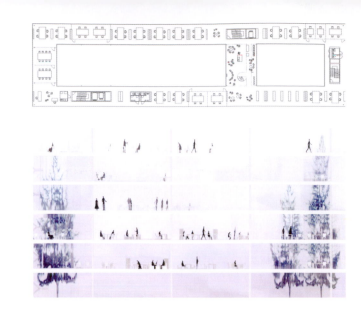

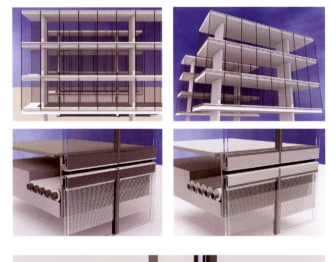

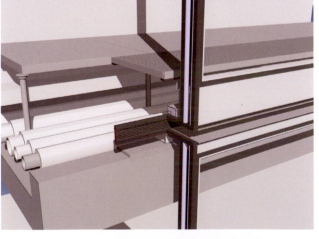

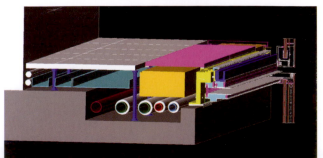

CONTINUOUS GLASS: NOVARTIS OFFICE BUILDING

The *Glass Pavilion* at the *Toledo Museum of Art* is a material manifestation of poetic minimalism. The office building *Sejima and Nishizawa and Associates* (*SANAA*) designed for *Novartis*, a global pharmaceutical giant, in Basel, Switzerland (2006) goes a step further as an example of *environmental minimalism*. The project was part of a reconstruction of an entire urban campus situated along the banks of the River Rhine, just south of the French-Swiss border. The building design focused on a specific human work experience, with a high level of transformability, and a high environmental performance. The simple, rectilinear plan features a linear central courtyard (figure 22.17). The floor plate was a continuous ribbon only 5.8 m wide and was conceptually envisioned as being entirely clad in glass (figure 22.18). The building had to meet or exceed the Swiss energy code, while maintaining a frameless glass expression, with a 100 percent naturally ventilated air system, and a dynamic façade.

With Matthias Schuler's team from *Transsolar*, and building structural engineer Klaus Bollinger of *Bollinger & Grohmann*, we set out to collectively achieve a vision. The starting idea was to simply clamp the glass at the base, thus reducing deflections and obviating the need for a metal frame. To achieve a reasonable energy performance, it was a given that the glass be double-insulated (meaning three layers of glass and two gas filled cavities), with double *low-e* coatings and argon-filled cavities.[1] The outermost cavity contains an integrated motorized blind which is centrally controlled by the building management system. The blinds are fully retractable and tiltable in their deployed position.[2] As each floor is fully flanked by two walls of glass in close proximity, one wall can be completely shut down, achieving a shading coefficient of 0.05, while the other wall, not having any direct sunlight, is left wide open, allowing an abundance of indirect natural light (figures 22.19a–d) to flow in. The building has all architecturally exposed cast-in-place concrete work for walls and ceiling and uses raised floor systems throughout. The bubble-deck concrete structure spans 10.5 m. There is no distribution ductwork; the perimeter of the façade is lined with fan coil units drawing air from a continuous fresh air intake along the edges of every floor. Alternating with the fan coils are simple direct air intakes delivering untreated air directly from the exterior to interior.

As with the *Toledo Glass Pavilion*, the size of the panels would have resulted in excessively large vertical silicone joints. In addition to the steel clamp at the base, we introduced a pin-rocker detail that changed the movement

22.22.
Holt Renfrew flagship store in Vancouver, Canada (2007), designed with *Janson Goldstein Architects*.

22.23.
Holt Renfrew: detail of the façade, showing heat-slumped glass panels.

22.25. (below)
Holt Renfrew: laminated glass was heat-slumped over a slightly irregular grid.

22.26. (above)
Holt Renfrew: a close-up view of one of the prototypes of the heat-slumped glass.

22.24. (right)
Holt Renfrew: the façade system is an aluminum unitized curtain wall supporting heat-slumped glass panels.

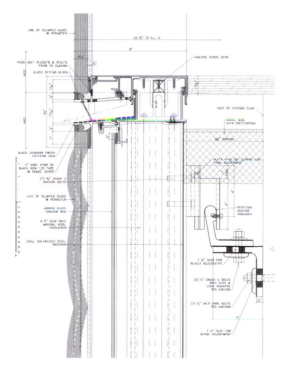

characteristics of the façade panels, and thus allowed us to minimize the joint sizes. Copious renderings were produced during the development process to study verified engineered dimensions (figure 22.20). We also conducted extensive modeling of the services-to-façade interface to ensure that all the work was properly coordinated (figure 22.21).

SLUMPED GLASS:
HOLT RENFREW FLAGSHIP STORE

The material exploration of glass was continued in a new flagship store for Canadian fashion retailer *Holt Renfrew* in Vancouver, Canada (2007, figure 22.22), designed with *Janson Goldstein Architects* of New York. The challenge was to develop a beautiful and iconic façade that contributed to the urban experience of Vancouver, while branding *Holt Renfrew* in a subtle, yet unequivocal manner. The team was interested in Vancouver light conditions, which are often subdued. As with many department stores, there is limited transparency to the exterior with much of the façade being opaque and lifeless. A strategy to develop a specular, translucent surface with an active reflective layer behind the exterior glass (figure 22.23) emerged. Drawing on several precedents including Pierre Charreau's *Maison de Verre* in Paris (1932), Renzo Piano's *Hermes* in Tokyo (2001), SANAA's *Dior* in Tokyo (2003), and our work with the *Office for Metropolitan Architecture* (*OMA*) for the *Beijing Books Building* (unbuilt), we chose to use custom slumped and frosted glass panels.

At the detail level, the basic system was developed as an aluminum unitized curtain wall, drawing on established detailing principles, and serving as a chassis to hold horizontally supported (on two sides) heat-slumped glass panels, free spanning 10 ft in the vertical axis (figure 22.24). The back panel, *per se*, is a mirrored glass that combines with the slumped translucent finish to create an illusion of depth. The façade glows and sparkles in low light (figure 22.22).

With Barry Allan of *Nathan Allan Studios*, an art-glass workshop in Vancouver, we developed several slumping variants, settling eventually on a technique to slump laminated glass over a slightly irregular grid (figure 22.25). This was an artisanal process – the art being in the temperature control, allowing the glass to sink at its slumping point for a period of a few seconds, and then quenching it, arresting any further deformation in the glass beyond the stipulated 10 mm. There was an extraordinary amount of structural testing and physical prototyping (figure 22.26) during this fast-track process (with the owner accepting the risk of having to spend several hundreds of thousands of dollars on physical testing). The building opened in June 2007 with resounding success.

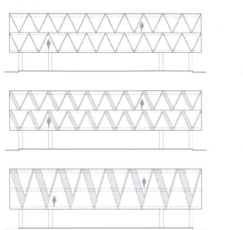

V-PATTERN

X-PATTERN

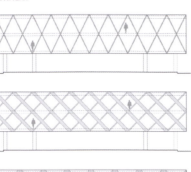

SLUMPED STRUCTURAL GLASS: VAKKO HEADQUARTERS

The headquarters building for the *VAKKO Fashion Group* in Istanbul, Turkey, designed by *REX* in New York (Joshua Prince-Ramus and Erez Ella) is another fast-track slumped glass project, deploying many of the lessons learned from previous projects. The façade design is based on an adapted version of clamped insulated glass used in the *Novartis* project, blended with a unique slumped glass approach based on wind resistance and structurally derived performance. The glass slumping can be read as cross-stiffeners (figure 22.27), thus partly making the stress diagram legible in the glass itself (figures 22.28a–b). This allows optimization of the glass thickness (and also of cost), while achieving a frameless, insulated, abstract, slump-curved architectural result (figures 22.29a–b). The project is under construction, with the expected completion in 2008.

22.27. (above) Cross-stiffening studies for the façade of the *VAKKO Headquarters* building in Istanbul, Turkey (expected completion in 2008), designed by *REX* (Joshua Prince-Ramus and Erez Ella).

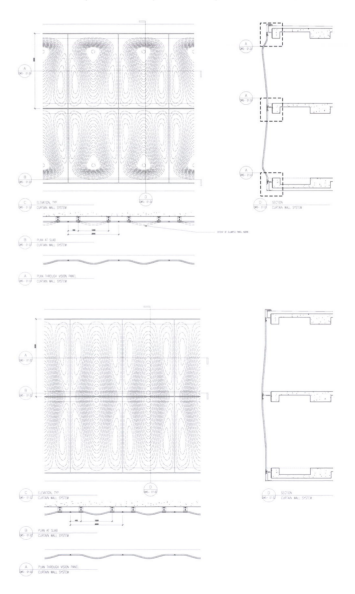

22.29a–b. *VAKKO Headquarters*: Rendering of the two different designs for glass panels.

22.28a–b. *VAKKO Headquarters*: Two different versions of the cross-stiffening, slumped glass panels.

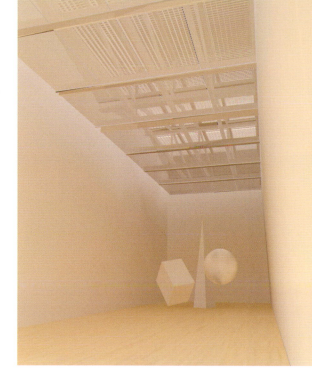

22.30.
The exhibition gallery in the extension of the *McNay Museum of Art* in San Antonio, Texas (expected completion in 2008), designed by the French architect Jean-Paul Viguier.

22.31.
McNay Museum of Art: the roof of the gallery is conceived as a series of layers, including a semi-transparent glass lay-lite (to the interior).

22.33.
McNay Museum of Art: the full-scale prototype of the exhibition gallery.

PATTERNED GLASS: MCNAY MUSEUM OF ART

In the new *Jane and Arthur Stieren Center for Exhibitions* at the *McNay Museum of Art* in San Antonio, Texas (expected completion in 2008), designed by the French architect Jean-Paul Viguier, the principal space is a top-lit special exhibition gallery that must allow manageable light levels, controlled for curatorial reasons, for sculpture, paintings, prints, drawings, and video installation artwork (figure 22.30). The roof is conceived as a series of layers including fixed, custom-engineered aluminum louvers, a translucent insulated low-e skylight with drainage, a set of double horizontal fabric roller blinds for solar control and blackout functions, and a semi-transparent glass lay-lite (to the interior) that defines the interior experience of the gallery space (figure 22.31). All layers were required to be configured in such a manner that they do not change the color rendering index beyond strict thresholds.

The lay-lite is a triple laminated assembly comprised of low-iron glass and three separate ceramic frit treatments of differing patterns with distinct densities of white. The result is a diaphanous filter that further diffuses natural light coming from above (figure 22.32).

The glass defines the experience of the special exhibition gallery. The full-scale prototype of the multi-layered skylight assembly was produced by *Sanxin Glass* in China in order both to ascertain fully the true architectural quality of the space (figure 22.33) and to use in fund raising. The prototype contributed in a significant way to the successful capital campaign for the museum extension.

22.32.
McNay Museum of Art: the triple laminated lay-lite panel with differing patterns.

269

22.34.
The *Beijing Books Building* in Beijing, China (unbuilt), designed by *OMA*.

22.35a–c.
Beijing Books Building: the façade is conceived as a suspended, steel-mesh reinforced, cast-glass block wall.

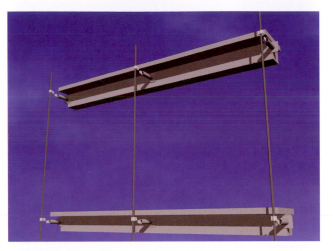

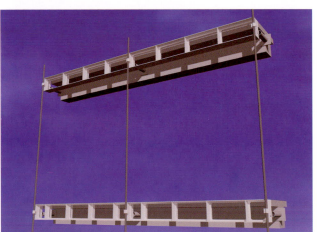

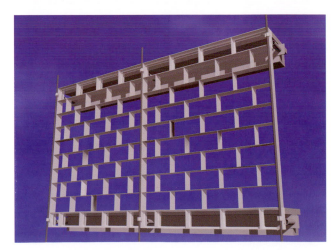

22.36a–c. (below)
Beijing Books Building: the cast blocks were 500 mm x 1000 mm in size.

GLASS BLOCKS: BEIJING BOOKS BUILDING

Working with the *Office for Metropolitan Architecture* (*OMA*) in Beijing on the *Beijing Books Building* (figure 22.34), we developed a façade approach that was quite delightful and playful, but which regrettably will not be built. Nonetheless, the exploration was very rewarding, and many developed ideas and relationships were evolved through other projects. The façade was based on the iconography of the bookcase, resulting in a pixellated, constantly changing appearance. It was conceived as a completely suspended, steel-mesh reinforced, cast-glass block wall (figures 22.35a–c). The cast glass blocks double as bookcases; visitors to the building could change its appearance by placing or removing books from the glass "bookshelves." The cast glass blocks were 500 mm x 1000 mm, designed and produced in collaboration with Nathan Allen and *Fusion Glass* (figures 22.36a–c). The blocks were prototyped using both ceramic and graphite molds.

22.37a–b. (left)
The pixellated bottle wall for the *Morimoto Restaurant* in New York (2006), designed by Tadao Ando and Stephanie Goto.

22.38. (right)
Morimoto Restaurant: the bottle wall is tension supported.

22.39. (right)
Morimoto Restaurant: the bottle wall is made from *Ty-Nant* bottles.

22.40.
Morimoto Restaurant: one of the bottle wall prototypes.

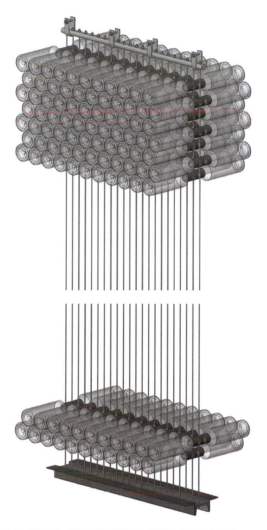

BOTTLE WALL: MORIMOTO RESTAURANT

For the *Morimoto Restaurant* in New York (2006, figures 22.37a–b), designed by Tadao Ando and Stephanie Goto, we designed a tension-supported, pixellated bottle wall (figure 22.38) made from 17,400 half-liter plastic bottles, filled with mineral water, and screwed into couplers. The vertical stainless-steel rods hold the couplers, while the horizontal bracing carries LED point lights, producing a backlit shimmering effect reminiscent of a waterfall. As part of the material research, we tested many water bottles, settling eventually on the acrylic *Ty-Nant* bottles (figure 22.39). This company makes a twisted acrylic water bottle, the base of which has a beautiful profile. We developed numerous prototypes to study the patterning, loading, and lighting effects (figure 22.40).

22.41.
LMVH Paradise
building in Osaka,
Japan (2005),
designed by
Kengo Kuma.

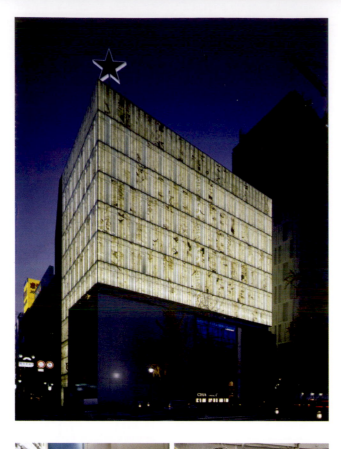

STONE GLASS:
LVMH PARADISE

The façade of the *LMVH Paradise* building in Osaka, Japan (2005), designed by Kengo Kuma, blurs the normative, dichotomic distinctions of the wall (opaque) and window (transparent). The office floors are wrapped in a continuous skin made from "stone glass," i.e. laminated stone and glass. The stone is a green onyx, effective with light transmittance. The stone-glass skin makes the building appear opaque from the outside during the day, but takes on a lantern-like appearance at night (figure 22.41).

The stone panels are used in three thicknesses and produced with three different techniques. One type is the "stone glass" – a laminate comprised of a 4 mm (1/8") thin layer of stone sandwiched between two sheets of glass using vacuum-injected cast resin. To fabricate the stone glass, the slab of onyx was cut and ground down to the desired thickness. Both sides were polished flat and laminated with glass using vacuum injected cast resin (figures 22.42a–d). A second type is a 30 mm (1") thick, acid etched luminaire side lite, with an onyx pattern printed onto glass. A third type is a 75 mm (3") thick slab of onyx laminated onto a 75 mm-thick PET film. With the natural patterning of the green onyx, these three variations create subtle changes around the building (figures 22.43a–b). The system also uses a customized steel mullion, with integrated vertical lighting in every mullion. The façade is the perfect realization of the design ambition – an abstract glowing block of onyx branding LVMH within the city fabric.

22.42a–d.
LMVH Paradise:
the slab of onyx
is ground down to
desired thickness,
polished flat on both
sides, and laminated
with glass using
vacuum injected
cast resin.

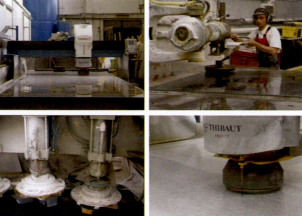

22.43a–b.
LMVH Paradise:
there are three
types of "stone
glass" panels
on the building
façade.

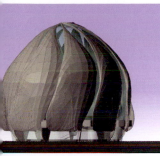

22.44.
Rendering of the *Baha'i Mother Temple of South America* in Santiago, Chile (not yet built), designed by *Hariri & Pontarini Architects*.

22.46.
Baha'i Mother Temple: the alabaster panels would be milled with a 5-axis CNC milling machine.

ALABASTER:
BAHA'I MOTHER TEMPLE OF SOUTH AMERICA

The *Baha'i Mother Temple of South America* in Santiago, Chile (not yet built), designed by *Hariri & Pontarini Architects*, features a dome with nine translucent alabaster and cast glass "sails" (figure 22.44). The exterior skin is conceived as cast glass, with interior surfaces rendered as CNC-milled alabaster (figure 22.45). For each material, a different and unique production technique was developed. For the alabaster, which is quite brittle, a translucent fiberglass reinforcing was laminated to the back of an alabaster panel to stiffen it and to secure mechanical anchors. Significant testing was required to implement such a technique. For the cast glass, a technique was developed to cast large regular slabs, and use these "gingerbread" slabs as raw material. Each panel would then be CNC water-jet cut to the correct geometry and edge bevel. The alabaster production would employ 5-axis milling equipment (figure 22.46).

22.45. (above)
Baha'i Mother Temple: the exterior skin is conceived as cast glass, with the interior surfaces rendered as milled alabaster.

CONCRETE:
LOUISVILLE MUSEUM PLAZA

Louisville Museum Plaza, a 62-storey skyscraper proposed for downtown Louisville, Kentucky (expected completion in 2010, figure 22.47), designed by *REX*, features a next generation pre-cast concrete curtain wall, with a very uniform rectangular wall system, driven by the design intentions and economics of the project (figure 22.48). Working with concrete, we developed a pre-cast panel that had the thinness of steel, and the cast surface and geometrical quality of concrete. Using concrete fins as exterior mullions, the result in the interior is a flush, smooth glass surface, with no mullions projecting into the space (figure 22.49). With *Island Industries* in Calverton, Long Island, we engineered and built two mock-ups, one in black and one in white concrete, using *Ductal*, a high strength fiber-reinforced concrete product. The scale and slenderness are remarkable (figure 22.50).

22.47. (right)
Louisville Museum Plaza, a 62-story skyscraper in Louisville, Kentucky (expected completion in 2010), designed by *REX*.

22.48. (right)
Louisville Museum Plaza: rendering of the pre-cast concrete curtain wall.

22.50. (left)
Louisville Museum Plaza: the scale and slenderness of the concrete panels are remarkable.

22.49.
Louisville Museum Plaza: concrete fins act as exterior mullions, resulting in a flush, smooth interior surface.

GLASS PATTERNS:
100 11TH AVENUE RESIDENCES

The *100 11th Avenue* project, a 23-storey residential
tower, described by its architect Jean Nouvel as "a vision
machine," will be located along West Side Highway in
Manhattan, New York (completion expected in 2008),
adjacent to Frank Gehry's *IAC/Interactive Headquarters*
building. The building features a faceted façade (figure
22.51), composed of glass panes of varying sizes,
shapes, and materials, tilted along different axes within
a complex steel and aluminum framing system (figures
22.52a–b). The design intent was for a façade with a
single composition, as opposed to a traditional curtain wall
with discernible panels. Our challenge was to introduce a
regulating order to the façade, and resolve it into a system
that makes sense in terms of sound construction practices.

The façade was designed using *CATIA* and the
related *Digital Project*, and locating "vision" panels
and operable windows based upon the interior of the
residential units; the envelope was designed from the
inside out and outside in. Groupings of glass panes were
organized into megapanels (figure 22.53), whose overall
dimensions conform to the rooms they cover. There are 192
megapanels, 87 of which are unique. Seven megapanels
cover each floor. The entire façade wall features 1,351

22.53. (above)
100 11th Avenue: one of
the megapanels.

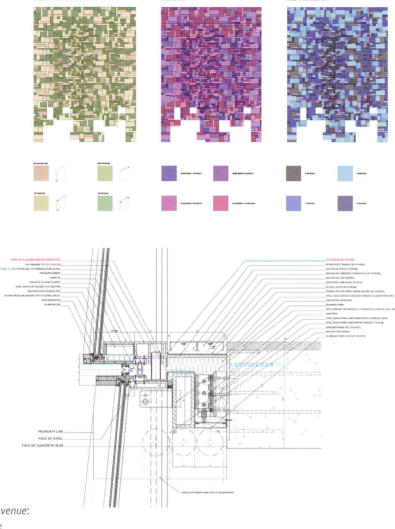

DIRECTION - OF ROTATION - MAP   MATERIALITY MAP   ANGLE - OF ROTATION - MAP

22.54.
100 11th Avenue: the façade wall comprises 1,351 individual glass panes, composed of four different material variations, with each pane tilted on one axis by several degrees.

individual glass panes, composed of four different material variations, with each pane tilted on one axis by several degrees (figure 22.54). The "fractured" framing system presented a significant set of design challenges, because there were no linear load paths. The traditional moment-connected aluminum mullion system could not meet the slim profiles desired by Nouvel. The frame was instead constructed from steel mullions, which would carry the loads when formed into the irregular patterns of the façade design. The mullions vary in width from 3 to 6 inches to support the various tilts of the glass panes. A system of aluminum cassettes, welded to the steel mullions, holds the individual glass units and provides a thermal and acoustic break (figure 22.55). Three-dimensional modeling in CATIA enabled the definition of fully associative parametric assemblies (figure 22.56), which in turn facilitated the automatic production of two-dimensional shop drawings.

Finding a fabricator to manufacture the steel and aluminum megapanels proved challenging. After an unsuccessful search for a cost-effective fabrication and assembly, we formed a contracting company, *CCA Facade Technologies* that included *KGE*, one of China's largest fabricators (figures 22.57a–b), and *Island Industries*, a local company that erects large panel systems. This collaborative effort cut the costs by 25%, saving the project.

22.55.
100 11th Avenue: detail of the façade system.

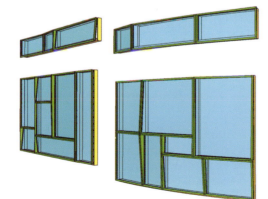

22.56.
100 11th Avenue: three-dimensional model of the mock-up megapanel in CATIA.

22.57a–b.
100 11th Avenue: full-scale mock-up of one megapanel produced in China.

22.58.
Headquarters building of the
Central Chinese Television
(*CCTV*) in Beijing, China
(expected completion in
2008), designed by *OMA*.

22.59.
CCTV: the original
regular diagrid of
the brace frame was
changed to reflect the
distribution of forces
across the surface of
the building.

22.60.
CCTV: the structural
analysis of the initial,
regular diagrid pattern
(unfolded).

22.61.
CCTV: the adapted,
irregular pattern
of the diagrid
(unfolded).

22.62.
CCTV: the structural
analysis of the adapted,
irregular diagrid pattern
(unfolded).

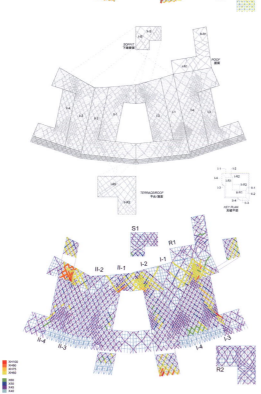

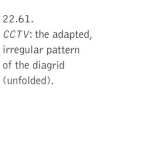

DIAGRID CURTAIN WALL: CENTRAL CHINESE TELEVISION HEADQUARTERS (CCTV)

In 2002, the *Office for Metropolitan Architecture* (*OMA*) won the competition for the headquarters of the *Central Chinese Television* (*CCTV*) in Beijing, China. According to Ole Scheeren, a partner at *OMA*, the building was conceived as a "loop folded in space," which is formed by a 90-degree bent low-rise at the bottom, two towers situated diagonally from each other and sloping at an angle of 6 degrees in different directions, and a connecting, cantilevered "bridge" volume at the top, also bent 90 degrees, leaving a large hole in the center (figure 22.58). The 230 m-tall building, to be completed in 2008 before the start of the *Summer Olympic Games*, has a floor area of over 500,000 m² in its 51 stories. The project combines administration, news, broadcasting, program production, and studios in an interconnected sequence of activities (i.e. the program loop).

The building's structure defies the normative conceptions of skyscraper design and the standards for the engineering of gravity and lateral loads. A brace frame, in the form of an irregular diagonal mesh, engineered by Cecil Balmond and Rory McGowan of *Arup*, is wrapped around the building, and acts as a primary structure, creating a structural "tube" of diagonal supports. The irregular pattern of the "diagrid" on the building's façades is an expression of the distribution of forces across the surface of the building, i.e. it is denser in the areas where the structural loads are higher (figures 22.59 to 22.62).

The steel curtain wall, designed by *Front Inc.,* is intended and engineered to be a blast screen for the primary diagonal structure. With a 1 million sq ft overhang subject to gravity, seismic, wind, and blast forces, there had to

22.63a–d. (below)
CCTV: the curtain wall consists of large chevron elements, attached to the primary structure at node locations.

22.64.
CCTV building under construction.

22.66. (above)
CCTV: component of the diagrid arriving on the construction site.

22.67. (below)
CCTV: a full-scale mock-up of the curtain wall segment.

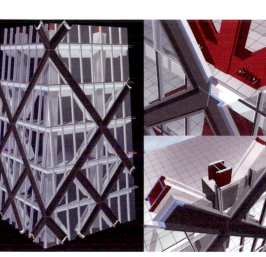

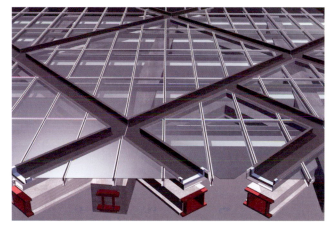

22.65. (right)
CCTV: the structural diagrid under construction.

be sufficient redundancy in the structural system. To mitigate one level of risk, the façade steelwork follows the primary diagonal bracing of the building, serving as a blast screen with a sufficient crumple zone to reduce the risk of any lateral impact on the bracing elements. The resultant diagonal façade structure reads as a series of chevron elements, and can only be attached to the primary structure at the node locations (figures 22.63a–d). As a result, the strength of the steel façade diagrid is adequate to support the self-weight of the curtain below, within a specific diamond grouping. Each element may weigh up to about 8 tons per single piece – in a façade structure, not the primary structure. The façade system is sufficiently strong that each of the large steel mullions is actually suspended up to nine floors inside the building. The principal reason behind this design strategy is that every second floor is not nodal, meaning there are diaphragm and non-diaphragm floors that move in opposite directions if an earthquake occurs, which would tear the curtain wall apart. As a consequence, the entire diamond grid forms a separate curtain wall, locked up as a diaphragm, creating a massive stack joint at the base. Conceptually and structurally, this is a radical high-rise curtain wall. What is exciting about it is its materiality – the interior expression is very muscular with the exposed steel, thus making its own performance very expressive. There is a legibility and authenticity to the experience of the façade from the interior that is not as present on the exterior. The negative reveal reading of the diagrid is a play – abstracting the façade into a series of floating diamonds rendered against the internal structural stress diagram (figures 22.64 to 22.67).

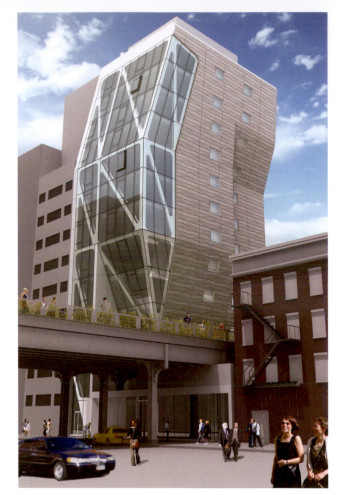

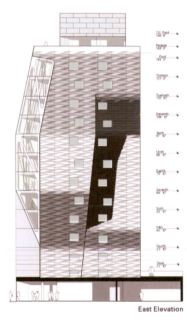

South Elevation | East Elevation | North Elevation

22.70.
The surface effect produced by pre-cast concrete panels.

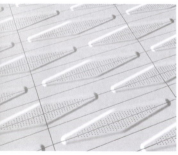

22.71.
A prototype of a pre-cast concrete panel.

FIELD EFFECTS IN CONCRETE AND METAL: HIGH LINE 23

High Line 23 is a 13-storey residential building (figure 22.68) along the *West Side High Line* in New York (expected completion in 2008), which is a continuous elevated bridge structure that will be transformed into a unique linear urban park. According to architect Neil Denari, the building is "precisely shaped by a confluence of forces" and is a "combination of both found and implanted ecologies," like the High Line itself. The east façade facing the High Line (figure 22.69) is formed as a sculptural surface with framed views of Manhattan. A curtain wall of glass and stainless steel panels hangs on a complex cantilevered steel frame, generating an expressive form and surfaces with economy. Since the building is located in the middle of the Arts District, the attempt is to deliver a highly crafted object that is also commercially viable.

Front's collaboration with *Neil M. Denari Architects* (*NMDA*) was intensive for every part of the enclosure. The fabric-like, embossed panels on the east façade facing the High Line have gone through several material explorations. The façade development started with a preference for thin cast concrete as a material (figure 22.70). Full-scale panel samples were fabricated using high-strength fiber-reinforced concrete (figure 22.71). Even though the production process was successful, and the cost of production acceptable, this material solution was rejected; the physical quality and the visual appearance of panels under different light conditions were not entirely satisfactory, and the long-term weathering effects on appearance and material performance were deemed detrimental.

The process continued with various metal materials (figure 22.72) and finishes, including stainless steel, aluminum, and zinc. The team worked closely with *A. Zahner Company* in Kansas City on several prototypes. A range of folded, origami-like panels were developed that could easily be cut from a single sheet and break-formed into a folded and embossed panel with sealed return edges (figure 22.73). The folded geometries were compelling (figure 22.74), but were ultimately unsatisfactory for the desired, "fluid" quality of the building. The team proceeded to develop stamped panels using subtle surface undulations (figures 22.75 and 22.76a–b). That exploration yielded a preference for stainless steel, an understanding of the ideal

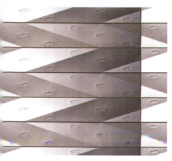

22.73.
High Line 23:
a stamped
metal panel
alternative.

22.72. (below)
High Line 23:
rendering showing
the metal clad
façade as seen
from the High
Line below.

22.77a–b.
High Line 23:
the building
systems
assembly.

22.74. (above)
The surface effects
produced by metal
panels.

22.75. (below)
Another stamped
metal panel alternative,
with subtle surface
undulations.

22.76a–b. (right)
High Line 23: different
field effects produced
by different tiling
patterns and panel
orientations.

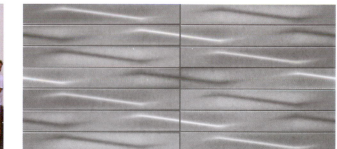

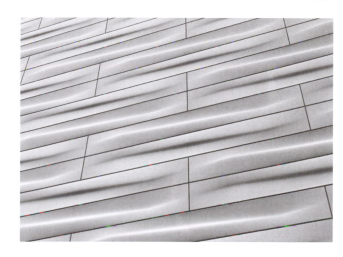

gauge of metal, and the slope ratio by which the metal could be safely drawn under the stamping process. In the end, the fabrication contract for the metal panel system was awarded to *Dante Martinez* from Argentina; *Thyssen* in Buenos Aires, Argentina, was sub-contracted to make the stamp, a process they typically employ in the local automotive sector.

The glass façade was developed over dozens of iterations. The final design employs a panelized façade with framing elements from milled steel that was over-clad with fine break-formed stainless steel profiles. Custom aluminum cassette profiles are "skinned" onto the steel, holding structurally siliconed glass panels. The glass is low-iron, low-e, floor-to-ceiling, laminated, and insulated, with the majority of panels having a custom applied silk-screen pattern. The pattern was developed as a projected shadow of the primary structural steel behind the façade; it reinforces the building's structural configuration, which has an offset core with irregular steel columns and diagonal bracing elements (figures 22.77a–b). The frit pattern is a super-graphic, but does in fact correlate directly to the structural diagram of the building, yielding a certain level of legibility and abstraction, and simultaneously giving the building one of its strongest iconic drivers.

22.78.
Rendering of
the *Walker Art
Center* expansion
in Minneapolis,
Minnesota (2005),
designed by Herzog
& de Meuron.

STAMPED METAL MESH: WALKER ART CENTER

The expansion of the *Walker Art Center* in Minneapolis, Minnesota (2005), designed by *Herzog & de Meuron*, articulates a large volume clad in lightly stamped aluminum, which provides a remarkable visual counterpoint to the Center's original brick-clad building designed by Edward Larrabee Barnes (figure 22.78). In collaboration with *Herzog & de Meuron*, we investigated several different material options, including slumped glass (figures 22.79a–b), tensioned backlit *Teflon* fabric (figures 22.80a–b), and stamped anodized expanded metal mesh (figures 22.81a–b) for the studio theater box – a largely opaque volume with shards of light cutting through the

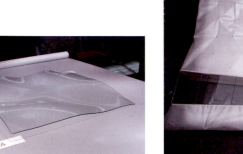

22.79a–b. (above) *Walker Art Center*: material studies – slumped glass.

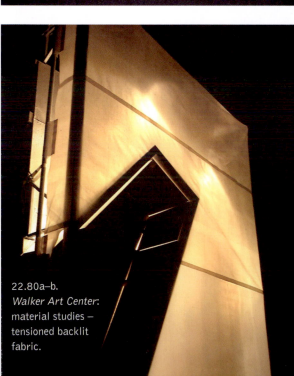

22.80a–b. *Walker Art Center*: material studies – tensioned backlit fabric.

22.81a–b. *Walker Art Center*: material studies – stamped anodized expanded metal mesh.

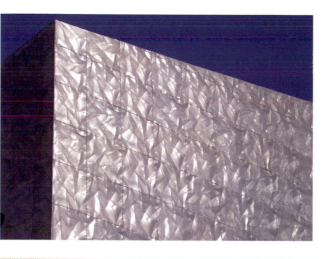

22.82a–b.
Walker Art Center: the façade panels were made from stamped, expanded aluminum mesh.

22.83. (below)
Walker Art Center: the panels reflect the ambient light during the day to create a shimmering, changeable façade.

façade. The slumped glass proved too expensive. While the fabric-covered façade produced a beautiful lantern-like effect when illuminated, the client rejected it, questioning its permanence and implications of its materiality (it looked to the client like an archeological site in Rome that had never been unwrapped). While the fabric did not succeed as a material choice for the *Walker Art Center*, it resulted in a spectacular success (without *Front*'s involvement) on the *Munich Allianz Stadium*.

Herzog & de Meuron have already experimented with fabric and stamped mesh enclosures on several buildings. Collectively, we continued to explore these ideas for the *Walker Art Center* with stamped, folded, repeatable patterns. In the end, stamped, "crumpled" expanded aluminum mesh panels were chosen to clad the building (figures 22.82a–b). During the day, the panels reflect the ambient light to create a shimmering, changeable façade (figure 22.83). As with the *Holt Renfrew* project in Vancouver, the specular surface borrows ambient and low-level winter light to achieve a highly present and iconic building. By night, irregularly shaped windows and illuminated aluminum panels create a glowing effect (figure 22.84).

22.84.
Walker Art Center: by night, irregularly shaped windows and illuminated aluminum panels create a glowing effect.

SANDWICHED METAL MESH: SEATTLE CENTRAL LIBRARY

The *Central Library* in Seattle, Washington (2004), designed by *Office for Metropolitan Architecture* (*OMA*), was built on a steeply sloped site on Fourth Avenue, one of Seattle's busiest and most important downtown streets. The faceted planes of the building outline the extended platforms of the "book spiral" that defines the programmatic and spatial articulation of the building. This distinctive exterior skin is defined and unified by the diagonal, diamond-shaped grid (the "diagrid") that wraps the entire building with a continuous, transparent glass layer (figures 22.85a–b), exposing the interior to sunlight – something libraries typically avoid.

The thermal performance of the envelope was integral to the design development of the diagrid curtain wall. Approximately half of the glazing panels have high performance low-e coatings, and were fabricated with airspaces filled with krypton gas. To deal with solar heat gain in the summer months, an aluminum expanded metal mesh interlayer was inserted into the glass panels with the most exposure to the sun. The mesh shields the interior from direct sunlight and simultaneously provides views to the exterior. The micro-diamond pattern of the mesh also related directly to the larger diagrid of the curtain-wall mullions.

Originally laminated between sheets of glass, the expanded aluminum mesh is encapsulated within a 2 mm layer of air. Clear, low-iron glass is used in front of the mesh to brighten its appearance from the outside. Considerable

22.86a–d. (below) *Seattle Central Library*: early studies of the laminated, expanded aluminum mesh.

22.87a–b.
Seattle Central Library: mock-ups of the different glazing panels.

effort (and a considerable part of our fee) were invested in determining how to insert off-the-shelf expanded metal mesh between two sheets of glass (figures 22.86a–d). A couple of precedents helped. Paul Andreu's *Glass Dome* in Osaka Harbor used laminated perforated metal developed by *Asahi*, but they refused to supply it to the US and therefore would not participate in the development. *Isoclima*, based in Padua, Italy, one of the best glass fabrication companies in the world, was already fabricating metal and glass composites for high-speed train and automotive products with 20 years of experience. Alberto Berolini, general manager and owner of *Isoclima*, successfully fabricated a high performance laminated glass panel with the expanded metal mesh based on our approach. Working with *Isoclima*, we further investigated customizing the stretch of the metal in order to selectively optimize the micro-sunshade by façade orientation and inclination. Regrettably, the laminating and optimizing process was too expensive for the client. In the end, *Okalux* collaborated in the development of an encapsulated version of the panel, which was their strength. They produced a glass panel that sandwiched the metal mesh within a 2 mm air-space using a polysulfide edge seal. No lamination was used in suspending the mesh between the sheets of glass. Mock-ups were constructed to provide a comparative understanding of the mesh/glass appearance relative to a tinted/coated appearance (figures 22.87a–b). Mock-ups were used in fund raising to pay for the library's expressive skin, and were essential to convey the desired quality of light within the library (figure 22.88).

22.88.
Seattle Central Library: interior view.

22.89.
The *New Museum of Contemporary Art* in New York (2007), designed by *Sejima and Nishizawa and Associates* (*SANAA*).

MAXIMUM METAL MESH:
NEW MUSEUM OF CONTEMPORARY ART

Kazuyo Sejima and Ryue Nishizawa of Tokyo-based *SANAA* designed the shimmering seven-storey structure of the *New Museum of Contemporary Art* in New York (2007) as a dramatic, shifting stack of metal boxes. The design intent was to reduce the building mass on a narrow site (figure 22.89). Its exterior cladding involves two interacting metal surfaces, combining extruded aluminum wall panels with an expanded metal mesh covering. The base layer was designed as very subtle corrugated, corduroy-like textured extrusions to create a slightly vibrant backdrop and reflective surface for the outer metal layer. The layer was made from the largest expanded mesh available, with 300 mm wide diamond-pattern openings (figures 22.90a–c). While industrial materials are used, the geometrical layout and the attachment system were perfectly indexed and coordinated. The large panels, which are 10'–3/4" wide by up to 28'–4" long, were designed with a gutter system for drainage, and an extruded clip attachment that allows the panel system to move independently of the building. The panels are also sufficiently strong to withstand typical wind loads, and support ice and dead loads of the polished anodized mesh. The panels are mounted 1'–1/2" away from the surface of the underlying wall panels. The final outcome is a building façade that achieves an ethereal quality rarely realized.

22.90a –c.
New Museum of Contemporary Art: the building is covered with an expanded metal mesh.

22.91.
Model of the
*Television Cultural
Center* (*TVCC*)
in Beijing, China
(expected completion
in 2008), designed by
OMA.

22.92a –b.
TVCC: the pixellated
glass façade.

MONUMENTAL METAL CORRUGATION: TELEVISION CULTURAL CENTER (TVCC)

The *Television Cultural Center* (*TVCC*) in Beijing, China (expected completion in 2008), is part of the *CCTV Master Plan*, also designed by *Office for Metropolitan Architecture* (*OMA*). The 1.25 million sq ft building houses a *Mandarin Oriental Hotel*, a flexible media/performing arts space, a conference center, and the press release area for the CCTV broadcasters.

The building envelope is an abstract series of folding planes of corrugated zinc, conceived and executed at a monumental scale (figure 22.91). The glass façade is "pixellated," whereby each pixel corresponds to one hotel room (figures 22.92a–b). The corrugations scale to approximately 450 mm per edge, with geometry as a subtle aspect of the fabrication. The line of the profile is continuous while traveling across fold lines between planes. When the profiles cross over a fold line, they do not exit at a mirrored angle from which they came. The corrugations are all parallelograms, which change every time they switch from one surface to another, as they ramp up over the building. Mock-ups were constructed using naturally weathered raw zinc panels (figure 22.93). To optimize the yield of material from a typical zinc coil, the corrugations were sized for maximum efficiency.

22.93.
TVCC: mock-up of
the corrugated zinc
skin.

22.94a –b.
(right and below)
The *Dee and Charles Wyly Theater* in Dallas, Texas (expected completion in 2008), designed by *REX*.

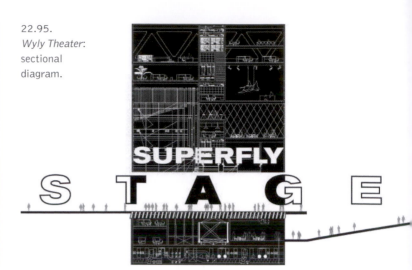

22.95.
Wyly Theater: sectional diagram.

TAPERED ALUMINUM EXTRUSIONS: DEE AND CHARLES WYLY THEATER

The *Dee and Charles Wyly Theater* in Dallas, Texas (expected completion in 2008), designed by *REX*, is a large abstract volume that is largely opaque (figures 22.94a–b). It has specific areas of fenestration, including a theater space at grade, a lobby glass wall below grade, and several apertures in the upper volume corresponding to specific functional spaces. The interior spaces are configured as interlocking programmatic volumes hinged around necessary adjacencies. At the base of the building mass, the stage conceptually runs through the landscape, with the fly tower and all rehearsal, auditorium, and lounge/public spaces above it (figure 22.95). The lobby areas are below the stage.

Much of the budget was allocated to the proper functioning of the theater. The façade was secondary, thus it was beneficial to have a large expanse of opaque material to offset the cost of the glazed area of the façade. Based on ideas present in the *Walker Art Center* and the *New Museum of Contemporary Art* projects, we developed, together with *REX*, a variant of simple clapboard siding, the principal challenge being to find an economical way to achieve this solution. In collaboration with Dante Martinez of *Tisi* and Bill Zahner of the *A. Zahner Company*,[3] we developed a system of custom aluminum extrusions in six profiles (figure 22.96) that were engineered to span precisely 16 ft vertically. The material in each extrusion was optimized to perform this limited structural function. As a result, no vertical sub-framing was required. The extrusions were also engineered for top-down installation, locking one extrusion to the next with a hairline splice detail. The extrusions, in aggregate, span up to 90 ft vertically, with all self-weight of aluminum resolved at the head bracket. The result is a seamless curtain functioning as a gasketed rain-screen with each panel interlocking to the next. Next, we developed variations in extrusion associations to generate randomness in profile (figure 22.97). Working with *Tisi*, we collectively developed the exact profiles, taking into consideration such factors as maximum diameter of the dies and ease of manufacture (figure 22.98). As an additional layer of refinement, for the large area of fenestration, we developed customized, tapered pieces, fabricated out of developable curves into a resultant ellipse (figure 22.99). These elements serve as transitions between the typical aluminum profiles and the elliptical louver profiles that selectively extend across the face of the glazed areas.

22.96.
Wyly Theater: a system
of custom aluminum
extrusions in six
profiles.

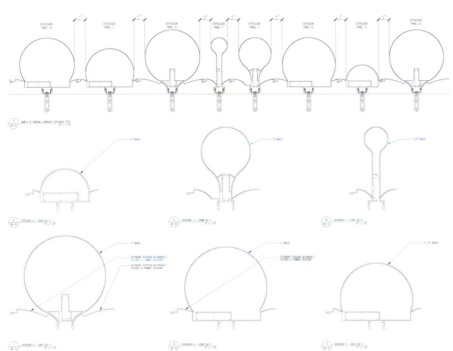

22.98.
Wyly Theater:
mock-up of the
extrusion system.

22.97.
Wyly Theater:
variations in extrusion
associations.

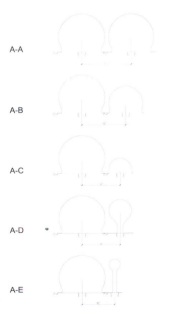

A-A	B-B	C-D
A-B	B-C	C-E
A-C	B-D	D-D
A-D	B-E	D-E
A-E	C-C	E-E

22.99.
Wyly Theater: tapered
extrusions are used in
large fenestrated areas.

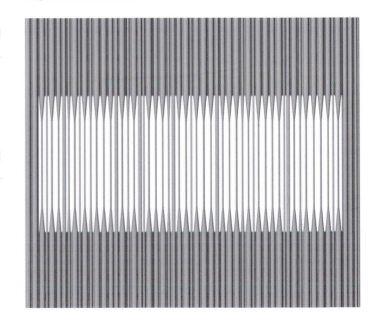

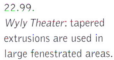

CONCLUSIONS

The discussion about scale and legibility, relative to materiality and material effects, often simply comes down to issues of material processing and handling. For example, the economics of aluminum curtain wall frequently require a nominal, standardized aluminum glass panel size of 5 x 8 ft. The weight of aluminum, glass panel thicknesses, available coatings, trucking, and the site–labor matrix conspire to yield certain ranges for sizes, weights, and patterns that are optimized financially. An economic imperative drives these normative results, yielding buildings that converge on at least one order of general uniformity. Developing an acute awareness of the economic metrics is essential to creatively find value in projects, relative to the achievement of specific architectural desires.

Every façade legibly embodies a set of values and priorities that should be understood, perhaps in ideological terms, as being established by the organization or individual bringing resources to bear when realizing a building project, according to their needs and desires. We recognize where our projects succeed and fail relative to the goals established by sponsors, lenders, and the priorities, understood in universal terms to be socially responsible. For example, a project may be a spectacular success as a branding effort, yet it fails considerably according to any reasonable standard of environmental responsibility; or a project achieves a rare holistic synthesis of divergent constraints yielding superior (perhaps sublime) architecture. We have worked on both kinds of projects. As we participate in each project, prior knowledge gained and judgments made cycle through future work as we strive to influence the process to enhance the work and serve the common good.

We have no distilled summary or incisive conclusions to offer. We barrel forward in our work, collaborating where and when we may, operating as chameleons, artfully inhabiting the agendas and artistic programs of our clients. We stand strong in our commitment to the richest conception and idealized execution of the work. We provide mostly façade design and consulting, occupying the territory between patrons, lenders, designers, makers, and builders. This is a fertile domain, which allows us to work on high ground, low ground, upstream, and downstream.

We are not digital apologists (being closer to the nuts and bolts), although we do recognize out of practicality the essential and defining nature of digital tools and their profound impact on the architecture, engineering, and construction (AEC) industry. We have adopted these digital tools in a pragmatic fashion, as a matter of necessity, and are now developing digital work processes tailored to our non-linear, iterative, and increasingly vertically integrated working methods. This includes the development of associative parametric building assemblies, accurate to the millimeter, and fully verified for fabrication, resulting in the capture and accumulation of the intellectual effort associated with industrial design. Such digital assemblies are tailored to project specific aesthetic and performance parameters and are instantiated into parametric wireframe armatures, with each instance intelligently adapting to its geometrical constraints and allowing the effective extraction of fabrication data from the model.

The Holy Grail, as we see it, is to structure practice in such a way as to overcome the inefficiencies rendered by the fact that those who pay for buildings do not design buildings, and those who design buildings do not build buildings. It is an encouraging sign that the world is currently exploding with organizations bridging across these boundaries, and that new project delivery systems are regularly being experimented with. The normative condition, however, remains – the economic benefits of full integration will elude the AEC industry until circumstances are generated where risks are shared and interests are aligned. Aerospace and automotive industries, among many others, see regular productivity enhancements as individual companies (profit centers) are responsible for the full lifecycle process from concept through design, testing, fabrication, sales, delivery, and post-contract maintenance and support. Change is now upon us, and as the AEC industry restructures to capture its lost efficiency in the order of 30% (as some say), digital technology will continue to be deployed at an accelerating pace in the service of that goal. Economics will win. It will be interesting to witness (and in some way impact) how fragmentation gives way to integration. The catalytic effect it will have in further transforming the practice and art of building will be formidable.

NOTES

1 This achieved a reasonable insulating value for the building envelope of approximately 0.7 W/m²k or R8.

2 The exterior glass lite is demountable in the event that the motorized blinds require servicing.

3 *Tisi* is the fabricator working collaboratively with the design team and Zahner's team, who will assume responsibility for installing the cladding.

SENSIBILITIES AND SENSITIVITIES

DONALD BATES
DAVID ERDMAN
ACHIM MENGES
FABIAN SCHEURER
SHOHEI SHIGEMATSU
MARC SIMMONS
KEVIN KLINGER
BRANKO KOLAREVIC

KEVIN KLINGER: Marc Simmons set up a provocative first question when he said "this form changes your idea of what stone is about." When we consider forms, skins, and structures, and we have an idea of some effect that we want to achieve, what happens if the industry is not able to provide that kind of material or manufacturing operation? Also, the technological capacity of the steel industry is very different from the stone industry. What is the impact of working with different materials and manufacturers in order to achieve a design intention?

FABIAN SCHEURER: I have been looking at wooden materials for the past two years. From my central-European perspective (Swiss-German, to be exact), the wood industry is very advanced; CNC machinery is available in most places, especially the joinery machines of timber engineering. They do what they have always been doing, just quicker and more exact. They are actually lacking ideas from the architects and designers who want to use their equipment. The machinery and CAD/CAM systems are capable of producing amazing work; detailing in timber construction is coming back, which has been more or less lost, because it was much cheaper to just use nails than do detailing. There is a tremendous potential in working with these industries.

DONALD BATES: It depends to some degree on where you are located. Jeanne Gang talked about opportunity for more employment, in light of automation and robots. In fact, with the projects we have been working on in China and the Middle East, the job sites are actually filled with masses of workers because labor is very cheap in both locations. So these are different conditions in which the work actually takes place. The buildings are just as sophisticated as anything built in Europe, but they are constructed by a lot of hands. There exists a much more hybrid condition. On the site, particularly with concrete construction and formwork, there are many people working 12-hour days wrapping reinforcement bars, and spending time hand-crafting and hand-cutting floor tiles. I do not think that there is a ubiquitous transformation. One has to realize there are huge pockets of differentiation where this may come in. Simultaneously, at another level, it is really eighteenth- or nineteenth-century production technology.

MICK EEKHOUT: Should we not make a difference between off-site and on-site production? Donald Bates described on-site production. We have mainly talked about off-site pre-fabrication. There is a large gap between architects accelerated in design computation in the last ten years and what is considered normal in the traditional industry. It is fantastic that the industry is catching up and is automating itself. Yes, the architect can bring a spark over and bridge the gap. The architect can imagine all kinds of complicated elements, more than ever before, and the manufacturer is able to manufacture them. Originally, there was no gap up to ten years ago. Then, there was a giant acceleration by clever architects who wanted to make sophisticated buildings and direct the whole building industry with them, or at least the frontrunners of the building industry. But the question of engaging industry also depends upon what percentage is pre-fabricated on or off the building site.

DAVID ERDMAN: There are some similarities, but also differences that relate to scale. One of the similarities is that, whether you are working at a small or large scale, working with a liaison such as *Front, Inc.* or managing those assets on your own in a smaller project, there is an ambition, seen in many of the presented projects, to get involved with a number of resources much earlier on. The ambition is to have direct feedback – material feedback – on any digital work, whether through digital modeling or mocking things up. There seems to be a much more robust exchange between the digital and material realms. I think some of the differences are present in smaller-scale projects, where I may have to manage that information directly with sub-contractors with which I am working, such as with *Warner Brothers* or the automotive industry cutting molds, or getting installers involved earlier to look at prototypes in my studio. At a larger scale, that happens through a liaison. In the same spirit, there is an increasing awareness that the material realities and tolerances can impact the design. There are very interesting elements to play with, such as seams, and how you can populate them, or texture, and how it can become something that allows for certain kinds of connections.

BRANKO KOLAREVIC: What we have seen over the past two days is an amazing capacity to engage material technique and technology. It is mesmerizing what one can do nowadays. I think the reason Shohei Shigematsu is with us is not accidental; one could say that at *OMA* there is a kind of underlying ideology of resisting technology and resisting complexity for the sake of complexity. It is an issue that merits some examination. Should we embrace complexity? Should we embrace technology for the sake of technology? We know what are the affordances, and what are the resistances. Should these resistances be productive?

SHOHEI SHIGEMATSU: Well, I do not think we are closed to the technology; we use many technologies, but ...

BRANKO KOLAREVIC: How do you resist the temptation?

SHOHEI SHIGEMATSU: I think we are just ignorant. That is why we collaborate with someone like *Front, Inc.* or *Arup*, who have more expertise in that field. In our best works, one cannot tell if it is either an engineering project or an architectural project. We do want to integrate technology, but not on our own, because we have to spend so much time on designing. We still believe in designing a good space. I do not think we are closed, but I am just so ignorant about the digital fabrication. Does it imply automation, and consequently reduce the fee of the architects? Shall we reveal to clients that we are working with digital technology? Is there any kind of precedent of a relationship with the client communication, because I did not really hear that except for the kind of aesthetical rejection. I did not hear discussion about any fee issues.

DONALD BATES: But it does not really reduce the work.

SHOHEI SHIGEMATSU: Right.

DONALD BATES: As everybody said, in many ways, digital fabrication takes much longer, because it requires more preparation. One of the things it provides is an increase in material options. Conventional architecture is about a lack of options, almost like narrowing down, or saying we will do

it this way, because we have always done it this way, therefore we do not have to think about it. Actually, most of what has been said is about increasing thinking, and therefore increasing responsibility, which is hardly a lessening of the role of the architect relative to time and client. There is partly some disquiet that I have, which can be characterized by a difference between a tendency to specialization or generalization. Some of my concern is that some of the work that we are seeing is becoming so specific and specialized, that it seems like it is leaving off a whole range of other architectural expression. In *OMA*'s office, you do a very good job of making it sound like you are ignorant, peasant architects. But, you do huge amounts of research. You have something like a thousand students in the background going out and finding out about different materials; it is a characteristic of most work that you are experimenting with simple materials used in non-simple ways, or unfamiliar ways. I do not think you are not part of the game either, although it sounds like a good story. I know that all of us at various times have gone through a research phase looking at certain things, narrowing it down as a quasi-specialization, but then it opens up again. I know there was some sensibility that was coming through, fixated on a very particular way of producing a very particular thing that has a very particular effect, that seems to be counter to what is one of the benefits of an architectural sensibility, which is to be open enough to see new possibilities everywhere, not just within one train of development.

KEVIN KLINGER: I wonder if we are not in the nascence of these expressions, and that over the next ten to fifteen years we will see even better informed processes. Certainly, the potential of parametric and associative modeling can include things other than just material effects. It is very promising. We are making progress. Right now many architects are interrogating the material potentials and manufacturing issues. But we are also directly engaging the information that underlies the process. What do you have to say about working with code, particularly how you craft the code, as if you were working it like a material? Information is now vital to "making." I can only imagine in ten years a very rich future where this totality of information is available to us in very particular ways. How do we prepare for that future?

ACHIM MENGES: I absolutely agree that what we are trying to do is to focus on particular aspects, especially the ones related to basic research. This is the consequence of recognizing the fact that, in architecture, we are still missing some of the essential sensitivity required to understand and unfold the possibilities and qualities latent in the engagement with these tools and technologies far beyond the currently omnipresent, parametrically decorated shed. Many architects have absorbed this technology with a speed that is hard to believe. For them, parametric and associative modeling is a fantastic machine for universalizing every kind of building typology. We have to face the fact that employing parametric design does not necessarily add a particular spatial or architectural quality. On the contrary, most of the time, parametric approaches actually mean a new kind of standardization of relationships geared towards efficient work flow and affordable production. This results from a one-dimensional understanding of the opportunities offered by these technologies, only seen within an established design process and a preconceived value system. What we are trying to do is raise the level of awareness of how we can create a different *sensitivity* and *sensibility* of what the additional qualities of these technologies may be. What strikes me is that currently many students and architects alike are longing to deal with this technology, yet ultimately, hardly anyone has a clue why they engage. What really is the vision that comes with that technology? One could even argue that this is one of the first major technological paradigm shifts in architecture that is neither driven by nor drives a related socio-cultural vision. I rather like to think that it may not be there yet. CAM is old, CAD is of old too, but the level of integration we are promoting and instrumentalizing is a relatively recent phenomenon. It has not yet brought about an additional architectural vision, and that is why we actually take a step back. Much of the work we do is based on a certain suspicion of directly engaging with these technologies on the level of uncritical application as the premature employment of these technologies will prevent us from understanding their greatest potential, which in my eyes is the capacity to question many preconceptions that we have about design. However, I assume it will take a lot of basic research to unfold the critical and radical paradigm shift innate in these technologies. This development is now in a decisive phase, with the relevance of these technologies being undermined by uncritical, premature applications, and it runs the risk of just becoming yet another architectural style or fashion.

SHOHEI SHIGEMATSU: I totally agree. However, there is a certain kind of confusion still in the pedagogical sense, not even as a vision, but some kind of preference. I interview many students or applicants, but the most difficult thing to get out of them is to know what they like, and it is not even about a vision, but just a preference. All of the projects in their portfolios look amazingly nice and complicated with interesting surfaces, but when I ask them what kind of architecture they like, they cannot answer. One of the most difficult things in design process is to choose. You can create millions of options. What I have seen in the presented projects is very nice; you are all talented, but in a normal standard practice, I do not know if it is encouraging people to have their own opinion. Of course, they can research, develop, and go further, but at the simple level, questions about preference for glass mullions, glass or wood balustrades, they cannot answer.

ACHIM MENGES: I assume it is very difficult for many people in the academic world to actually teach decision-making at this moment in time, mainly because, first, they would have to understand what the criteria are for creating an alternative, critical value system within the context of the new possibilities and constraints of these technologies. To turn it in a positive sense: this may well be one of the fantastic opportunities this technological development may bring about; it allows you to revisit and radically rethink the way you establish criteria for choice.

SHOHEI SHIGEMATSU: But do you think students are aware of that potential? Don't you think you have to be responsible to bridge the gap between the actual practice and your lab?

DAVID ERDMAN: There is a much bigger question of how one addresses issues of "difficulty." *OMA* has a tendency to present itself as having an agnosticism about difficulty. It has a highly refined aesthetic that says difficulty is not part of what we do, however, they achieve uncanny effects at particular scales that are very difficult to replicate as an architect. These effects take a very specific set of decisions to produce. There are different sensibilities about the idea of difficulty as an architect: things that quiver, or spaces that have a longer duration due to shifting qualities within them. I do not think these are tied to specific technologies. They require decision-making, and having an agenda about what you are doing with the building. A lot of people think difficulty means that it is difficult to do, it is difficult to produce, and therefore it is good. That is where the confusion of values lies. Architecture should have cultural value, because it is difficult to perceive in a space. There are moments when it might be worth being difficult because it is difficult as a space in terms of spatial typology and experience of space. Otherwise no; if it is easy to do, make it easy. That is something that is not being addressed aggressively. All of us need to get better about talking about that in our own way, so that confusion does not persist. Otherwise, architects will not be understood as being people that are good at producing those kinds of experiences – which I would suggest is where architecture *is* valued for being difficult.

DONALD BATES: There is something very interesting about the question of "responsibility." Achim Menges talks about "fitness criteria." But the fitness criteria he mentions were about self-referentiality. That is to say, fitness criteria were about fulfilling a mathematical description of what they were trying to do. Most students end up giving you a chronology of work. They do not tell you what came out of the work, they do not tell you the consequential nature of the work, they tell you the sequence: "I did this, and then I did this, and then somebody told me how to try this, so I did it … Do you like it?" They do not say what it did, or this is what came out of it that I never thought would happen. One of the queries, or the unease that I have, is that we are not yet describing with these techniques and technologies their consequential nature beyond the self-referentiality of their emerging as techniques and technologies.

CHRISTIAN PONGRATZ (from audience): I would like to cite Peter Eisenman when he referenced in the mid-1990s the Deleuzian terms of the "*machinic.*" He was developing a discourse on the processes of the interstitial, saying that you have to have a machine – a design machine – running, and then you need to learn when to stop it. Eleven years after, we are still learning when to stop it, and he did not have an answer as well. But he also said that as an architect, you should establish your own discourse through the work of somebody else, which may be that kind of self-referentiality (Eisenman–Terragni). This then helps you to set up your own machine, and working with it you may find some kind of solution to fine-tune the decision process.

ACHIM MENGES: What we discuss requires a different model of thinking about design. The evolutionary processes underlying most of our research are driven by specific fitness criteria yet they are not geared towards any kind of single parameter optimization. What may appear as self-referentiality in the experiment results from an essentially open-ended process and requires a different sensibility compared to established design processes and methods. How do you establish criteria for evaluating results, additional qualities and performative capacities beyond the initial fitness criteria that you embedded as a designer? The particular experiments I presented explore possibilities of embedding the logics of materialization within the fitness criteria driving the form generation. However, I would argue that one can find additional architectural possibilities and qualities in the resulting material systems and prototypes – far beyond this initial goal of being able to make and produce them. While being often mistaken as merely a process of structural optimization, one of the truly fascinating aspects of Frei Otto's work is the way he instrumentalizes the behavior innate to materials through a limited number of influences set by the designer. As a result of working within the inherent constraints of materials and related processes of making, the designer operates within a very narrow frame; however, within that frame, there still is an infinite amount of possibilities. Consequently, one first needs to define this frame and establish criteria. Only then those additional qualities, capacities, and some of the more mundane performative aspects can be assessed.

DONALD BATES: The tendency when one talks about Frei Otto is that it still ends up being a kind of quasi-engineering criteria – what he could do with a certain kind of shell, etc. I am interested in looking at what his work did spatially, as an open plan with irregular surfaces, which imply densities within a flat surface. The way that these surfaces would move up and down gave quality to the space, which was not the same as a big shed. We all know about the *Maison Domino* of Le Corbusier from the engineering aspect – a series of columns and slabs different from previous load-bearing masonry walls. It also enabled the "free plan" which allowed the way we now contemporarily live; having kitchens open to living rooms, which are open to bedrooms. Loft living comes out of *Maison Domino*, not the other way around. The cognitive possibility of a lifestyle of an open area where there is no differentiation between living, eating, sleeping, publicly conversing, is a new way of living in the world arising from a technology. We should not be afraid to talk about the consequential condition of these technologies in that same way, or at least even speculating on what they should be. My worry is that we have so much work to do, that we will do this for the next ten years, and then figure out how we can use it. That is the reason why we should talk about it now.

DAVID ERDMAN: The Eisenman question is an important one, because there is one school that sees mathematical rigor as producing an emergent sensibility that comes along with technique, and another school that thinks no matter how rigorous and mathematically technical you are, you always have to go into that, being aware of your own sensibilities. Achim Menges' collaborative work demonstrates an amazing ability to produce highly continuous surfaces and build up depth within a minimum thickness. It is latent with very particular sensibility that is not being foregrounded. That work, to my mind, has a very narrow and useful set of sensibilities about it that can begin to evaluate what they mean spatially and expand into other architectures. I do not think Peter Eisenman ever intended to suggest that there is not a degree of authorship or sensibility behind the automation of things. I would say that it was actually the opposite. His article "Toward a Conceptual Architecture" was supposed to imbue you, make you more self-aware of your sensibility going into that kind of process, and make use of it rather than assume that it is somehow emergent. This is perhaps where a general confusion lies. Emergence entails a set of things that begin to design themselves, that help

the design process, but I would suggest that emergence does not necessarily mean that your sensibility should be emergent.

KEVIN KLINGER: Someone earlier alluded to a trend for anti-intellectuals in our education system right now. I wonder if anyone else on the panel shares that view. Along those lines, are these processes just about making and production? Is there an incredible sensibility of pragmatism, or just the ecstasy of process?

MICK EEKHOUT: Technology is the focus of our discourse. But, actually, it is also an excuse. Just after the introduction of good modeling programs, architecture focused a bit on the capacity of manufacturing. The quality of architecture is not established by the complexity of making it. The quality is established by viewing or experiencing architecture. We can make new possibilities, and open it up to the rest of the world, and it is up to architects whether they catch up with the technical parts. Frei Otto was mainly engaged in pavilion-like ground floor spaces, and the *Maison Domino* is a concept that is vivid for eighty years. Every one of those decision impulses was a timely impulse. It is an excellent way to show that cladding may be spaces, or the form of buildings, and can be much more complicated and conceived than ever before. We can also almost perfectly make it. So, do not be afraid! Ten years ago, we did not dare to make it because there were 50 percent errors. Now, there is hardly any error. Yes, it is still expensive, but it will gradually go down. Finally, it is not a new style, only a means.

MARC SIMMONS: Although not particularly academic at *Front Inc.*, what drives us are the two brackets. First, we are very interested in the relationship with the client – who they are, and the fact that they are an entity, a person, a group, a culture that has the resources and the desire and the need to manifest its agenda. Second is the end result, and ultimately how to measure the final result, which is the actual, exquisitely executed building in all of its varieties relative to the original ambition. As consultants, we are only interested in working with people at the beginning and their interests and ambition...

MICK EEKHOUT: You should not confuse your sales thinking with the capacity that you have to astonish the world with something that was not there before. That is what I meant. I am not interested in your relationship with *Prada*.

MARC SIMMONS: I understand. Whether it is *pro bono*, for a social entity, or something for education, matters, and we have façades that range from $10 a square foot to $1,400 a square foot. I agree with you that ultimately the thing in the middle is only the means, but for me, it is also the exquisite process of living – it is what we do every single day, it is what we live and breathe for. I do not care whether we use a computer or not. I am interested in finding out what we want to build, how it needs to perform, and then tire-kicking until we get the building that everyone dreamt about. That is our agenda.

MICK EEKHOUT: ... and make it in a very intellectual way so that you know that *Front Inc.* was there and not somebody else?

MARC SIMMONS: Perhaps, but it is the client for us, the collaborator that gives us the most latitude to engage and make a difference on the project. That is a very powerful thing, because we have the ability. We are not a façade consultant that does not comment on design. We are very comfortable telling somebody when we think their building is lazy, or is a pig, or is irresponsible, or that they are not living up to certain expectations. We will remove ourselves from a project if we do not agree with the certain kind of values.

GREG MORE (from audience): I am interested in the way in which these processes might be changing the signature of the architect, and the homogeneous nature of these processes working at a global scale – how things start to look very similar versus the way in which one defines a distinct position in the marketplace.

SHOHEI SHIGEMATSU: It is a very interesting question. What we showed in Dubai is also polemical in the sense that now this kind of blobby architecture is catching up and flourishing in Dubai. That is why we made a slab. Probably we would not make a slab in North Korea. It cannot be either/or. That is also why I think the "no default" thinking is important; that we do not generalize architecture as always related to the site, client, economy, etc. That is the only way to go: personal objective aesthetics. In all the conferences that I attended, it ends here. I really want to talk about what is next after this.

MARC SIMMONS: One thing that is next is a process. We talked about *associative parametrics* ... It is not a foundation of our practice, we just found our way into it because it seemed very interesting to us. I like the word DNA; we could take every single façade system, or perhaps structure that was presented over the past two days and deconstruct it to its fundamental DNA to the point where we could program every single portion of that façade in an associative parametric environment. As long as we do not modify the DNA too much, it can adapt itself to any one project, as long as the DNA is actually still relevant. What will happen is evolutionary. If a model does not work the way we modeled, and fabricated the steel, we can adapt that portion. The intellectual property that begins to evolve is actually achievable. The question is, who is going to own it? Who is going to develop it? What I would like to see is a democracy, where basically every single architect, fabricator, contractor, or owner has the tools to do these sorts of things. Expertise is essential, so in all likelihood it is going to concentrate in the hands of *Seele and Gartner*, *Permasteelisa*, *Benson*, *Hyundai*, and *Zhongshan Shengxing*; these are the companies that are basically going to own it. They will own no longer the off-the-shelf catalog components, but the DNA of a hundred thousand different types of façade systems which can be propagated. Already, we have two of these associative models, where if someone gave me a steel cassette system to instantiate into a certain kind of frame, I could model every panel within a day or so, and I can extract it all to fabrication. I can export it for analysis. I can run thermal analyses on it. I can send it to China, Germany, or the Netherlands for pricing, and then have it fabricated and shipped. And, I guarantee the speed with which that will happen. In five to ten years it is going to be shocking. Therefore, it is critical that these tools are in the hands of designers.

KEVIN KLINGER: So, what is next?

DAVID ERDMAN: Intellectual production is important. There are things that are nascently on the table. For instance, who is doing the most boundless continuous spaces right now as a result of this technology? – Kazuyo Sejima and SANAA. Because of their particular sensibility, we see walls that have the least amount of lines in them than we have ever seen in the history of architecture. What does that mean in terms of a "threshold" when you are rethinking the wall? Historicizing it, looking at the intellectual tools we have to evaluate the specific architecture that results from these technologies is absolutely how you can formulate a signature for it. There are a lot of people who are not discussing it at that level, who are totally content talking about it as technical innovation and not architectural innovation, or geometrical innovation and not architectural innovation. It is important to ask, what are the specific architectural attributes that are happening as a result of these surfaces? You could talk about shimmer. You can talk about the *Maison Domino* as being as much about

a critique of a wall and a surface as it is about posts and slabs, but that kind of discussion about architecture is not the focus of how these innovative projects tend to be presented. I think if that discussion stops, that is an intellectual crisis. The more we talk about architecture, the more you can begin to distinguish different new onsets of authorship among the younger generation, which, to be honest right now, is totally blurry. Many clients have no idea how to evaluate who is better or worse in terms of who they are going to hire. Few people – if any – are articulating what these differences are, and that absolutely has to happen. Part of that is just being more intellectual, and a little bit more mundane and humble in terms of the history of what we are doing, like simply talking about walls and discussing what is at stake in a wall. After all, it is about what you are doing with the technology not the technology itself.

KEVIN KLINGER: I learned from a very good friend a number of years ago that the best way to close a good panel discussion is to cut it off just when it gets interesting.

APPENDIX
AUTHOR
BIOGRAPHIES
PHOTO CREDITS
INDEX

BIOGRAPHIES

BRANKO KOLAREVIC
Haworth Chair in Integrated Design
University of Calgary
Calgary, Canada

Branko Kolarevic has taught architecture over the past two decades at several universities in North America and Hong Kong. He is currently an Associate Professor of Architecture at the University of Calgary, where he holds the Haworth Chair in Integrated Design. He was previously the Irving Distinguished Visiting Professor at Ball State University in Indiana.

He has authored, edited or co-edited several books, including *Performative Architecture: Beyond Instrumentality* (with Ali Malkawi, Spon Press 2004) and *Architecture in the Digital Age: Design and Manufacturing* (Spon Press 2003). He is the past president of the Association for Computer Aided Design in Architecture (ACADIA) and is the recipient of the ACADIA 2007 Award for Innovative Research.

In recent years, Branko has given more than 50 lectures worldwide on the use of digital media in design and construction and was twice (in 2005 and 2007) a featured speaker at the Innovation conferences in New York, organized by the *Architectural Record* magazine.

He holds doctoral and master's degrees in design from Harvard University and a diploma engineer in architecture degree from the University of Belgrade in the former Yugoslavia.

www.ucalgary.ca/evds/kolarevic

KEVIN R. KLINGER
Director, Institute for Digital Fabrication
Ball State University
Muncie, Indiana, USA

Kevin R. Klinger is the Director of the Institute for Digital Fabrication and an Associate Professor of Architecture in the College of Architecture and Planning at Ball State University. The Institute for Digital Fabrication (IDF) through the Center for Media Design acts as a catalyst for interdisciplinary applied research and industry immersive education, which examines the impact of digital fabrication in architecture and the allied arts. As such, IDF serves as a conduit between students, design professionals, and the manufacturing sector.

Kevin R. Klinger served as a two-term President (2003 to 2005) of the Association of Computer Aided Design in Architecture (ACADIA). Recent publication highlights include "Visualizing the Operative and Analytic: Representing the Digital Fabrication Feedback Loop and Managing the Digital Exchange," published in 2006 in the *International Journal of Architecture and Computing* with co-author, Josh Vermillion. In 2005, Klinger authored "Retooling the Architecture Machine: Innovations of Digitally-Driven Architecture" for the *Blueprints* journal of the National Building Museum in Washington, DC, in conjunction with the Tools of the Imagination Exhibition. Professor Klinger is the author of numerous conference publications and has lectured extensively in universities and industry organizations on the topic of digital fabrication in architecture, including the 2007 Architectural Record Innovation Conference: "Architecture in an Age of Transformation."

In his teaching appointments, Professor Klinger encourages explorations in digitally driven design enabled by techniques of digital fabrication. The digital exchange of information in this inventive process has led to new forms of architectural production that take designers deeper into the complexities of making, assembly, and material formulation, and encourage new forms of collaboration with industry, challenge conventional methodologies, and suggest a future in which designers are much more engaged in the total process of architecture.

www.bsu.edu/imade

FRANK BARKOW
Principal
Barkow Leibinger Architects
Berlin, Germany

Regine Leibinger and Frank Barkow's practice can be characterized by the interaction of practice, research and teaching. Their interdisciplinary, discursive attitude allows their work to expand and respond to advancing knowledge and technology. Recent designs include a gatehouse and factory-campus event space in Stuttgart, Germany, and the *TRUTEC Office Building* in Seoul. Recent research projects include revolving laser cutting; CNC-cut translucent concrete formwork; façade systems, pre-cast concrete and ceramic elements.

Digitally tooled material no longer "accessorizes" construction but contributes to essential components including skins and structures. Their research folds into ongoing construction projects focusing on a "trickling down" of these technologies, informing the construction of everyday building types, including office buildings, factories and pavilions. This method favors expanding building systems (part to whole) leading to form and phenomenal/physical material effect.

Frank Barkow is currently teaching at the University of Wisconsin, Milwaukee, in conjunction with the practice winning the *2007 Marcus Prize for Architecture*. He is a former visiting studio critic at Harvard and Cornell and was a former unit master at the Architectural Association in London. The work of the office has been published worldwide; drawings and other practice materials are included in collections at the Pompidou Centre, the Deutsches Architektur Museum, and the Heinz Architecture Center, among others. They have recently published a book edited by Andres Lepik, MoMA, entitled *Reflect: Building in the Digital Media City, Seoul* (Hadje Cantz 2007).

Barkow Leibinger will construct a digitally cut installation for the *11th Biennale di Architettura* for the exhibition, "Out There: Architecture Beyond Building", in Venice, at the *Arsenale Show* in September 2008.

www.barkowleibinger.com

DONALD BATES
Director
LAB Architecture Studio
Melbourne, Australia

Donald Bates studied architecture at the University of Houston, graduating with a Bachelor of Architecture (with honors) in 1978. He attended graduate school at Cranbrook Academy of Art, under the tutorship of Daniel Libeskind, gaining a Master of Architecture degree in 1983. Also in 1983, Donald Bates joined Raoul Bunschoten to form intermediate unit 10 at the Architectural Association, serving as sole director of the unit from 1986–9. In 1987, Bates acted as design assistant to Daniel Libeskind on the prize-winning *City Edge* project, Berlin. In 1989, he was an associate to Libeskind for the competition design of the *Jewish Museum*, Berlin. Bates has been a guest lecturer, visiting professor and critic, and workshop coordinator at more than 55 universities and schools of architecture throughout Europe, North America and Australia.

In 1994, Peter Davidson and Donald Bates formed LAB Architecture Studio, beginning work on a number of speculative competition entries. In 1995, LAB was a short-list finalist for the Wagga Wagga Civic Centre competition, and in the summer of 1996, LAB initiated the Berlin architecture workshop, bringing together students from 16 countries for a three-week urban design workshop. In 1997, LAB Architecture Studio won the international design competition for *Federation Square*, Melbourne, the largest urban, civic, and cultural project recently completed in Australia.

labarchitecture.com

PHILLIP G. BERNSTEIN
Vice President, Autodesk
Lecturer, Yale University
New Haven, USA

Phillip G. Bernstein is a Vice President at Autodesk,
a leading provider of software for architecture and
engineering. A practicing architect with over twenty years
of experience, he leads Industry Strategy and Relations for
the AEC Division where he is responsible for setting the
company's future vision and strategy for technology serving
the building industry. Phil was formerly with Pelli Clarke
Pelli Architects, where he managed many of the firm's most
complex commissions. Phil teaches professional practice
at the Yale School of Architecture where he received his
B.A. magna cum laude with Distinction in Architecture and
his M.Arch. He is a Fellow of the American Institute of
Architects, a Senior Fellow of the Design Futures Council
and former Chair of the AIA National Contract Documents
Committee.

autodesk.com

MICK EEKHOUT
Director, Octatube International GV
Professor of Product Development, TU Delft
Delft, Netherlands

Mick Eekhout founded his company Octatube Space Structures
bv in 1982. In 1989, he received a PhD degree and in 1992 he
was appointed as Professor of Product Development at TU Delft.
The Octatube group, with Professor Mick Eekhout as the general
managing director, is formed as a holding with several companies.
Octatube Netherlands bv does the design-build projects in the
Netherlands. Octatube Engineering bv takes care of all design
and engineering in the projects. Octatube International bv covers
the export projects and has expanded considerably over the years,
into countries such as Saudi Arabia, the Emirates, Germany,
Israel, England, Ireland, Portugal, Belgium, Romania, Hong Kong,
Singapore, Malaysia, India, and Spain. The main plant in Delft,
the Netherlands, houses 50 to 60 personnel, spread over three
departments: Design & Engineering, Production & Subcontracting,
Assembly & Supervision. Close contact between these departments
is maintained throughout the entire production process, which we
regard as a necessity. The "Design & Build" approach stimulates the
growth of the body of knowledge in experimental projects that flow
from design to building under one roof and with a single point of
responsibility.

octatube.nl

DAVID ERDMAN
Principal, davidclovers
Design Faculty, UCLA Dept of Architecture and Urban Design
Los Angeles, USA and Hong Kong, PRC

David Erdman was the principal of servo's Los Angeles office before establishing davidclovers in 2007 with partner Clover Lee. With servo he designed and completed numerous projects in the USA, including exhibitions for Nike and the Santa Monica Museum of Art and a small residence in upstate New York. Projects currently in development with davidclovers include a photography studio/residence in Malibu, a series of live–work condominiums in Beijing and a collaborative project with artist C.E.B. Reas, entitled 07 Masses.

David Erdman received his architecture degrees from Ohio State University and Columbia University. Erdman has been teaching at UCLA's Department of Architecture and Urban Design since 1999 where he continues to develop research with graduate students in both design studios and seminars. Erdman held the Visiting Esherick Chair at Berkeley's College of Environmental Design during the Fall of 2006 and was the Cullinan Visiting Critic at the Rice University School of Architecture, Fall 2007.

Erdman has lectured at Harvard, Yale, UCLA, UC Berkeley, Tulane and Rice as well as other national and international venues. His work has been exhibited at the Centre Pompidou, San Francisco MOMA, MOMA, Artists Space, and Biennales in Venice, Korea and Beijing. His projects have been published in the *New York Times*, *The Los Angeles Times*, *Architectural Record*, *A+U*, *Esquire Japan*, *Icon*, *Interior Design*, *Frame*, *Monitor* and in several collected books such as *10x10_2* (Phaidon) and *Next Generation Architecture* (Rizzoli). The French Architecture Collection, SFMOMA and the MAK Center in Vienna have acquired selected works.

www.davidclovers.com

JEANNE GANG
Principal
Studio Gang Architects
Chicago, USA

Jeanne Gang is design principal architect and leads Studio Gang Architects, a practice that has designed award-winning projects since its inception in 1998. Ms. Gang's design in the field of architecture is supported through a mode of working that combines practice, teaching, and research. As adjunct professor at the Illinois Institute of Technology, she has taught architecture since 1998. She was visiting professor at the Harvard Design School in 2004, and held the Louis I. Kahn visiting professor chair at the Yale College of Architecture in 2005.

As design principal, Ms. Gang is responsible for leading the design throughout all phases of the project. Through exploration and research early in the design process, her work has staked out new creative territory in materials, technology, and sustainability.

Her recent projects include the winning entry for the *Ford Calumet Environmental Center*, now under development, and the 80-story, mixed-use residential "Aqua Tower" under construction in downtown Chicago. The work of Studio Gang has received numerous awards and has been published and exhibited widely. Studio Gang's work has been featured at the International Venice Biennale, the National Building Museum of the Smithsonian Institution and the Art Institute of Chicago. Ms. Gang was chosen to lecture as one of the Architecture League of New York's *Emerging Voices* in Spring 2006 and received an Academy Award from the American Academy of Arts and Letters in the same year.

studiogang.net

MARK GOULTHORPE
Principal, dECOi
Associate Professor, MIT
Cambridge, MA, USA

In 1991, Mark Goulthorpe established the dECOi atelier to undertake a series of architectural competitions, largely theoretically biased. These resulted in numerous accolades around the world, which quickly established dECOi's reputation for thoughtful and elegant design work suggestive of new possibilities for architecture and architectural praxis. Significantly, such work was presented under the rubric "dECOi," which was intended to allow for the possibility of collaborative practice, and which has latterly become essential to a digitally networked creative enterprise.

dECOi has received awards from the Royal Academy in London, the French Ministry of Culture, and the Architectural League of New York, and has represented France three times at the Venice Biennale and at the United Nations 50th Anniversary exhibition. They were selected by the journal *Architects Design* in its international survey of 30 *Emerging Voices* at the RIBA in London, the Architectural Record's *Design Vanguard* in the USA, as well as The Architectural League of New York's *Emerging Voices* selection. dECOi was invited to exhibit in the International Pavilion at the Venice Biennale 2000, and to exhibit 10 years of work at FRAC depot in Orleans 2001. dECOi won the prestigious international FEIDAD Digital Design Award 2002 and again in 2004, and was invited to the *Non-Standard Architecture* manifesto at the Centre Pompidou in Paris in 2003.

Mark Goulthorpe took a professorship at MIT in 2003 to teach digital design in architecture, and has recently been awarded the national Rotch Travelling Scholarship. Books of dECOi's work and writings are forthcoming from Hyx Publications/FRAC (Centre Pompidou), collected essays appear in *Haecceity* (Routledge), and *The Parametric Turn* (Birkhauser). While at MIT, the *HypoSurface* was established as a new interactive display medium, and the *Bankside Paramorph* fully developed as a parametric prototype.

architecture.mit.edu/people/bg/cvgoulth.html

FABIO GRAMAZIO / MATTHIAS KOHLER
Principals, Gramazio & Kohler Architecture and Urbanism
Assistant Professors, Chair in Arch. and Digital Fabrication, ETH
Zurich, Switzerland

Fabio Gramazio and Matthias Kohler are joint partners in the architects' office Gramazio & Kohler in Zurich. Their works include the contemporary dance institution *Tanzhaus* and the Christmas illuminations for the prestigious Bahnhofstrasse in Zurich as well as the *sWISH* Pavilion* at the Swiss National Exposition *Expo.02*.

Since 2005, they have been assistant professors at the Department of Architecture at ETH Zurich. Their research and teaching focus on architectural design strategies for full-scale robotic fabrication. Highly informed non-standardized architectural elements are explored for their sensual, constructive, and economic potential. They are developing additive fabrication processes in a unique research set-up which features a 3 m robotic arm on a 7 m linear track, permitting the direct construction of building parts on a real-world scale.

Together with their team, which combines the different expertise of architects, craftsmen, physicists, and computer programmers, they explore the concept of "digital materiality," the interconnection of data and material, and the resulting implications on architectural design. Their aim is to develop criteria for a new system of structural logic that, by the direct introduction of material and production logic into the design process, will extend the reach of the architect into the production process and thus increase creative freedom and validate a new aesthetic.

gramaziokohler.com

DAVID J. LEWIS
Partner
LTL Architects
New York, USA

David Lewis is a founding partner and principal of Lewis.
Tsurumaki.Lewis (LTL), an architecture and research
partnership based in New York City, dedicated to exploring
the inventive possibilities of architecture through a close
examination of the conventional and the overlooked. LTL
Architects has received numerous awards and honors,
including representing the USA at the 2004 Venice
Architecture Biennale, participating in the Architectural
League of New York's *Emerging Voices* lecture series, and
being selected by *Architectural Record* as one of ten firms
representing the vanguard in contemporary architecture
in 2000.

David Lewis received a Bachelor of Arts from
Carleton College in 1988, a Master of Arts in the History
of Architecture and Urbanism from Cornell University
in 1992, and a Master of Architecture from Princeton
University's School of Architecture in 1995. He has been
an Assistant Professor at Cornell University's College of
Architecture, Art, and Planning from 1997 to 2001 and
is currently the Director of the Master of Architecture
Program at Parsons New School for Design. David has
also taught at the University of Pennsylvania and Ohio
State University.

ltlarchitects.com

MARTA MALÉ-ALEMANY / JOSÉ PEDRO SOUSA
Principals
ReD
Barcelona, Spain / Porto, Portugal

Co-founded by architects Marta Malé-Alemany and José Pedro
Sousa in 2004, ReD | Research + Design is an award-winning
research and design studio in architecture and digital technologies.
Operating internationally from Porto and Barcelona, ReD merges
research and design endeavors in both academia and professional
practice. Specializing in implementing cutting-edge digital
technologies to assist design conception, engineering, and fabrication
(CAD/CAE/CAM), ReD is committed to exploring the new design
opportunities that emerge from the cultural and technological
context of today's digital era. With built projects in the USA, Austria,
Italy, Spain, and Portugal, ReD's work has been presented regularly
in lectures, selected for architecture exhibitions, and recognized
in international publications. In 2006, ReD was the winner of the
prestigious FEIDAD Award, and winner of the Portuguese prize in
Ephemeral Architecture "Outros Mercados." In 2007, ReD received
the NEOTEC grant from the Portuguese Agency for Innovation, to
develop an entrepreneurial project with a technological basis.

Marta Malé-Alemany is a licensed architect who graduated
from ETSAV-UPC (Escola d'Arquitectura del Vallès, Universitat
Politècnica de Catalunya). She holds a Master's Degree in Advanced
Architectural Design from Columbia University and is doing her PhD
in the Department of Visual Communication in Architecture and
Design at the ETSAB-UPC (Escola Tècnica Superior d'Arquitectura
de Barcelona, Universitat Politècnica de Catalunya).

José Pedro Sousa is a licensed architect who graduated from
FAUP (Faculdade de Arquitectura da Universidade do Porto) and
holds a Master's in Genetic Architectures from ESARQ-UIC (Escola
Tècnica Superior d'Arquitectura, Universitat Internacional de
Catalunya). Since 2003, he has been a PhD candidate in Architecture
at IST-UTL (Instituto Superior Técnico, Universidade Técnica de
Lisboa) with the support of FCT (Fundação para a Ciência e a
Tecnologia) and AMORIM.

re-d.com

ACHIM MENGES
Professor, Stuttgart University, Germany
Studio Master, Architectural Association
London, United Kingdom

Achim Menges studied at the Technical University, Darmstadt, and graduated from the Architectural Association (AA) with Honors. He has taught at the AA as Studio Master of the Emergent Technologies and Design MSc/MArch Program since 2002 and as Unit Master of Diploma Unit 4 from 2003 to 2006. Since 2005, he has been Professor for Form Generation and Materialization at the HfG Offenbach University for Art and Design in Germany. Recently he has been appointed as Professor at Stuttgart University, leading an institute for computational design.

His research focuses on the development of integral design processes at the intersection of design computation, parametric design, biomimetic engineering, and computer aided manufacturing that enables a highly articulated, performative built environment. His research projects have been published and exhibited in Europe, Asia, and the United States. Achim Menges recently received the FEIDAD (Far Eastern International Digital Architectural Design) Outstanding Design Award in 2002, the FEIDAD Design Merit Award in 2003, the Archiprix International Award 2003, RIBA Tutor Price 2004, the International Bentley Educator of the Year Award 2005, and the ACADIA 2007 Award for Emerging Digital Practice.

Recent publications include *Emergence: Morphogenetic Design Strategies* (AD Wiley, London, 2004), *Techniques and Technologies in Morphogenetic Design* (AD Wiley, London, 2006), *Versatility and Vicissitude: Performance in Morpho-Ecological Design* (AD Wiley, London, 2008), and *Morpho-Ecologies* (AA Publications, London, 2006).

achimmenges.net

FABIAN SCHEURER
Principal
designtoproduction
Zurich, Switzerland

Fabian Scheurer graduated from the Technical University of Munich after studying Computer Sciences and Architecture. He worked as assistant at the CAAD chair of TU Munich, as a software developer at Nemetschek Programmsystem GmbH, and as new media consultant for Eclat in Zurich. Between 2002 and 2006 he was researching and lecturing as an assistant at the Chair of CAAD at the Swiss Federal Institute of Technology (ETH Zurich). His scientific work focused on the practical aspects of artificial-life methods in architectural construction and has been applied to a number of collaborative projects between architects, engineers, and fabrication experts. In 2006, he teamed up with his ETH colleague Christoph Schindler and architect Arnold Walz to found designtoproduction, a consultancy firm for the digital production of complex designs with offices in Zurich and Stuttgart.

designtoproduction.com

CHRIS SHARPLES
Principal
SHoP Architects
New York, USA

SHoP Architects is a New York design firm with five partners whose education and experience encompass architecture, fine arts, structural engineering, finance, and business management. Founded in 1996, SHoP was awarded the 2001 *Emerging Voices* Award by the Architectural League of New York and the 2001 Academy Award in Architecture from the American Academy of Arts and Letters, as well as a Progressive Architecture Citation in 1999. In 2000, SHoP was the winner of the annual Museum of Modern Art and P.S.1 Contemporary Art Center Young Architect's Awards Program. Most recently, SHoP's design for The Porter House was recognized by a 2006 Lumen Award, a 2005 AIANY Housing Design Award, a 2005 AIANY Honor Award in Architecture, a 2005 Chicago Athenaeum American Architecture Award, a 2005 Building Design and Construction magazine Building Team Project Award, as well as a 2004 AIA New York State Merit in Design. Work produced by SHoP is published and exhibited internationally, and is in the permanent collection of the Museum of Modern Art.

Christopher Sharples received his Bachelor of Fine Art and Bachelor of History degrees from Dickinson College, and his Master of Architecture from Columbia University (1990) where he graduated with honors for excellence in design. He has worked in the offices of Richard Meier and Partners in New York and Aoshima Sekkei in Nagoya, Japan, prior to establishing his practice in New York City. He has taught at Columbia University, Parsons School of Design, The City College, City University of New York, and at the University of Virginia.

shoparc.com

SHOHEI SHIGEMATSU
Director
OMA*AMO
New York, USA

Shohei Shigematsu graduated in 1996 from the Department of Architecture at Kyushu University, Fukuoka. After studying at the Berlage Institute, Amsterdam (Postgraduate Laboratory), he joined the Office for Metropolitan Architecture in 1998. He has been the director of OMA*AMO New York since 2006.

During his time at OMA, Shohei Shigematsu has acted as lead architect for many projects in various phases including the *Whitney Museum Extension* in New York (2001), and the *Shenzhen Stock Exchange Tower*, China (2006). Having led the team that won the design competition in 2002, he served as project architect for the *Central Chinese Television Headquarters* in Beijing.

He is currently in charge of the Cornell University *Paul Milstein Hall* project in Ithaca, New York, a high-rise condominium-hotel complex in Jersey City, and a high-rise condominium and screening room for CAA (Creative Artist Agency) in 23 East 22nd Street, New York.

oma-amo.nl

MARC SIMMONS
Partner
Front Inc.
New York, USA

MAKAI SMITH
Product Manager
Bentley
Exton, USA

Marc Simmons is a founding partner of Front Inc., a specialist façade consulting practice in New York City. Front is a cross-disciplinary collective of creative individuals with professional backgrounds in architecture, structural and mechanical engineering, product design and computer science. The firm provides design and technical advisory services to realize projects through intensive collaboration and in pursuit of innovative, responsible design.

In recently completed projects Front has had successful collaborations with a number of well-known architects and firms, such as Office for Metropolitan Architecture (OMA), Sejima and Nishizawa Associates (SANAA), Renzo Piano Building Workshop, Herzog & de Meuron, REX, Gehry Partners, Zaha Hadid, David Chipperfield, Asymptote Architecture, Neil Denari, Ateliers Jean Nouvel, and many others. Front has recently won an invited design competition for the design of the Louis Vuitton flagship store in Singapore, extending its multi-disciplinary range across full design and engineering.

Marc holds both Bachelor of Environmental Studies and professional Bachelor of Architecture degrees from the University of Waterloo, Canada, and lectures widely on the subject of façade design. He is a faculty member at the Princeton University School of Architecture and has given presentations at Columbia University, Yale University, University of Pennsylvania, MIT, SIUC, Rice University, University of Houston, UCLA Los Angeles, Georgia Tech, Cornell University, University of Wisconsin, the Green Build Conference, and various AIA events including the 2004 AIA/ACADIA Fabrication Conference. Most recently Front were featured presenters at the 2007 Architectural Record Innovation Conference.

frontinc.com

Makai Smith is Product Manager for Generative Components at Bentley. He was previously Director of Digital Fabrication for Kreysler and Associates, an architectural composites fabricator located near Napa, CA, where he oversaw digital pattern making operations, integrating large-scale CNC milling, 3D laser scanning, and additive fabrication processes into the manufacturing process. Prior to joining Kreysler, Makai practiced at Venturi, Scott Brown and Associates in Philadelphia. Makai has taught at the Southern California Institute of Architecture (SCI-Arc), the University of California – Berkeley, and Philadelphia University and has lectured at a number of universities including the University of Pennsylvania, and the School of the Art Institute of Chicago. He holds a Master of Architecture from Arizona State University, Tempe, and a BS in Design from the University of Florida, Gainesville. He is a member of the Association for Computer Aided Design in Architecture (ACADIA), the Association for Computing Machinery's Special Interest Group on Computer Graphics (ACM SIGGRAPH), and the American Institute of Architects (AIA).

bentley.com

BRETT STEELE
Director
Architectural Association School of Architecture
London, UK

Brett Steele is the Director and Head of School of the
Architectural Association School of Architecture, in
London. In 1996, with Patrik Schumacher, Brett founded,
and for eight years directed, the AA DRL (Design Research
Lab). The AA DRL is the first-ever full-time MArch graduate
design program in the 150-year history of the AA. Brett
designed and maintains www.aadrl.net as an open-source
online application that extends the innovative team-based
design pedagogy of the AA DRL, and the site currently
contains more than 13,000 downloadable image, model,
scripting, video, and other files related to the work of the
AA DRL, which has during the past five years participated
in more than two dozen exhibitions and symposia around
the world. Brett is a Partner of DAL, desArchLab, an
architectural office in London, and has taught and lectured
at schools in the USA, Europe, Hong Kong, China, and
Japan. His recent articles have been published in *LOG*,
Arch+, *A+U*, *Archis*, *AA Files*, *Harvard Design Magazine*,
Hunch, *World Architecture*, *Daidalos*, and are online at
www.brettsteele.net. He is the editor of *Corporate Fields*
(London, 2005) and *DRL R&D* (Bejiing, 2005).

aaschool.ac.uk

RUBEN SUARE
Vice President
3form
Salt Lake City, USA

Ruben Suare, Vice President of 3form's Architectural Division,
is a pioneer in the architectural industry. Graduating with a BA
in Architecture from the University of California at Berkley in
1993, Suare held leadership roles in the design, construction, and
fabrication of award-winning architectural projects. He worked
with companies such as CTEK, a multidisciplinary, multi-industry
engineering and fabrication firm specializing in automotive,
aerospace, and architectural applications, and Studio Suare, a
private architectural firm. He went on to achieve an MBA from the
Paul Merage School of Business at the University of California at
Irvine in 2004, with a desire to question and challenge the way
manufacturers and architects communicate and do business, and
dispel the perceived limitations of both industries. Joining 3form in
2004, Suare is building a visionary portfolio of innovative projects
and products that utilize digital fabrication technologies and that
challenge traditional building methodologies, as it is the case for
projects like the *Alice Tully Hall* at the Lincoln Center (with Diller
Scofidio + Renfro), where a real translucent wood panel was
developed as the complex wall surface; the *Fidelity Finance Board
Room* (with Perkins + Will), where compound geometries are used
to shape the ovoid walls; and the *Sunset Boulevard Façade* (with
Patterns), where resin is used to build the twisting façade curtain
wall of a three-story building.

3-form.com

L. WILLIAM ZAHNER
President and CEO
A. Zahner Company
Kansas City, USA

L. William Zahner is internationally recognized as one of the foremost experts in both metallurgy and architectural metals. He is a lecturer and trusted consultant in all disciplines relative to architectural metals. He is also the author of two books: *Architectural Metals: A Guide to Selection, Specification and Performance* (Wiley, 1995) and *Architectural Metal Surfaces* (Wiley, 2004).

L. William Zahner has been recognized locally, regionally, and internationally for his services to the industry. He is the past president of the Sheet Metal Association in the United States, a Trustee for the Kansas City Art Institute, and is on the advisory board of the Nerman Museum of Art and the School of Engineering at the University of Kansas. The American Institute of Architects (AIA) has recognized and awarded his company more than a dozen times for their many innovative contributions to the advancement of the architectural metal industry. He was recently made an Honorary Member of the AIA.

L. William Zahner is a graduate of the University of Kansas, School of Engineering, with a degree in civil engineering.

azahner.com

PHOTO CREDITS

COVER	Barkow Leibinger Architekten
1	**Kolarevic & Klinger**
1.1	Roland Halbe
1.2	Áron Losonczi / Litracon
1.3a–b	Michael Silver
1.4a–c	Thom Faulders Architecture
1.5a–b	UN Studio / Christian Richters
1.6a–f	dECOi / Mark Goulthorpe
1.7	Barry Halkin
1.8	Heinz Emigholz
1.9	Branko Kolarevic
1.10–11	Franken Architekten
1.12	Future Systems
1.13	Greg Lynn FORM
1.14	Branko Kolarevic
1.15	Margherita Spiluttini
1.16–18	Roland Halbe
1.19	Branko Kolarevic
1.20a–b	Thom Faulders Architecture with Proces2
1.21	Branko Kolarevic
1.22	Matsys / Andrew Kudless
1.23	Cecil Balmond / Arup
1.24	Matsys / Andrew Kudless
1.25	Serpentine Gallery / Stephen White
1.26	Cecil Balmond / Arup
1.27	Arup Sports
1.28	PTW Architecture, Planning and Interior Design
1.29	Wikipedia
1.30	OMA
1.31	Georges Fessy
1.32a–b	Bernard Cache
1.33	Greg Lynn FORM
1.34	Marotte
1.35	Belzberg Architects
1.36	Matsys / Andrew Kudless
2	**Klinger**
2.1	Harrieta171 / Wikimedia Commons
2.2	Matsys / Andrew Kudless
2.3	Richard Ketchum / Wikimedia Commons
2.4	Claude Ledoux / Wikimedia Commons
2.5	Matsys / Andrew Kudless
2.6	A. Zahner Metals
2.7	Robert Horner
2.8-9	Institute for Digital Fabrication / Ball State University
2.10a–b	Robert Horner
2.11–12	Institute for Digital Fabrication / Ball State University

2.13–15	Robert Horner
2.16–22	Institute for Digital Fabrication / Ball State University
2.23	Jamie Owens
3	**Sharples**
3.1–25	SHoP Architects, except:
3.1	Seong Kwon
3.8	Seong Kwon
3.13–14	Seong Kwon
3.16	Seong Kwon
4	**Suare**
4.1–24	3form, except:
4.3	Marcelo Spina / PATTERNS
4.12	Perkins + Will
4.20	Diller & Scofidio + Renfro
6	**Zahner**
6.1–24	A. Zahner Company
6.25–28	Kevin Klinger / Ball State University
7	**Gang**
7.1–23	Studio Gang Architects, except
7.1	Bob Harr, Hedrich Blessing
7.2	Jim Tetro
7.3	M.F. Ashby (original drawing)
7.13	Scott McDonald, Hedrich Blessing
7.19	David Seide
8	**Barkow**
8.1	David Franck
8.2	Corinne Rose
8.3	Barkow Leibinger Architekten
8.4	Marie-Lan Nguyen / Wikimedia Commons
8.5	Jaqueline Yeo / Diploma Unit 8 (1998), AA, London
8.6	David Franck
8.7–11	Barkow Leibinger Architekten
8.12	Werner Huthmacher
8.13	David Franck
8.14	Marc Eggimann / Vitra
8.15	David Franck
8.16	Barkow Leibinger Architekten
8.17	Werner Sobek Ingenieure
8.18	Werner Huthmacher
8.19–20	David Franck
8.21–24	Barkow Leibinger Architekten
8.25	David Franck
8.26	Amy Barkow
8.27	Christian Richters
8.28	Barkow Leibinger Architekten
8.29	Barkow Leibinger Architekten

9	**Gramazio & Kohler**
9.1–5	Gramazio & Kohler, Architecture and Urbanism
9.6	Viola Zimmermann
9.7	Roman Keller
9.8–11	Gramazio & Kohler, Architecture and Urbanism
9.12–13	Ralph Feiner
9.14–17	Gramazio & Kohler, Architecture and Digital Fabrication, ETH Zurich
9.18	Ralph Feiner
9.19–36	Gramazio & Kohler, Architecture and Digital Fabrication, ETH Zurich
10	**Kolarevic**
10.1–2	Nia Garner / Univ. of Pennsylvania
10.3	Herzog & de Meuron
10.4a–b	Bernard Cache / Objectile
10.5–9	Carmen McKee and Fuyuan Su / Univ. of Pennsylvania
10.10–15	Jill Desimini and Sarah Weidner / Univ. of Pennsylvania
10.16–17	Virginia Little and Maggie McManus / Univ. of Pennsylvania
10.18	Dustin Headley and Mickel Darmawan / Ball State Univ.
10.19–20	Dustin Headley / Ball State Univ.
11	**Malé-Alemany & Sousa**
11.1–27	ReD, except:
11.3a–p	ReD, Amorim, Lasindustria
11.6a–b	ReD, Escofet
11.7–8	Inês d'Orey / Almamate
11.12	Inês d'Orey / Almamate
11.13a–b	Inês d'Orey / Almamate
11.14a–b	Habitat Actual Arquitectura
11.17–18	Inês d'Orey / Almamate
11.21a–d	ReD, Procedes
11.22–23	Inês d'Orey / Almamate
11.26	Inês d'Orey / Almamate
11.27	Lackner / Kunsthaus Graz
12	**Goulthorpe**
12.1	dECOi
12.2a–c	dECOi
12.3	John Norton
14	**Bates**
14.1	From "Federation Square International Architectural Design Competition" booklet, State Government of Victoria

310

INDEX